PRAISE FOR
New Feminist Christianity: Many Voices, Many Views

"Both a rich, colorful sampler for those unfamiliar with feminist Christian work in the U.S. and an invitation to all of us to continue liberating Christianity from hegemonic 'isms.' This is a welcome resource for all who care about justice in the church and in the world."

—**Rev. Dr. Rita Nakashima Brock**, coauthor,
Saving Paradise: How Christianity Traded Love of This World for Crucifixion and Empire and *Casting Stones: Prostitution and Liberation in Asia and the United States*

"What is new about *New Feminist Christianity* is the depth and breadth and scope—Diann Neu and Mary Hunt do not shy away from all the intersectionalities that feminism in the context of Christianity contains. The inclusion of such powerful, diverse voices that deal with body, art, and ministry, as well as rich crosscultural lenses, will make this a powerful, required text for anyone wanting to understand Christianity or feminism today!"

—**Rev. Nancy Wilson**, moderator,
Metropolitan Community Churches

"Too often in monogendered theology, male eyes looked through the wrong end of the telescope and saw a world writ small. In this volume, woman-spirit that has long been rising comes of age, and Christianity is dynamically reimagined. This is the real, not the fictive, radical orthodoxy."

—**Daniel C. Maguire**, professor of religious ethics,
Marquette University

"A rich mix of topics and perspectives that clearly conveys where feminist Christianity has been and where it needs to go."

—**Judith Plaskow**, author, *Standing Again at Sinai: Judaism from a Feminist Perspective*

"The twenty-eight authors in this collection give us a rich menu of voices, perspectives, and insights. They demonstrate that feminist Christianity is far from monolithic; rather it is diverse, thoughtful, incisive, pastoral, prophetic and, above all, deeply faithful."

—**Emilie M. Townes**, Andrew W. Mellon Professor of
African American Religion and Theology, Yale University

"With smarts, wit, and tantalizing moral vision, feminist movers and shakers illustrate how transforming patriarchy, religiously as well as socially, requires 'changing the subject,' both the 'who' that speaks (and is listened to) and the 'what' that's spoken about. For women and men invested in a justice-centered Christianity that delights in women's empowerment globally, this collection provides truly nourishing bread for the journey."

—**Rev. Marvin M. Ellison, PhD**, Willard S. Bass Professor of Christian Ethics, Bangor Theological Seminary; co-editor, *Sexuality and the Sacred: Sources for Theological Reflection*

"Almost forty years after the emergence of feminist theological analysis and ministry, we have here a rich collection of some of the best and most cutting-edge thinking from academics, practitioners and activists. They call upon us to do together the hard yet hopeful work of dismantling sexism and domination—both within and among us—so that God's earth and all who dwell upon it can be saved."

—**Rev. Loey Powell**, executive for Administration & Women's Justice, United Church of Christ

"An important—and exciting—book with both power and poignancy. Its power lies in its ability to put the reader down into the very vortex of the struggles women endure in their search for equality in churches that proclaim justice but deny it in practice. Its poignancy lies in its ability to teach us all about the other we do not know. This book makes a new community of us all. It is a very banquet of ideas big enough to reinvigorate the life of the Spirit. More than that, it is a catalyst for the ongoing process of achieving it."

—**Joan Chittister, OSB**, co-chair, Global Peace Initiative of Women; author, *Heart of Flesh: A Feminist Spirituality for Women and Men*

"The voices in this book offer living proof that feminism has shaken the Christian patriarchal mindset to its core—from theology and Scripture studies to ethics, liturgy, art and ministry. With its multiracial and multiethnic array of authors, it is a must read for anyone interested in the future of Christianity in the twenty-first century."

—**Maureen Fiedler**, host, *Interfaith Voices* (on public radio nationwide); editor, *Breaking Through the Stained Glass Ceiling: Women Religious Leaders in Their Own Words*

New Feminist Christianity

New Feminist Christianity

MANY VOICES, MANY VIEWS

Edited by Mary E. Hunt and Diann L. Neu
Cofounders of the Women's Alliance for Theology, Ethics and Ritual (WATER)

Walking Together, Finding the Way®
SKYLIGHT PATHS® PUBLISHING
Woodstock, Vermont

New Feminist Christianity:
Many Voices, Many Views

2010 Hardcover Edition, First Printing

The editors gratefully acknowledge the following for permission to reprint previously published and/or recorded material: Doris J. Ellzey, "The Ones Who've Gone Before Us" © 1975 by Doris J. Ellzey. Doris J. Ellzey, "We Are Gathered" © 1974 by Doris J. Ellzey. Doris J. Ellzey, "We Are Women" © 1974 by Doris J. Ellzey. Carolyn McDade, "Move, Sister, Move," words and music by Carolyn McDade © 1975 by Surtsey Publishing. Carolyn McDade, "We Might Come In a-Fightin'," words and music © 1973 by Carolyn McDade. Diann L. Neu, "Commissioning for Feminist Ministry" © 2005. Diann L. Neu, "Eucharistic Banquet of Divine Wisdom" © 2007. Alicia Partnoy, "Bread," from *The Little School: Tales of Disappearance and Survival in Argentina* © 1986 Cleis Press. Miriam Therese Winter, "Blessing Song," first published in *WomanPrayer, WomanSong: Resources for Ritual* (Wipf & Stock Publishers) © Medical Mission Sisters 1987.

Library of Congress Cataloging-in-Publication Data

New feminist Christianity : many voices, many views / edited by Mary E. Hunt and Diann L. Neu.

p. cm.

Includes bibliographical references and index.

ISBN 978-1-59473-285-0 (hardcover)

1. Feminist theology. 2. Feminism—Religious aspects—Christianity. I. Hunt, Mary E., 1951– II. Neu, Diann L., 1948–

BT83.55.N53 2010

230.082—dc22

2010013618

SkyLight Paths Publishing is creating a place where people of different spiritual traditions come together for challenge and inspiration, a place where we can help each other understand the mystery that lies at the heart of our existence.

SkyLight Paths sees both believers and seekers as a community that increasingly transcends traditional boundaries of religion and denomination—people wanting to learn from each other, *walking together, finding the way.*

10 9 8 7 6 5 4 3 2 1

Manufactured in the United States of America

Jacket Design: Jenny Buono
Jacket Art: "Rideau 2," fotolia.com, © by Marie Hacene.
Interior Design: Kristi Menter

Walking Together, Finding the Way®
Published by SkyLight Paths Publishing
A Division of LongHill Partners, Inc.
Sunset Farm Offices, Route 4, P.O. Box 237
Woodstock, VT 05091
Tel: (802) 457-4000 Fax: (802) 457-4004
www.skylightpaths.com

In gratitude and with deep respect for
the women scholars and activists
who led the way.

Contents

Acknowledgments

This anthology owes its existence to Jewish women. Rabbi Elyse Goldstein edited the wonderful collection *New Jewish Feminism: Probing the Past, Forging the Future* (Jewish Lights Publishing, SkyLight Paths Publishing's sister imprint). The many authors in that book prove that it takes a lot of voices and a lot of different views to change millennia of religious patriarchy. We follow their good lead with appreciation.

Marcia Broucek came to us from SkyLight Paths with the invitation to craft a similar volume bringing together feminist Christian authors. Her enthusiasm was contagious and we embarked on the task. Deep thanks to her for thinking generously and creatively about this volume. She got the process started.

We are grateful to the twenty-six women who wrote the chapters in this book. They did so in record time, with good humor, and with openness to crafting their individual work in relation to the whole. We come away from the process with renewed appreciation for the complexity and struggles of individual women's lives that make such books all the more precious. *Gracias mil. Merci beaucoup. Danke vielmals. Xièxie. Asante.* תודה *(toda). Ābhārī hōn. Muito obrigada.*

Lauren Hill was the ideal editorial colleague. Emily Wichland and the creative staff at SkyLight Paths made working together a pleasure. Their cover art and book design reflect the message here—bold and spirited, inviting and solid. Our hats go off to them for capturing the spirit of the volume in its form.

Laura Bernstein is the Women's Alliance for Theology, Ethics and Ritual's (WATER) eagle-eyed editor. We are grateful to her for careful, competent work. Thank you also to WATER summer interns Nellie Beckett, Ikhlas Saleem, and Elizabeth Speigle, who edited the final manuscript.

WATER is an extensive alliance and a dynamic force that puts people and ideas together. Our goal is to actualize feminist religious values in the service of social justice. This book is part of WATER's work, which in its fullness includes men as well as women, and people from a range of religious traditions worldwide. We give thanks for all of our collaborators—interns, donors, colleagues, and staff—who make such work possible.

Introduction

Feminist Christianity is something new under the sun. While some may argue that both feminism and Christianity share many of the same values and commitments, the history of the movements demonstrates that their connections are not always obvious. A more accurate analysis is that feminists have been skeptical of patriarchal Christianity and patriarchal Christianity has distanced itself from feminism. Yet, there is the phenomenon called new feminist Christianity that is apparent in churches and seminaries, in the press, and on the front lines of most justice struggles. How did it emerge and where is it going? These are the questions underlying the chapters in this book.

Feminist Christianity is a hybrid notion in the twenty-first century. Christianity has been a source of the oppression of women, as well as a resource for unleashing women's full humanity. Women's oppression takes many forms, with race, age, ethnicity, nationality, sexuality, ability, and other factors all interwoven. Feminist analysis and practice have recognized this, such that what began as a concern for gender is now a widely differentiated way of seeing structures that privilege some and marginalize others.

The result, feminist Christianity, is the product of far-reaching scholarship and wide-ranging practices. Without allowing any one approach to be emblematic, the movement of feminist Christianity is reshaping religious institutions and religious life in more holistic, inclusive, and justice-focused ways. It is influential across the board, in varying degrees, from Catholics to Unitarians, from Baptists to African Methodist Episcopal Zion members.

For the purposes of this book, we have narrowed the scope of our writers and their topics to the U.S. reality in order to focus sharply on one social location. There are drawbacks to this approach, since feminist Christianity is a worldwide phenomenon. The hegemonic nature of the U.S. culture in the world and the equally hegemonic nature of Christianity in the United States give us pause. But we decided it was better to focus on a manageable part of a huge agenda, to look at the reality in one—albeit large and diverse—country, rather than try to cover the world. That way our authors make no claims beyond their own situations, though they do offer insights from them as illustrative of global trends. We await similar work in other countries and regions, where the results will differ and be instructive for us.

This book is meant to be a snapshot, not a movie. We invited the writers to describe what the future of feminist Christianity looks like from their various starting points. Some are scholars teaching in the academy, while others are ministers working in churches; still others are activists running centers or working in their denominations. To accomplish the same task, some have emphasized history; others have deepened the scholarship on their topic, while a few have chosen personal narrative as their primary mode. The variety of their methods and the range of their conclusions illustrate some of the many strands of feminist Christianity, which, when taken together, have an impact well beyond their own circles.

Feminist Christianity in the United States is the result of multiple factors. Chief among them is the role of global feminism in the lives of U.S. women. In the nineteenth century, some of the U.S. women's suffrage leaders, especially Matilda Jocelyn Gage and Elizabeth Cady Stanton, understood the nexus of religion and politics. They advocated for religious changes because they realized that without them no secular changes would take place. Prejudices against women were deeply rooted in the Christian fabric of their society. Stanton's project, *The Woman's Bible,* made clear some of these glaring problems and showed that women were interested in and capable of rectifying them.[1] From the beginning, feminist Christianity has been and remains a political as well as a religious movement.

In the middle of the twentieth century, as the so-called second wave of feminism gathered steam, the questions of religion emerged anew. By that time, there were some Protestant women in ministry, both ordained and lay. Lots of nuns and Catholic lay women were working in schools, colleges, and hospitals, many of which had been built by the women's own congregations. Being able to vote was simply the beginning of women's expectations of full civic and ecclesial citizenship. These religious women were in the vanguard of feminist Christians who gradually dealt with the spiritual dissonance created by what they knew intellectually about the equality of women and the second-class citizenship they were forced to endure in their churches. It would not last long without reply. However, racism and class differences were not taken as seriously as they ought to have been in those early years, something that has taken generations to rectify.

Women began to enter the ordained ministry in significant numbers throughout the twentieth century in many mainstream Protestant churches, though still not yet in the institutional Roman Catholic Church. They studied in seminaries that had theretofore been virtually all male in both faculty and student body. They worshiped in services that were rife with male-exclusive language and imagery both for the divine and for humans, words and symbols that were chosen without sensitivity to gender, race, ability, and the like. Because of women's persistent efforts, that gradually began to change.

In an early 1960s essay, theologian Valerie Saiving clarified that women's social situation caused women's religious lives to differ from men's.[2] It was not because women were physically different, but because of oppressive social conditions that women's sins were the opposite of men's: instead of sinning on the side of power, women, she argued, sin by not taking themselves and other women seriously enough, by doing too many things at once, by lacking focus. So to preach to women that they should be "meek" and "gentle" is to reinforce damaging stereotypes. To counsel them per the

Christian Scripture to "turn the other cheek" is to risk women's lives. Thus the gendered nature of religion came into sharp focus just as liberation theologians highlighted the class-based nature and black theologians the racialized nature of religious experience.

Secular feminist writings and actions emerged apace. Simone de Beauvoir's *The Second Sex* and Betty Friedan's *The Feminine Mystique* were cultural landmarks that expressed the spirit of the day.[3] Groups of women began to work for equal pay for equal work, for the passage of the Equal Rights Amendment, for improved childcare and family leave. It all seems rather quaint now, but the 1960s' anti-war, civil rights, and nascent gay/lesbian rights movements all erupted in a postwar culture that was intent on replicating the pre-war patterns, but this time with the economic and political clout of an emerging superpower. Social change was contested and slow in coming, but a new American society was being shaped and feminist religion was a part of it. Again, the political and religious dimensions are clear in the work of feminist Christians.

Feminist theologian and philosopher Mary Daly published *The Church and the Second Sex* in 1968, outlining the scandal of women's exclusion from full participation in Catholicism.[4] At the same time, Rosemary Radford Ruether began her lectures in feminist theology, in which she articulated the contradictions between male chauvinism and women's equality.[5] All of this work in English came several years after Elisabeth Schüssler Fiorenza had published in German her thesis on women's ministry and church leadership.[6] Others were working at the same time in churches and communities where the exclusion of women from leadership; the passing over of women in Scripture, church history, and theology; as well as the active disavowal of women's moral agency began to dawn on millions of Christian women. Once the issues became clear, the American can-do spirit kicked in and women set about to fix the problems with a boldness that some in other countries found astonishing.

The intellectual pillars of the movement were solid, as many scholars began to problematize gender in the various subspecialties of theology: feminist revisions of church history; feminist ethical analysis; feminist biblical and theological renewal; pastoral theology and counseling; practical theology, preaching, and liturgy all looked at through various feminist lenses. Pioneers including Nelle Morton, Anne McGrew Bennett, Pauli Murray, and others laid a firm foundation in the real lives of those who struggled to bring about the inclusion of women and to end racism, heterosexism, war, ecocide, and the oppression of animals.[7]

Many feminists in the 1970s were rightly suspicious of religion, especially Christianity, which they, like their nineteenth-century foresisters, viewed as oppressive of women. With the rise of Christian fundamentalism, both Catholic and Protestant, that suspicion turned to contempt as right-wing bishops and televangelists became the voice of a patriarchal god for all to hear. Some feminists looked askance at feminist Christians, considering them misguided at best, part of the problem at worst. It is easy to see the logic of their position. At times, even now, there is reason to believe that their suspicions are well founded, especially in the face of continued recalcitrance on the part of many churches to embrace the ideas of feminism. But as a growing number of well-trained feminist Christians began to give the churches a run for their money from the inside as well as from the margins of the institutions, even skeptical feminists began to include religion among the social institutions that required feminist change.

Women ministers emerged as one strong cohort living the contradictions of feminism and Christianity. Some came out of seminary programs that included feminist work in the curriculum. Others met at a series of summer institutes called Seminary Quarter at Grailville, a living/learning program held in the mid-1970s at the Grail in Loveland, Ohio. There, dozens of women students from around the country took part in a plethora of workshops, lectures, and liturgies that shaped them as decisively as any seminary course. Still others were lone rangers in their denominations, struggling for what they knew to be more differentiated forms of Christianity.

Women got together in working groups such as those sponsored by the National Council of Churches and later the Re-Imagining Conference to discuss and assess feminist issues, mainly from Protestant perspectives. The women-church movement reflected similar concerns among Catholics. Women began to bring their ideas into the mainstream of many Christian denominations. While structural changes were few and far between, ideological changes, including reforms of language and imagery, new thinking on ethical issues, challenges to theological givens, and new appreciation for women's historical contributions to the faith, emerged in many arenas.

Backlash against these efforts was vehement and virulent. Many women ministers found themselves assigned to small, far-flung congregations, making ministry as much an endurance sport as a profession. Feminist Catholic sisters were sanctioned. Efforts to diversify language and imagery, to create more horizontal forms of team ministry, and to experiment with innovative forms of worship and preaching were often met with resistance. Gradually, some women made inroads in some denominations, including access to leadership in larger churches. But the road has been rocky and the results mixed.

By the 1980s, what had been a predominantly white women's feminism became a more racially and ethnically diverse movement in Christian circles. African American women theologians including Katie Geneva Cannon and Delores Williams made clear that concern for the well-being of women and children was at the heart of their work, which was profoundly antiracist and attentive to class differences.[8] They and their womanist sisters challenged white feminist women on matters of race and economics such that all subsequent feminist critiques included these issues as substantive dimensions of their analysis.

Likewise, Latin American women in their *feminista* and *mujerista* work demonstrated how community-based (versus more individualized) approaches to theological work enhance the projects. Asian American colleagues took on feminist work from the perspective of those who could parse the complexities of colonialism. Native American women have been more focused on their own traditions than on feminist Christianity per se. In each instance, feminist work has been challenged, changed, and indeed enhanced by taking account of more factors and by including and being shaped by more women's realities.

Issues of sexuality have always been among the most contested parts of feminist work in religion. Lesbian, bisexual, gay, queer, and transgender voices are central to the discussion. Some of the most difficult and unfinished work has been to convince rank-and-file Christians who are led by allegedly heterosexual men that women should be able to make their own sexual and reproductive decisions. Now same-sex marriage is being challenged by some of the same kind of conservative thinking that restricts reproductive choice to a privileged few. These struggles are worldwide, with a lot of the opposition headquartered and funded in the United States. That is why U.S. feminists are so vocal on issues such as maternal mortality and rights of same-sex partners around the world—because we take responsibility for dealing with the despicable U.S. export of organized bigotry. The work of groups such as Catholics for Choice, the Religious Coalition for Reproductive Choice, and the Religious Institute reflects the impact of feminist Christianity in concert with colleagues of other faiths and nations.

Feminist Christianity is but one new religious approach. Feminists in Jewish, Buddhist, Hindu, Muslim, pagan, and Wiccan traditions are exerting similar pressures in their circles. Religious pluralism is a given in the United States such that the new gold standard for feminist work in religion is multireligious. What began as a white concern for gender in one religious tradition is now a multiracial concern for many interlocking forms of oppression as they relate to many religions around the world.[9]

There is a growing number of resources for feminists who wish to deepen their study and practice. Academic groups include the American Academy of Religion, the Society of Biblical Literature, the Society of Christian Ethics, the Catholic Theological Society of America, and the American Academy of Liturgy, where annual gatherings, both nationally and regionally, are occasions for presenting and responding to papers and panels. While there are some denominational groupings, the women's sections of these associations have generally become multireligious. It is in these settings that contemporary feminist Christian scholars do their work.

Publications mirror the same dynamic. The *Journal of Feminist Studies in Religion,* for example, is now the journal of record in the field. It is multireligious and global in its reach. The same is true of centers that have nurtured feminist Christianity in the United States. For example, the Resource Center for Women and Ministry in the South "weaves feminism and spirituality into a vision of justice for the world."[10] The FaithTrust Institute encourages "working together to end sexual and domestic violence."[11] The Women's Alliance for Theology, Ethics and Ritual (WATER) brings together "justice-seeking people who promote the use of feminist values to make religious and social change."[12] These groups have their roots in Christianity but are now broadening their scope and enriching their offerings by working in multireligious settings where many feminists dwell.

This is the context in which the authors of the following chapters live. Whether born in the United States or immigrants, whether part of the academy, the not-for-profit sector, or the churches, these writers are grounded in a new reality in which the parochial limits of denomination and the patriarchal constraints of male dominance have been transcended. They are also active in their respective local communities where feminist work in religion combines with feminist efforts more broadly to shape a new, more just, and more inclusive social fabric. Insofar as these essays contribute to that goal, this volume will serve its purpose.

Part I

FEMINIST THEOLOGICAL VISIONS

Theology is contested intellectual and spiritual space. Women were systematically excluded from asking and answering questions of ultimate meaning and value in Christianity for millennia. Only recently have women been part of the conversation, and even now feminists are not always welcome. But feminists persist in the process, changing both content and method of the field.

In the hands of feminists, theology is increasingly more participatory and accountable to groups beyond the theological guild. The net results are more exciting and accessible, intimately connected to the daily struggles of those who have been marginalized.

It is remarkable to fathom the theological development of the pioneers, of those who picked up the task in mid-century, and now those who continue to deepen and sharpen the analysis. Their visions are grounded in hard-won advances. Particularity and real-world connectedness are characteristics of contemporary feminist Christian theology. Our writers are scrupulous about naming their own starting points, differentiating themselves from others, and acknowledging their part in a larger whole. It is the theological gestalt that changes as new voices and new views come to the fore.

We begin with a postcolonial view as Kwok Pui-lan lays out the contours of a feminist vision for Christianity that overcomes historical barriers. Rosemary Radford Ruether looks at how theological education is renewed by feminist theology, telling the history and emphasizing the strategic moves that will keep the gains in place. Nancy Pineda-Madrid looks ahead, from a Latina feminist perspective, at what next steps are necessary.

Wanda Deifelt contrasts the U.S. scene with Latin American feminist theological communities in a comparison that illuminates both. María Pilar Aquino concretizes one Latina perspective in the work of peacebuilding as part of the creation of a just world. W. Anne Joh seeks to name and sketch some of the elements of a feminist theological vision: gender, race, sex, class, global reach, queer issues. Letha Dawson Scanzoni offers an equally systematic approach, in her case looking at the rich and varied history of evangelical feminist Christians.

This broad section offers an abundance of history, data, and imagination. It proves that the future of feminist Christianity will not be shaped in the United States alone, but in a globalized, multilingual effort where myriad voices articulate critical issues, and even more voices contribute to rethinking them. The children and grandchildren of those colleagues will live out the new reality.

Kwok Pui-lan is the William F. Cole Professor of Christian Theology and Spirituality at Episcopal Divinity School. Dr. Kwok's many publications include *Postcolonial Imagination and Feminist Theology* and *Introducing Asian Feminist Theology.* She has edited *Off the Menu: Asian and Asian North American Women's Religion and Theology* and *Empire and the Christian Tradition: New Readings of Classical Theologians.* She is active in professional societies, including the American Academy of Religion, where she was elected as president.

A Postcolonial Feminist Vision for Christianity

Kwok Pui-lan

You may be wondering whether Christianity has any future, since membership in mainstream denominations in North America and Europe has been in decline, and the churches seem to care for nothing else except human sexuality. If you are feeling dispirited, I invite you to take heart and look further. Today, a "typical" Christian is no longer living in the North Atlantic, but in a village in Nigeria or in a Brazilian shantytown. Africa has the fastest growing number of Christians, and by 2025, the Christian population in Africa, estimated to be 635 million, will surpass that of Europe. In 2050, only about one-fifth of the world's 3 billion Christians will be non-Hispanic white.[1]

We are suffering from myopia if we fail to see that Christianity is becoming a non-Western religion and its center of gravity is shifting to the global South. This demographic shift presents new challenges as well as opportunities to rethink what a new feminist Christianity would look like.

The shift of Christian demographics means that we must begin to envision a postcolonial Christianity that is beyond the colonial legacy, and to welcome the prospect that many cultures will contribute to shaping its future. In the beginning, Christianity had to borrow from and adapt to the language and social structures of the Roman Empire. Since the time of Constantine, church and state became closely intertwined with the imperial patronage. The Roman Catholic Church became the world's first globalizing agent when it sought to create a new world order through the Latinization of the world. The alliance between the cross and the sword has led to genocide and atrocities inflicted upon indigenous peoples. The Protestant missionary movement, likewise, shared a colonial mindset when it supported cultural imperialism in its "civilizing mission."

Today, sadly, the colonial legacy can be seen in the hierarchal and patriarchal structures in many churches in the global South. This is most evident in the recent schism within the Anglican Communion over the issue of homosexuality. Several African bishops, notably Archbishop Peter Akinola of Nigeria, have vehemently condemned homosexuality as a sin and an abomination. Some even argue that homosexuality is only found in the West and that there are no gay men or lesbians in Africa. These church leaders behave as if they could speak for all the African churches, while the voices of dissenting clergy and laity are being excluded.

The future of Christianity looks rather grim if we focus only on patriarchal leaders and the cooperation between the conservative wing of American churches and churches in the global South. But if we conceptualize the churches not as bureaucratic structures, but as movements of base Christian communities in the struggle for justice and peace, a different picture emerges. For example, we will see that the Circle of Concerned African Women Theologians, formed in Accra, Ghana, in 1989, is expanding, and has done important work fighting the HIV/AIDS epidemic that has wrecked havoc on its continent. In Asia, Catholic women have formed the Ecclesia of Women in Asia for networking with feminist grassroots and theological movements and for creating feminist scholarship. In Latin America, Colectivo Con-spirando (the Con-spirando Collective) in Santiago, Chile, is the liveliest ecofeminist group in Latin America. More recently, Latina theologians in South, Central, and North America gathered to exchange ideas and develop a feminist intercultural theology that would contribute toward a shared future of justice.[2]

The future of feminist Christianity is not located at the center of the bureaucratic church, but at the margins and in other subversive spaces. Throughout the centuries, Christian women have created alternative spaces and developed their own organizations and movements, such as the Beguines, the female monastic orders, Mother's Unions, and women's missionary societies. They have exercised religious leadership and carved out spheres of influences at times when women's roles were much more limited than in our time.

Should Christian women continue to knock down the barriers in the church or should they focus their energy on creating something new? This was a question posed by Ivone Gebara, a leading Latin American feminist theologian from Brazil. Gebara was "silenced" by the Catholic Church because of her radical views on ecofeminism, women's reproductive rights, and feminist theology. She observes that feminist critical analyses of patriarchal power have so far not brought about changes in the official structures. She notes, "The power remains the same, although it may seem at times a bit more flexible."[3] Moreover, it has been difficult for women to stay in positions of power without compromising their feminist ideals and practices. Women can easily be co-opted to serve existing religious institutions, and even bring in some small changes, but the patriarchal set-up remains very much the same.

Even in Christian denominations in which women can be ordained to the priesthood, the battle for equality is far from over. Women priests find it difficult to balance family life and work and they experience discrimination in their work and in their career development. If the ordination of women simply means that women are performing the roles of men, with the liturgy, language, and church structures remaining almost the same, this does not bring much hope for the future.

How have feminist theologians helped us rethink the doctrine of the church and its mission? For Mercy Amba Oduyoye, a pioneer in feminist theology in Africa, "the Church is God's household, it is a place where God reigns and where all God's children are at home."[4] The image of household has particular connotations in the African extended family system. She says that ecclesiology is not studying and talking about church. It is being the church. "The Church is the Church when it seeks justice,"[5] she proclaims. Women become church in Africa when they respond to Jesus's call, "Daughter, arise," by taking care of HIV/AIDS victims and female sex workers and combating centuries-old myths and biases against women.

The late Letty Russell, former theology professor at Yale Divinity School, offers the beautiful image of the church "in the round" where all are invited to join the open table fellowship. The church is a place where radical hospitality toward the stranger and the marginalized is practiced.[6] Russell practiced this radical hospitality throughout her life, in her leadership in combating racism in the church, in seeking recognition for lesbians and gay men, and in mentoring and providing support for racial minority women as well as women in the two-thirds world.

How can such egalitarian and prophetic visions of the church be embodied? What are the infrastructures necessary to realize such visions? Can such visions be found within the existing structures, or must women look somewhere else? I imagine there will be no uniform answers to these questions, as much depends on concrete situations. The church as a movement will never be static and must adjust to different circumstances. I have friends who have changed denominations in order to find a spiritual home so that they will feel a sense of belonging and not need to compromise their integrity.

In my own work teaching courses on spirituality, I have found that there is a deep hunger among women for rituals and liturgies that will sustain and nourish them. Our Sunday services have become so repetitive and sometimes so deadening that there is no life and energy to them. One of the things I enjoy most when I attend Asian women's ecumenical gatherings is the aesthetics and sensuality of women's rituals. I remember the Asian women's meeting held at Garut-Bandung in West Java, Indonesia, in 2005. We gathered in a small, beautiful retreat center, called the House of Jars because the focal point of the center has big jars filled with running water. We had bird of paradise flowers on the altar, which was decorated with an exquisite brown and white batik cloth. Each morning the worship leader would introduce the liturgy using symbols, rituals, and movements from her country.

As we envision a new feminist Christianity, we have to find spaces to develop liturgies and symbols that will honor our bodies and rejuvenate our souls. It is when we gather to tell our stories, celebrate our lives, and mourn our losses that rituals become a place to touch the divine. Carmelita Usog, a professor of theology and women's studies in the Philippines who has a gift for leading feminist rituals, writes, "Using an embodied ritual and liturgy allows participants free expression for prayer.... This embodied ritual is also an actualization of the call to reconstruct the meaning of woman's body, which is the seat or locus of exploitation, and reclaim it as hallowed ground and a temple of the spirit."[7]

When I went to South Africa several years ago, I had the opportunity to participate in the worship service of an African Instituted church. The service included the usual reading from Scripture and preaching, but it also included singing, dancing, and swirling. The worship lasted for several hours, and the bodies—young and old, female and male—were fully engaged. The Pentecostal churches are fast growing worldwide. It is a tradition that allows the freedom of bodily expression. In contrast, many Christian women sit through their worship services out of a sense of duty rather than out of joy. They have no wish to invite their children to join the church and thus the mainstream churches are not growing.

In addition to feminist rituals and liturgies, we need to develop spiritual practices for our crazy, busy modern life. In North America, many Christian women are interested in Asian spiritual practices, such as yoga, tai chi, meditation, and other forms of healing exercises. According to a poll conducted by the Pew Research Center's Forum on Religion and Public Life, large numbers of Americans engage in multiple religious practices, mixing elements of diverse traditions. About 25 percent of adults believe in some tenets of Asian religions and 23 percent believe that yoga is not just an exercise but also a spiritual practice.[8] Some have called this New Age spirituality a kind of spiritual buffet that fits into the individualistic style and consumerism of middle-class Americans. I certainly understand the danger of shopping here and there, without religious commitment and accountability, to satisfy your spiritual hunger. But I suspect that, deep down, many women who have grown up in the Christian tradition are dissatisfied with their religion and are looking for something else.

The popular Asian spiritual practices adopted by Americans emphasize the integration of the body and the soul and the release of physical and mental stresses. The body is a living organism with centers of energy, or chakras. It is a site of spiritual knowledge, and must be fully engaged in the spiritual practices. This is in sharp contrast to the Christian spiritual tradition we have inherited, which emphasizes that the soul must be liberated from the body in its spiritual ascent. The women mystics, who have received a lot of attention in feminist spirituality, often denied themselves food and inflicted pain on their bodies in their spiritual pursuit. Their body-denying practices find a strange parallel in the modern-day regimens of dieting, the most popular sport in American society.

To counter the centuries-old Christian misgivings about the body, I am proposing that we understand the Christian notion of incarnation not as a religious belief but as a spiritual practice. Incarnation is the divine meeting the body, so that the body can fully reveal the grace of God. Incarnation is not once and for all, but an ongoing process. We need to develop spiritual practices so that the body can come alive and reflect the image of God in its plurality and multiplicity. My friend Greer Anne finds writing Chinese characters with an ink brush a deeply spiritual exercise because she believes the energy flows through her body and from her fingertips to the paper. Another friend, Liz—with a small physique—shattered a friend's image of her when she took up rock climbing in middle age. Rock climbing challenges her fears and tests her potential. These activities have spiritual qualities because they offer new ways to connect with the body, revitalize the spirit, and actualize unexplored potentials.

It is unfortunate that faith communities are sidelined in the current spiritual revival. Christian spirituality is not living on the mountaintop, dwelling in those rare moments in which we catch a glimpse of eternity. Christian spiritual practices are grounded in the everyday, in the mundane. As the Vietnamese Zen master Thich Nhat Hanh once said, "The miracle is not to walk on water. The miracle is to walk on the green earth."[9] We need to cultivate a new generation of spiritual leaders who can rekindle the sense of awe, wonder, and beauty in encountering the divine, and to attract others to follow.

A new feminist Christianity must find ways to appeal to younger women; otherwise, the wisdom we have gained cannot be passed on. Generation Y, born in the seventies and eighties, is by current accounts the most globally aware and racially diverse generation in history. The sixty million members of Generation Y do not know a world without instant messaging, cell phones, and chat rooms. Many young women who belong to Generation Y think that feminism is outdated, something that belongs to their mothers' generation. They talk openly about queer or intersexed orientations, and often enjoy subverting identities. They are interested in finding ways to integrate sexuality and spirituality, while the church tells them, "Just say no." Feminist Christianity must help them understand that sexuality is a gift from God, intended to help us enter into intimate communion with ourselves and others. We need to help young women honor their bodies and their selves in their sexual relationships.

The Internet and social networking sites allow us to connect with Christian women in other parts of the world with ease. I imagine virtual communities will form around different issues, as well as new alliances and solidarity among Christian women's grassroots movements. For example, the Catherine of Siena Virtual College has been established as an interreligious, not-for-profit education enterprise specializing in gender justice education for women and men.[10] I have a female student who has established a virtual church on the social networking site Second Life for those marginalized because of their sexual orientation.

Today more than ever, the world needs women with courage and vision. We have a responsibility to walk gently on this earth and to make the world a better place for the generations to come. A new feminist Christianity that is green, egalitarian, and exuberant will fulfill the spiritual longing of women and meet the crying needs of the world.

Rosemary Radford Ruether taught for twenty-seven years at the Garrett-Evangelical Theological Seminary and Northwestern University and for six years at the Graduate Theological Union. Dr. Ruether is an emerita professor at Garrett-Evangelical and the Graduate Theological Union. She is the author or editor of more than forty books and numerous articles, including *Sexism and God-Talk: Toward a Feminist Theology; Women-Church: Theology and Practice of Feminist Liturgical Communities;* and *Gaia & God: An Ecofeminist Theology of Earth Healing*. She teaches at the Claremont Graduate University in Claremont, California.

Feminist Theology in Theological Education

ROSEMARY RADFORD RUETHER

In the 1960s feminist theology did not exist. A small but growing number of women worldwide began to invent it. My own first talk on feminist theology, given at a conference in 1968, was "Male Chauvinist Theology and the Anger of Women."[1] It expressed the unwillingness of women to tolerate any longer male theological language inferiorizing women. In 1972–73 I was invited to teach at Harvard Divinity School by Harvey Cox under the Chauncey Stillman Chair of Roman Catholic Theological Studies. I took the opportunity to gather basic resources for feminist critique of theology from the ancient Near Eastern, biblical, and Greco-Roman periods and from nineteenth- and twentieth-century Europe. I taught a second version of this course at Yale Divinity School in 1973–74.

Around 1975 I put together my first course on feminist theology that dealt with the full range of the topics of systematic theology (God, creation, anthropology, good and evil, Christology, redemption, church, and eschatology). No text existed for such a course, so I created a handbook of texts from the ancient Near East and Greco-Roman worlds, Scripture, and early Christian and Western thought organized around these topics. I got the students to write their own feminist biblical *midrashim* (stories), myths, and prayers or poems. Each year we put these together in a booklet distributed to all the students. The lectures for this course were published in my *Sexism and God-Talk: Toward a Feminist Theology* (1983). The handbook of texts was published two years later as *Womenguides: Readings toward a Feminist Theology,* with some of the students' stories and poems. I still teach this course in an ever-expanding version.

From 1968–80 the trickle of feminist theology became a gushing stream. Mary Daly published her first feminist book, *The Church and the Second Sex,* in 1968. She came out with her more radical *Beyond God the Father* in 1973. Letty Russell brought out her first feminist work, *Human Liberation in a Feminist Perspective,* in 1974. Carter Heyward began to pour out articles during this time as well. Her autobiography on her journey to priesthood, *A Priest Forever,* appeared in 1976 and her pioneering theological work, *The Redemption of God,* in 1980.

Feminist theology was also being produced in Europe. Kari Børresen's foundational study of the gendered anthropology of Augustine and Thomas Aquinas was published in French in 1968, although American feminists did not read it until it appeared in English in 1981. Catharina Halkes called for inclusive ministry in her 1964 book *Storm after the Silence* and published her major book on feminist theology, *Met Miriam is het Begonnen* (It All Began with Miriam), in 1980, but, being in Dutch, it was not read by most Americans. Dorothy Soelle was reluctant to embrace a feminism she saw as "American" and lacking class analysis, but changed her view after teaching at Union Seminary in New York. Her *Strength of the Weak: Toward a Christian Feminist Identity* was published in English in 1984.

In the 1980s African American women began to arrive in growing numbers in theological seminaries. African American women's critique of feminism goes back to the beginning of the seventies with articles such as Toni Morrison's 1971 "What the Black Woman Thinks about Women's Lib,"[2] but formal theological work awaited their presence in theological schools. African American women adopted from Alice Walker the term *womanism* to refer to their distinctive context for doing theology from black women's perspectives. One of the first major womanist works was Jacquelyn Grant's *White Women's Christ and Black Women's Jesus: Feminist Christology and Womanist Response,* which appeared in 1989. In the 1990s womanist theological works would abound from writers such as Delores Williams, Kelly Brown Douglas, Emilie Townes, and Katie Cannon. They were joined by Latina feminist (*mujerista*) theology from writers such as Ada María Isasi-Díaz and Asian women such as Chung Hyun Kyung, whose first major book on Asian women's theology was published in 1990.[3]

The story of the development of feminist theology has sometimes assumed that the feminist theologians of the late sixties and seventies lacked race and class analysis and that this was only corrected by the second wave of theology coming from women "of color." This is somewhat misleading. The feminist theologians of the late sixties and seventies, such as Letty Russell, Beverly Harrison, Carter Heyward, and myself, were deeply shaped by the civil rights movement's critique of racism and classism, and sought to integrate a gender analysis *within* class and race critique. What we could not do is speak for black (or Latina or Asian) women's experience. Women theologians from these contexts brought this perspective in the late eighties and nineties to today.

The eighties and nineties also brought a critique of heterosexism in the voices of lesbian feminist theologians and ethicists, such as Carter Heyward, Mary E. Hunt, and Virginia Ramey Mollenkott. The Christian context of feminist theology also saw its critics. Carol Christ and Naomi Goldenberg embraced the Wiccan religious perspective that saw Christianity itself as part of a history of patriarchal religion, beginning sometime in the fourth millennium BCE, which had repressed an earlier religious worldview based on an immanent, earth-centered Goddess. Carol Christ laid forth her claim on "why women need the Goddess" and defined her religious vision in major books, such as her 1987 *Laughter of Aphrodite: Reflections on a Journey to the Goddess.* Both Christ's and Jewish Wiccan priestess Starhawk's writings (such as her 1979 *The Spiral Dance: A Rebirth of the Ancient Religion of the Great Goddess*) were and are widely read by American and European feminists. The Wiccan movement brought vibrant worship communities and spiritual practices that many alienated Christians and Jews found attractive.

Feminist reflection was not limited to the discipline of theology. Feminist critique also developed in all the other theological disciplines. Most important here is the work of Elisabeth Schüssler Fiorenza in New Testament studies. Schüssler Fiorenza is a New Testament critic focusing on hermeneutical methodology that overlaps with feminist theology. Her pioneering work *In Memory of Her: A Feminist Theological Reconstruction of Christian Origins* (1983) has been followed by many other monographs and articles and is foundational reading for any work in feminist theology. Other feminist biblical interpretations, such as Phyllis Trible's work in Hebrew Scripture, *God and the Rhetoric of Sexuality* (1978) and *Texts of Terror* (1984), and Mary Rose d'Angelo's in the New Testament, should also be counted as indispensable for doing feminist theology.

Feminist church historians, who may write more comprehensively or may focus on particular periods, are also key for laying the interpretive foundations for feminist theology. Feminist women working in pastoral psychology, Christian education, liturgics, and preaching interact with theology and its practical applications in Christian life. Feminist work in theological education thus is not the focus of one theological field, but covers the whole scope of the curriculum of theological education.

The late eighties and nineties also saw a burgeoning internationalization of Christian feminist theology, with voices from Latin America, Asia, and Africa, impelled by both the development of liberation theologies in those areas and the lack of gender analysis in those theologies. Women theologians from Latin America, Africa, and Asia called for their own "women's commission" within the Ecumenical Association of Third World Theologians in 1982 and began to develop a series of national, regional, and global conferences to contextualize their own perspectives on theology as "third world" women. Latin American women, such as María Pilar Aquino, Elsa Tamez, and Ivone Gebara; African women, such as Mercy Amba Oduyoye and Teresia Hinga; Asian women, such as Marianne Katoppo, Mary John Mananzan, and Sun Ai Park, developed journals and networks of communication, organized conferences, poured forth their own monographs, and edited volumes. Some of this work goes back to the seventies. Marianne Katoppo's *Compassionate and Free: An Asian Woman's Theology* was published in 1974 and Mary John Mananzan's *Women in Asia: Status and Image* appeared in 1979. Sun Ai Park founded the all-Asia feminist journal *In God's Image* in 1980.

Feminist theology also began to develop from Jewish, Muslim, Buddhist, and Hindu perspectives. The pioneering expression of Jewish feminist theology is Judith Plaskow's 1990 classic, *Standing Again at Sinai: Judaism from a Feminist Perspective*. Rachel Adler's *Engendering Judaism: An Inclusive Theology and Ethics* (1998) reflects her close study of rabbinic texts. Jewish religious feminism is deeply tied to a quest for an inclusive practice of Judaism, as reflected in Lynn Gottlieb's feminist liturgical perspective in her *She Who Dwells Within*. Marcia Falk's *Book of Blessings: New Jewish Prayers for Daily Life, the Sabbath, and the New Moon Festival* reflects her work as a liturgical poet who has developed inclusive prayer language in Hebrew (and Yiddish). Jewish feminism also exists in Israel, but its religious expression is hindered by the fact that only Orthodox Judaism is recognized in Israel. Most Israeli Jewish feminists interested in religion work more as sociologists and anthropologists than as rabbinic exegetes.

Buddhist feminists in the United States have been heavily influenced by the fact that most of their writers are American converts to

Buddhism, and so stand outside the Asian cultures in which Buddhism was shaped. Rita Gross, a Lutheran and then a Jew before becoming a Buddhist, has sought to do the foundational work in theological reinterpretation of Buddhism from a feminist perspective in her *Buddhism after Patriarchy* (1993). Sandy Boucher's *Turning the Wheel: American Women Creating the New Buddhism* (1988) documents the way that American women converts are reshaping Buddhism in North America. She highlights the struggle for full ordination for women in the Buddhist tradition in the United States, as well as conflicts that have arisen over issues of sexual abuse of women followers by male Buddhist leaders. Feminism is not absent from Buddhism in countries such as Taiwan and Thailand. Here, too, the restoration of the full ordination of women becomes a defining issue for Buddhist women.

Muslim feminism is also a movement that is developing very fast. One of the first Muslim women to work on an inclusive Islam has been Riffat Hassan, who in the early 1990s began to study carefully the anthropology of gender in the Quran and discovered that the Quran does not teach that women were created secondary to the male and from his rib. This is a view that a later Islam took over from Christianity. She has written numerous articles and given talks worldwide that enunciate a gender-inclusive Islam. A number of other books and articles from Muslim women holding up an inclusive Islam have followed. In a volatile situation in which radical Islamists seek to enforce a strict subordination of women as an anticolonialist revolt against Western "decadency," while the West seeks to exploit the issue of women to attack the Muslim world, Muslim feminists walk a difficult middle path, critiquing misogynist Islamism, while holding up a vision of Islam as an egalitarian tradition that needs to be rediscovered in its original potential and redeveloped anew today.

This brief overview shows that feminist theology and religious studies have experienced a remarkable development in the last forty-plus years. Books and articles have poured from presses around the world, expressing feminist rethinking of theological categories from the context of many different ethnic-cultural contexts and religious perspectives. In 1970 there were virtually no recently published texts we could use for the bibliography of a course on feminist theology in Christian or other religious contexts, such as Judaism, Buddhism, and Islam. Now references in this area would fill a sizeable book.

Not only are there many new writings that have appeared in the last forty-plus years, but there has also been a remarkable recovery and republication of many earlier feminist religious writings that were unknown to us in 1970. We have discovered medieval women mystics, such as Hildegard of Bingen and Julian of Norwich, who express an inclusive spirituality. We have come to know the dynamic feminism of seventeeth-century English writers, such as Quaker Margaret Fell, with her 1666 treatise *Women's Speaking Justified, Proved, and Allowed of by the Scriptures,* and Anglican Mary Astell, with her 1694 work *A Serious Proposal to the Ladies.* We have realized that these two writings were not isolated exceptions but expressions of a developed perspective among women in these religious communities.

We have also rediscovered the vibrant feminist religious thought of our nearer ancestors in the nineteenth-century United States. We have studied the writings of the Shaker tradition, which claims that Christ appeared as a woman in Mother Ann Lee to complete the revelation of the female side of God. We have been delighted by the pithy writing of Sarah Grimké, such as her *Letters on the Equality of the Sexes and the Condition of Women* (1838), where she proclaims, "All I ask of our brethren is that they will take their feet from off our necks and permit us to stand upright on the ground which God has designed for us to occupy."[4] We have been amazed by the almost fifty years of public lectures of Quaker Lucretia Mott as she expressed her race- and gender-inclusive theology (1830–78). We were moved by Elizabeth Cady Stanton's *Woman's Bible* (1895, 1898), as well as her many other writings. These and many other feminist religious writings of earlier eras are now integral to our remembered history. We are no longer alone as feminists thinking thoughts that women have never thought before.

What is the status of feminist theology and feminist women in theological education today? Clearly the availability of resources for teaching across the theological curriculum from a feminist perspective has changed dramatically since 1968. Resources now abound in all theological fields. There has been an enormous creation of new work in this field, as well as recovery of forgotten traditions. There has also been a great increase in women as theological students and as faculty. In mainstream Protestant theological schools, women students are present in equal numbers, in more progressive schools sometimes comprising nearly two-thirds of the students. Women faculty are also well represented in these schools. For example, in the Graduate Theological Union schools, which range from very liberal to moderately conservative, Protestant, and Catholic, we note the following faculty figures in 2006–7: the three Catholic schools had three women faculty to twelve men, six women to eighteen men, and three women to eleven men. The five Protestant schools had ten women faculty to eleven men, six women to seven men, five women to eight men, ten women to eleven men, and six women to fourteen men. The Unitarian school had five women faculty to one man. The Protestant schools had more equal numbers, more than equal in the case of the Unitarians, who also have a woman president. In the Catholic schools men greatly outnumber women, but women are present in some numbers and in important fields, such as history, ethics, biblical studies, and theology.

Thus the presence of women in theological education as students has been a resounding success, and as faculty a fair success in mainstream to liberal schools. I have no experience of conservative evangelical and Catholic diocesan theological schools, but I would expect lesser numbers of women students and fewer faculty, although women would not be absent in either category. Attendance at professional societies of theology is also significant. The Catholic Theological Society of America was a male clerical bastion in 1966 when

Elizabeth Farians, one of the first Catholic women with an advanced degree in theology, sought to crash its doors. Today the CTSA has close to equal numbers of women and men, and offers a feminist-friendly environment.

However, all is not well for feminist theology in theological education. There are still many male students who never read feminist work, much less take a feminist course. Many male faculty also do not read feminist work and do not integrate it into their courses. When they teach an overview of theology, they may create their syllabus with no feminist work at all. When this is pointed out to them by students, they may respond by creating a "lady's day" in the syllabus, with one lecture devoted to feminist work. This was the experience with the foundational course in theology taught at the School of Religion of the Claremont Graduate University, despite having a feminist woman dean and the only doctorate program on women and religion in the country.

This kind of token inclusion of feminism in foundational courses is far from feminist goals. From a feminist perspective, women are and have been present in all societies throughout history. Even when they have been excluded from male preserves of power and knowledge, they are present through ideologies and strategies that enforce their absence. Thus it is impossible to teach any subject responsibly without analyzing how women are present or how they have been made absent. We cannot talk about women and a feminist perspective only when discussing feminist theology written by women. When teaching theologians such as Augustine, Thomas Aquinas, Calvin, Luther, Barth, and Tillich, we must look at their implicitly or explicitly gendered anthropology and how this affected their view of God, creation, good and evil, Christ, church, and ministry. A theological curriculum that integrates feminist critique should integrate it throughout the curriculum and in every field. It does not content itself with one specialized course in feminist thought and token representation in the foundational curriculum.

Thus there is still much work to be done in feminist thought in religion. The story has still only begun to be told. Since women have been excluded from male elite culture for at least five thousand years, there is work to be done recovering their history for endless years to come. But there is also the important task of maintaining the gains that have been made in the last forty years. Women wrote theological critique in the past and it was forgotten. It is crucial that the work that has been done in our time not suffer the same fate. Just as the price of liberty is constant vigilance, so too is constant vigilance the cost of making women and feminist critique present in theological education, and in education and culture in general. We must be alert to see that when a feminist theologian retires, she is replaced by another feminist theologian, and that feminist work pervades the curriculum. Male students and faculty, as well as women students and faculty, should be expected to read and know feminist thought in religion as an integral part of their education and teaching.

Nancy Pineda-Madrid is assistant professor of theology and U.S. Latino/a ministry at Boston College's School of Theology and Ministry. She holds a doctoral degree in systematic and philosophical theology from the Graduate Theological Union. Dr. Pineda-Madrid is working on a book that examines the problematic intersection of suffering and the quest for salvation from a Latina feminist perspective.

Latina Feminist Theology

Charting Future Discourse

NANCY PINEDA-MADRID

Latinas began writing feminist theologies during the late 1980s, the earliest accounts penned by Ada María Isasi-Díaz and María Pilar Aquino.[1] This theological voice emerged from a consciousness of Latinas' experience as gendered, racialized, classed, heterosexualized, and colonized; these dimensions of Latina experience have together served as a point of departure for Latinas' theological constructions. While Euro-American feminist theology, Latin American liberation theology, Latino theology, and womanist theology have all contributed to Latina feminist theological reflection, Latinas' own history of struggle has shaped Latinas' consciousness of themselves in relation to God. Indeed, Latina feminist theology is located within a long history of Latina resistance to dominant political, economic, and ecclesiastical powers that dates back to the work of Mexican intellectual Sor Juana Inés de la Cruz (1648–1695), and arguably much earlier.[2] This history predates the late twentieth century's women's movement, Chicano movement, and other civil rights movements.

The term *Latina* is used by the majority of feminist theologians of Latin American ancestry writing in the United States. It is an umbrella term chosen for political as well as strategic reasons, and includes the writings of feminists who are Mexican American, Puerto Rican, Cuban American, and many others of Latin American ancestry. In addition, *Latina* highlights the Latin American roots of this group of theologians. It recognizes the Spanish, Amerindian, African, and Portuguese origins of contemporary Latina/o communities, and it is a self-selected term.[3] Other terms frequently used are *mujerista, Hispanic, mestiza, mulata,* and *Chicana*. *Mujerista* is a type of Latina feminist theology that employs the social science method of ethnography and has been developed by Ada María Isasi-Díaz.[4] The term *Hispanic,* while used by some Latino theologians, is not used by most Latina feminist theologians. The U.S. government designated this term for Spanish-speaking and Spanish-surnamed people, and intended, by its use, to focus almost exclusively on the Spanish ancestral roots, thereby dismissing Amerindian and African roots. *Mestiza* means a woman whose identity emerges from the biological, cultural, and religious mixing of the Spanish and the Amerindian, and *mulata* from the mixing of the Spanish and the African. *Chicana* has a more narrow focus because it primarily designates a woman born in the United States of Mexican or Mexican American heritage who critically assumes a class/race/gender political consciousness as orienting her worldview. These last three terms are not inclusive of all women of Latin American heritage.

Latina feminist theologians assume that theological work needs to reflect critically on the lived experience of Christian faith for the sake of liberation. In short, theology must be relevant and emancipatory. These theologians write *from within* the experience of Latinas, that is, this work begins with the questions, concerns, and issues of Latinas today. It, then, considers how God is speaking in the midst of Latinas' lived experience and how this particular experience of God might suggest a fresh approach to the insights and wisdom of the Christian tradition. All of this reflection is done with the aim of realizing a world freer of whatever is dehumanizing and unjust.

However, these theologians do not value all Latina experience equally. They privilege the experience of those who know poverty and oppression most acutely, which means that the injustices of the world are to be understood first from the vantage point of the most vulnerable among us. Accordingly, the theological task is an intellectual endeavor in service of bringing about a more just, transformed, God-filled world not only for Latinas/os but for all humanity and creation.

Since its beginnings more than two decades ago, Latina feminist theology has expanded and deepened. Today, this growth finds expression in a wide array of concerns that will shape Latina feminist theology for decades to come.

Patriarchy, Kyriarchy: A Latina Angle of Vision

Even though feminist theologies each critique *patriarchy*,[5] how patriarchy is understood and what constitutes patriarchy varies substantially among them. Latina feminist theologians take seriously the interlocking nature of sexism, racism, classism, heterosexism, and colonialism as the context out of which they develop their theological constructions. As a consequence they are critiquing not only "the rule of the father" (patriarchy) but also the interstructuring of a broad range of oppressions—in a word, *kyriarchy*.[6] While not widely used, *kyriarchy* nonetheless distinguishes the critique Latina feminists are advancing.

Even so, for Latina feminist theology to mature, these theologians will need to understand more deeply the particular character of Latina/o patriarchy and sexism. To date this has not been sufficiently clarified. When Christianity took root in Latin America in the sixteenth century, Marian devotions began to form, and along with them grew a distinctive expression of the patriarchal feminine.[7] In the process Mary was falsely but powerfully interpreted in a way that idealized woman as passive, silent, obedient, and subordinate. This distorted interpretation of Mary has served to structure and legitimize an unjust social order, and has had profound and wide-ranging consequences. Today, it finds expression in the ideology of *marianismo,* which promotes the so-called veneration of Mary. It encourages women to follow the "example" set by Mary, that is, to model "self-sacrifice, self-effacement, and self-subordination" and by so doing, become "spiritually superior."[8] "Superiority" is achieved through "submission and invisibility."[9] *Marianismo* is but one manifestation of oppression. Far too often, the structure of the family (*la familia*) has been interpreted in a conventional manner. This symbol of efficacious power reflects a heterosexually circumscribed universe. When this symbol is used to uphold conservative norms, it serves to exclude the validity of "female sexuality generally and male homosexuality and lesbianism specifically."[10] In the process, *la familia* no longer serves to further the humanization of either women or men. Latina feminist theologians need to analyze more deeply how ideas such as *marianismo* and *la familia* function within the social and imaginative worlds of U.S. Latina/o communities. This effort will make clear the ways in which Latinas/os have internalized oppressive social structures.

Violence, Suffering: A Bodily Reality

Many feminist theologians have recounted the problems attributed to Descartes's famous pronouncement "I think, therefore I am." Out of the ashes of their critiques, they have created new theological constructs that attend to emotions, to intuitions, and to the psyche. But what of the human body? Latina feminist theologians need to turn to questions of violence and human bodies. In alarming numbers, girls and women know the experience of rape, abuse, torture, murder, and dismemberment. Theologians must focus more sharply on bodies materially rather than exclusively in a symbolical, figurative, or metaphorical fashion. To be sure, the incidents of feminicide in Mexico (especially Ciudad Juárez), Honduras, and Guatemala,[11] not to mention all manner of violence girls and women experience in the United States, each demand attention, as do the many other ways female bodies are being crushed or destroyed. When it comes to female bodies and the legacy of Christian theology, questions of power move quickly to the fore. We must ask: What are the theoretical tools that can dismantle the legacy of misogyny that continues to shape the public imagination of today? No task is more urgent for brown female bodies.[12]

"Undocumented" Immigrants and Civil Society

Latina feminist theologians have committed themselves to writing theology from the standpoint of the most vulnerable, which means the situation of "undocumented" immigrants, most of whom are Latinas/os. "Undocumented" is in quotes because these immigrants do, in fact, have documents recognizing them as citizens of countries other than the United States. However, their presence in the United States demands that Latina feminist theology engage in a more thorough, broad-based social analysis to better understand the experience of these immigrants. They represent a significant portion of U.S. Latinas/os who, according to the *New York Times,* number some 47 million, an estimated 8 million of whom are "undocumented" immigrants.[13]

The plight of these immigrants remains largely invisible in the public arena. An enduring fear of being discovered marks their lives and overshadows their experiences of physical violence, economic betrayals, and every manner of abuse. These brutal realities continue unabated because "undocumented" immigrants are persona non grata before the law. Without question, their daily lives are marked by unmitigated vulnerability. Their experience of structural violence defies description. It eludes us because while they live in close physical proximity to us, their culture, their language, their life histories remain distant from most of us who are U.S. citizens and professed Christians. Consequently, the experience of these immigrants can be, disastrously, less affecting. We find it next to impossible to relate to it. "Undocumented" immigrant women are far more likely to suffer abuse.[14] The story of these immigrants is a story of enslavement. It calls into question the United States' formal abolition of slavery in 1865 (in the Thirteenth Amendment to the U.S. Constitution). Latina feminist theology is uniquely positioned to address this atrocity.

Interculturality and Diversity

Recently, many Latina feminist theologians have begun reflecting on diversity both internal to the Latina/o community and external to it, that is, the Latina/o community's relation to other racial and ethnic communities. While the word *Latina* functions as an umbrella term, it is coming under increased scrutiny. These theologians have begun analyzing the challenge associated with the term *Latina,* in large part due to the enormous differences—in histories, in cultures, in religious beliefs and practices, in racial and ethnic mixing, in intellectual histories, in economic circumstances, and so forth—that this term attempts to straddle.[15] For example, in 2006 the Pew Hispanic Center conducted a survey and determined that of all Hispanics/Latinas/os living in the United States, 68 percent are Roman Catholic, 15 percent are evangelical Protestant, and the third largest group, making up 8 percent, identifies as "no affiliation," agnostic, or atheist. In addition, there are huge differences in terms of the relative size of the Latina/o communities residing in the United States. Again, according to Pew, for 2005, of all Hispanics/Latinas/os living in the United States, 63.9 percent are of Mexican origin, 9.1 percent are Puerto Rican, 3.5 percent are of Cuban origin, 3 percent are of Salvadorian origin, 2.7 percent are of Dominican origin, and all other Hispanic/Latina/o groups make up less than 2 percent of the U.S. Hispanic/Latina/o population.[16]

The challenge of diversity extends beyond the bounds of the Latina/o community. Latina feminist theologians have begun engaging in conversations with womanist and African American feminist theologians as well as feminist theologians from various Latin American and Caribbean countries.[17] Naturally, these exchanges have led Latina feminist theologians to discover overlapping areas of interest and some similar historical concerns. These exchanges will continue to recontextualize Latinas' liberationist aims by concretizing what emancipation means in new ways. Questions of globalization, economic power, race, sexual identity, and imperialism have been cast in a new light as a result of these rich conversations.

A number of Latina feminist theologians have addressed the challenge of diversity through their use of the philosophy of *interculturality*. It will continue to shape the contours of Latina feminist discourse for many years.[18] Implicit here is a critique of "multiculturalism," which has far too often been used to gloss over significant differences and surreptitiously further an assimilationist agenda. Interculturality, by contrast, reframes how we understand diversity. It is an eschatological philosophy that can productively guide the construction of theology toward an emancipatory goal. In the words of German philosopher Raúl Fornet-Betancourt, interculturality entails "consciously knowing the finality for which we work … in order to know what we should take care of today and how we should do it."[19]

Intercultural philosophy foregrounds the historical context of each group of people, and promotes the value of living together transnationally. Living together necessitates a critical awareness of the material particularities of each group of people. It necessitates a reinterpretation of the notion of diversity such that it means not mere toleration or celebration of difference, but rather a call to grow by being in an ongoing relationship with the "Other," by being open to and deliberately seeking out the ways in which this relationship invites growth and transformation. This philosophy furthers a shift: cultural groups are invited to shift *from* relations of domination and subordination *to* relations that overtly recognize that all groups are participating in God's truth. Accordingly, this philosophical vision regards all ways of thinking as being relative, promotes a critical awareness of the politics of inequality and how this shapes group relations, and supports conceptual strategies that foster a culture of just and humanizing relations.

In the years to come, through the various challenges and concerns addressed by Latina feminist theologians, the Christian faithful in the United States will be invited to see Christianity with new eyes. The writings of these theologians will call Christians to work toward the realization of the gospel message of justice for the most vulnerable, especially "undocumented" immigrants and the victims of violence. In the process, Christians will develop a more acute vision, one that sees that being a committed Christian necessarily means critiquing the oppressive practices of American empire. Latina feminist theology—as it critiques violence, patriarchy, and kyriarchy and as it affirms interculturality—will likewise contribute to the internal transformation of the Christian tradition. This theological contribution will address the ways in which the Christian tradition has become domesticated, and will suggest a path toward a more righteous embrace of the gospel message.

Perhaps the most significant contribution Latina feminist theology will make is to invite Christians to develop a borderlands vision of the gospel message. This kind of vision has developed out of the experience of speaking two languages (English and Spanish), knowing two practices of faith (Latina/o popular religious practices and Euro-American church rituals), and experiencing two ways of being human (Euro-American and Latina/o). A borderlands vision is not unique to Latinas/os—many communities in the United States know this experience (for example, African Americans, Native Americans, LGBTQ communities, the differently abled, and others). In naming it, Latina feminist theologians stand for the proposition that this vision carries the possibility of expanding our understanding of what it means to be human. When we embrace a borderlands vision, we also grow in our embrace of the radical life to which God calls us. We learn to embrace others who are very different from ourselves. In the process, the world becomes a more humane place and a more God-filled place, a place of creativity, imagination, and transformation.

Wanda Deifelt is associate professor of religion at Luther College in Decorah, Iowa. She is an ordained pastor of the Lutheran Church in Brazil (IECLB). Dr. Deifelt taught at Escola Superior de Teologia in São Leopoldo, Brazil, from 1991–2004, where she held the Chair of Feminist Theology. She writes and lectures widely on liberation topics.

Crossing Borders

Feminist Christianity in Latin America

WANDA DEIFELT

As a Brazilian teaching in the United States, I find myself constantly crossing borders. I cross not the geopolitical borders that separate countries, but the borders of theory and praxis, social activism and academia, North Atlantic and Latin American theology. In my opinion, the scope and meaning of feminism requires building bridges and overcoming the boundaries imposed by geography, race, class, or religion. In my case, these bridges were built very early. I was deeply influenced by feminist theologians from the United States, even though my theological identification was with Latin American liberation theology. Feminist scholars in the United States helped women around the globe find their voices. In crossing borders, feminist Christianity intersected people, practices, and political movements.

A budding feminist theology found root in Latin America, helping to articulate how Christianity could deconstruct misogynist teachings that classified women as descendants of Eve (the second in the order of creation but the first one to sin) and construct more egalitarian relationships between women and men, following the examples of Jesus and his teachings.[1] Based initially on women's experiences but expanding to critically reflect also on men's gender conditioning, feminist theology gained space particularly within academic theological settings and helped reshape the face of Christianity on the continent.[2] Interestingly, the values of feminist Christianity—justice, equality, dignity, respect for creation, and the well-being of all—also grew outside the realm of organized religion in camps that are not markedly Christian—that is, in civil society.

The changes and contributions of feminist Christianity in Latin America are deeply connected to the development and future of feminist Christianity in the United States. Three Latin American experiences (or approaches) are worthy of attention because they offer further opportunities for crossing borders and deepening conversation within feminist Christianity from a global perspective.

The first is the academic setting that allowed feminist Christianity the freedom to criticize, explore, and creatively formulate theological truths through a feminist lens, presenting some of the most creative theological insights for the future of feminist Christianity. The second is the presence of feminist voices and practices within church settings, bridging the gap between feminism as a political movement and Christianity as an organized religion. This dialogue gives theological discourse and practice new impetus and relevance, offering new insights on the presence of the church in the world at large. The third experience is the feminist presence, motivated by Christian values and mores, in civil society. Although not bearing the ecclesial structure and perhaps not even being consciously associated with feminist Christianity, this approach embodies the possibilities and tensions of a feminist life and spirituality translated into social action. By using the experiences of Latin America, it is possible to draw parallels, gain new insights, and foment border crossing between Latin and North American feminist Christianity.

Feminist Christianity in the Academic Setting

In Latin America, the articulation of a feminist Christianity can be very clearly identified in the academic setting. This might seem contradictory, considering that feminism claims a grassroots approach reflecting on daily, embodied experiences, and empowering women and men to be agents of social, political, and economic transformation in light of Christian teachings. The reason for this academic emphasis has to do primarily with the long-lasting connection between feminism and education. Similar to what happened in the secular setting, education became a catalyst for larger changes within Christianity. Realizing women's absence from both the classrooms and the curriculum, Christian feminists realized the urgent need to train leaders, especially women and men in solidarity with women, who could rethink and reshape church practices.

It did not take long for the connection between theological education and ordination to be made. Advocating for the theological education of women required finding biblical and theological justifications for the presence of women not only in higher education but also in church rosters. This connection can be exemplified in a small document titled "Letter Regarding Women and Theology," resulting from the Third World Lutheran Theological Educators Conference, 1988, in Brazil. Although drawing from its particular denominational background, there are similar examples from other Protestant churches.

> As theologians we are especially concerned with women's access to theological education and the support available to women from our churches and the communities of their studies. We pledge to work for an increase in the number of women in theology—students as well as educators—responsible for theological training. We believe that the ordination of women is needed, just as is a theologically sound reinterpretation of Scripture. The Lutheran tradition, particularly the Lutheran understanding of justi-

> fication by grace through faith, and the universal priesthood of all baptized believers should lead to fuller human community. Therefore we pledge to work for the ordination of women in our churches and in all the Lutheran churches.[3]

Women's presence in theological education led to some auspicious initiatives. The creation of a chair in feminist theology at Escola Superior de Teologia (the Lutheran Seminary) in 1990 made classes in feminist theology mandatory in the curriculum of theological education, exposing future pastors to feminist biblical hermeneutics, feminist pastoral care, and the study of theological topics from a feminist perspective.[4] The nomenclature "feminist theology" to describe the initiatives taken by Latin American female scholars was adopted in 1993 at the regional meeting of the Ecumenical Association of Third World Theologians (EATWOT). Gender became a common theme in national and international theological conferences. Feminist theology in particular functioned as a catalyst for ecumenical gatherings, such as the ongoing annual congresses bringing together Lutheran, Roman Catholic, Anglican, and Methodist theological students in the state of Rio Grande do Sul, Brazil.[5] Young women and men preparing to enter ordained ministry have met since 1990 to discuss issues such as women in the Bible, ecofeminism, and queer theology.

The new contributions of feminist Christianity in Latin America come through the work of theologians and scholars engaged in interdisciplinary work. We can foresee that the dialogue across disciplines will continue to bear fruit in the future. Publications and conferences building bridges between theology and fields as diverse as economics, politics, art, and ecology offer new insights not only on the way to be a Christian in Latin America, but also on how feminist theological insights contribute to these fields. This interdisciplinary approach benefits all fields of knowledge involved. An example of this is the research on gender, sexuality studies, and reproductive rights.[6] Given the role of religion in conditioning human sexuality, feminist Christianity will continue to be a liberating voice in this field.

The use of gender as a category of analysis has led to a new wave of publications and reflections on men's experiences.[7] Because the early stages of feminist Christianity focused primarily on women, significant work was done to affirm women's presence in Scripture, in the early Christian movement, and in society at large. A new and ongoing tendency is the appropriation of feminist Christian rhetoric to include a deeper reflection on masculinities, a much-needed process in light of the *machista* (chauvinistic) culture that permeates Latin America. The discussion on masculinities is also influenced by queer theory, which opens yet other possibilities for feminist Christianity.

The close ties between academic feminist endeavors and grassroots movements have been constant. Feminist Christianity in Latin America will continue to benefit from this partnership. Social and political movements such as the landless workers, indigenous peoples, and Afro-Caribbean groups have shaped feminist theological discourse, and this will continue in the future. This innovative work can already be seen in the works of ecofeminist theologian Ivone Gebara, Afro-Caribbean biblical scholar Maricel Mena Lopez, and Aymaran theologian and grassroots activist Vicenta Mamani Bernabé.[8] In the future, we can expect more collective work on religious pluralism as Christianity engages in conversation with ancestral religions and practices.

There are many parallels between the Latin American experience and the development of feminist Christianity in the United States, including the fact that, in spite of ongoing struggles, feminist Christianity found a home in the academic setting. Feminist Christian scholars achieved recognition and offered theological contributions that are now considered historical landmarks. Of particular importance is the imperative that feminist Christianity branch out and cross borders in order to engage in dialogue with multiple social, cultural, and disciplinary perspectives. Similar to the Latin American endeavor, feminist Christianity in the United States has learned from the contributions of womanist, *mujerista,* queer, and indigenous perspectives, and it must continue to dialogue with theologies from the global South.

Feminist Christianity in the Churches

In Latin America, the past decades have witnessed a tremendous shift in the mentality of churchgoers over issues such as women's ordination, women's leadership in local congregations, and women's presence in seminaries as theological educators. This shift was not accidental, but is part of a longer and greater feminist movement. Although the entrance of the first woman to study at any seminary or theological college is remembered as a historical event, this is a reality taken for granted by women in the twenty-first century.[9] Similarly, if the first women working as pastors in local congregations were perceived as pioneers, ordained ministry is no longer unattainable for women in many Christian denominations.

In many churches, women have changed from being those who listen to sermons to those who preach them; from being spectators in liturgy to those who administer the sacraments; from being completely absent from seminary classrooms to being admitted to theological institutions, and eventually comprising nearly half of student bodies. Women's ordination became a reality in mainstream Protestant churches and also in many independent Pentecostal churches in Latin America. Although not ordaining women, the Roman Catholic Church also saw a significant increase in the number of women teaching and studying in its undergraduate and graduate theological schools.

Several ecumenical initiatives boosted feminist Christianity in Latin America. The World Council of Churches (WCC) declared 1988–98 the Ecumenical Decade of Churches in Solidarity with Women. The decade provided a space for women to articulate their aspirations for church and society and to establish a wider network among women across countries and denominations. It also promoted the possibility of women exercising leadership, made discrimination against women more visible, and publicly denounced that discrimination.[10]

The Decade to Overcome Violence (2001–10), also a WCC initiative, led to awareness and debate not only about violence in the public space but also about violence inside the home: gender violence, violence against women and children, and more.[11] These ecumenical activities fostered a greater feminist presence in the churches because feminists had the necessary socio-analytical tools and the theological insights to make these ecumenical activities more relevant and effective.

In terms of ecclesial organization, the Protestant denominations have undergone more visible changes, even though similar discussions are also found (even if not implemented) within the Roman Catholic Church. Nevertheless, mainstream Protestant churches do not represent the majority of the population. In Latin America, Catholicism still prevails as the leading denomination, although it is losing terrain to the fast-growing neo-Pentecostal churches.

Most women in Latin America do not enjoy the benefits of qualified theological education, access to the decision-making bodies in their church, or even full participation in the community. Feminist Christianity will need to be particularly attentive to the growth of fundamentalist ideas associated with prosperity theology, charismatic religious movements, televangelism, and literal readings of Scripture. An ongoing concern will be advocacy for the ordination of lesbians and gays in the churches that already ordain women, and the ordination of women and abolishment of compulsory celibacy in denominations that do not yet engage in these practices.

The strength of feminist Christianity within the churches will continue to lie with more democratic, participatory, and lay-centered initiatives. This is true for both Latin American and North American contexts. Theological training for lay leaders, liturgically innovative worship, inclusive and expansive metaphors to address the divine, the connection between personal spirituality and social justice, and an overall attentiveness to the life of the church as it relates to the seasons of people's lives will be the greatest contributions of feminist Christianity in the churches.

Feminist Christianity outside the Churches

Both in the United States and throughout Latin America, there is a significant number of Christians who identify with feminism. But there is probably an equally large number of feminists who have left organized religion (in this case, the church) because they saw their energy seep away while attempting to reform a patriarchal institution and they decided to focus on civil society instead. This is particularly true with feminist organizations, whose members are often ostracized by religious leaders due to their stances on issues such as abortion, reproductive rights, sexual pleasure, and the like. In Latin America, the initiatives of feminists in civil society are often closer to the message of the gospel than the churches themselves. This leads to the experience of feminist Christianity outside the churches.

To identify these initiatives as feminist Christianity outside the churches is not done lightly, especially because these feminists do not always claim to be Christians. It is done, however, to recognize that feminist nongovernmental organizations engage in a ministry that follows in Jesus's footsteps: uplifting the rights of the poor and disenfranchised, healing the sick, welcoming the stranger and outcast, denouncing violence and abuse, and speaking words of comfort and hope.

In making this comparison, the idea is not to legitimize their work by naming it Christian or to grant it acceptability through Christian credentials. The future of feminist Christianity lies in establishing welcoming bridges to social feminist initiatives and leading church bodies to realize that the gospel is preached and practiced in unlikely places. To name not-for-profit feminist organizations as feminist Christianity outside the churches is a provocative description to confront churches about their own prophetic work in the world at large. The organizations named here are only a small sample of the rich networks active in Latin America that represent feminist Christianity dancing to a different tune.

The initiatives undertaken by Las Dignas–Asociación de Mujeres por la Dignidad y la Vida (Association of Women for Dignity and Life), an organization formed in El Salvador in 1990 in the aftermath of the armed conflicts that assailed that country, are described as contributions to eradicate women's subordination in society and to foster democratic participation with social and economic justice.[12] Las Dignas focuses on education, legal advice, and therapeutic services for women. Its educational resources are geared toward empowering women who have experienced violence and discrimination to become participants in society. Las Dignas challenges feminist Christianity and the churches to rethink the role of theological education. If education is a means to empower human beings with the knowledge, positive attitudes, values, and skills necessary to develop critical thinking, assertiveness, self-confidence, and full participation in society, how can theological education do the same for churches? In other words, if education fosters citizenship in society, how does theological education foster citizenship in the churches?

Colectivo Con-spirando (Con-spirando Collective) in Chile has a closer connection to religious discourse and practice.[13] Its main publication, *Con-spirando,* addresses feminist rituals and reclaims a broader notion of the divine than that broadcast by the churches. It focuses on inclusive, poetic, and holistic approaches to the sacred and challenges churches to deconstruct idolatrous imagery of God. It also confronts churches with the urgency of the Christian message in light of social, political, economic, and ecological crises. Why is traditional Christianity holding God hostage to conformist and often outdated schemes? How can feminist Christianity help propagate the inventive approaches proposed by feminists outside the churches, such as Con-spirando?

SOS Corpo, Instituto Feminista para a Democracia (Feminist Institute for Democracy) is a Brazilian organization engaged in a variety of activities that promote full participation in the social, political, and economic decision-making processes.[14] By promoting gender equality, human rights, and social justice through education, research, and political action, SOS Corpo has been a leader in health education, particularly in light of the HIV/AIDS pandemic in Northeast Brazil. It works to involve women and girls in shaping effective policies and programs in relation to reproductive rights and sexual education. Through initiatives such as SOS Corpo, feminist Christianity finds new partners for advocacy and social engagement.

The work undertaken by Iniciativa de Mujeres Colombianas por la Paz (the Colombian Women's Initiative for Peace) addresses the painful reality of women and girls affected by the armed conflict in Colombia.[15] Among other services, the organization provides legal support for the women and girls who have been sexually violated by Colombian paramilitaries. It also works to safeguard the victims whose lives are threatened for going public and to denounce the atrocities committed in the situation of warfare. Iniciativa de Mujeres Colombianas por la Paz challenges feminist Christianity to engage in proactive political networking that goes beyond geographical location, but sees patterns of violence in a wider perspective. It reminds Christian feminism that the scope of its activities is not only *ad intra,* that is, to transform the space of church and seminaries, but also a prophetic commitment to the world at large.

The future of feminist Christianity is being shaped in the obvious places: in academic theological institutions, women-centered organizations, and gender programs within the churches. Across the border, these experiences emphasize the "Christian" aspect of feminist Christianity. But the new feminist Christianity is also found in less obvious settings. By seeking closer proximity to the "feminist" arena and reclaiming feminism as a political movement, feminist Christianity continues to establish close partnerships in civil society. It constantly crosses borders when it affirms teachings that are shared by Christians and feminists alike: justice, equality, dignity, respect for creation, and affirmation of well-being for all. A new feminist Christianity is already taking shape as it moves beyond geographical borders and claims its global citizenship.

María Pilar Aquino is professor of theology and religious studies at the University of San Diego. Dr. Aquino was a visiting professor of theology at Harvard Divinity School. She is the author of *Our Cry for Life: Feminist Theology from Latin America; La teología, la iglesia y la mujer en América Latina* (Theology, the Church and Women in Latin America); and *Teología feminista Latinoamericana* (Latin American Feminist Theology). She organizes and convenes Latina feminist scholars and activists in religion.

Analysis, Interconnectedness, and Peacebuilding for a Just World

MARÍA PILAR AQUINO

No future is possible without justice for women. No future is feasible without human rights for women. No future is viable without meeting women's basic human needs. No future of feminist Christianity can flourish without a just world. I begin my contribution to this book with phrases that serve to articulate, initially in negative terms, that which precludes a positive realization of a desired future in feminist Christianity.

To speak about the future from my perspective as a Latin American feminist Christian theologian involves at least three aspects. First, thought about the future involves awareness about my hopes and aspirations for something that I consider to be good and desirable for myself, as well as for my loved ones and others around the world. Second, it implies giving a name to a positive reality that centers my personal and social life, guides my choices and decisions, and provides meaning and orientation to my activities and work. Third, it entails taking a deliberate, constructive position as I seek possibilities and opportunities to transform that which prevents an envisioned future from being. In short, to speak about the future in feminist religious terms involves making explicit my hopes, aspirations, and tasks for actualizing positive realities that enable wholeness, fullness, justice, and well-being for all.

Feminist Christianity can only affirm a just world as its desired future for the ultimate goal of liberation. From my perspective, a just world is the name for that reality that encapsulates the motives of existential hope and the reasons for dedicating our energies to bringing about, from the existing circumstances, those positive realities that ought to exist in the world. The vision of a just world is not only consistent with critical feminist reason but also with the core of liberating Christianity. In the biblical tradition, such a world becomes the object of hope as the fulfillment of a renewed world and humanity in G*d's grace and blessing and, as embodied by the Christ event (Wis. 7:27; Mark 1:15; Luke 7:22–23; Rom. 8:18–25; Rev. 21:5–6), it becomes for Christians the reference point for their lives, values, and commitments.

In the works of early feminist theologians from the United States, the future is named with different but related terms. As an understanding of what it means to be human and as a social event, Letty M. Russell articulates the feminist vision of the future as "a new cooperative social order," "a humane society" that actualizes G*d's goal of liberation through "righteousness, peace, and justice in community."[1] As the ultimate point of history, the feminist vision of the future is articulated by Rosemary Radford Ruether as a "livable, as distinct from unlivable, environment," as a "state of peace and justice."[2] It is a "just and livable future."[3] As the reality free from kyriarchal domination and dehumanization as "intended by the life-giving power of G-d," Elisabeth Schüssler Fiorenza articulates the feminist vision of the future in terms of an "alternative world of justice and well-being."[4] She calls it "an alternative society and world."[5] She claims it was inaugurated "by the vision of equality, wholeness, and freedom expressed in Gal. 3:27 ff."[6] These approaches point to affirming visions of a just world as the future of feminist Christianity.

The affirmation of a just world as the defining mark of the future in feminist Christianity consistently makes reference to bringing about realities of justice and peace. While justice is the primary goal of liberation, peace is the fruit and outcome of justice.[7] According to Russell, the word *peace/shalom* "represents a summary of all the gifts that God promises to humanity; the fulfillment of God's intention for all creation."[8] For her, peace as a blessing and "as a gift of total wholeness and well-being in community" sets the ground for "all humanity to have a future and a hope."[9] Thinking about hopes and aspirations for a positive future, I ask how a society and world rooted in peace would look. I find a helpful response to this question in the document on peace of the famous Medellín Bishops Conference (Medellín, Colombia, 1968), which is also considered to be a pioneer of Latin American liberation theology. This document characterizes the Christian concept of peace not as "the simple absence of violence and bloodshed," but provides content for justice to be achieved in the following terms:

> Peace is, above all, a work of justice. It presupposes and requires the establishment of a just order in which men [and women] can fulfill themselves as [humans], where their dignity is respected, their legitimate aspirations satisfied, their access to truth recognized, their personal freedom guaranteed; an order where [a person] is not an object, but an agent of [her/his] own history. Therefore there will be attempts against peace where unjust inequalities among [humans] and nations prevail.[10]

In my view, the vision of a just order presented by this document is consistent with the vision of a just world as the future of feminist

Christianity. This commonality of vision also allows the assertion that the feminist struggles for justice, human dignity, and human rights in both society and church bring credibility and authenticity to Christian thought and practice. Feminist religious and theological work for a just world must transform *injustice* that engenders destructive human relationships, hateful human interaction, violent conflict, dehumanization, and exploitation of humans and their environment.

In religious terms, *sin* is the name for injustice that causes harm to humans, leading humans to damage their own world. Naming sexual violence as sin in the work of Marie M. Fortune is particularly relevant as a feminist theological approach.[11] The radical destructiveness of injustice in contemporary times is exposed in the pervasive practices of rape and sexual violence against women in contexts of armed conflict. In this light, the establishment of a just world presupposes and demands the elimination of sin by changing sinful relationships and realities. Historical and spiritual liberation demand the elimination of sin as a theological necessity.

The vision of a just world rooted in peace as the work of justice for the well-being and liberation of humans and the world is also demanded by the current historical reality from which feminist religious visions and practical orientations emerge. This demand is highlighted by the unmitigated realities of poverty, destructive conflict, sexual violence, and deprivation of basic human rights and needs lived by the majority of women and children around the world. Ruled by kyriarchal globalization and dominated by kyriarchal cultures and religions, the current structure of the world does not offer the material conditions for actualizing social justice, human rights, and fulfillment of basic human needs. Thus, in the interest of the future, contributions to systemic change in religious terms continue to be the main task of feminist Christianity. To the extent that feminist Christianity continues to develop visions and resources for constructive transformation of personal and structural realities, it asserts its relevance to the present and future for the aim of reaching a just world. I turn now to two aspects to strengthen our work in bringing about a positive future in feminist Christianity.

Critical Analysis and Tangible Interconnectedness

If a just world is the name I am giving to the type of society that feminist Christianity is seeking to build, such an intended future can and should serve to increase clarity about the destructive impact of today's global market capitalism on both humans and the environment. This aspect calls feminist Christianity to continue developing systemic analysis to promote intervention in processes of social change with greater creativity and effectiveness. Taking into account the ethical value and principle of interconnectedness, such analysis provides sociopolitical and religious strategies for transformative action that benefits equally the local and global contexts. Based on my knowledge of the U.S. feminist religious and theological field, I am confident in saying that only a few scholars in this field deliberately adopt a critical feminist analytic of domination.[12] Along with this, only a few scholars engage in developing critical approaches to U.S.-led global market capitalism, to its pernicious effects on the marginalized populations of the two-thirds world, and to its imperial, idolatrous ideology that continues to cover up the harm done by U.S. financial and militaristic foreign agendas.

It is important to continue to develop a critical feminist analysis. Feminist religious intervention for change at the local level is needed to prevent the future of humanity and the world from collapsing. According to two-thirds-world social analysis, the current phase of global capitalism, with its dramatic financial crisis caused by irresponsible decisions of the greedy, speculative financial sector, is resulting in deteriorating conditions not just for the poor in the Southern Hemisphere but for everyone else excluded from shaping the face of the world. This phase of global capitalism, called "oligopoly market structure," is ruled by large financial corporations.[13] It constructs a social reality in which only a few elite social actors concentrate products, investment, consumer goods, trade, and essential resources in such a way that provides them the greatest profit while excluding everyone else from participation in decision making and a share in the market. This is a social system marked by a high level of competition between firms for positions of dominance and control in the global setting. As a societal system, it must be named kyriarchal capitalism. For a kyriarchal market system, promoting human rights, meeting human needs, and creating sustainable environments are not primary concerns. In fact, they are not concerns at all.

In the world today, the human aspirations for sustainable environments to meet basic human needs and promote human rights become once again asphyxiated by focus on corporate profit. This is a significant source of conflict that cannot be resolved by rescuing banks through leaving marginalized people in ever more precarious circumstances, and continuing to increase levels of social instability and human insecurity around the world. Systemic social injustice multiplies a pervasive reality of conflict as massive inequalities become key factors in deepening social divisions. Therefore, the future of feminist Christianity can and should have something to say and something to do in response to this environment. Contributing to building the future as a world of justice and well-being for women and for others around the world entails work to ensure that material conditions are created to cover the basic human needs and protect the human rights of all, not just to provide for the needs and rights of those located in the economically and financially powerful United States of America.

In bringing forth the religious and political implications of interconnectedness, I am increasingly convinced that U.S. feminist scholars would benefit greatly by connecting actively and directly with communities and colleagues located in the two-thirds world. Personal encounters with the individuals who actually live and work in that world will enhance our ability to identify the interwoven character of both systems of domination and opportunities for joint transformative action. Sharing common experiences and engaging together in critical reflection will facilitate a more lucid understanding of the challenges and tasks for the future of feminist Christianity. It will help us tangibly sense the global magnitude of social injustice and human deprivation, and their effects on women in their own communities. It also helps clarify how, in the words of Letty Russell written many decades ago, "many of the goals are held in common and need to be worked on in mutual respect and solidarity."[14] Learning and fostering a broader knowledge of the impact of kyriarchal Christianity on the lives, particularly the sexual lives and sexual health, of marginalized women in the setting of two-thirds-world communities offer opportunities for devising shared activities of partnership and mutual cooperation for transformation.

This is not a way of promoting a kind of tourism of poverty, but a sensible way to foster tangible feminist interconnectedness and solidarity in the interest of shaping a just world together. In expressing this issue, I have in mind the enormous disparity between the United States' and the two-thirds world's academic settings in access to means, benefits, and resources to develop our scholarly work. The articulation of feminist theologies of liberation in the United States must consider and establish links with the realities of marginalization affecting women of the Southern Hemisphere. Although our social location and material conditions are simply not the same, tangible experience and dialogue become venues for partnership as equals as we develop together feminist religious knowledge infused by shared values and goals for liberation. Also, being actually in touch with colleagues and communities around the world that are exposed to the miseries engendered by the weapons, markets, and policies of U.S. global capitalism gives a better sense of the implications and reach of feminist Christianity as we engage opportunities for a shared alternative future. Many of my friends and colleagues, U.S. feminist theologians and biblical scholars who are regularly connected to marginalized communities in the Southern Hemisphere, find that this type of tangible sharing of experiences enhances their desire to work for an intended future of justice. Such lived experience does have an epistemological and hermeneutical impact on your own feminist theological activity.

Feminist Peacebuilding

As of the time of this writing, I am confident in saying that the large majority of feminist scholars of religion and theology have not yet connected to, much less made an impact on, the emerging field of peacebuilding and conflict transformation studies. This rapidly growing field of study was born in the context of contemporary societies seeking constructive responses to human atrocity, genocide, destructive conflict, and war as experienced by a large number of countries in the past few decades. In this context, sexual violence against women and rape have been used on a massive scale as a tool of war. In many instances, peacebuilding was born in connection to the constructive intervention of religious actors and faith-based communities that, under the precarious circumstances of violent conflict, committed themselves to seeking change, healing, restoration, truth-finding, reconciliation, and reparations.

I understand peacebuilding as a dynamic process and framework involving a multiplicity of interdependent actors, approaches, functions, and activities that work simultaneously on different levels of community and society to transform constructively all forms of violent interaction. For the purpose of shaping just relationships and social systems, peacebuilding actors engage in collaboration and partnership to build conditions and capacities for "societies that affirm human dignity through meeting basic human needs and protecting human rights" within sustainable environments.[15]

In spite of the pervasiveness of destructive conflict and war around the world, in spite of the fact that many of those wars are instigated and supported by the dominant U.S. weapons industry, in spite of the fact that those weapons and destructive confrontations affect women and children disproportionally, and in spite of the fact that a large population of immigrants (documented and undocumented) residing in the United States is directly connected to situations of destructive conflict and war, an explicit approach to religious peacebuilding by experts in the sciences of religion and theology remains weak. I cannot fail to note that in spite of those situations, while scholars from a variety of other academic fields are strongly engaged in the task of studying the intervention of religion in international peacebuilding, scholars of religion and theology have insufficiently addressed the actual and potential contribution of religion to conflict transformation through frameworks of religious peacebuilding. This is also true for feminist theologians and biblical scholars.

In my view, the future of feminist Christianity must be closely involved in both the social processes and the scholarly works that give shape to peacebuilding and social transformation. This is an ethical, religious, and political implication of my previous section on critical analysis and tangible interconnectedness. But this intervention is also demanded by the contemporary dynamics of conflict in which religion has been and continues to be an important factor in conflicts, especially in terms of shaping human identities and of validating societal systems. Violence and dehumanization, hateful human interaction, and abuse of women have been legitimated by religious and theological rhetoric, Christian included, for centuries. I believe that concerns about the constructive intervention of religions in processes of conflict involve not only concerns about the immediate response to the calamities of military power and war, which are crucial indeed, but also larger concerns about the present and future of humanity and the world.

If a just world is the name of the future that feminist Christians envision for ourselves and others around the world, then the historical advent of such a world requires from us greater involvement in peacebuilding processes. But naming the type of world and society that feminist Christians are seeking to build is already here and now an act of affirming our choice for justpeace (peace efforts with attention to social justice). John Paul Lederach, a Mennonite pioneer of peacebuilding and conflict transformation studies, asserts that it is important to name that world because, in peacebuilding processes, "if we do not know where we are going it is difficult to get there."[16] As individuals and as feminist religious actors, we need to give an account of where we are and where we are going from here. In this light, I suggest that, from today's context of destructive conflict and massive misery instigated by kyriarchal capitalism, if religion is to contribute to the restructuring of the world in constructive ways, the community of feminist scholars of religion and theology can and should devise conceptual and social practices for intervention in conflict transformation and for working together to fashion paths conducive to a desired future of justice and peace. While personal and social transformation is a core aim of feminist theologies of liberation, transformation is also at the heart of peacebuilding. As noted by Lederach, "transformation provides a clear and important vision because it brings into focus the horizon toward which we journey—the building of healthy relationships and communities, locally and globally. This goal requires real change in our current ways of relating."[17] The development of feminist religious peacebuilding is an urgent historical necessity.

Conclusion: Aspiring toward Peace and Justice

My hope is that we engage in constructive interaction about the most urgent and effective ways to shape the future of feminist Christianity. I also hope that you, the reader, will join me in recognizing that hope in a different future is as necessary today as it was for the countless women of the Christian tradition who preceded us with their aspirations and struggles for a just world. But for us today, being in a turbulent world, I suggest that we keep in mind that situations of destructive conflict and violence will neither go away soon, nor during our lifetime. This is true not only because poverty and environmental instability are growing, but also because the only industry that remains quite healthy in the midst of a deep financial crisis is the weapons industry. Among the G-8 countries controlling global arms sales (Canada, France, Germany, Italy, Japan, Russia, the United Kingdom, and the United States), the United States continues to be the largest supplier of weapons; overall, more than 68 percent of arms sales are to the global South, to countries in which violation of human rights is persistent.[18]

Given the impact of destructive conflict and of weapons on women, and given the relentless practice of sexual violence against women, the potential future offered by kyriarchal capitalism is not positive. From the heart of divided societies, by taking seriously the demands of critical analysis, of tangible interconnectedness, and of feminist peacebuilding, we contribute by affirming a constructive future of feminist Christianity focused on building a just world.

W. Anne Joh is associate professor of theology at Garrett-Evangelical Theological Seminary. Dr. Joh's research interests lie at the intersection of postcolonial theory, feminist theology, cultural studies, psychoanalysis, and critical race and queer theories. Her latest project is postcolonial theological anthropology in conversation with feminist theology and Gayatri Spivak, Giorgio Agamben, Jan Mohammed, and Michele Foucault.

Race, Class, Gender, Sexuality

Integrating the Diverse Politics of Identity into Our Theology

W. ANNE JOH

> The production of knowledge must be supplemented by the training of the imagination.
>
> GAYATRI CHAKRAVORTY SPIVAK, *OTHER ASIAS*

> Building oppositional practices within and across multiple simultaneous sites is imperative in political struggle as is the cultivation of the discipline of freedom.
>
> M. JACQUI ALEXANDER, *PEDAGOGIES OF CROSSING*

At the heart of Christian theology is the radical notion of divine incarnation. If you were to think on this very concept, you might become amazed at the fantastic imagination and dreaming that would conjure up such a radical sense of hope—of divine becoming incarnate in the midst of people's suffering and despair. How might feminist theologians continue the tradition of envisioning radical incarnality, in which the divine becomes infused in all of creation? Would such an epistemological shift ensure a more just and sustainable existence? Would it create space to envision our understanding of transcendence differently? Or even a keener awareness of how we are bound to one another? What might be the breadth and depth of our feminist imagination for the present and future? Feminist theology must not be apart from other critical discourses but, as it has done so recently, must continue even more than before to engage in theoretical analysis at the intersections of gender, race, sexuality, and colonialism (empire) so that the kinds of theologizing we do may be relevant to our world.

We cannot forget those whom Frantz Fanon refers to as the "wretched of the earth."[1] In the sufferings, wrongs, and injuries we inflict upon others and ourselves, we must remember that those who are the most vulnerable are often forgotten. As we remember the past and the present, we must also work to forge an incredibly hope-filled world where there is deep recognition of our interdependence. This takes a tremendously—almost fantastically—active imagination and rigorous production of knowledge that will shift our epistemological outlook of how we are to be in this world with one another.

Whether we are actively involved in them or not, we are nonetheless bound to the sufferings of others. How do we theologize the unequivocal fact that too often "my comfort is at the expense of others' discomfort"?[2] How do we reflect on the truth that whatever small sense of invulnerability we think we have achieved is accomplished by maintaining a predatory stance toward "Others"? Amid so much dismay, violence, and suffering, what might a feminist theological vision encompass? How might we participate in the unmaking and remaking of this world into one that is hospitable to all who live in it? How do we hold despair and hope together?

Many dimensions can be highlighted as part of our ever-shifting understanding of self and the differing historical events that contribute to the formation of our ever-becoming self. I immigrated to the United States from Korea with my parents when I was very young. Having lived through their childhood of Japanese occupation that, among many other things, forbade them to speak their mother tongue, my parents lived through the traumas of the Korean War, then the desperate move toward national reconstruction and military dictatorship, and then eventually crossed the Pacific Ocean into a land they had never visited, a language they did not speak, and a culture they did not know. All this was before the electronic age that has revolutionized our ability to connect with the world.

My own experience as an immigrant is intermingled with that of my parents'. Even though I did not even know the English alphabet before coming to the United States with my parents, only a few months after we came to this foreign land I began to serve as the sole translator for all their negotiations and transactions; I basically functioned as a social service person navigating the structures and systems of the United States. For most immigrants, coming to a foreign land and learning to live there is a traumatic experience. In hindsight, I realize that my experiences were even more complex and complicated because as a translator from a young age, I witnessed the injustices of systemic oppression against those deemed "other" or "foreign." Serving as my parents' and their friends' negotiator made me conscious from the beginning of the brutal and yet routine ways that some people exercise power over others. As a feminist postcolonial theologian, I am especially alert to the ways that our experiences and interlocking historical parallels and connections affect how we understand and negotiate differences, power, and oppression.

In this essay, I muse on several important factors. I do not even attempt to name the multiplicity of diverse dimensions that are crucial for any holistic feminist theological vision. I will merely highlight several vital dimensions that I feel must be included as part of an ongoing feminist theological vision that requires, as the beginning epigraph notes, a robust "training of our imagination."

Gender

Writing specifically as a *feminist* theologian, I continue to be haunted by the dominance of heteropatriarchy in Christian theological tradition. Feminist theology, foremost among other forms of theology, must continue to grapple with the reality of sexism in the lives of women and men. I say both women and men because at the heart of sexism is the construction of gender polarization, in which femininity and masculinity are assumed to be clearly delineated and any transgression of this pattern warrants punitive measures.[3]

The structural and systemic disciplinary and regulatory measures that are in place work effectively to curb any desire to transgress boundaries, making the gender binary much more rigid. The construction of genders along a binary division must be critiqued and problematized not only because of various ways in which it feeds into other misogynistic social impulses, but also because it is linked to the ways that men have come to understand their identity. While in the past, sexism was justified based on essentialist and biological notions of what constituted gender, feminist scholars today are arguing for anti-essentialist views: a person is not "born a female but becomes one." I extend this argument further to say that a person is not "born a male but becomes one" and even further to say that a person "is not born as a 'woman of color' but becomes one."[4]

The social construction of gender and racial identities is important to examine not only because of the powerful ways that it influences us and how we come to know ourselves, but also because any kind of polaristic essentialist stereotypes limit us to one-dimensional identities. Second, it is crucial for feminist theologians to continue to examine the ways that the concept of gender fails even within theological traditions that look very patriarchal. What and who are the instances in which essentialist gender constructions have failed, thus testifying to the slippages within supposedly rigid gender constructions? To be sure, rigid gender boundaries have always been transgressed and it is the task of feminist theologians to uncover those transgressive occasions. Third, as I suggest below, a sustained and thorough investigation of how gender is also "raced" must continue to generate a wider conversation among scholars from all different racial and ethnic backgrounds.

Gender is also raced, that is, people of various racial and ethnic groups experience gender differently.[5] Heteronormativity (the default assumption that everyone is heterosexual until proven otherwise) is not often extended to people of color. Likewise, racialized men of color, those from marginalized racial or ethnic groups, are often demasculinized or overtly feminized. (Under Western colonialism, what constituted "rational" patriarchal masculinity was not extended to men of color. In contrast to the agency, rationality, progress, and reason that constituted white masculinity, colonized men were often depicted as effeminate, childlike, emotional, and incapable of reason; others were hypermasculinized as again irrational, uncontrollable, incapable of reason, uncivilized, libidinous, and sexually promiscuous.)

A white woman's experience of heteropatriarchy cannot be universalized but must be particularized. Likewise, one Asian American woman's gendered self is understood differently from other Asian women, and from Latina and white women. Moreover, a white Euro-American male's understanding of masculinity is quite different from an Asian male's experience. Any kind of feminist theological vision must take seriously the ways in which becoming gendered infiltrates, in a problematic way, how we understand what it means to be complex creatures, and equally, the ways we understand all of creation.

Race

Although some biologists argue that there are not different races within our human species, the experience of race is a concrete reality. Structural and systemic oppression based on notions of racial hierarchy and superiority is present in our history and in our current reality. In the history of settler colonialism in the United States, white racism rooted in white supremacy gave birth to the colonization of this land and its peoples as well as institutionalized slavery. This is attested to in the weight of our nation's history. In fact, white racism worked to define who was and was not even considered to be *human.* White racism continued throughout U.S. history. Even today it is at the core of beliefs that build and rebuild our national identity.[6] White racism and sexism work simultaneously to marginalize particular peoples in routine daily practices of humiliation and degradation.

Second-wave feminists have already criticized the fallacy within white feminist movements that universalized white, heterosexual, middle-class women's gendered experiences as normative. Women scholars of color have argued that feminists come in all different shades. Because of how those shades have determined our experiences, we have asserted and continue to contend that racialization changes the ways in which we experience sexism. Racism constructs what it means to be a "woman" differently based on our "race." This is also true of the ways it constructs how a "man" is understood based on his "race."

Negative racial and gender stereotypes, unsurprisingly, work as the means by which the dominant group constructs its identity in contrast to the marginalized group. For example, men of color are often depicted as lazy, whereas white men are considered hard-working and grounded in the Protestant work ethic. Women, in contrast to men, are constructed as overly emotional and incapable of reason. Usually, the dominant group is aware at some level that these stereotypes are fallacious. However, the possibility that these negative traits might also belong to part of the dominant group causes the dominant group anxiety. This anxiety shows how racism and sexism are intermingled. It works to sustain the dominant identity, creating stagnant essentialist metanarratives about "them" and "us." From a "city upon a hill" to manifest destiny, this nation is founded on white supremacist beliefs that excluded many and continue to create wreckage haunting the lives of many people. A feminist theological vision must continue to insist on destabilizing white supremacy and the ways it sustains itself through continual deployment of gender and race, and criticize the presumed solidities and clear demarcations of each.[7] Because patriarchy and white racism are so intimately linked, any feminists who ignore the debilitating effects of racism in the lives of other women do so at great peril.

While the black-white dyad in critical race theory is important and must be sustained, we also need to develop such conversations even more by examining how white racism deploys race differently against different groups of people. There is no uniform strategy against *all* people who are racialized, but rather racism's insidious nature is due to its diverse strategies of deploying racism against different peoples differently.[8] Ultimately, it is important to recognize that racism so saturates heteropatriarchy that even white women are not exempt from being racialized.

Feminist theologians also need to examine how the ongoing heteropatriarchal Christian theological framework continues to racialize and genderize women and men of other religious traditions. Christian supremacy is deeply connected with the underpinnings found in white supremacy and misogyny. Christian dominance is rooted in its history of imperialism and continues its trajectory in modern times as it works insidiously to racialize and genderize other religions as unruly, deviant, dark, irrational, feminine, weak, passive, and having homosexual proclivities.

Christian supremacy and assumptions that Christianity is the normative religion often go unnoticed in public space and in public discourse in the United States.[9] Our public space and discourse are littered with assumed Christian words, concepts, and practices. Thus, rather than cultivate religious tolerance, feminist Christian theologians need to collaborate with people of other faith traditions so that the multiplicity of religious traditions is celebrated rather than harassed or, at best, lived in the shadow of Christianity. All feminists, from a multiplicity of divergent and even contradictory backgrounds, should forge a theological vision that includes a continual examination of how heteropatriarchal ideology sustains itself through its various deployments of racialization and gender construction and maintenance.

Sexuality

If gender and race are problematic categories that need further and ongoing theorization and theologizing by feminists and womanists, then so too is there a vital need to reexamine how we construct and understand sexuality. If the ruse of gender and race as clear categories is deployed as a scaffolding to shore up and hold together structures of domination, then heteronormativity is yet another concept that links all these threads together.

Heteronormative, or "straight," sexuality works to sustain patriarchal power over women and men who transgress rigid sexual demarcations. If what it means to be women and men is to be gendered and raced, so too is it to be sexualized. In a heteronormative power structure, those who are deemed "Other" are often seen to be sexually transgressive, degenerate, and deviant, and in need of discipline and regulation. Not only are other racialized and gendered people then constructed as non-heterosexual, but so too are those of other religions constructed by heteropatriarchal ideology as sexually deviant. We might ask if there are any differences between being a practicing white lesbian Christian and, say, a practicing lesbian Sikh.[10] How do race and gender get deployed here?

In a critique of heteronormativity, queer theorists argue that sexuality is political. However, is there a chance that even within the queer movement, racism still exists between LGBTQ people of color and white queers? According to the "straight" epistemology, all those who are not heterosexual are deviant and queer. But, there is also a lingering and persistent tendency even within queer communities to deploy race and gender against other queers of color; this needs further examination. Moreover, we need to ask the question of how and in what ways those who identify with LGBTQ communities often fail to examine their complicity in the global capitalist project. Perhaps the very notion that we live in a straight world is already problematic in itself, and feminist theological vision must participate in constructive work of "queering" our theological reflections—that is, embracing a radical epistemological and theological shift through a critique of how notions of race, gender, and sexuality are deployed to sustain heteropatriarchal power.

Class and Globalization

In an age of rapid globalization, it is not surprising to say that feminist theology must also focus on finding ways to create a just and sustainable existence. Colonization, imperialism, and neoliberalism have left an indelible mark on many lives and nations. Race, gender, and sexuality have been used and deployed to mark the bodies that have been excluded and even abandoned. Nevertheless, there is an additional dynamic. In the age of globalization, which has shifted and is shifting the way we define global power in our time, we are learning to recognize the emergence of "financialization" of the globe, in which the masses of the global poor far outnumber those few global elites whose access to wealth is far-reaching.[11] This is a situation of massive devastation of vulnerable people and creation. A privileged few accumulate wealth and resources beyond their needs. So we face an unprecedented crisis of hunger, forced migration, disease, and death and, out of this mix, defiance and violence.

How do we theologize in ways that take life—all life—as sacred? How do we theologize so that our world can continue and flourish? What deconstructive and reconstructive theological moves must be made so that we begin to reimagine the divine and this creation as sacred, as living in abundance rather than rooted in competition and scarcity? In the West, there is a saying that "might does not make right." Yet, tragically, belief that power confers moral authority is at the base of our impulse for waging war on others, stealing their resources, exploiting their labor, and colonizing their lands, all in the name of progress and democracy. The caveat here is not simply that the "West" is fast becoming the only practitioner of such modes of being in the world, but also that other powerful global elites have joined its ranks.

Feminist theology must give critical attention to the ways that the financialization of the globe is deepening the suffering of masses of people worldwide. For theologians who argue that *all* life is sacred, how do we make sense of a world that no longer counts some lives as worthy of saving but demands that others should be made safe and secure no matter what the costs?[12]

It's a Queer World after All: A Queer Feminist Theological Aesthetic

I close by introducing elements of postcolonial theory, suggesting how they aid reflection on this tangled and complex world. In arguing for a postcolonial deconstructive move, I want to insist that even when identity (whether gendered, raced, or sexualized) is provisional, we must engage in a persistent self-critique in order to avoid over-determined authorization of identity and claims to authenticity. For example, the question of who the "authentic inhabitants" of margins are challenges us to criticize ourselves in order to avoid monolithic and homogenous notions of, say, who or what we mean when we use the term *Asian American* or *feminist, queer,* or *womanist.* The instability of all rigid identities must give way to identity as always positional and provisional in time and space. How, then, do we narrate our experiences without reifying certain essentialist stereotypes or without reifying a particular narrative as a metanarrative? How do we speak about all the plurality, ambiguity, multiplicity, and provinciality of ways that identity is understood without allowing our particular speaking and theorizing to feed into a particular imaginary, be it white imaginary, or that of a particular feminist imaginary, or for that matter even Asian American queer feminist imaginary? We must be mindful of just how interdependent our lives are even when we live a "world" apart from one another.

We cannot speak of the West or the East precisely, because geopolitical histories cannot be so easily packaged. While unique and specific peoples and national formations exist, there are also historical parallels and global links between different formations, due to the ways that those formations are gendered, raced, or colonized.

Postcolonialism is a discourse that emerged after the grand periods usually designated "colonization." However, as many scholars have argued, this does not mean that we live today in a "post" world, in some aftermath of colonial practices. Postcolonialism as a discourse functions as a reading strategy that criticizes not only past experiences of colonization but also its legacy. Given the breadth and depth of feminist theologies and postcolonial studies, and the limitations of this essay, I conclude by suggesting that postcolonial discourse might become a strategic reading of feminist/womanist experiences in the United States. To that end, cultural critic and literary theorist Edward Said's notions of the fugue and contrapuntality are useful metaphors.[13] The fugue is a metaphor that helps us understand not only the integrity of singularity but also that of plurality. In music, a fugue is a polyphonic composition sometimes described as a texture rather than a form. In essence it is a contrapuntal composition in which many voices enter, then fade and reenter, and often overlap with one another. Fugue is a musical practice that becomes a useful theological practice, showing us the possibilities and the conditions that might make singularity and plurality possible even as it recognizes interdependent histories that point toward textual sociality.

Contrapuntality—reading against the grain—blurs the line of center/periphery, straight/queer, male/female, East/West, citizen/noncitizen by questioning assumed binaries so that we begin to recognize the depth of our "worldliness"—the inevitable fact of the hybrid nature of all cultures and identities. Postcolonial contrapuntal reading of U.S. history then sheds light on how race, imperialism, colonization, gender, and sexuality all work to form the ideal "hetero-patriarchal American" who does not transgress clear boundaries in the dominant white imagination. How do we begin to theologize the ways in which we must right all the wrongs? Perhaps we must heed the words of people like Gayatri Chakravorty Spivak, an atheist, who notes that "one needs some sort of 'licensed lunacy' from some transcendental Other to develop the sort of ruthless commitment that can undermine the sense that one is better than those who are being helped."[14]

A continuous and sustained effort must be generated to move away from unilateral global feminist theologies and toward the building of coalitions and solidarities across differences—even those that seem insurmountable to some. By doing so, we will generate a worldview that embraces heterogeneity, multiplicity, and differences among and within us, and moves toward our recognition that all life is worthy of dignity and respect.[15]

Feminist theologians then need to enter into a wider and more deeply textured conversation about what dreams we can dream together and what dreams can bring healing of our injuries to and with one another, continuing our labor to find ways to create a just and sustainable existence. In order to widen and deepen our feminist theological conversation, we must also be open to interdisciplinary learning and teaching. Given the complex world in which we negotiate, feminist theology cannot isolate itself. It must be in lively conversation with other creative areas that will give birth to feminist theological aesthetics. In doing so, I hope we unlearn much of our gendered, raced, classed, imperialist-based knowledge; learn through the lens of those who have been segregated, marginalized, ghettoized, demonized, or terrorized; and come to realize that we already live in a queer world and we desperately need to see, know, and live in this world otherwise. Indeed, we must train our imaginations to dare to dream such fantastic possibilities.

Letha Dawson Scanzoni is an independent scholar. She is the editor of the Evangelical & Ecumenical Women's Caucus's quarterly publication, *Christian Feminism Today*. She is the cowriter with Kimberly B. George of the cross-generational Christian feminist blog *72-27*, at www.eewc.com/72-27. She is the author or coauthor of numerous books, including, with Nancy Hardesty, *All We're Meant to Be*, which helped launch the biblical feminist movement within second-wave feminism, and *Is the Homosexual My Neighbor?* with Virginia Ramey Mollenkott, which opened the LGBTQ conversation among evangelicals.

Why We Need Evangelical Feminists

LETHA DAWSON SCANZONI

To say that evangelical feminists play a significant role in the broader category of Christian feminism or feminist Christianity—or even feminism in general—may come as a surprise to some readers, first, because many people are unaware that evangelical feminists even exist (and in fact have been around for a long time), and second, because combining the terms *evangelical* and *feminist* strikes some as an oxymoron.

The negative reaction stems in large part from media portrayals of evangelicalism as a distinct, easily delineated, homogenous population of people characterized by right-wing politics, anti-intellectualism, intolerance, self-righteousness, incitement of culture

The author wishes to thank Nancy A. Hardesty and Linda Bieze for reading this essay in manuscript form and offering helpful suggestions.

wars, authoritarianism, a preoccupation with sexuality issues, biblical literalism, and a narrow conception of family values. Although the description fits a significant segment of what has come to be known as evangelicalism, more fitting terms for that particular subgroup would be "militant fundamentalism" or "reactionary Christian conservatism."

Defining *Evangelicalism*

Evangelicalism is not easy to define. The word comes from the Greek, meaning "good news" or "gospel," and the roots of the evangelical movement may be traced to eighteenth- and nineteenth-century revivalism along with the seventeenth-century pietistic movement. Historically, evangelicalism's emphasis has been on the authority of the Bible, the Reformation doctrine of justification by faith through God's grace, the importance of an individual's personal relationship to God through Christ, and living out a commitment to Christ in daily life. Today, evangelicalism is a cross-denominational Protestant community that may also be viewed as a religious subculture, with its own institutions of higher learning, book publishers, periodicals, parachurch organizations, and outreach through specially produced radio, television, and motion picture productions as well as the Internet.[1]

Evangelicalism and Gender over the Previous Two Centuries

"Although the term *evangelicalism* is often used synonymously with *fundamentalism* in general references to conservative Protestants," writes sociologist Sally Gallagher, "it has historically been a more socially engaged orthodoxy, providing both a strong sense of normative truth as well as an impetus for social and evangelistic mission."[2] The same point is made by historian and religion professor Nancy Hardesty concerning the nineteenth-century woman's rights movement. "Most woman's rights leaders—whether in the church, education, reform organizations, or the media—were products of evangelical backgrounds or were deeply influenced by evangelical culture, whether or not they acknowledged that debt or maintained any allegiance to it in later life."[3] A theology that stressed the free moral agency of the individual helped women recognize themselves as equal human beings in the sight of God and not as secondary to men. In revival services, women were encouraged by evangelists to speak and pray publicly even though, at the time, it was considered a breach of propriety for women to address audiences in which men were present. Thus emboldened, many women extended their speaking beyond revival services, working diligently for the abolition of slavery and for women's rights.[4] When hostile clergy hurled Scripture verses to keep them in their place, the women had ready answers.[5]

Historian Janette Hassey has written of the widespread acceptance of female preachers and evangelists at the turn of the last century and how fully their public ministry was praised and promoted—even within many of the most conservative churches and schools that would later do a turnabout and use biblical and theological arguments to bar women from public ministry and church leadership.[6] Religion professor Betty A. DeBerg has shown how the fundamentalist-modernist controversies marking the 1910s and 1920s were inextricably linked to social changes in the conception of gender: "The rhetoric used by fundamentalists in their attacks on modern or liberal theology expressed the same deep uneasiness with new currents in gender roles and social codes as did their language in the evolution and inerrancy debates. It was not so much traditional theology they were defending as it was traditional gender ideology."[7] Sociologist Julie Ingersoll has found a similar pattern in more recent divisions among Southern Baptists, particularly in what amounted to a litmus test used at Southern Seminary in Louisville, Kentucky, to separate conservatives from those perceived as liberals. "What was 'really' at issue," she writes, "were the larger symbolic values that conflict over gender evokes; gender conflicts now function in the same way that conflict over inerrancy did a generation ago."[8]

For fundamentalists in the early twentieth century, women's increasing freedom in obtaining educational and career opportunities was viewed as promoting immorality and the breakdown of the family. At the same time, many fundamentalist clergy feared the "feminization" of the church and claimed that an emphasis on love and tenderness (what they considered "softness") must be replaced by a virile, muscular, militaristic image of Christianity. Further, they emphasized, God had ordained a natural order that gave men authority over women and that order must not be violated by increased rights in marriage, opportunities in education and the marketplace, or women's ordainment as pastors.

Questioning Assumptions

Religion can be primarily *limiting* or *liberating* in its gender ideology. Nineteenth-century revivalism illustrated the liberating aspect with its emphasis on women's moral agency and the use of their spiritual gifts in public speaking and reform work. Later in the nineteenth century and into the twentieth, evangelicalism stressed the more limiting aspect. It became taken for granted that a more limited role for women was the only view true to Scripture and that all evangelical Christians believed the same.

But beginning in the 1960s and 1970s, a new wave of evangelical feminists began to raise questions about what Scripture teaches and, like women in the nineteenth and early twentieth centuries, to critically examine assumptions, biblical interpretations, and church traditions. In seeking answers, these evangelical women (and a number of supportive men) examined translations of Scripture, the historical-cultural contexts of the passages used to keep women in a subordinate role, and the meaning of words and phrases in the original Hebrew and Greek languages. At the same time, they shared their experiences of rejected talents and gender-limited service in fundamentalist and evangelical churches, organizations, and academic organizations.[9]

In any area of life, questioning previously undisputed assumptions can be unsettling. As questioners go about their task of seeking answers, their opponents go about the task of forming arguments to discredit the questioners and refute the issues they raise. I first experienced such efforts to discredit my work after one of my earliest articles, "Woman's Place: Silence or Service," was published in February 1966 in *Eternity*, an evangelical monthly magazine. Angry letters to the editor poured in, led by one that said, "Mrs. Scanzoni's article ... is a perfect example of why a woman is admonished to be silent in the church. Most women seem to be incapable of consistent logic when their emotions are involved." My article had consisted entirely of a logical series of questions about why churches proclaimed one thing and then practiced something different when it came to the role of women. But hurling charges of emotionalism is only one of numerous tactics used to keep women's voices quiet and their arguments ignored.

By the time the same magazine published my second article, "Elevate Marriage to Partnership," in July 1968, followed in 1974 by the publication of *All We're Meant to Be: A Biblical Approach to Women's Liberation,* coauthored with Nancy Hardesty, efforts to quash feminist voices within evangelicalism were growing stronger.[10] One reviewer falsely accused us of despising the home and ended his harsh critique by saying, "We were long ago warned that the 'ignorant and unstable twist the Scriptures to their own destruction.' Readers must determine for themselves whether or not this book fits that description."[11]

Nancy and I were, of course, not the only ones who were espousing gender equality. One example was a study group of Chicago-based evangelical women who called themselves Daughters of Sarah and began publishing *Daughters of Sarah* magazine in 1974.[12] They and we shared names of like-minded women and looked for ways to put such women in touch with each other. When, in 1973, a group of socially conscious evangelicals from all over the country came together in Chicago for a gathering called Evangelicals for Social Action (ESA), in which they would discuss a progressive approach to social justice and peace issues, Nancy made sure that the issue of gender equity was included. At a follow-up ESA gathering in 1974, one of the break-out discussion groups or "caucuses" at the gathering was the women's caucus, thus laying the foundation of what later became the Evangelical Women's Caucus (EWC).

Trajectory of Social Movements

In a speech I gave at the EWC organization day in 1978, I talked about the trajectory of social movements, loosely drawing upon the theoretical framework of sociologist J. Victor Baldridge, who showed how social movements go through an awakening stage, a building stage, and an influence stage.[13] Here, I want to expand on that framework by suggesting a simplified cycle of forward and reverse ABCs to describe what I see happening today and show why I think evangelical feminists have an important role to play in the overall mission of feminist Christianity. The cycle I have in mind moves through five stages: awakening, building, catalyzing change, backlash, and awakening again with a new set of players. This A-B-C-B-A pattern happens over and over again.

Awakening

As evangelical women were awakening to the injustices of a gender-based system in the home, church, and society that restricted them from being all that they could be, they began finding each other. By sharing their personal experiences, they began seeing a pattern of *systemic* discrimination. No longer would they accept the notions that they were to blame for their discontent or that wanting something more than straitjacketed gender roles indicated a rebellious attitude toward God.

Building

Like their counterparts in society in general and in mainstream manifestations of Christian feminism, evangelical feminists began organizing. The Evangelical Women's Caucus had numerous chapters in various states, held biennial conferences, and published a newsletter. In 1986, after the group had adopted several resolutions, including one that affirmed civil rights for gay and lesbian persons, a large group of members broke away and formed Christians for Biblical Equality (CBE) to dissociate themselves from what they considered an unbiblical endorsement of homosexuality.[14] From that time forward, there were two major evangelical egalitarian organizations. In 1990, as EWC was attracting a more theologically diverse membership of both Protestants and Roman Catholics and was increasingly known for its inclusiveness, it added another E to its name and became the Evangelical & *Ecumenical* Women's Caucus (EEWC).

Catalyzing Change

Both EEWC and CBE have been engaged in scholarship and activism within and outside the larger evangelical world of churches, academic institutions, and parachurch organizations, presenting an alternative to the traditionalist insistence that the only true biblical view is male dominance and female subordination. Each group has produced periodicals, books, and online resources presenting a message of biblical egalitarianism. The two groups, while not abandoning their evangelical roots, overlap in some respects but also differ in their respective audiences, with CBE's outreach concentrated more directly on the moderate evangelical community (taking great care to remain within certain theological and socially conservative boundaries), whereas EEWC has a more expansive outreach, offering a safe and welcoming place to those who have felt emotionally and spiritually abused by conservative churches (both Protestant and Catholic), or have been marginalized because of their gender identity or sexual orientation, or have been ready to give up on Christianity because of its teachings on women, or whose general doubts and theological questioning have not been welcome elsewhere.

How much influence have evangelical feminists really wielded in our day? Our major impact has been to demonstrate to conservatives that individuals can take the Bible seriously and maintain a strong faith and personal relationship with God while believing in the full equality of women and men in every aspect of life. Conservatives can no longer disregard evangelical feminists as those who have "left the faith," nor can conservatives expect to be persuasive in presenting their caricature of what feminism is and means.

Additional signs that evangelical feminism has been catalyzing change are everywhere. A few examples:

Evangelical feminism has catalyzed change in the use of inclusive language in preaching, teaching, and writing. Replacing the generic use of male nouns and pronouns (such as *men* or *he*) with gender-neutral terms (such as *people* and *he or she*, or recasting sentences into the plural and using *they*) is now common in evangelical circles—even in Bible translations, in spite of traditionalists' protests.

Evangelical feminism has influenced how evangelicals study the Bible and do theology. For its fiftieth anniversary in 2005, the evangelical magazine *Christianity Today* included a list of the "top fifty books that have shaped evangelicalism." At number twenty-three on the list was *All We're Meant to Be* along with this comment: "Scanzoni and Hardesty outlined what would later blossom into evangelical feminism. For better or for worse, no evangelical marriage or institution has been able to ignore the ideas in this book."[15]

Evangelical feminism has helped change how evangelicals conduct their daily lives. Sally Gallagher's sociological research shows that although evangelical feminism holds a marginal place in evangelicalism as a whole, what she calls a "pragmatic egalitarianism" is common among evangelical married couples, who though staying within traditional evangelical boundaries by giving lip service to a belief in male headship, nevertheless tend to practice partnership marriages that are characterized by democratic decision making and shared parenting responsibilities. Observing this and other egalitarian attitudes and practices, she concluded that evangelical feminism is being given wider attention than ever before.[16]

Evangelical feminism has provided an empowering climate for evangelical women to respond to God's call to ministry. Evangelist Anne Graham Lotz, daughter of Billy and Ruth Graham, was featured on a *Washington Post* online video in which she spoke of having people walk out of meetings, turn around and put their backs toward her, or withdraw invitations because they do not believe a woman should preach. But she said she is following a calling from God and that the Scripture shows that Jesus chose a woman, Mary Magdalene, to be the first to tell the news of his resurrection. Anne Lotz said that she is accountable to *God,* not to those who disapprove of her calling, and that if people have a problem with it, they should "take it up with Jesus."[17]

Evangelical feminism has catalyzed an opposition movement. Worried traditionalists began recognizing the influence of evangelical feminism, saw it as a threat, and mobilized against it. In 1987, a group of conservative pastors and scholars met "to address their concerns over the influence of feminism not only in our culture but also in evangelical churches."[18] To resist the momentum, they formed the Council on Biblical Manhood and Womanhood. In contrast to gender egalitarianism, which considers women and men equal in all areas, they proposed what they called *complementarianism,* "which affirms that men and women are equal in the image of God, but maintain complementary differences in role and function." It is a softer term to promote male dominance and female subordination, while hoping to avoid charges of discrimination and chauvinism, and this in itself shows the influence of cultural and religious feminism.

Evangelical feminism has put complementarians on the defensive. The new preface to the 2006 edition of the conservative book *Recovering Biblical Manhood and Womanhood: A Response to Evangelical*

Feminism laments that many pastors and congregations are embracing feminist ideas and that "many evangelical publishers (once bastions of conservatism regarding gender roles) are publishing books from a feminist perspective, and some of them now refuse to print anything that assumes or advances complementarianism." The writers of the new preface also expressed concern over signs of "functionally egalitarian patterns of ministry" in evangelically based Christian campus organizations, and evidence that many evangelical faculty members, "even in the most conservative of institutions," are now favorable toward egalitarianism.[19] Among complementarian writers, fears are frequently expressed that evangelicals who embrace feminist ideas are sliding down a slippery slope or are being overtaken by a tsunami that sweeps people up in heresy.[20] Others, echoing the fears of many pastors in the nineteenth century, are now warning that the church is becoming "feminized."[21]

Evangelical feminism has caused opponents concern about defeat. Worry about actually losing the battle is now admitted by those opposed to gender egalitarianism. For example, Russell D. Moore, dean of the School of Theology at Southern Baptist Theological Seminary, gave a talk at the Evangelical Theological Society titled, "After Patriarchy, What? Why Egalitarians Are Winning the Evangelical Gender Debate."[22] He argued that the gains made by feminists within evangelicalism have led to a softening in how male authority is presented even among traditionalists and has since expressed a wish that the word *patriarchy* could replace the term *complementarian.*[23]

Backlash

As evangelical feminism continues through the A-B-C-B-A cycle, a stepped-up backlash is a sign of the impact of the *catalyzing change* stage. Today's backlash to evangelical egalitarianism is taking the form of conferences, workshops, and a proliferation of books and articles written by traditionalist women declaring familiarity with feminist history and women's studies courses, some claiming to be "ex-feminists" themselves. Their presentation of feminist history is superficial and distorted, and the tone of these materials tends to be alarmist, warning young women that the seductive ideas of feminism can lead them away from God and into immorality.[24] Feminism is presented as selfish, anti-God, antimale, antifamily, and dangerous to society. The website of Radical Womanhood, a traditionalist organization, includes a four-minute video claiming to provide "an overview of feminist history" and showing the danger of feminist ideas.[25] The recently formed True Woman organization (which boasted an attendance of more than six thousand at its first conference in 2008 and has a goal of eventually reaching membership of one hundred thousand women worldwide) has accessible on its technologically sophisticated website a sign-up for the "True Woman Manifesto" (sample statement: "We are called as women to affirm and encourage men as they seek to express godly masculinity and to honor and support God-ordained male leadership in the home and in the church"). This website also offers a free thirty-day online "True Woman Makeover" (based on Prov. 31, 1 Tim. 2:9–10, and Titus 2:1–5), as well as video, audio, and text of conference speeches.[26]

These books and organizations are but a small sampling of antifeminists' urgent efforts to counteract evangelical egalitarianism. Some gender-traditionalist pastors are requiring engaged couples to read books on male headship and female submission. The Southern Baptists, America's largest Protestant denomination, issued an amendment to the "Baptist Faith and Message" statement in 1998 saying that "a wife is to submit herself graciously to the servant leadership of her husband."[27] A simple Internet search will show the myriad sites emphasizing the need to be a "Titus 2 woman," based on a biblical passage in which older women in a specific cultural situation were instructed to mentor younger women in homemaking, childcare, and submissiveness to their husbands.

Awakening Again

Christian feminists who know the language and subculture of evangelicalism have an important role to play in reaching out to a new generation of young women who have grown up in conservative churches or who are spiritually seeking on their own but become exposed to workshops, Bible study groups, conferences, and widely available books that purport to tell them how God has designed them for a specific and limited role.

Many of these young people are asking the same questions today that we were asking as the biblical feminist movement emerged in the second half of the twentieth century. There is a new awakening to the damage done to young women's self-esteem as they are told that God made them to be secondary and subordinate to men, that they may not use their gifts fully in the church, and that it is selfish to aspire to anything more. They often don't know that there are alternative interpretations and helpful resources available based on excellent biblical and theological scholarship. These women don't want to throw out their faith as the price they must pay for rejecting patriarchal teachings (although some feminists have felt they have no other choice). They need what those of us who understand their evangelical background, their desire to follow Jesus, and their love of Scripture can offer them in a unique way.[28]

At the same time that a *new* awakening of evangelical feminism is taking place, the work of second-wave evangelical feminism continues. We who are from that tradition want to continue and enlarge our vision, while welcoming the third wavers to share their creative visions and work together with us as we learn from them and they from us. We also want to reach out to secular feminists and feminists of other faith traditions and explore our mutual concerns.[29]

In addition, serious biblical and theological scholarship is underway among many women and men within the evangelical sector of Christian feminism, just as it is in mainstream Protestant and Roman Catholic feminist circles. Many evangelical feminists are addressing such topics as biblical interpretation, our concepts of God and language for God, Christology, spiritual metaphors, worship and devotional practices, feminist rituals, racial and ethnic diversity, sexuality questions, and ordination and other church leadership matters. Some are working to stop rape, verbal harassment, and other acts of violence against women; seeking to prevent child abuse and helping those who have been abused; facing up to issues of justice, peace, and empowerment in a world of wars, poverty, and income disparities; taking seriously the stewardship of the environment; seeking answers to questions about marriage partnership, reproduction, and parenting among both heterosexual and LGBTQ persons and families; trying to find ways to work together for and with girls and women in developing countries; and so much more.

It is encouraging to see young third-wave feminists so deeply concerned about intersectionality, the link between all forms of discrimination, and their determination not to let any of us forget that every effort to promote human dignity and equality is interconnected with all the others. While pursuing gender justice is basic, it is only one part of what feminism is all about.

Like all feminism, the mission and tasks of Christian feminism in its various manifestations (including the streams of feminism within evangelicalism) are exciting, challenging, inspiring, humbling, gratifying—and endless!

Part II

FEMINIST SCRIPTURAL INSIGHTS

Text-based religions have some of their greatest controversies over the interpretation and application of their scriptures. Christianity is no exception. Feminist biblical scholars have discovered powerful meaning in texts long ignored by the patriarchal tradition; discerned the presence of women hidden, indeed buried, under the weight of patriarchy in both the Hebrew and the Christian Scriptures; and explored new ways of interpreting classical texts.

Their work has shaped the preaching and teaching of a generation of feminist ministers and professors who now speak routinely of Sophia (Wisdom), the Jesus movement, and a "discipleship of equals." It is hard to exaggerate the importance of the imaginative feminist deconstruction and reconstruction of texts as they have opened the way for more inclusive and politically helpful theological resources.

Again, particularity and real-world connections are key. Texts are sacred to individual communities where their meanings take shape. So postcolonial feminist readings are crucial to seeing how many groups, especially women, have been held captive to patriarchal interpretations. It is just as important to see how liberating the words can be when understood in relation to marginalized people. Their survival and thriving becomes the measure of the text.

We begin this section with Gale A. Yee's query about identity, how an Asian American biblical scholar, indeed how every scholar, finds her place in the field. Elisabeth Schüssler Fiorenza reflects on the development of critical biblical studies, a field she shaped and developed, focusing on the struggles that configure the future. Surekha Nelavala brings an Indian Dalit feminist perspective, that is, the view of those on the bottom of society, to bear as she teases out the matters of inclusivity and distinctions. Shelly Matthews offers a future-oriented perspective, acknowledging the stunning progress and production in the field of Scripture studies but warning of the power of kyriarchal backlash to resist or undo it.

There are many more feminist scriptural perspectives to explore. But this group represents a good cross-section of the particularities that abound and the concrete application of biblical texts to sites of struggle.

Gale A. Yee is Nancy W. King Professor of Biblical Studies at Episcopal Divinity School. Dr. Yee is the author of many articles, essays, and books, including *Poor Banished Children of Eve: Woman as Evil in the Hebrew Bible*. She is currently working on a book putting the Bible in the service of the U.N. Millennium Development Goals.

Where Are You Really From?

An Asian American Feminist Biblical Scholar Reflects on Her Guild

GALE A. YEE

YOU: Where are you from?
ME: I'm from Cambridge, Massachusetts.
YOU: No, where are you really from?

We get this a lot, those of us who are American-born Asians: people requesting further clarification about where we are from, even after we have just informed them. Asians who have an accent usually aren't asked this. Their Otherness is already flagged as soon as they open their mouths. The question "Where are you *really* from?" implies that those Asians born in the United States have not been fully assimilated into the collective consciousness of what it means to be an American. Even though I am a third-generation Asian American, the perception of being a stranger in the land of my birth is difficult to dislodge. Asian American studies has a name for this syndrome, that of the "perpetual foreigner."[1] My social location as a perpetual foreigner is further marginalized by being a female who had to endure both the patriarchal attitudes of her Chinese ethnicity and those of her U.S. context. To complicate matters even more, I am also an outsider in a Chinese context, as my recent stint as a visiting professor in Hong Kong revealed. People realized that I was not a "real" Chinese as soon as I opened my mouth. There are very few Asian and Asian American female biblical scholars in the U.S. context. Not all of these would describe themselves as feminist or even acknowledge that their ethnicity has any bearing on their study of the Bible. Therefore, the place where I am "really from" in contributing to this volume about the future of feminist scriptural studies is one that is quite marginal in terms of my gendered, racial, geographic, and ideological social locations and as a member of my guild. However, it is precisely because I do not fit the mold of the "typical" biblical scholar that I am aware that the future of biblical studies must reckon seriously with the diversity of places where readers of the Bible are "really from."

When I first began my masters and doctoral studies in Bible in the 1970s, I could have been from the planet Xanadu, insofar as my social location as an Asian American female was a nonfactor from the guild's perspective. With respect to my own self-consciousness, I was not a feminist at the time, one of those "women's libbers," as they were called back then. Biblical studies was firmly immersed in the historical critical method and its male- and Euro-centric vortex, and I had to sink or swim in its waters. Things changed in the late seventies, and I was caught up in the paradigm shift from historical criticism to a literary-critical study of the Bible. This shift moved critical analysis beyond the search for the ancient author's meaning to the literary examination of the rhetorical beauties of biblical narrative and poetry. What resulted was the startling discovery that the Bible is open to multiple interpretations, just like any other work of art. The Bible contained not just one single meaning, which under the historical paradigm was the author's intended meaning. Rather, the text itself engages readers to see multiple and even conflicting interpretations of the same text. This is really a can of worms for those who think there is only one correct interpretation of the biblical text, usually their own.

Literary theory developed in the 1960s in the United States and Europe in a climate of student unrest and rebellion, leftist politics, and the questioning of traditional structures. Power became a variable in the literary analyses of texts. Who has power in the text? Who has power to create and produce the text? Who has power to read and interpret the text?[2] What therefore developed in literary theory is a whole series of postmodern approaches to the Bible that rejected the idea that we can examine the text in a totally objective, value-neutral, or disinterested way.

In biblical scholarship, the paradigm thus shifts to viewing the Bible as a site of struggle among competing interpretations. Here, the Bible is not simply a product of a particular historical context. Neither is it merely an object of literary art. It is something that directly shapes and influences the past and present historical contexts in diverse and often conflicting ways. For example, the Bible has been used in the United States by white slave owners to legitimize their possession and mistreatment of African American slaves. That same Bible offered African American slaves hope for the end of slavery and for their liberation. The creation story in Genesis 1–3 has been used by misogynists to enforce the subordination of women, and paradoxically by feminists to exalt the status of women to proclaim that women, too, are made in the image and likeness of God.

People approach the Bible from different places, and its interpretation depends heavily on where the reader is "really from." And where someone is "really from" depends on the complex interconnections of her or his gender, racial-ethnic identity, class status, and sexual orientation, among many other factors. In contrast to the other two paradigms, biblical scholars operating under this one acknowledge in varying degrees that these factors play important roles in how we interpret the text. These scholars try to identify the potential of a text for oppression or liberation depending on the context in which it is used, acknowledging that our readings of the Bible have obvious ethical implications, depending on where we are from: Who is helped by my reading? (The rich? The colonizer? The white master? Men?) Who is hurt by my reading? (The poor? The colonized? The black slave? Women?) Far from being value-neutral, this paradigm is consciously very partisan and biased. It is intentionally embedded in the ethics of reading.

In biblical studies this paradigm falls under the general category of ideological criticism, whose various approaches highlight and theorize the inequalities of power in different types of social relations. For example, feminist criticism addresses gender disparities. Liberation criticism focuses on economic and class differentials. Minority criticism explores the categories of race and ethnicity. Sexuality and sexual orientation are spotlighted by queer criticism. The special focus of postcolonial criticism is the power relations and disparities between empire and colony, between center and periphery. Although these different criticisms highlight a particular set of relations, this does not mean that the other categories of analysis are ignored. In fact, the "isms" of racism, classism, sexism, and colonialism interconnect, implicate, and reinforce each other in a cruel web of domination. Each of these criticisms must incorporate the other approaches to some degree in order to accomplish its interpretative task. White feminists were challenged painfully in the late 1980s and throughout the 1990s by feminists of color, particularly African American feminists, for privileging gender to the exclusion of race and class in their analyses. Both first-world white feminists and feminists of color were criticized by third-world feminists for their complicity in the exploitative workings of colonization and global capitalization, and by queer feminists for their heterosexism and homophobia.

African American theorist Patricia Hill Collins refers to these interlocking categories of experience as a "matrix of domination," in which the fundamental issue in each of these oppressive social relations is the domination of one group over another.[3] For me, the matter of feminism and race hit me emotionally during the summer of 1989, when I was invited to contribute to a festschrift for Rosemary Radford Ruether and meet with other authors at Maryknoll School of Theology. (It was there that I first met one of the codirectors of WATER, Dr. Mary E. Hunt.) It was an explosive occasion during which black feminists confronted white feminists with their racism, and white feminists were plagued with white guilt. Everyone was weeping. I was crying, too, but for different reasons. I remember tearfully expressing to Rosemary Radford Ruether that, as an Asian American, I belonged to neither group, black or white. The black/white binary did not conform to my experience, and it put me outside both of these groups of women in racial matters. This experience of being a racial outsider left an indelible mark on me and became significant for my understanding of Asian American biblical hermeneutics later on.

In light of my own particular "place" within my guild, how do I see feminist biblical criticism shaping up in the twenty-first century? First, I predict that feminist biblical criticism's methodology will become increasingly interdisciplinary. This is not a new development. Feminist biblical critics have already taken up narratology, deconstruction, and psychoanalytic criticism.[4] The history of biblical women in art, literature, music, and film has been the focus of several feminist cultural studies.[5] Feminist biblical scholars are beginning to use queer theory to analyze the construction of gender in biblical times, as well as provide readings from LGBTQ perspectives.[6] Ancient Israel has endured colonization and conquest by a number of ancient empires, including Egypt, Assyria, Babylonia, Persia, Greece, and Rome. Therefore, a number of feminist biblical scholars have utilized postcolonial criticism to explore the construction of gender under empire reflected in the Hebrew Bible and the New Testament.[7] Much more needs to be done in this area, however. In the special field of reception history (the history of a text's interpretation), some feminists have recovered the forgotten voices of women on the Bible through the ages.[8] Even traditional historical criticism is getting an overhaul, as scholars continue to expose its pretense of offering an objective, value-neutral inquiry and subject it to postmodern, cultural, Marxist, and feminist criticism.[9]

In addition to an increasingly interdisciplinary methodology, my hope is that feminist biblical studies will better integrate gender with issues of race, class, and colonial status in the analysis of biblical texts. The exclusive focus on gender and sexism in the Bible sometimes can mask sexism's complex links with classism, racism, colonialism, heterosexism, and so forth. Any further study of gender must encompass a broader systemic analysis of the matrix of domination embedded in the text and the society that produced it. Most recently, Asian American, African American, and Latino/a biblical scholars have collaborated in a joint effort to develop minority criticism of the Bible that foregrounds race but deliberately intersects with gender, class, colonial status, and sexuality.[10]

Finally, I believe that feminist biblical criticism can develop further by incorporating scholarship into new modes of discourse. In some ways, this development is a form of Elisabeth Schüssler Fiorenza's hermeneutics of creative imagination, which seeks to communicate alternative, liberating interpretations that allow biblical women to emerge, utilizing historical imagination, elaboration of narrative, artistic recreations, and liturgical celebrations.[11] Dissatisfied with the traditional focus of biblical studies on recovering "the past," Athalya Brenner, professor emerita of Hebrew Bible at the University of Amsterdam, the Netherlands, declares, "Let's face it: much academic writing tends to be dull to the point of dryness, often incomprehensible to those uninitiated into a given discipline, and thus inaccessible to many." She asks, "What would happen, in short, if we turned the tables and retold a biblical story, using our own intellectual and scholarly tools while openly voicing our own concerns rather than desperately alleging exposure of the implied biblical author's intentions in a less-than-distinctly-specified past?"[12]

Brenner wants to recreate an autobiographical voice for different female characters of the Hebrew Bible, incorporating into these voices modern issues about nationalism, ethnicity, war, sexuality, class, and culture. Eleanor Beach, professor of biblical studies at St. Ambrose University, Iowa, and a participant in archaeological digs at Tel Zeror, Gezer, Tel Halif, and Tel Miqne-Ekron, has authored a semi-fictional first-person account of Queen Jezebel by integrating her historical and archaeological expertise.[13] I have taken Beach's approach a step further, drafting a mystery novel set against the succession narrative of Solomon in 1 Kings 1–2. My protagonists are two sisters who are part of the contingent of virgins brought to Jerusalem as potential concubines to keep King David warm in his old age (1 Kings 1:1–4).

I applaud these efforts to leave the ivory tower and make our scholarship more accessible to a wider public. Particularly when religious discourse in our country is being held hostage by the religious right, the more we can make our work intelligible to the congregations in our churches and synagogues and even the secular world itself, the better we will be able to break this stranglehold and confront the "isms" that have been legitimated by this religious discourse.

I began this essay reflecting on my marginal place within my guild. My field has moved a long way from the place where I began almost forty years ago, and it is still developing. Furthermore, I myself am in a really different "place" from where I began long ago. I am much more conscious of the place I am "really from" when I analyze a biblical text as an Asian American female biblical scholar. As my field becomes more interdisciplinary, recognizing and confronting the intersections of all the systemic "isms" that were involved in the production of the text and in its current interpretation, I look forward in hope as feminist biblical scholarship emerges into the twenty-first century.

Elisabeth Schüssler Fiorenza is the Krister Stendahl Professor at Harvard University Divinity School and the founding coeditor of the *Journal of Feminist Studies in Religion*. Dr. Schüssler Fiorenza's many books include *The Power of the Word: Scripture and the Rhetoric of Empire* and *Democratizing Biblical Studies: Toward an Emancipatory Educational Space*. Her groundbreaking *In Memory of Her: A Feminist Theological Reconstruction of Christian Origins* has been translated into many languages. She is active in the women-church movement.

Critical Feminist Biblical Studies

Remembering the Struggles, Envisioning the Future

ELISABETH SCHÜSSLER FIORENZA

> Wisdom has built Her house,
> She has set up Her seven pillars …
> She also has set Her table.
> She has sent out Her wo/men ministers
> to call from the highest places in the town …
> "Come eat of my bread and drink of the wine I have mixed.
> Leave immaturity, and live,
> And walk in the way of Wisdom."
>
> PROVERBS 9:1–3, 5–6

In the past four decades, feminist Christians have heard this call of Divine Wisdom.[1] They have been sent out as Her wo/men ministers to proclaim Her invitation.[2] We have come together as the *ekklēsia* of wo/men to celebrate our common struggles for a just church and to renew our vision for a world free of oppression. We have assembled around the world to envision and live the discipleship of equals, to celebrate our baptismal call, and to share with each other our lived and variegated gifts.

Feminist Analysis

Because of the many different forms of wo/men's discrimination and our diverse struggles for full citizenship in church and society, there are many divergent and even contradictory articulations of feminism (for instance, womanism, *mujerista*, Latina, black, Asian, or Native American feminism) so that it is appropriate to speak of "feminisms" in the plural.[3] Most of them agree that contemporary feminism is not only a political movement that is akin to other emancipatory movements; it also is an intellectual and religious methodology both for investigating and theorizing the experiences and structures of wo/men's dehumanization and for articulating norms of well-being and visions of change. The diverse articulations of feminism, I suggest, come together in their critique of kyriarchy—that is, the domination of the Lord, emperor, slavemaster, father, elite male; they hold that gender—like race, class, and nation—is socially constructed rather than innate or ordained by G*d.[4] In my understanding, feminism is not just concerned about gender but also about race, class, heteronormativity, and imperialism. It is concerned about kyriarchal power relations of domination.

In the past forty years or so, feminist scholarship has amply documented that wo/men were apostles, missionaries, prophets, community leaders, and healers not only in early Christianity but also throughout church history.[5] Like them, feminists in the churches have insisted on their birth- and baptismal right to equal citizenship in society and church. Yet, like the Galilean wo/men disciples, we are often passed over with silence; like the wo/men prophets of Corinth, we are censured by autocratic hierarchies. Like Miriam, the sister of Moses and Aaron, we are often punished and shunned in our struggles for equal citizenship when we ask: "Did G*d not also speak with us?"[6] It is a critical feminist the*logy of liberation that has enabled us to ask this question.[7]

Feminist biblical scholars have enabled us to remember our biblical foresisters in the struggle who have been eliminated from public church knowledge or deformed in the interest of cultural femininity: Miriam, the sister of Moses and Aaron, who asked: "Did G*d not also speak with us?"; the wo/men prophets in Corinth who insisted on speaking G*d's word in the assembly, the *ekklēsia;* the Syrophoenician wo/man who challenged Jesus to get rid of his prejudice and to heal her daughter; the wo/men disciples, such as Mary of Magdala, who were with Jesus in Galilee, witnessed Jesus's execution, and became the primary witnesses to the resurrection.[8] We reimagine them and remember their struggles in order to receive strength in our own struggles for the future.

As the*logical inquiry, a critical feminist biblical interpretation of liberation therefore focuses on the imperial power relations inscribed in Scripture as the Word of G*d in and through andro-kyriocentric language and imagination. In order to lift into consciousness the linguistic violence of so-called generic, andro-kyriocentric (that is, male/Lord-centered) language that eliminates wo/men from the cultural and religious records, I use the term *wo/men,* and not *men,* in an inclusive, generic way. I suggest that whenever you read *wo/men,* you understand it in the generic sense. *Wo/men* includes *men, she* includes *he,* and *female* includes *male.* Feminist studies of language have elaborated that Western, kyriocentric, male-centered language systems (using words such as *slavemaster, lord,* or *father*) define language as both generic and gender-specific.

In such an andro-kyriocentric language system wo/men always must think at least twice, if not more, and adjudicate whether we are meant or not by so-called generic terms such as *men, brothers, humans, Americans,* or *Catholics.* To use *wo/men* as an inclusive generic term invites men to learn how to "think twice" and to experience what it means not to be addressed explicitly. Since wo/men always must arbitrate whether we are meant or not, I consider it a good spiritual exercise for men to acquire the same sophistication and to learn how to engage in the same hermeneutical process of "thinking twice" and of asking whether they are meant when the word *wo/men* is mentioned. Since, according to Wittgenstein, the limits of our language are the limits of our world, such a change of language patterns is a very important step toward the realization of a new feminist consciousness.

A critical feminist the*logy of liberation understands wo/men as the people of G*d and indicts the death-dealing powers of religious exclusion and oppression as structural sin and life-destroying evil. Hence, feminist the*logies and studies in religion have the goal not only to alter fundamentally the nature of malestream knowledge about G*d, the Self, and the World, but also to change institutionalized religions that have excluded wo/men from leadership positions throughout the centuries.

Feminist History as Memory

Reclaiming the authority of wo/men to shape and determine biblical religions, feminist the*logies ask new questions and employ new ways of seeing in order to recover the histories of wo/men's religious leadership and struggles that have been forgotten or diminished. In the past fifty years, feminist scholars have elaborated how church teaching and scientific historiography have been shaped by gender and the interest in nationalist domination. Malestream historical scholarship has prioritized men's history over wo/men's, white history over the history of people of color, the political history of Western domination over the history of struggles against it. Thus malestream historiography has produced scientific historical "facts" about wo/men that construct wo/men's historical absence and second-class citizenship.

Church teachings and religious dogmas have equally relegated wo/men to the fringes, indicted leading wo/men as heretics, or seen them as helpmates of the leading men in history. Biblical texts about wo/men have been forgotten, excluded from the lectionary, or interpreted in feminine, subordinate terms. Hence, feminist scholars of early Christianity have argued that the story of Christian origins must be retold not just as the story of leading men, but also as the story of wo/men from all walks of life, wo/men who have made history. In order to accomplish this project, much of feminist work has first focused on texts about wo/men without questioning their androcentric (that is, male-centered) rhetoric.

My own work has insisted that such marginalizing rhetoric must be critically analyzed, since "biblical wo/men" are constructs of andro-kyriocentric texts. A feminist reconstruction of Christian beginnings, I have argued, needs to investigate critically both androcentric biblical texts as to the androcentric imagination and the*logy that undergirds these texts, as well as the scientific models of historical reconstruction.

Compelled by the feminist critique of andro-kyriocentric language and historiography, I set out in my book *In Memory of Her* to show that the early Christian story could be told—and must be told—to move wo/men from margin to center.[9] My question has been: Do we still find traces of egalitarian emancipatory tendencies in andro-kyriocentric (that is, Lord-centered) early Christian sources? Do we still have sufficient information and source texts to tell the story of the movement carrying Jesus's name *otherwise*? Do we still have enough information in andro-kyriocentric records to enable us to tell early Christian history as a story about the equal discipleship of wo/men and men, slaves and freeborn, Jews and barbarians? Can the early Christian story still be told in terms of equality rather than in terms of kyriarchy (since egalitarian relations are the most obvious alternatives to dominance-submission relationships)? The task, I argued, involves not so much discovering new sources as recognizing the andro-kyriocentric rhetoric of our available sources and rereading them in a different key.

Not only was there plenty of material that could be read in an egalitarian frame of interpretation, but such an egalitarian reading could also do more justice to our sources that speak about wo/men's leadership in ways that malestream scholarship and church teaching felt compelled to explain away, overlook, or interpret in terms of cultural femininity. Two examples illustrate my point: 1) The malestream interpretation of Phoebe in Romans 16, for instance, was notorious for depicting her as a helpmate at Paul's meetings rather than as the leader of a house-church; 2) Mary of Magdala and the other wo/men were usually understood as supporting Jesus and his itinerant male disciples emotionally and financially, doing the necessary "housework" and helping the men with their monetary resources.

If we understand the mechanisms of andro-kyriocentric language, we cannot simply focus on texts about wo/men but must problematize the rhetoric of the text as well as place wo/men as historical agents into the center of attention. In so doing, we must avoid an "add wo/men and stir" approach. Instead, we need to engage in a feminist re-vision of early Christian history in the interest of liberation that presupposes a con-version, a turning-around of wo/men from self-negation to self-affirmation.

This critical feminist approach not only challenges malestream historical scholarship and hierarchical teachings to recognize that they have engendered prejudice and exclusions of wo/men from the historical record, but it also calls for a feminist conversion. For instance, it is often argued that Jesus chose only men as apostles and not wo/men. Hence, it is maintained, wo/men cannot be ordained and become successors of the apostles. Yet, this argument overlooks, on the one hand, that wo/men were disciples and apostles in the beginnings of Christianity, and on the other, how Jesus himself was not ordained and did not ordain anyone, male or female. In order to sustain this feminist argument, it is important that wo/men learn how to affirm ourselves and our foresisters.

If feminist biblical knowledge is to foster the self-recognition and self-determination of wo/men, then we must participate in re-envisioning "early Christian origins" as an alternative memory to that of domination. To do so, we must avoid the apologetic fallacy that argues that the leading men of early Christian beginnings (for instance, Paul) accepted wo/men. We should not continue to ascribe all agency, power, and authority to Paul, for example, and conceive of wo/men only as followers of the male apostles and leaders. To argue in this vein would mean to reinscribe the andro-kyriocentric mindset of malestream teaching that places men at the center of attention and sees wo/men only in relation to men, dependent on their approval and power. Instead, we need to shift our attention away from the image of the authoritative and powerful apostle Paul to the Corinthian wo/men prophets and to other early Christian wo/men leaders such as Priska, Phoebe, and Junia, who were founding figures of early Christian communities, although we have no records written by them.

In short, early Christian history must be retold, I have argued, as the memory of the struggles between those who envisioned and practiced a "discipleship of equals" and those who advocated the kyriarchal order of domination and subordination, between those who sought to realize the *ekklēsia* of wo/men and those who championed church as modeled after the kyriarchally organized imperial household that was stratified by gender, class, race, slavery, and caste as part of the "natural order" of the universe and seen as divinely ordained.

I am often asked whether it would matter if it could be shown that, in fact, wo/men did not participate in the early Christian movements or that there was no impulse whatsoever toward radical equality in antiquity. Does it matter whether or not history provides us with any examples of emancipation, equality, and justice? In response I point out that since history shapes identity and our view of the world, it matters whether wo/men and other subjugated peoples have a history, not just of violence, subordination, and exploitation, but also a history of liberation, agency, and equality—a history that is not just utopian, but one that has already been partially realized in the past and is again and again realized in the present.[10]

Egalitarian Reconstructive Models

The past is never simply discovered but is always reimagined and reconstructed in order to link the present with the past and the future. The remembered past always seeks to provide traditions, models, and visions for living communities today.[11] If memory shapes individual and collective identity, then it is important to scrutinize the reconstructive models that scholars or churchmen use to tell the story of the remembered past. Such models and frameworks need to be tested out not only as to how much they can make wo/men visible as historical agents but also as to how much they are able to transform kyriarchally defined collective memory. Only the presumption of wo/men's historical and religious agency (slave and freeborn, rich and poor, Jewish, Greek, Asian, or Roman) will allow us to read the ambiguities, gaps, and silences of androcentric (that is, grammatically masculine) texts against the grain.

Consequently, I have proposed two feminist models or frameworks for reimagining early Christian beginnings: one frame is "*ekklēsia* of wo/men" and the other is "discipleship of equals." They are guiding images that seek to inspire religious communities to feminist action in the present and the future. Discipleship of equals harks back to the language of the Gospels, whereas *ekklēsia* of wo/men seeks to correct and radicalize the democratic political tradition that has left its marks in the Pauline literature. Both expressions are like two sides of the same coin.

Ekklēsia *of Wo/men*

In the 1980s, I coined the notion of the *ekklēsia gynaikōn* (translated into English as "wo/men-church") and conceptualized it as an in-between space that sought to overcome the dualistic feminist alternative of either exodus from church and religion, or acceptance of church and religion, uncritically, as home, forgetting the violence that often takes place in the kyriarchal home. By introducing the radical democratic notion of the *ekklēsia* of wo/men as an alternative religious symbolic space and biblical image to those of exodus from patriarchy and patriarchal home, I sought to reframe the feminist binary (either feminist or religious, either moving out of church or remaining beholden to its hierarchy), a binary that reinscribed the dualistic division between religion and culture, religion and democratic rights, or religious and secular wo/men's movements.

The expression "*ekklēsia* of wo/men" picks up the early Christian communal self-designation *ekklēsia* (that is, the democratic assembly of full citizens) and qualifies it with *wo/men* in order to express the radical equality in the Spirit-Wisdom community.[12] All members have received the gifts of Spirit-Wisdom, but not all are the same. The members of the body of Christ—or, better, of the messianic corporation—are all equal and at the same time different because of their manifold gifts.

Ekklēsia is best conceptualized as an alternative space—not as a counter- or antispace but as an alternative space—to domination and empire because it is constituted not by super- and subordination but by egalitarian relationships. Elizabeth Castelli, professor of religion and women's studies at Barnard College, has rightly likened the notion of the *ekklēsia* of wo/men to a utopian space of "texts, institutions and worldviews that critique the historical or contemporary situation and promote an alternative vision of social and individual existence."[13] Moreover, within the context of social movements for change, we can understand the *ekklēsia* of wo/men not only as a virtual utopian space but also as an already partially realized space of living community and radical equality, as a site of feminist struggles to transform social and religious institutions and discourses.[14]

Discipleship of Equals

Whereas the notion of the *ekklēsia* of wo/men belongs to the language context of the Pauline letters, the notion of the discipleship of equals is rooted in the language world of the Gospels.[15] The genitive "of equals" that qualifies *discipleship* introduces a philosophically loaded and highly contested concept of rhetorical power. Equality is often misunderstood as sameness. But whereas identity means sameness, equality signifies a correspondence between a group of different persons or things that have the same quality in at least one respect but not in all respects—that is, they differ in many respects.

Equality has close links with justice. It expresses the fundamental moral principle or idea of equal dignity that is the equal worth of all persons, and requires equal respect for all persons. Equality does not imply the adaptation or assimilation to a standard kyriarchal male norm, but rather is a radical democratic challenge to it. Discipleship of equals, then, signifies communities of persons with equal status, worth, and respect who follow a common vision of justice.

The notion of the *ekklēsia* of wo/men makes it possible to understand Jesus and early Christian beginnings as shaped by the agency and leadership of Jewish, Greco-Roman, Asian, African, free and enslaved, rich and poor, elite and marginal wo/men. Those who hold the opposite view that, for instance, slave wo/men were not active shapers of early Christian life, would have to argue their point. If we shift from a kyriarchal frame of reference to that of the discipleship of equals, we no longer can hold, for instance, that wo/men were not leaders or even members of some early Christian communities. If we cannot prove that wo/men were not leaders or members, we need to give the benefit of the doubt to the textual traces suggesting that they were. Rather than take the kyriocentric text at face value, we must unravel its politics of meaning.

We need to be careful not to follow the androcentric and kyriocentric narrative lead of the Gospels, which put Jesus in the center of the story. Such an interpretation that focuses on Jesus reinscribes the cultural kyriocentric gender frame that places an elite man, the kyrios-Lord, into the center of attention and defines wo/man in relation to him as either subordinate or secondary. Hence, it is important to recognize this kyriocentric pattern. In order to overcome it, we need to imagine a discipleship of equals in which Jesus was first among equals. In this frame of a discipleship of equals, the movement that is named after Jesus is best understood as placing not Jesus but the vision of the *basileia* (that is, of G*d's "different" world of justice and well-being) in the center of its struggles. Because of this vision, Jesus was executed by the Roman Empire.

The *Basileia* of G*d

The central symbol of the movement named after Jesus is the *basileia,* the kingdom or, better, the commonwealth of G*d. This term expresses a Jewish religious-political vision that spells freedom from domination and is common to all the different movements in first-century Israel. However, it is difficult to translate the Greek term *basileia* adequately because it can mean "kingdom," "kingly realm," or "domain," or it can be rendered as "empire," "monarchy," "kingly rule," "sovereignty," "dominion," or "reign." In any case, the word has not only monarchic but also masculinist overtones.

To lift the political meaning of *basileia* into consciousness, I suggest that *basileia* is best translated as "commonwealth" or "commonweal." Such a rendering of the word *basileia* underscores linguistically the oppositional character of the empire/commonweal of G*d to that of the Roman Empire that crucified Jesus. Since such a translation is generally not understood, however, in an alternative sense but as ascribing to G*d imperial monarchic power, I have tended *not* to translate the Greek word *basileia,* but to use it as a symbol that evokes a whole range of the*logical meanings. Leaving the term *basileia* untranslated seeks to bring to the fore its political impact and eschatological significance in the first century CE, while at the same time problematizing its kyriarchal politics of meaning.

Exegetes agree that the Roman form of imperial domination signified by the term *basileia* has determined the world and experience of all Jewish movements in the first century, including that of which Jesus and Mary of Magdala were a part. Jesus and his companions, wo/men and men, sought for the emancipation and well-being of Israel as the people of G*d, a kingdom of priests and a holy nation (Exod. 19:6). They announced the *basileia* of G*d as an alternative to the empire of Rome.[16]

The *basileia* of G*d is a religious symbol proclaiming G*d's power of creation and salvation. This term also connotes a political vision that appealed to the oppositional imagination of people victimized by the Roman imperial system. It envisions an alternative world free of hunger, poverty, and domination. This "envisioned" world is already anticipated in the inclusive table-community, in the healing and liberating practices, as well as in the domination-free kinship community of the discipleship of equals that found many followers among the poor, the despised, the ill and possessed, the outcasts and sinners.

In short, discipleship does not mean that the wo/men disciples followed the great male master Jesus, but it means that, like Jesus, they followed the vision of the *basileia,* the "alternative world" of G*d. It also means that the discipleship of equals derives its meaning from its political context in first-century Palestine under Roman occupation.

Feminist remembering of the early Christian wo/men disciples, therefore, cannot simply focus on texts about wo/men and Jesus. Rather, it must imagine early Judaism and nascent Christianity in such a way that it can make marginalized wo/men such as Mary of Magdala visible as central agents of the *basileia* movement. This requires a reconsideration of the dominant the*logical reconstructive framework that—as Rosemary Radford Ruether has aptly put it—has produced Christian anti-Judaism as the left hand and divine masculinism as the right hand of Christology.[17] This framework has engendered the elite masculine church structures of domination that exclude wo/men from proclaiming the Word, from apostolic succession, and from church leadership.

Undergirding this reconstructive frame of the discipleship of equals are four basic assumptions:

First, anti-Judaism is contrary to a feminist Christian the*logy because such a prejudice does not recognize that Jesus and the movement of which he was a part were Jewish wo/men. They were *not Christian* in our sense of the word. Rather, as Jewish Galilean wo/men they gathered as the discipleship of equals for common meals, the*logical reflection, and healing events. They did so because they had the "dream" of the well-being of creation, the *basileia* of G*d, and followed a vision of liberation for everyone in Israel.

Second, who Jesus was and what he did can *only* be glimpsed in the interpretations and memory of the discipleship of equals understood as a first-century Jewish movement. Therefore, the movement of which Jesus was a member must not be separated from other messianic movements in first-century Judaism.

Third, this emancipatory movement of Galilean Jewish wo/men must be seen as a part of the variegated *basileia* movements that in the first century sought for the "liberation" of Israel from imperial exploitation. The concrete political referent of these movements was the colonial occupation of Israel by the Romans. Some of them, such as the Pharisees and Essenes, stressed the notion of "priesthood and holy nation." Others, such as the apocalyptic prophetic movements, stressed the political notion of the *basileia* of G*d as alternative to the Roman Empire.

Fourth, the emerging variegated, predominantly Galilean, movement in which Jesus and Mary of Magdala had leadership may have understood itself as a prophetic movement of Divine Wisdom. That it named itself after Jesus, the Messiah—Christ—was probably due to the conviction that had emerged after Jesus's execution that he was the Vindicated or Resurrected One. This conviction has its roots in the wo/men's tradition of the "empty tomb," which centered around the proclamation in Mark 16:7 "that Jesus is *going ahead* of you to Galilee," the site where the antimonarchical prophetic traditions were still alive.

This tradition manifests the self-understanding of the inner Jewish, Galilean *basileia* of G*d movement as an ongoing and inclusive movement of prophets and messengers sent to Israel by Divine Wisdom. The discipleship of equals is thus best understood as a Wisdom/Sophia movement, as is the *basileia* movement, whose members, such as John the Baptizer and Jesus, can be quite different in their strategies for change, but have in common their work to make present and experientially available G*d's different world of justice and well-being.

Such an egalitarian, reconstructive historical model is able to place the beginnings of the Galilean prophetic-wisdom *basileia* movement within a broader historical frame of reference. This frame allows us to trace the tensions and struggles between emancipatory understandings and movements in early Christianity, inspired by the democratic logic of equality on the one hand, and the kyriarchal structures of imperial Roman society and religion on the other. It allows us to do the same in our society.

Yet, it must not be overlooked that ancient movements of emancipatory struggles against exploitation and domination do not begin with the movement around Jesus. Rather, they have a long history in Greek, Roman, Asian, and Jewish cultures. The emancipatory struggles of biblical wo/men must be seen within the wider context of cultural-political-religious struggles for freedom from oppression. Such a historical model of emancipatory struggle sees the Jesus of history and the movement that has kept alive his memory not over and against Judaism but over and against structures of domination in antiquity and today. The wo/men friends of Jesus have been "going ahead" of us in the emancipatory struggles for a world of justice, liberation, and freedom from kyriarchal oppression.

Surekha Nelavala received her doctorate from Drew University. Dr. Nelavala's dissertation is titled *Liberation beyond Borders: Dalit Feminist Hermeneutics and Four Gospel Women.* She engages in biblical scholarship as a way of doing justice work. She is the author of *Paradigms of Authority in the New Testament: Women's Perspective,* as well as articles in international journals.

Inclusivity and Distinctions

The Future of Dalit Feminist Biblical Studies

Surekha Nelavala

"Inclusion with respect to distinction" has been one of the primary motifs of third-wave feminism. It is a simple concept, yet it demands virtual transformation in perspective. Most often, unity is used as a solution for inclusion and the two are perceived to go hand in hand. But is this always the case? Did everyone find justice under the umbrella of unity? Over the years, the attributes of oneness and unity have been challenged for their potential for perpetrating a universality that ignores certain particularities that demand attention and justice. Speaking as an Indian Dalit feminist scholar, I argue that the future of feminist scriptural work must keep people and justice at the center. Given the plurality and specific needs that arise from diversity, how can such a future be possible?

I believe that it is not merely theological jargon or linguistic extravagance that will create just and inclusive communities, but the people-oriented theology that emerges from the simple lives of those people who are excluded, those who have no voice, and those who are unheard. It is an obligation for feminist scriptural scholars to listen to the unheard voices crying for justice, and become their voice. However, can inclusiveness be replaced by unity to attain justice? What is unity and what is inclusiveness?

My understanding of justice, unity, inclusiveness, or any other concept, for that matter, is certainly influenced by my identity and how it is carried in multiple ways. I have been known mostly as an Indian Dalit feminist Christian scholar to the outside world, whereas my two other major roles, as wife and mother, are usually considered less important, even though they demand most of my time, presence, and attention. It may be odd to speak of or emphasize those two roles, because I am expected to write in the role of a feminist biblical scholar. As I am trying to reflect on the concepts of unity and inclusiveness, the two images that come to my mind are milk and salad, which Indians consume on a daily basis. On the one hand, the scholar in me is warning against my instincts to get insight from the home environment, but on the other hand, the mother and wife roles from which I drew the insight dictate that I include these simple concepts to explain unity and inclusiveness. I present these images especially in relation to the status of simple Indian Dalit women.

Milk and Salad: Images to Convey the Status of Dalit Women

In unity, at times one part of the whole completely loses its identity, as in the case of a mixture of milk and water. Although water can thin the consistency of milk and thus has its impact on the whole, its identity is minimized, because it can no longer be called water once it is united with the milk. Therefore, water risks losing its identity completely in being united with milk. Many people and communities in this world have similarly lost their identities in the name of oneness and unity. The milk-and-water image thus calls us to redefine our goals of unity and oneness, while asking that any model we use ensures justice for all.

If the image of milk and water symbolizes unity, then the image of salad can explain inclusiveness. The image of salad symbolizes a community where no one ingredient overshadows the other; each ingredient contributes to enhancing the flavor of the salad, but each maintains its identity. Regardless of quantity, each added item contributes to the whole while asserting its uniqueness.

Is this a utopian model that can exist only as a concept, not as reality? If so, it challenges feminist Christian spirituality. How can we move from the milk-and-water image of a community to the salad image of a community? Inclusiveness not only seeks similarities but also provides space for differences. Having experienced the milk-and-water image as a Dalit woman, both in the Dalit and women's communities, and having lost my identity like the water, I resist such unity and seek inclusiveness, where participants' contributions are acknowledged and appreciated, their cries are heard, and their issues are attended to.

I represent Dalit women and seek inclusiveness and justice for Dalit women. I am challenged by questions more than by solutions: How can a Dalit woman be heard when she is forced to be mute and invisible? How can she find justice when her very survival is at stake? How can she experience true inclusiveness when she has lost her identity? Furthermore, how can churches respond and react to a Dalit woman's situation and affirm justice? Is it through theological reflection, biblical interpretations, or social theories? Of course, yes to all. Feminist studies can be relevant only when it has a practical approach, where one of its norms is the reality of people's experiences. Feminist studies helps only when women's stories are heard, and only when there is transformation.

Dalit Women's Standpoint: Biblical Interpretation

Who are Dalit women? Broadly speaking, Dalit women in India are simple, mostly illiterate, hard-working, innocent, and poor laborers who are considered untouchable and are marginalized and discriminated against in every aspect of their lives; they cannot voice or theorize their issues. Being a voice for the broad spectrum of Dalit women, I affirm my difference from those who are stereotypically described as Dalit women. I situate myself as a Dalit feminist biblical reader. My subjective experience is what shapes my standpoint in theological reflection and biblical interpretation.

Dalit feminist interpretation of the Bible, which shapes theological reflection from the standpoint of Dalit women, begins with the question, Can the biblical text give Dalit women dignity and affirm their identity? When there were mass conversions of Dalit men and women to Christianity, the Bible was regarded and honored as a liberating holy book for Dalits. However, initially, the Bible slipped into the hands of upper-caste converts and later into the hands of Dalit males who interpreted the Bible primarily through their lens of caste hierarchy and patriarchy. Thus Dalit theology was loud, clear, and sharp with regard to discrimination of caste, but paid little attention to gender issues even though there was an underlying concern for all the marginalized.

Dalit theology has emerged as a countertheology to caste theology, which is known as Indian Christian theology.[1] Dalit theology has struggled to become an academic discipline; it is sometimes reduced to a theoretical method or mere intellectual inquiry. In the process, it has lost its connection to the roots of Dalit people even though from the very beginning Dalit theology claimed to be founded on Dalit experience and personal suffering. For example, Arvind P. Nirmal, a Dalit who was a pioneer of Dalit theology, wrote, "I would say that a Christian Dalit theology will be produced by Dalits. It will be based on their own Dalit experiences, their own sufferings, their own aspirations, and their own hope. It will narrate the story of their pathos and their protest against the socioeconomic injustices they have been subjected to throughout history. It will anticipate liberation which is meaningful to them."[2] Another leading theologian, V. Devasahayam, states that theology starts from an analysis and reflection of our own context and seeks to interpret the Word of God in relation to that context. He goes on to say, "In our context, we could boldly affirm that no theological method is adequate if it does not recognize caste as the contextual reality and a major structure of oppression."[3]

What is the Dalit experience? Is it a monolithic experience? Can it be homogenized? By now, it is familiar from the identity standpoint that "Dalit experience," as it is in the case of "women's experience," in its generalized sense is considered problematic.[4] Today, with deeper sensitivity to the differences in Dalit identity due to the gender, social, and economic distinctions, the use of the term "Dalit experience" demands words of caution and explanation. Dalit experience is not homogenous and thus calls for attention to other identities that qualify it, such as class, gender, subcaste, and sexuality.[5] Dalit feminist theologians and biblical readers find it hard to accept any theories or theologies that do not pay attention to caste-gender dynamics.

While upholding the contributions of Dalit theology and crediting the positive influence of feminist theology in the church and society, Dalit feminism emphasizes the need to resolve the question of the perpetual discrimination and marginalization of Dalit women. A Dalit feminist biblical approach seeks to provide a forum for the issues of Dalit women to be discussed by hearing the stories of Dalit women, which are otherwise unheard. A Dalit feminist perspective invites constant debates of the issues of casteism and patriarchy, regarding both systems as inherently oppressive and equally autocratic in nature. Thus, a Dalit feminist standpoint challenges both feminist movements and Dalit movements, not just to include Dalit women but also to properly analyze caste-gender dynamics and their discrimination in multiple and overlapping patriarchies of caste communities in order to create a just and inclusive context.[6]

The Power of Personal Stories in Biblical Interpretation

As a Dalit feminist reader, my goal is not only to make the biblical text relevant to the context of Dalit women but also to enhance and bring the text alive through the real stories of Dalit women. Dalit feminist biblical interpretation authenticates and allows the life situations of Dalit women and their stories to be in active conversation with the text. In Dalit women's contexts, each story is closely linked to their community. Similarly, the text has a particular message and relevance to the contexts and questions of Dalit reality. Therefore, autobiographical stories of Dalit women that are otherwise unheard, unseen, and unnoticed can counter patriarchal and caste violence powerfully, and bring rich nuance and a critical base for interpreting the text.

In the past, autobiographies were typically confined to famous people and celebrities until the emergence of personal voice in the academic literature. Many marginalized groups that did not find space in traditional histories of those cultures have embraced autobiographical narrations as a method.[7] These stories are a tool for presenting an alternative view of history by theorizing the relation between the dialogical self and its context.[8] Similarly, for a Dalit woman, it is a paradox even to have an opportunity of any writing, much less autobiographical writing. But autoration (speaking about self) is common among women. It is part of women's culture and it has been seen as a potential method to release pain and suffering.

Stories of other women play a crucial role in women's lives in terms of how they respond to particular situations. Being surrounded by information on the life situations and stories of others, people spontaneously relate to personal experiences, particularly when they have encountered similar situations, perhaps in a film, in literature, or even in Scripture. Stories of one another are always transmitted from friends, neighbors, sisters, and evidently from mothers to daughters. The stories and the suffering of the mother are passed on to the daughter, much as family name, fame, and property are passed on from the fathers to the sons. For Dalits, the significance of testimonials or autobiographical narrations is that they raise awareness about the perpetuation of untouchability and its insidious effects on the outside world and thus bring visibility to their voice against the unjust structures.[9]

Conclusion: Exposing Injustice and Inviting Change

The autobiographical element in Dalit women's writings creates narrative authority for Dalit women to be heard in a culture of writing. It helps claim their subjectivity, which has always been undermined in writings, including Dalit writings. Dalit women's autobiographies provide dissident spaces within the literary public in which they can speak out against untouchability and patriarchy. Personal narratives of the marginalized also serve as sociocultural records of their community as well as literary forms of social protest. In autobiographical form, these facts become uncontestable truth, because no one knows more about an individual's life experience than the individual herself. Thus, the clear narrative agenda of Dalit autobiography is to expose the reality against popular notions that simplify casteism, patriarchy, and their effects. Autobiographies reiterate the contemporary occurrence of untouchability, which is otherwise ignored in public discourse. Exposing continuous untouchability unites everyone who has similar experiences and those who identify with such experiences of exclusion, insult, or discrimination. However, for those who stand on the other end, autobiographies of painful experiences bring a challenge and an invitation for change, reconciliation, and transformation. This is a Dalit feminist contribution to biblical studies.

Shelly Matthews is the Dorothy and B. H. Peace Jr. Associate Professor of Religion at Furman University. The Reverend Matthews is ordained in the Dakotas Area Conference of the United Methodist Church. She is the author of *First Converts: Rich Pagan Women and the Rhetoric of Mission in Early Judaism and Christianity* and *Perfect Martyr: The Stoning of Stephen and the Construction of Christian Identity.*

The Future of Feminist Scripture Studies

SHELLY MATTHEWS

I speak of the future of feminist Scripture studies from my social location as a teacher of undergraduates in a liberal arts college in the southeastern region of the United States, a region where a fiercely kyriarchal reading of biblical texts holds sway. As an ordained United Methodist minister steeped in Social Gospel traditions and a feminist Christian, as well as a college professor schooled in academic approaches to Scripture study, I am something of an alien to many of my students, who do not identify with a branch of the Christian tradition so much as with a particular posture toward the Bible. This significant majority of students would identify themselves as "Bible-believing Christians," and a number of these would go so far as to suggest that the only true Christians are those who are so categorized. To these students, traditionalist readings are sacrosanct, and critical readings suspect. Reading from this place, I see the future of feminist scriptural studies as a territory that will be continually contested. Though I acknowledge below that progress has been made, and thus that I can find reasons for continuing optimism about the future, my optimism is tempered by awareness of the strength of kyriarchal biblical interpretations and institutions, and the tendencies of these forces to push back.

I note that good reason for hope in the future of feminist scriptural studies comes from assessing what has been accomplished in the past. Thanks to the endeavors of feminist biblical scholars, especially over the past thirty years, we have access to many more interpretive tools and a significantly broader textual base from which feminist work can proceed. In my own field of New Testament studies and Christian beginnings, I point to the work of Elisabeth Schüssler Fiorenza, along with Ann Wire, Bernadette Brooten, Jane Schaberg, and many others, as providing a foundation for future work while also nurturing a new generation of Scripture scholars. One of the happy results of the groundwork laid by these feminist scholars is that they have given us resources for decentering the male figures who have held primary significance in Christian Scripture studies (including Peter, Paul, and, yes, even Jesus), so that we might hear a fuller range of voices that contributed to the early Jesus movement, and to the development of early Christianity.[1] These results may be highlighted through the articulation of some basic ground rules for feminist Scripture studies.

1. *What we see in the Scriptures will depend on our theoretical framework—on the lenses we use to read the text.* One of the revelations that caught many by surprise in the seventies and eighties was that there were actually women "in plain sight" in Christian Scriptures, women who seem to have been key agents and actors in the Jesus movement, but who had gone little noticed simply because no one was looking for them. Romans 16 serves as an illustrative text in this regard. Operating on the unarticulated assumption that if there were women mentioned in the Scriptures, they could not be leaders, and conversely, if there were leaders in the church, they could not be women, traditional androcentric scholarship had not registered the significance of the women hailed in this closing chapter of Romans as

Paul's coworkers, ministers, and apostles. Owing to the androcentric translation of the leadership titles *diakonos* and *prostatēs,* Phoebe of Romans 16:1–4 had been traditionally rendered a mere hostess—a "deaconess" or "helper"—to an *ekklēsia,* rather than a presider and minister in Cenchraea. Likewise, Junia, a female name, was rendered as the male name Junias in textual tradition, on the assumption that since this person was hailed as an apostle, "he" must be male. Only upon reading the text within a different framework, one that allows for the possibility of wo/men's agency, can women's leadership roles be properly recognized.[2]

2. *Biblical texts are rhetorical texts, constructed with an aim to persuade. Thus, it is possible, through rhetorical criticism, to reconstruct the arguments of the audience to whom a text is written.* This principle has been most usefully employed in feminist interpretations of the letters to the Corinthians. Paul's many references to gender issues and spiritual gifts suggest the presence of confident, enthusiastic women prophets and leaders of the *ekklēsia* in Corinth. Thus, his arguments about mutuality in conjugal relations (1 Cor. 7), head coverings (1 Cor. 11), and the ordering of spiritual gifts (1 Cor. 14) may now be read as carefully calibrated attempts to modify the behavior of these women. His own ordering of spiritual gifts in 1 Corinthians 12:28, in which (not by coincidence) apostles such as himself are placed first in the hierarchy, may be read with a "hermeneutics of suspicion." The subsequent defense of his own authority in 2 Corinthians may be read as a sign that these Corinthian women prophets were not convinced by his earlier arguments.[3]

3. *Prescriptive language should not be read as descriptive language. When we come upon prescriptions for wo/men's behavior, and especially upon stark prescriptions, we may assume that the author is in a bit of a panic about the "misbehaving" wo/men he knows.* With this principle firmly in place, feminist Christians no longer need despair when contemplating texts such as 1 Timothy's proscriptions against women speaking in church, or the exhortations in the household codes of Colossians and Ephesians for slaves and women to obey

their masters/husbands. Instead of reading these words as inspired ideas for proper behavior, we may read them as signs of resistance by those who did not obey, and did not keep silent, and whose struggles prompted the clampdown initiated in these texts. In this way, those at the receiving end of the proscriptions become for us inspiration for our own struggles.[4]

4. *The* basileia *movement that came to focus on Jesus was a communal movement and part of a larger Jewish struggle for justice in the first century.* Many of the sayings attributed to Jesus centered on justice for the poor and marginalized do not stand in opposition to first-century Jewish teaching from other quarters. In fact, they echo those sentiments—as readings from texts with utopian impulses such as the Song of Solomon and the Dead Sea Scrolls attest. Moreover, it is good to celebrate the relatively positive treatment of women in the Gospels not as owing to Jesus's uniqueness, but to the positive position of women in the Judaism of his day.[5]

5. *While we can recognize and celebrate many utopian impulses that animated the early Jesus movement, this celebration is tempered by acknowledgment of the limitations of these utopian struggles and visions.* Feminist work in past decades that has taken up the call to be sensitive to issues of race, ethnicity, sexuality, and social status, as well as gender, has also taught us to keep our eyes on the whole story, not just the parts of it in which liberating struggles can be glimpsed. I point to Gay Byron's *Symbolic Blackness and Ethnic Difference in Early Christian Literature* as a persuasive argument that early Christian rhetoric of universal love did not preclude ethnic prejudice based on color differences among Christians.[6] In addition, Jennifer Glancy's *Slavery in Early Christianity* reminds us that utopian Christian visions did not extend to full embrace of slaves in many quarters.[7] Many of the parables attributed to Jesus assume the violence of the master/slave system; the churches of the Pauline orbit seem not to have resisted the widely held cultural assumption that slaves were subject to sexual use by their masters.

6. *The boundaries of the canon do not fix the boundaries of the resources we may utilize to reconstruct the struggles and agency of wo/men in the Jesus movement.* In feminist Christianity, the Scriptures now extend beyond the boundaries of the twenty-seven books of the Christian Testament. For example, it is simply impossible for me to imagine teaching my undergraduate introductions to the New Testament, or any adult education seminar on early Christian diversity, without considering the Gospel of Mary and the Acts of Thecla. In these two texts, one associated with Jesus traditions and one with Pauline traditions, we have access to voices that have long been silenced. We now have access to Mary Magdalene as she is depicted in the Gospel of Mary, as a visionary teaching the disciples the mysteries that lead to salvation, as the one who has the fortitude to comfort the disciples in their distress, as the one who weeps in the face of Peter and Andrew's scorn, as the one who serves as the inspiration for the defensive question raised by Levi on Mary's behalf, "If the Savior made her worthy, who are you indeed to reject her?" To be sure, this text is also wrapped in a kyriocentric frame: the fight depicted here is between the "boys," who argue about her worthiness. As the narrative progresses, the voice that is first used for authoritative teaching and comforting exhortation turns solely to weeping; Mary weeps, Levi defends. But still, the text gives us a new angle of vision, provides us a fragment—a shard—of what Mary Magdalene must have meant in some quarters of the *basileia* movement. Holding this shard up to the light, we can also see traces of a story behind the story in John 20, the scene between Mary and the resurrected Jesus in the garden; we read with indignation Luke's dismissive condemnation of Mary in Luke 8:2 as the woman "from whom seven devils had come out"; we mourn the complete silence concerning Mary Magdalene in the Acts of the Apostles, the only canonical story of the postresurrection *ekklēsia*, as the silence of repression.[8]

We have the Acts of Thecla. While there are debates about whether Thecla was an actual historical figure or merely a character in a work of fiction, we do not need proof of her historicity to recognize that the text speaks against societal norms of the patriarchal household, against the notion of marriage as cementing bonds between elite families within a city and preserving that city's status quo. As a text that defies the status quo, it offers the possibility of agency to one who might otherwise have been sequestered and silenced within the patriarchal house. Thecla opts for Paul over her fiancé, for the communal life of the *ekklēsia* over the stability of household; she baptizes herself. She goes forth teaching the Word of God. To be sure, as with the Gospel of Mary, so with Thecla the utopian impulse is trapped within a kyriocentric frame. The negative connotations of female/body/sexuality in this text allow for Thecla's agency only as predicated on her continence, and her "manliness." Thecla renounces her sexuality and cuts her hair to signal her newfound virility. Although she baptizes herself, her authorization to "go and teach the Word of God" comes from Paul. Again, this is not a perfect model for the feminist Christianity we would like to see in the future, but still it is a fragment of a tradition from the past that sheds new light on canonical texts and ecclesiastical traditions.[9]

The fact that feminist Scripture studies begins with these principles in hand bodes well for even more intellectually exciting, energizing, and spiritually enriching work in the future. But these tools and this work already accomplished do not guarantee feminists a place at the table, either in the academy or in the church. While forward progress is possible, it is not inevitable. What is inevitable, at least in the place where I stand, is kyriarchal resistance to feminist work. I end with a story of two different students from my introduction to the New Testament class, whom I will call Hannah and Sarah, one open to the promise of feminist Scripture studies and the other resistant to it.

Hannah is one representative of the future of feminist Scripture studies. She studies Greek and loves the classical world and all things related to early Christianity. She embraces progressive Christianity and spirituality. She questions received traditions. She plans to pursue ordination in the Presbyterian Church USA, and also possibly to pursue doctoral work in Scripture studies. She presented in my introductory New Testament class on the Gospel of Mary, utilizing the resources given to her by Jane Schaberg and other feminist Magdalene scholars. She expressed surprise over the strength of Mary Magdalene in the text, tempered by awareness of the text's androcentric framing. She questioned traditions of female exclusion in the church in light of Mary's privileged role in early Christianity.

Sarah represents the many young women I teach who regard the exhortations to wives' submission in the household codes as the high mark of Christian duty for women. Her presentation for my course was on Philo's proscriptive text limiting women to the private sphere and reserving the public life for men.[10] I offer this text to my students to help them contextualize the household codes in the New Testament—so that they might see how these kyriarchal scriptural proscriptions are crafted within a world that would restrict any public role for women. Sarah is an A student, but by no means a feminist. She anticipated how I would direct a conversation relating Philo's proscriptions to the household codes, and she recognized clearly that in order to defend these Scripture codes, she would also need to defend Philo. Thus, in her presentation, Philo's draconian exhortation that women remain sequestered within the walls of their houses, never speaking in public, was hailed as a sign of Philo's "respect" for women's nature. Like Philo, and the author of the household codes, Sarah affirms two spheres and two natures: an active one for men and a submissive one for women.

In Sarah, and countless students like her, I see what Elisabeth Schüssler Fiorenza has identified as the "tenth roadblock" to engaging in feminist Scripture interpretation, the emotional heaviness of reading Scripture critically among those for whom such readings violate a sacred taboo.[11] The sacred taboo of the Scriptures, and especially the sacred taboos of exhortations to wifely submission, weigh heavily on many of the students I teach in Greenville, South Carolina. It is the roadblock that may prove most difficult to remove, and therefore the one of which those engaged in feminist scriptural study would do well to be mindful.[12]

Part III

Feminist Ethical Agendas

Ethical issues are the daily bread of religions. Everyone has an opinion. Votes are cast on the basis of religiously informed views. So feminist theo-ethical discourse is the most obvious place where the conflicts of values and commitments are played out.

Feminist scholars and activists are nearly unanimous in insisting that women's well-being and the well-being of dependent children must be the ethical bottom line. In U.S. society, abortion and same-sex love have been cast as the litmus tests of orthodoxy in many Christian denominations. More ink has been spilled on them than on the wider ethical agenda items of ecology, economics, and violence, which surely shape the world more decisively.

Feminists have developed a wealth of experience in sifting through the morass of arguments that would keep women, people of color, and those who are poor, young, ill, or elderly from thriving. They have collaborated with organizations and movements for change, adding their insight and energies to the resources for social justice. Feminist scholars and activists have set their own agenda, refusing to be boxed into responding and reacting, insisting on naming for themselves the priorities and principles that emerge from feminist Christianity even when they conflict with the churches. Structural change is equally as important as personal change.

We open this discussion with Traci C. West's challenge to develop antiracist feminist Christian social ethics, since nothing less is worthy of the name. Then we turn to Virginia Ramey Mollenkott's exposition of trans experience that leaves behind the old gender binaries and embraces a far more fluid, inclusive sexual agenda. Marie M. Fortune makes the life-saving case for antiviolence work as essential to a feminist Christian agenda.

Rachel A. R. Bundang takes on the challenge of laying out a feminist ethical agenda in the complex and multilayered reality of contemporary society. Kate M. Ott thinks carefully about the implications of feminist Christian ethics in the lives of children and young people, who are moral agents in their own right.

So much more needs to be discussed from feminist Christian theo-ethical starting points. This sample shows the products and the promise of a method that assumes women's moral agency and encourages women's ethical thinking. Multiple struggles characterize the agenda that emerges from the integrity of committed women's lives that can and must have an impact on public policy.

Traci C. West is professor of ethics and African American studies at Drew University Theological School. Dr. West is the author of *Wounds of the Spirit: Black Women, Violence, and Resistance Ethics* and *Disruptive Christian Ethics: When Racism and Women's Lives Matter,* and editor of *Our Family Values: Same-sex Marriage and Religion.* She is an ordained elder in the United Methodist Church.

What Does Antiracist Feminist Christian Social Ethics Look Like?

TRACI C. WEST

Issues of race and ethnicity represent some of the most exciting horizons for developing political solidarities and expanding theological imaginations in current discussions taking place within feminist and womanist Christian social ethics in the United States. Two examples come to mind immediately. I think that antiracist approaches to globalization and sexuality represent profound opportunities for the development of liberationist Christian social ethics by feminists and womanists. As a black feminist scholar/activist whose work bridges the church and the academy, I must also admit the difficulty of seizing these opportunities.

I grew up in New England in a predominately white, so-called mainstream Protestant denomination: the United Methodist Church. During the 1980s, I was among the first group of black women to be ordained and serve as a local church pastor in the New York Conference of my denomination. I now teach at a United Methodist–related seminary and maintain an activist commitment to antiracist, woman-affirming social justice. A particular focus of my scholarly/activist work includes the persistently inadequate responses by churches and the broader society to male-perpetrated violence against lesbian, bisexual, transgender, and heterosexual women of color. The realization of antiracist, feminist aspirations within actual practices remains, however, a thoroughly challenging endeavor in academia, churches, and the broader U.S. society, including the feminist enclaves within these arenas.

Nevertheless, I believe that there is more to be found in recognizing our racial and cultural plurality besides the challenge of conflicts, resentments, and struggles to maintain hierarchies of power and status. A renewed global consciousness about humanity's ecological and economic interdependence is steadily gaining traction in U.S. culture. This growing awareness has boosted the possibilities for joint global feminist strategizing with a more coordinated global impact. Also, late-twentieth-century immigration patterns have had an undeniable impact on the cultural geography of local community life in the United States.[1] Significant concentrations of immigrant families of color, especially from the global South, are now found in most U.S. cities, both large and small, from Texas to Maine and Florida to Oregon. Their adult family members are not always marginalized laborers. The degree of class stratification within immigrant groups varies.

As a result of these societal trends, the cultural and racial assumptions have broadened even within U.S. Christian feminist and womanist ethics. Deliberations over which strategies and conversation partners are essential to create an agenda for safeguarding women's bodily integrity and freedoms have been impacted. Awareness has grown steadily about the need for a conceptual shift that expands Christian feminist ethics beyond its former white-dominated, monocultural starting points.[2] Likewise, womanist ethics has grown beyond its initial analytic presumptions of a primary white-black cultural dichotomy.[3] Also, the nature of religious language at the heart of feminist and womanist Christian ethics must now find a mode of articulation that allows for the possibility of consultations with Hindu, Sikh, or Muslim women to address effectively shared local community needs, such as domestic violence intervention and access to health-care services for women and children.

There is, in addition, a slowly dawning realization about the necessity for a more complicated understanding of cultural identities that exist within racial/ethnic minority groups usually lumped together as one cultural monolith. For example, in feminist and womanist Christian social ethics, simplistic references to "black women in the black community" that assume an exclusively Christian church base with southern U.S. cultural roots have to be amended.[4] They must be broadened to also reflect U.S. black women who are Caribbean American, African immigrants, Afro-European, Afro-Latina, as well as the wide range of distinctive cultural backgrounds within those groups. Without acknowledging longstanding traditions such as the Muslim religion or African-based traditional religious practices of "black women in the black community," the construction of antiracist Christian feminist and womanist ethics that refers to black American religious life will be erroneous. The inaccuracy of these cultural generalizations about blacks, hopefully, becomes more obvious with an ever-increasing consciousness of global interrelatedness and the transmigratory patterns of populations in U.S. culture. Most important, analytical attention to the range of diasporic cultural identities of U.S. women of African descent can bring invaluable insights. It can help us learn more about the politics of transnational antiblack racism as well as the nature of religious collusion with it and religious resources for resisting it.

Any blanket conceptualization of a uniformly disempowered status for all U.S. black women asserted within feminist and womanist Christian ethics must be reconfigured in light of ever-widening socioeconomic disparities among blacks. Powerful elites, such as former U.S. Secretary of State Condoleezza Rice, billionaire Oprah Winfrey, and First Lady Michelle Obama, are positioned at the opposite end of the social spectrum from the numerous single, poor black women who struggle to care for their families and depend upon some form of public assistance. Such differences in socioeconomic class divisions exemplify differential degrees of political power among blacks, as well as gradations in the impact of antiblack racism experienced by black women. Of course, the crushing economic and educational inequities of class barriers stretch across racial and ethnic groups. Each one of the African American women mentioned above—Rice, Winfrey, and Obama—albeit in differing ways, has greater global influence and power than most people in the U.S. from any racial or ethnic group, including most white men and women. The privileged status of such individuals must be factored into generalized feminist and womanist Christian ethical claims about the subordinate group status of black womanhood in U.S. society. Consideration of such examples also corrects a naïve vision about the extent to which the inclusion of more black women within existing power relations can foment just societal practices and antiracist attitudes, particularly for poor women.

The ability to maintain an ongoing dialogical relationship between universalized moral claims and particular ones is a necessary skill for developing liberatory Christian social ethics. We need moral commitments that are universal, such as a commitment to the elimination of violence against women. By *universal,* I refer to moral commitments that contribute to a common good that crosses cultural boundaries within our communities. The *particular* moral commitment to end the intimate violence against impoverished U.S. immigrant women, for example, requires attention to the particularities of racist, anti-immigrant U.S. cultural sentiment, as well as to the complicity of the state in this violence. A solely universalized moral commitment to the elimination of violence against women leaves out and can even erase such essential but particular moral concerns. Ideas about the kinds of practices that build the common good can only be discovered through a dialogical understanding of how culture shapes both universal and particular moral claims. An antiracist feminist Christian social ethic can only formulate a commonly shared notion of justice that operates with experientially informed fairness, compassion, and historical memory if it is mindful of the cultural complexities of and injustices experienced by women in particular marginalized groups.

Globalized community realities that reflect permeable international borders offer promise for learning about how we formulate such principles of justice. Currently, justice proposals in antiracist, feminist, and womanist Christian ethics that address male-perpetrated sexual violence against women, for instance, must include varied instances of nation-state border crossing, even when the proposals are limited to criticizing U.S. perpetrators and culture.

A focus on U.S. sexual violence should include concern about incidents such as those perpetrated in foreign nations by male U.S. military and civilian contractor personnel against local women. An examination of sexual violence at home in the United States should consider incursions onto Native American tribal nation lands where so many of the assaults are committed by non-Native males against Native American women.[5] An adequate antiviolence Christian ethic must also attend to victim-survivor experiences of internationally trafficked women laborers en route to and trapped in the United States, as well as impoverished migrating Mexican women at border-crossing zones near Mexico.[6] A challenge for feminist and womanist Christian ethics is to create antiviolent Christian moral understandings of right relation, that is, to create relationships that honor the dignity, wholeness, freedom, safety, and well-being of women while fostering the empowerment of racially and socioeconomically marginalized groups. We must also redress the response to the broad nexus of global cultural values at issue within incidents of sexual assault, including the multiple religious values.

Feminist and womanist Christian ethicists can utilize the complicated sociohistorical layering of Christian religious heritage and the moral problems related to that complexity as a resource. Oddly, several unique traits of Christianity resonate with the task of recognizing multiple globalized cultural values within our visions of justice. Contemporary Christians are gentiles who claim a Jewish leader as divine. We claim the sacredness of ancient Christian writings that focus on describing how Christian communities seek to extend the religious heritage of one cultural group, Jews, to non-Jews. Hopefully, Christian ethicists also come to our contemporary antiracist feminist projects humbled and instructed by a critical view of a long, troubling history of global struggles where Christian cultural supremacy has been wielded as a strategic weapon. This history includes claiming the Hebrew Scriptures of Judaism as the Old Testament of Christianity and a Jewish man as God, while committing genocide against Jews, Muslims, and indigenous peoples all over the globe in the name of the Christian man-God.

The transatlantic slave trade illustrates a major project featuring European and Euro-American Christian greed justified by racialized Christian supremacist claims. For subsequent generations of peoples of African descent in the Americas, this Christian-supported commercial project bequeathed a long-lasting legacy of tolerance for their dehumanization.

In addition, feminist Christians have tried to interpret the Gospel stories about Jesus as conveying some positive, liberating regard for women, in spite of his surrounding patriarchal culture. Feminist Christians have struggled with constructing a woman-affirming interpretation that avoids a false separation of Jesus from his own Jewish cultural identity.[7] The goal of this effort has been to steer clear of the temptation to teach an erroneous narrative about a Christian feminist Jesus whose salvific qualities can be recognized in his liberation of ancient Jewish women in the Gospels from sexist Judaism. Therefore, quite problematically, Jesus, the Jewish man-God, is used to teach anti-Judaism to contemporary Christians in the service of promoting Christian feminism.

In short, a commitment to a distinctively Christian cultural identity without supremacist claims, imperialist ambitions, or historical amnesia about Christian atrocities generates a vital, liberationist Christian faith. For feminist and womanist Christian scholars and activists, participating in this everyday commitment to creating and nurturing countercultural Christian faith equips us for crafting antiracist, globally conscious Christian social ethics that is useful to church people. Churches need this kind of Christian social ethic in order to enable their members to be effective partners in working for the common good in the culturally pluralistic communities that surround them.

Just as numerous issues surround globalization, there are also contemporary ethical issues related to sexual identity and public life that offer opportunities for producing innovative, woman-affirming Christian social ethics. Heated legal battles about the civil rights of gay men, lesbian women, and transgender persons have been raging in U.S. public life throughout the early twenty-first century and, I believe, will continue throughout this century. Antiracist, Christian feminist, and womanist social ethics must be formulated in terms that can make ongoing, supportive contributions to these movements for broader inclusion and equality in secular society as well as those taking place in the churches. It is essential feminist work to try to end social and religious evaluations of moral worth on the basis of sexual and gender identity, together with the severe consequences for safety, dignity, and freedoms that result from such judgments for devalued groups.

Public policy struggles in government arenas have ranged from state-level battles over issuing new birth certificates that reflect accurately the identities of transgender persons after their sex-reassignment surgeries to equal access for same-gender couples who wish to obtain the legal marriage licenses that heterosexual couples now have. In federal legislative arenas, battles have been waged over adding hate crimes against gay, lesbian, and transgender persons to existing federal hate-crimes statutes.[8] Statutory protections banning employment discrimination against gay, lesbian, and transgender persons remain to be mandated.[9] Church leaders have frequently played an active public role in these political battles, identifying their Christian faith as central to their advocacy positions on both sides of the question.

Public discourses framed by the mass media frequently offer distorted racial depictions of blacks teaching a white racist logic in their representations of blacks.[10] Headlines from the *Los Angeles Times* provide an example of this phenomenon. In the case of California's Proposition 8 in November 2008, the voters passed a state constitutional amendment defining marriage as the exclusive right of heterosexual citizens of the state. A *Los Angeles Times* article described local community disputes over Proposition 8 that appeared on the day of the referendum. The newspaper's headline read: "Why gays, blacks are divided on Prop. 8: For many African Americans, it's not a civil rights issue."[11] The juxtaposition of "gays" versus "blacks" makes it appear, misleadingly, as if there are no black gay men and lesbians.[12] The headline's assertion that for many African Americans, Proposition 8 is not a civil rights issue adds to the impression that "blacks" uniformly stand together against "gays." However, in the coverage by the *Los Angeles Times,* blacks were not always portrayed as a homogenous unit.

Another *Los Angeles Times* headline in October 2008, weeks before the vote, asserted: "Black clergy both attack, defend Prop 8; Rallies focus on the measure to block same-sex marriage."[13] Even in this headline noting divisions among blacks, racial identity remains the primary category for identifying black clergy. They are still represented as a black racial mass, unlike white Christian leaders who are often referred to with particular religious identifiers such as Southern Baptists, Catholic archbishops, or Church of Jesus Christ of Latter-day Saints (Mormon) leaders. With a circular logic, a view of blacks as primarily motivated by racial group interests is reinforced by primarily (and repeatedly) referring to them in terms of their racial group identity. It seems almost impossible to conceive of cross-racial socioeconomic class groupings or levels of education as equally instructive for media headlines about political trends as racial categories seem to be when explaining the beliefs or behaviors of blacks.

For feminist and womanist Christian ethics, the task of conceiving and implementing antiracist approaches to ethical discourses on sexuality is desperately needed to advance justice-oriented political change and solidarity across marginalized groups. In our critical approaches to sexual morality and equitable gender relations within both church and society, how can feminist and womanist social ethics be more explicitly antiracist? The antiracist undergirding needs to be attached not only to inclusive understandings of sexual orientation and gender identity but also to the suggested strategies for nurturing those understandings.

Feminist and womanist Christian social ethicists are peculiarly equipped to make this contribution to the current political struggles about sexuality in churches and the broader society. There is such a rich recent feminist legacy of struggle to develop language, ideas, and institutional practices that unlink devalued human moral status from the gender identity of women. Many Protestant feminists and womanists, for instance, have been quite successful in their fight against patriarchal justifications for the exclusion of women from ordination and pulpit ministry. The late-twentieth-century feminist legacy of struggle also includes valuable racial lessons about why it is so harmful to maintain a white-dominated view of the kind of gender justice that is needed. While benefiting from this feminist legacy of struggle, we can simultaneously engage more contemporary, burgeoning knowledge that nuances its lessons. New awareness of the complexities of transgender and bisexual identities expands previous feminist assumptions about the immutable, singular nature of women's gender identities and sexual orientations.

There is an exciting synergy between the opportunities to address issues related to globalization and those related to sexuality. Recognition of plurality in racial, cultural, and diasporic identities of the global South can constructively reinforce the acceptance of plurality in sexual and gender identities. I can envision a mutually reinforcing chain reaction of constructive political and theological impulses. Feminist and womanist Christian social ethics nurture antiracist justice ideas and strategies that affirm women's dignity and human rights. Multifaith, multicultural women's alliances are necessary to generate relevant, community-rooted ideas and strategies. The skills and commitment to multifaith, multiracial, multicultural organizing for social justice strengthen the commitment to safety, equal freedoms, and respect for the multiple gender expressions and sexual orientations that constitute human identity.

To work together as multifaith women to stop hate crimes would mean, for instance, mobilizing to stop violence targeting Latino/a immigrants and transgender persons of color. Femicides must be included, too. Christians would be able to utilize examples from Christian history to illustrate the destructive role of religion in spawning hatred. They would need to incorporate the differing relationships of contemporary Christians with varying racial and ethnic backgrounds to that history. It would be possible, I think, for feminist and womanist Christian ethics to contribute to such a movement for change. It would be possible, with a strong tolerance for tensions that ongoing acknowledgment of differences in a community inevitably brings, with fluidity in identity boundary markers, and with enlivening spiritual celebrations that honestly nurture our socioreligious commitments.

Virginia Ramey Mollenkott is actively retired after forty-four years of university teaching where she specialized in Milton and seventeenth-century poetry. A pioneer feminist and LGBTQ activist, Dr. Mollenkott has published hundreds of articles and numerous books, most recently the updated versions of her groundbreaking works *Omnigender* and *Sensuous Spirituality*. She leads workshops at churches and retreat centers, including Kirkridge in Bangor, Pennsylvania.

Trans-forming Feminist Christianity

VIRGINIA RAMEY MOLLENKOTT

This essay concerns the way the transgender Christian movement is trans-forming feminist Christianity, and will continue to do so. I begin by quoting part of a late-nineteenth-century sonnet by Gerard Manley Hopkins:

> Glory be to God for dappled things—
> For skies of couple-colour as a brinded cow;...
> Landscape plotted and pierced—fold, fallow, and plough;...
> All things counter, original, spare, strange;
> Whatever is fickle, freckled (who knows how?)
> With swift, slow; sweet, sour; adazzle, dim;
> He fathers-forth whose beauty is past change:
> Praise him.[1]

Father Hopkins, a Jesuit priest, here praises God for everything that is queer, as is he himself. Hopkins was a closeted gay man, and I suspect by our standards, also transgender, since he loathed and detested being called by his middle name, Manley.

I quote this sonnet because it embodies a profoundly healthful attitude for LGBTQ Christians of the present and the future: glad acknowledgment that in all our uniqueness we are embodiments of a Creator who likes diversity so much that She created all sorts of spotted, freckled, in-between, counter-expectation, original, unusual, and strange landscapes and creatures. Who knows how all this queerness came about? Who cares? The tone of rejoicing in glad gratitude is, I believe, the tone with which LGBTQ Christians will most effectively impact our culture and heal its homophobia and transphobia.

When I learned the term *transgender*, I was empowered to claim my trans identity as a masculine woman. But long before that, I knew that I was lesbian and that I was drawn toward "all things [and people who were] counter, original, spare, [and] strange." When I was teaching at Nyack Missionary College in the 1960s, the senior class bequeathed me a box of crayons that were all shades of gray to honor my emphasis that conditions are rarely black or white, but somewhere in between, somewhere complex and ambiguous. I now think of myself as a psychic androgyne or a spiritual hermaphrodite, with a woman's body but a spirit that is male as well as female, neither or both. At the senior continuing-care center where I now live, sometimes people identify me as male, even when I am wearing a name tag with "Virginia" prominently displayed. So I catch glimpses of how men speak to other men, and I enjoy the times when a woman flirts with me. I make no corrections, because when one person sees me as male and another as female, that "reflects back to me my inward gender identity more accurately than if I were perceived as just one or [just] the other."[2]

I am glad to identify as a psychic hermaphrodite, because in Greek mythology Hermaphroditus was the offspring of Hermes (the god of communication) and Aphrodite (the goddess of love).[3] Accordingly, Hermaphoditus stood for the healing of the imagination.[4] Our society desperately needs healing from its illusion that there are only two "opposite" sexes, male and female. This false binary is the enemy of the real lives of real people, making millions afraid to disobey gender roles, telling transsexuals they cannot transition to the other sex, telling transgenderists we cannot engage in our gender in-betweenness, and telling intersexuals as little as possible in order to conceal what their bodies reveal—that humankind exists on an ever-changing continuum, with varying degrees of masculinity and femininity, maleness and femaleness. These false absolutes are beginning to crack under the evidence of open transgender lives and testimonies. In the future, continued research and education by transgender activists and Christian feminists will break through binary assumptions and trans-form society into a more inclusive, humane, mutually affirming gender landscape that I have called omnigender.[5]

I fully understand that transsexuals, transgenderists, and intersexuals do not always agree about terminology and strategies. Many transsexuals prefer to conform to the binary so that they can "pass" and feel that they "belong," whereas transgenderists do not want to conform, and intersexuals do not want to be forced into conformity through surgeries and medicines. I hope that trans-formed feminist Christianity will support everyone's right to wholeness, whether that wholeness is interior (subjective) or exterior (social). For instance, people would no longer be forced to choose a binary-gendered lavatory or declare themselves male or female on government forms. Incidentally, I would strongly urge provision of unisex lavatories that include a transgender symbol in between the familiar male and female symbols, because to leave the lavatories as they are and to add separate trans-facilities would force some people to "out" themselves when they are not prepared to do so. I am all for openness in order to make life easier for those who are coming along after us, but the openness should be freely chosen, not forced by social circumstances.

A trans-formed feminist Christianity will insist that clitoridectomies be abolished, not just in Africa but also in the United States, where they have been routinely and secretly performed to "correct genital ambiguity."[6] And Christian feminists will no longer tolerate the "recycled biological determinism" that bans "nongenetic women," such as transwomen and certain intersexuals, from women's events and withdraws support from lesbians as they decide whether to transition into transmen.[7]

One more disclosure about my social location: I was raised in Protestant fundamentalism and now consider myself a left-wing or progressive evangelical. I am an active member of the Evangelical & Ecumenical Women's Caucus and a frequent contributor to its journal, *Christian Feminism Today*. Certain evangelicals of the center and right have repudiated my sex and gender identities, inclusive God-language, faith in universal redemption, and confidence that God really is "above all, and through all, and in [us] all" (Eph. 4:6). But I got these ideas from the Bible and from my studies of the great Puritan poet and theologian John Milton, and I am not willing to cut myself off from my roots. So, to the consternation of some evangelicals, I still recognize my spirit as evangelical in my passion to share truth as I understand it, my love for Jesus as the firstborn among many sisters and brothers, and my respect for ancient mystical traditions. I deplore many of the political strategies used by self-proclaimed evangelicals, but I would argue that it is they, not I, who have departed from our biblical heritage.[8]

In fact, I live in the hope that as a result of trans-formed feminist Christianity, society will eventually learn to recognize Christian "conservatives" as political ideologues, instead of the holders of a self-evident universal perspective. Right now, "conservatives" get away with arrogant statements that bear little or no relationship to reality. For instance, the Evangelical Alliance, consisting of about a million British Christians, condemns sex-change surgeries because "an ongoing transsexual lifestyle is incompatible with God's will" so that "change from a person's given sex is not possible."[9] Such statements can be made only by ignoring mountains of evidence to the contrary, including the lives of thousands of sincere Christian transsexuals and the fact that God created not only human bodies, but also human souls and spirits, as well as the hormones, doctors, gender clinics, and technologies necessary for their laying claim to their own wholeness.

It will be wonderful to watch the trans-formation as society gradually learns that it is *evidence* that makes one opinion more valid than another. As more and more scholars turn their attention to history and hermeneutics, evidence is piling up that "objectivity" is hard to come by and therefore everyone must take responsibility for their interpretations of events and texts. For instance, the chair of the History of American Civilization program at Harvard University recently wrote that "[Abraham] Lincoln's soul-mate and the love of his life was a man named Joshua Speed," endorsing the extensive evidence offered by the late C. A. Tripp, a psychologist, writer, and gay activist, that Lincoln was "predominantly homosexual."[10] Yet most Lincoln scholars have ignored Tripp's solid evidence, rushing instead to embrace the idea that Ann Rutledge was Lincoln's youthful girlfriend, on the basis of one man's very questionable reminiscences thirty years after Rutledge's death. Apparently Lincoln scholars have "relaxed [their] evidentiary standards to accommodate a hetero-romance story in order to ward off homo-romance stories."[11] I yearn for the day when quiet, determined insistence on evidence—and truthful revealing of social location—make this sort of deception impossible.

Particularly in the area of biblical interpretation, queer scholars are amassing evidence that Christians can let go of their homophobia and transphobia without in any way disrespecting their Christian faith. For instance, Theodore Jennings Jr. has recently published irrefutable evidence that Christian homophobia and transphobia are based on the late writings of Plato and certain Hellenistic writers who followed. Plato's *Laws* (his last work before his death in 347 BCE) probably predated the holiness code in Leviticus (recodified after 358 BCE).[12] Plato's *Laws* introduced the most basic themes of phobic discourse: "the appeal to nature (including the appeal to animal behavior) [which has been thoroughly refuted by recent biologists], the appeal to appropriate gender performance, the appeal to divine abhorrence, the linking to incest taboos; and so on."[13] Plato's intention was to shame homosexuals and gender-variant people into committing suicide, or at least into keeping a silence that would not disrupt the societal consensus.

Despite the passion of Plato's phobic *Laws,* however, it was not until well into the sixth century CE, half a millennium after the epistles of St. Paul, that Christianity adopted Plato's phobias into the Justinian Code, a compilation of imperial laws codified by Eastern Roman Emperor Justinian I (ruled CE 527–65). And even then, Christian discourse was more moderate than Plato's. Not until the twelfth and thirteenth centuries did Christians begin to view homophobia and transphobia as "essential to [Christianity's] self-understanding." As Professor Jennings concludes, historical evidence proves that

> there's no essential connection between Christianity and homophobia [including transphobia]. The grafting of homophobia [and transphobia] onto Christianity is indeed "against nature" and as such it may be undone without damage to the rootstock of faith.... Moreover, this unnatural joining of Christianity must be undone if Christianity is not to continue to be guilty of the true sin of Sodom: the violation of the vulnerable. Too many lives have already been lost or incurably damaged by this unholy alliance. There was a time before homophobia [and transphobia] insinuated [themselves] into Christianity. It is long past due that we entered a new era.[14]

I believe that a trans-formed Christian feminism will lead the way back to that more humane, more egalitarian Christianity.

Queer biblical scholarship has shown that both the Hebrew and the Christian Scriptures are far more LGBTQ-friendly than anyone had heretofore imagined.[15] It is because of transgender Christian scholarship that we have begun to notice details like the fact that the Gospels, written after Paul, show Jesus subverting gender expectations by doing women's work such as cooking and washing the disciples' feet, and that the Christian epistles teach "feminine" virtues such as meekness and gentleness to men and call men "the bride of Christ," while teaching women "masculine" virtues such as courage and self-control and calling women "the sons of God." At this time, Christian "conservatives" are ignoring such scholarship, but evidence cannot be ignored forever. Eventually, Christianity will be forced to capitulate to the mountains of evidence that progressives will continue to uncover.

Perhaps the major change in Christian concepts will be a deepening of the understanding of incarnation and embodiment. Feminists have already done a great deal to recast society's gender framework by disproving the notions that biology determines destiny, that what is personal is not also political, and that males should be valued for "efficacious accomplishment" while females should be valued for attractive appearance.[16] But by revealing the dazzling diversity of creation's sex/gender continuum, the transgender movement is also changing society's concept of what nature is, who or what God is, and what authentic human experience looks like.

During the Renaissance, Shakespeare, Ben Jonson, and other playwrights mocked "in-betweens" (homosexuals, feminine men, eunuchs, and hermaphrodites/intersexuals) as very amusing freaks of nature. By the 1840s, Christian feminist Julia Ward Howe—yes, the very woman who composed "The Battle Hymn of the Republic"—wrote a novel she never published, titled *The Hermaphrodite*. In it, the intersexual protagonist is a "heavenly superhuman mystery" who feels crucified upon the cross of being both male and female, a state in which the society requires denial of the love of both men and women. This denial "tears [the intersexual's] bowels … utterly asunder."[17] By the 1940s and 1950s, same-sex lovemaking was criminal and a person could be jailed for not wearing at least three articles of gender-appropriate clothing.[18] Bisexual Carson McCullers was writing novels that were preoccupied with "human freaks and oddities," with lonely, yearning characters who break down "the rigid barriers between normalcy and abnormalcy, difference and sameness, likeness and other."[19] Is it too much to hope that by the 2040s and 2050s, artists and society will catch up with Gerard Manley Hopkins by expressing gratitude to God and nature for all things (and people) who are "counter, original, spare, [and] strange," and who are glad to claim themselves just as they were created?

No one can predict the timeline, of course, but if it is true that "freaks [or anomalies] function as outer physical manifestations of [humankind's] inner psychological fears and desires,"[20] then it follows that the more transgender people lay claim to our wholeness and open up about our lives, the more we will be helping to heal not only ourselves but also many people who have never before identified themselves with the queer community. Christians, especially, will be encouraged to learn the difference between egocentricity and healthy self-love and self-care. For instance, one transman described the connection between his fundamentalist training and his "initial repression of his trans-self." I could echo his words out of my own early experience of the evangelical right-wing: "Fundamentalist religion does not help you to develop your own sense of who you are. It's all about Jesus and forgetting yourself—you're regularly taught certain verses in the Bible along the lines of 'Don't trust yourself; you're too sick and sinful to trust your own thoughts.'"[21] By contrast, here is the testimony of a lesbian brought up Southern Baptist, now a progressive clergywoman in the Universal Fellowship of the Metropolitan Community Churches. She describes the transformations recently wrought in her consciousness by getting to know a variety of transgender people: "My image of God was changed and in the process my expectations of humanity were changed. I began to get a glimpse of what it means to allow the Christic presence to inhabit my spirit. I began to get a glimpse of the commonwealth of God coming alive in the midst of my human family. When I *pay attention to what God has created,* my image of God transcends the limits of the dominant culture and allows me to experience the incarnation of particular peculiarities that enrich my spiritual life."[22]

Above all, I hope that feminist Christianity will continue to be trans-formed in the direction of ever-fewer rigid categorizations and ever-expanding graciousness concerning fluidity. Lisa Diamond, who teaches psychology at the University of Utah, has conducted in-depth interviews with one hundred women over a period of ten years and has discovered an amazing sexual fluidity. Although the women's basic sexual orientation remains the same, "a predominantly heterosexual woman might, at some point in time, become attached to a woman just as a predominantly lesbian woman might at some point become attracted to a man."[23] And although "women appear to be more fluid than men," Professor Diamond has found that any individual human being is "capable of experiencing desires that run counter to his or her sexual orientation."[24] But for Diamond personally, the biggest surprise was that although she had never intended to deal with issues of gender identity, during the decade of her study four participants began to identify as transgender. These people raised into clear perspective the dilemma that both gender and sexual fluidity raises for all people, whether they are male, female, or otherwise, "namely, how do you live a noncategorical life in a rigidly categorical world?"[25]

I have noticed that as any group becomes more "conservative," its members become increasingly addicted to certainty and rigid categories. In the fundamentalism and evangelicalism of my youth, all doctrines and activities were labeled either as God's will (good) or not-God's-will (evil), and among the latter were such activities as dancing, spending time with non-Christians, attending the theater, and thinking subversive thoughts. No one, but no one, would have dared to question the assumption that whatever seems "fixed"—such as the male-female binary—is therefore biological and God's will and deserving of acceptance and protection, whereas whatever is variable is fully chosen, often rebellious against God, and "fair game for stigma and dissociation."[26] Never mind that such assumptions have been scientifically proven to be false. They continue to hold sway in popular opinion and among many Christians of the political center as well as the right.

But I am convinced that as intersexual issues are aired more and more openly, they will provide the wedge that will effectively "disrupt heteronormative systems of sex, gender, and sexuality." Intersexual conditions are hard to dismiss as a "choice" because individuals are *born* with them. These conditions refer to "multiple components including karyotype (organization of sex chromosomes), gonadal differentiation (e.g., ovarian or testicular), genital morphology, configurations of internal reproductive organs, and pubertal sex characteristics such as breasts and facial hair."[27] It is difficult to think rationally about all these components while insisting that it is God's will for all characteristics to be concordant in each individual. What of the one in every one hundred births that exhibits some anomaly in sex differentiation?[28] Who could be cruelly ignorant enough to declare that these infants were born in defiance of the will of God?

In the United States, a federal law and many individual state laws stipulate that marriage must be granted only to one man and one woman. But as these laws are challenged in the courts, it will become necessary to define *man* and *woman* in a way that applies to everyone unambiguously. What will be the deciding factor: chromosomes? genital shape? internal organs? pubertal characteristics? After decades of trying to find one legal, universally applicable definition of what a man is and what a woman is, the International Olympic Committee has given up on sex/gender analysis.[29] People may continue to defend the many privileges that go with having an unambiguous, obvious, sex/gender identity, but sooner or later intersexual and transgender evidence will prevail over defensive ignorance.

As trans-formative evidence continues to pile up, the complexities of human sex and gender will empower Christians to expand our understandings of God. As Reverend B. K. Hipsher puts it, "We need a trans-God … one that transgresses all our ideas about who and what God is and can be, one that transports us to new possibilities of how God can incarnate in the multiplicity of human embodiments, one that transfigures our mental images from limitations, one that transforms our ideas about our fellow humans and ourselves, one that transcends all we know or think we know about God and about humanity [as made in the image of God]."[30]

Queer theology, including the transgender movement within feminism, has already begun a continual questioning of norms and will continue to do so. We have the potential for acknowledging all human constructs as merely provisional, so that even our hard-won acceptance as women, men, or otherwise must be regarded as fluid, not rigid, and as important but not ultimate. Our essential humanity, our external selfhood, the divine light within us, reaches far deeper than any human category or label. What we need is a society that permits us to name and claim our diverse experiences, inner and outer, so that by our mutual listening we can create a language that clarifies all experiences that are "counter, original, spare, [and] strange." In turn, our trans-formed language will empower us to settle more comfortably into our authenticity as Christians and lovers of human equality.

Marie M. Fortune is founder and senior analyst at the FaithTrust Institute, where she addresses sexual and domestic violence in faith communities. The Rev. Dr. Fortune is ordained in the United Church of Christ. She is a pastor, an educator, an author, and a practicing theologian and ethicist. Her books include *Keeping the Faith: Guidance for Christian Women Facing Abuse; Is Nothing Sacred? When Sex Invades the Pastoral Relationship;* and *Sexual Violence: The Sin Revisited.*

Seeking Justice and Healing

Violence against Women as an Agenda for Feminist Christianity

MARIE M. FORTUNE

In the 1970s, the silence was deafening but women's voices were beginning to pierce it, particularly the voices of women survivors of violence and abuse. Often at great risk, women who had been raped or battered, or who had been sexually abused as children, began to tell their stories. Even at the risk of "having it bruised and misunderstood,"[1] one woman would tell another woman and then another. Some even tried to tell the powers and principals who were generally not interested in hearing about it. The police, the courts, the doctors, the therapists all were disbelieving the numbers of women beginning to come forward and tell their truths. But the eyes and ears of the church were closed to these women's voices. It was beyond the realm of most male theologians' and pastors' experiences and, so, not important. But even early Christian feminists who began to deconstruct the oppression of sexism did not speak about the violence behind it. In the beginning, rarely did they explicitly discuss the personal violence so many women had experienced.

I began to hear those voices as a seminarian and a young pastor. As a rape crisis volunteer, I spoke with victims and survivors who wanted to talk with their faith leader but were afraid, for good reason, to try. As a pastor, I would bring up the subject of violence against women with my congregants to a response of silent, knowing looks. The gap between newly organized advocacy services for victims and the victims' faith communities was huge. The fact that a victim or survivor would probably have to choose between these two resources was unacceptable. The fact that many battered women and children heard the justification of their abuse preached from the pulpit was unacceptable. The fact that clergy husbands were sometimes the abusers was unacceptable. The fact that Scripture was casually used to deny women and children the right to say "no" to abuse was unacceptable. The fact that women and children were often cut off from the spiritual resources of the Gospels, the Psalms, and the Prophets was unacceptable.

My ministry began in 1977 with the founding of FaithTrust Institute, not only to respond to victims and survivors within our churches but also to change the structures, teachings, and practices of our churches to intervene when necessary and hopefully to prevent the victimization of more women and children.[2] In other words, at FaithTrust Institute, we are working to ensure that the church is part of the solution, not part of the problem.

As we consider the history of feminist Christianity and where we as feminist or womanist Christians are going today, we must acknowledge the remarkable changes we have witnessed in the past forty years. Our efforts to deconstruct the dominant paradigm of patriarchy have succeeded, if only partially. But the contribution of feminist and womanist Christian leaders is not limited to deconstruction. Equally important is the work of reconstruction, that is, salvaging and lifting up the resources from our faith tradition that support, inspire, challenge, and nurture us in seeking healing and justice for individuals, families, and communities.

Biblical scholarship, ethics, theology, liturgy, homiletics, and church history are no longer male domains. Women's voices are now assumed, if not always appreciated. One of our goals, of creating space for women's voices and experiences, not only for ourselves but also as a critical contribution to the whole enterprise, has begun and been sustained with vigor. But it is not to be taken for granted. The default position remains patriarchal; vigilance is required to sustain the space we have created beyond the next generation. In other words, women's voices are present but are still at the margins.

Beyond the academy, we have created the largest space for women's voices in local churches. The presence of women leaders in ministry is now a fact of life within most of Protestantism. Roman Catholic women's voices are strong but not always acknowledged or appreciated, and Catholic women continue to be denied the sanctioned role of clerical leadership. The presence of women in leadership in no way guarantees a feminist/womanist voice, but our very visible presence in leadership roles has changed the experience of the faith community for our children and grandchildren. The question remains for the academy and the local church whether the presence of women's voices has resulted in attention to women's all-too-common experiences of personal violence. These results are decidedly mixed.

The visibility of scholarship addressing violence against women both within the American Academy of Religion and the Society of Biblical Literature remains sparse.[3] The dominant paradigm remains intact. But in teaching theology, ethics, and practical ministry within the seminary there is an effort by some to prepare future ministers with essential training. There are also some signs within some denominations and local churches of addressing domestic terror and battering as well as sexual assault and abuse, including abuse by clergy. But even here there remains a hesitation to acknowledge that these are common experiences among our members and not just unfortunate experiences of those outside the fold.

Violence is a common, shared experience of women of every ethnicity, class, age, sexual orientation, ability, and faith tradition.

Women share either the fear or the memory of personal violence, or both. This is a fact of life that all girls learn. The commonplace reporting of individual incidents of personal violence or of hate crimes against women in public reinforces our awareness that the threat of violence is the air we breathe. It is, however, also particular to culture and ethnicity, which provide context for behaviors of violence against and control of women. Although the individual's victimization may be particular, women's experiences of fear, and their memories of violence, are universal.

Yet, each of our voices is partial and incomplete. This fact compels us to understand the work on violence against women within Christianity to be in a much larger context of collaboration with other faith traditions. Our enterprise parallels that of women and men of many faiths who are also giving voice to victimization and challenging assumptions and practices that reinforce acts of violence against women. We are sisters and brothers in this work and, as such, we Christians have much to learn.

Sadly, an act of physical, emotional, or sexual violence against a woman creates a relationship between her and the perpetrator. It is not a relationship of choice, which is fundamental to the violation. It is intimate because it touches the core of her being. Even if it takes place within an established intimate partnership, or maybe especially if it takes place within an intimate partnership, the violence creates a dimension of relationship not chosen; it creates a "victim." An act of domestic terrorism or battering or of sexual abuse or violence is ethically a violation of oneself, of an existing relationship, and of community. Not only is another harmed, but also trust is betrayed and brokenness of self, relationship, and community result. This is the sin of violence against women.

One goal of feminist/womanist Christianity is to deny the misuse of Christian texts and teachings to justify violence against women, to respond pastorally to victims, to call perpetrators to account, and to change institutions that reinforce the norm of violence against women. To put it more succinctly, the goal is to remove the roadblocks created by the misuse of the faith tradition and instead to draw on the resources within the faith tradition that make for the abundant life promised by Jesus in John's Gospel.

The challenges to the dominant paradigm have been strong, especially in the work of Traci C. West (*Wounds of the Spirit: Black Women, Violence, and Resistance Ethics*), James Poling (*The Abuse of Power: A Theological Problem*), Nancy Nason-Clark (*The Battered Wife: How Christians Confront Family Violence*), Toinette Eugene (*Balm for Gilead: Pastoral Care for African American Families Experiencing Abuse*), Pamela Cooper-White (*The Cry of Tamar: Violence against Women and the Church's Response*), Carol Adams (*Woman-Battering*), Catherine Kroeger (*Women, Abuse, and the Bible: How Scripture Can Be Used to Hurt or Heal*), Al Miles (*Domestic Violence: What Every Pastor Needs to Know*), myself (*Sexual Violence: The Unmentionable Sin*; *Keeping the Faith: Questions and Answers for the Abused Woman*; *Is Nothing Sacred?*; *Sexual Violence: The Sin Revisited*), and others. These resources have provided a scriptural, theological, ethical, and pastoral foundation for women and men in the local church to develop programs not only to raise awareness but also to bring a change of practices, especially in pastoral ministry.

But, alas, there are still many church leaders who refuse to examine their assumptions and the impact of their teaching as they continue to preach and teach the headship of men in families, the unquestioned authority of clergy, the "value" of suffering and atonement theology, and the necessity of forgiveness as an immediate response to victimization. It is in these areas that feminist/womanist scholarship and practice of ministry have begun the deconstruction of the dominant paradigm and the reconstruction of resources within the Christian tradition to promote healing and justice.

Part of the Problem: Atonement Theology

Rebecca Parker and Rita Brock confront head-on one theological area that is foundational to the dominant Christian paradigm: atonement theology. With the publication of *Proverbs of Ashes*, Parker and Brock challenged one of the most basic tenets of mainstream and evangelical Christian theology.[4] They name clearly the roadblock created by atonement theology and advocate for salvaging life-giving resources from Christian theology:

> Religion can be an accomplice to violence. In Christian theology, doctrines of the atonement sanction violence. They interpret the execution of Jesus as divinely ordained and necessary for human salvation. These doctrines must be challenged; for we believe Christianity also offers theologies that resist violence and save life.[5]

Frankly, I have never understood atonement theology. I know that Jesus, a Jew, was executed by the Roman State in a definitive act of anti-Semitism. I believe that God was deeply grieved by the death of Jesus. And I believe that Jesus, in his prime as teacher and leader, knew and accepted the inevitable consequences of his teaching and his politics, both of which confronted the religious establishment and the state. I believe that Jesus lives again in the hearts and minds of his followers. I never attributed Jesus's death to God or saw in it a cosmic salvific event. It just never made sense to me.

It also never made sense to me to conclude that, because Jesus suffered death upon the cross, we, as his followers, were condemned to similar fates. Rather, Jesus shared in the extremity of human suffering even in premature death. Suffering happens. He knew the sufferings that we know and so, as a statement of faith, we believe that he is present with us in those times of suffering. Sin is an alienation from God and the subsequent moral choice to do harm to another human. Because of the limits of our imaginations and our capacities, brokenness unhealed begets brokenness.

This is what I understand and believe about Jesus, the crucifixion, and the reality of sin in the world. This is what I have seen repeatedly in my ministry with victims, survivors, and perpetrators of sexual and domestic violence. But I do understand that Christian traditions about the atonement have nonetheless been central to the dominant worldview of which we are a part. They represent Jesus's followers' struggles to make meaning of his death. Unfortunately, some of the meaning they have made has translated into a theology that ends up being misused to justify the abuse of vulnerable people and avoid confronting accountability for those who abuse others. This is especially salient for women and other marginalized people who are looking for a way to make sense out of senseless suffering and to change the circumstances that allow for that suffering. I have seen much suffering that has resulted from atonement theology.

Part of the Problem: Forgiveness

Reframing our understanding of forgiveness is a fundamental task of feminist and womanist theology, biblical studies, ethics, and pastoral care. The single most common pastoral concern that I hear expressed by victims and survivors of sexual or domestic violence is their anxiety about forgiveness, which often focuses on a sense of obligation regardless of circumstances.

In contemporary Christian teaching and practice, the burden to forgive seems always to be placed solely on the shoulders of those who have suffered physically and emotionally. This is the most common response that victims or survivors hear from family, friends, and the church. The first thing anyone who is trying to be helpful wants to discuss is forgiveness, meaning that the one victimized should simply forgive and then be rewarded magically with healing.

In Judaism, the burden rests with the one who causes harm. Medieval Jewish philosopher Maimonides explained that the Day of Atonement, Yom Kippur, provides corporate atonement for sins against God. But sins against one's neighbor (or intimate partner) are not pardoned unless the offender compensates the victim and apologizes. This means confession, taking responsibility, repentance, and restitution to the one harmed.[6] Repentance is real when there is an opportunity to repeat the offense and the offender refrains from it because of his or her repentance, and not because of fear.[7]

In fact, the teachings of Jesus in the Gospels are congruent with the teachings of Judaism on this issue. In Luke 17:3–4, Jesus says, "If another disciple sins, you must rebuke the offender, and *if* there is repentance, you must forgive." And then the seven times come in: if that one "sins seven times *and* repents seven times, you must forgive." Fundamentally, both Judaism and Christianity link the expectation of forgiveness on the part of the one harmed to genuine confession and repentance on the part of the offender. This is the context of justice that we shall examine as necessary for real forgiveness and healing to occur.

The problem for Christians is that somehow the notion and practice of forgiveness have been romanticized and placed in a vacuum due in large part to the canonization of "forgive and forget" theology. Although "forgive and forget" is not biblical, it has struck a resonant chord in the public psyche.[8] I believe that is precisely because it is simplistic and allows us to ignore the power dynamics of the situation in which harm has been done by one to another.

If the expectation of agency in response to harm done by one to another is passed to the one harmed and away from the one causing harm, then three things happen:

- No one (including bystanders) ever has to make the offender accountable. This is particularly advantageous for the non-repentant offender.
- Victims, whose priority is their own healing, can decide that they have the power to bring about this healing by their agency in the "act" of forgiving. This is a cruel hoax for victims.
- The bystanders (often ministers and many members of our churches) can stand by and do nothing, self-righteously reassured that we have no lines in this play.

As a result, the victim is shamed or cajoled into saying the magic words, "I forgive him," convinced by us that now she will feel better. Now God will love her, and now she can remain in good standing within her church. And the bystanders don't have to do anything.

Forgiveness is God's gift for victims and survivors. Any benefit that it brings to offenders is a bonus. Likewise, any benefit it brings to the bystander is a bonus. Forgiveness brings the possibility of healing to those harmed. But what, then, is it?

- It is not condoning or pardoning, making everything okay as if harm had not been done by the perpetrator (temptation to "heal the wound lightly, saying 'peace, peace' where there is no peace," Jer. 6:14).
- It is not the sole responsibility of the victim/survivor (for example, "Don't you think it's time you forgave him?").
- It cannot happen in a vacuum.
- It is difficult but not impossible when the accountability of the offender is absent.
- It is finally about letting it go and getting on with life.

Justice is a necessary precursor to forgiveness. As a pastor, I began to learn what justice looked like when I slowed down long enough to listen to survivors. I learned to ask them the question, "What do you need in order to find some healing and resolution from the abuse that you suffered?" If, as a helper and an advocate, we bother to ask this question, they will usually have a fairly straightforward answer. They say that they need:

- "my abuser to acknowledge what he did to me."
- "a chance to tell the bishop what the priest did to me."
- "an apology from my uncle."
- "to be sure that he won't do this to anyone else."
- "compensation for my expenses as a result of all this."

If we think categorically about these concrete requests, we begin to see what justice looks like:

- Truth-telling: the chance for the victim/survivor to tell her story.
- Acknowledgment: a response from someone who matters to the victim/survivor, who stands beside her as an advocate (for example, "What he did to you was wrong").
- Compassion: to suffer with the victim/survivor—not to pass by.
- Protection of the vulnerable: to do everything we can to ensure that no one else is harmed by this perpetrator.
- Accountability for the offender: to call the offender to account either in the church and/or legally.
- Restitution to the survivor: material compensation to the survivor for the cost of the harm done.
- Vindication for the survivor ("to be set free"; the outcome of justice making is to be set free and restored to one's community).

So, if we understand that some experience of justice (imperfect though it may be) is a prerequisite for forgiveness, then we see that forgiveness does *not* condone or pardon harmful behavior or assume any degree of future relationship with the person who caused the harm. Forgiveness is:

- letting go so that the immediacy of the painful memories can be put into perspective.
- possible in a context of justice making and the healing presence of the Holy Spirit.
- God's gift to those who have been harmed, for the purpose of healing.

Women who have been victimized do not need platitudes, sentimentality, and offers of cheap grace. They do not need to be urged "to forgive"; in fact, in many cases they need to be urged not to forgive so quickly. They need guidance and support to help them face head-on the painful realities and memories of violence and abuse in their lives. They need to hear about a God who stands with the exploited and abused; who calls the powerful to account; who offers justice and forgiveness as the tools of healing; who expects bystanders to support victims and call abusers to account.

Conclusion: Part of the Solution

Addressing violence in women's lives is an absolute necessity in the work of feminist and womanist theology. The voices of feminist and womanist Christians have pressed the academy and the church to listen, learn, and respond to the voices of those who have been victimized by domestic terror and battering and by sexual assault and abuse. Many of these voices have been those of survivors who have spoken out in the space created by feminist and womanist theologies. They are silent no more and are calling the churches to be the church. Ironically, if we do engage our experiences of personal violence from a theological perspective, the issues of language, images, leadership roles, structures, and more begin to fall into place as we are guided by a mandate to do no harm.

We have named the ways in which the teachings and practices of the Christian faith have and continue to be part of the problem of violence against women and children and we have begun to deconstruct these teachings and practices. But we are also lifting up and affirming the ways that the Christian faith, if it is true to the gospel that Jesus taught, is part of the solution and a bountiful resource not only for healing and restoration of body and soul, but also for justice and prevention.

As we consider the state of feminist/womanist theology in the early twenty-first century in the United States, we are reminded that a sailboat cannot sail directly toward its destination. Rather, it must tack its way, back and forth, but always moving forward. Those of us who are fortunate enough to sail these boats need only keep watch and keep faith and prepare to pass the tillers along to the next generation.

Rachel A. R. Bundang is on the religious studies faculty at the Marymount School in New York. Dr. Bundang earned her doctorate in constructive theologies, praxis, and ethics from Union Theological Seminary. She was a Bannan Fellow at Santa Clara University. Rooted in feminist ethics and Catholic theology, Rachel's work takes her from the academy to the parish and beyond.

Feminist Theo-ethics in Remix Culture

RACHEL A. R. BUNDANG

I consider myself very lucky to be a working ethicist. I say this as a way of beginning because the thing that brought me into feminist theological ethics and keeps me engaged in it as a scholar, teacher, and minister is that this body of knowledge enables me to meet people where they are. Whether you are religious or not, whether you are particularly educated or not, whether you are especially articulate or not about your beliefs matters little initially in a discussion of ethics. Everyone can have an opinion about what is good or bad, right or wrong, just or unjust, loving or indifferent for virtually any issue at hand. Scratching past the surface, though, such conversations inevitably get more interesting because we begin to share what matters most to us and why, and how these deeply held beliefs have been formed and continue to shape our decisions large and small in our lives each day.

Our moral lives develop through imagination, action, reflection, and experience and are yet more than the sum of these parts. What I have found useful in discerning my way through questions of ethical import, whether by myself or with groups, is to draw upon the moral and methodological resources of my own Catholic tradition. The bookends that frame my thinking are twofold: virtue as articulated in both classic and contemporary senses by ethicist James Keenan on the one hand, and commitments as articulated in a feminist key by ethicist Margaret Farley on the other. The work of Keenan and Farley has been formative and influential for me intellectually and spiritually. In considering virtue, we ask ourselves: What kind of people or community are we? Who do we want to become? Likewise, in considering commitment, we ask ourselves: What must we do—or what are we willing to do—in order to become the best we are called to be?

With virtue and commitment as the backdrop, the picture must be fleshed out a little with more detail, color, and shading. As an Asian/Pacific American theo-ethicist informed by multiple strands of feminism and the richness of the Catholic tradition, I believe there are three trends—three broad areas of concern that I consider important for the future of Christian ethics:

1. further complicating, multiplying, and remixing difference as seen, lived, and understood through feminist lenses;
2. using the metaphor of empire as a way to critique, resist, and transform institutions and practices of structural violence; and
3. rethinking what it means to be human.

These may each be considered separately, but they ultimately do all connect and inform each other, both in our private musings and in our relationships as lived out day to day.

In bringing all these considerations into conversation with contemporary cultures, communities, and concerns, the practice of "remixing," in particular, is a helpful one. Borrowed from hip-hop culture and analyzed carefully in scholarship on music, youth cultures, and cultural criticism, the term *remix* refers to the art and work of the DJ, who samples broadly from the variety of music available, weaves it into the sonic fabric of the occasion, and in the process creates a whole new musical experience. In borrowing from the culture, engaging with both tradition and experience, and imagining new worlds into being, the DJ demonstrates a kind of agency or process that may be a model for our moral lives. Just as the DJ is an agent, we too are all agents and can be remixers, trying to make the best sense of what we think, feel, and experience from the moment—trying to create and live in that groove. This is one way of understanding and bringing into being a theo-ethic from the ground up.

Difference Rendered More Complex

In the academy and on the ground, we have witnessed the passing of the torch from one generation of feminists to another: first, second, and third wave, and onward. Along the way, though, the encouragement and support have commingled with tension and questioning: Is the younger generation giving the respect and honor due to the previous one? When may any generation freely and legitimately question the generations that preceded them and articulate their own vision of how the world is and should be? How closely must they hew to the traditions they have inherited? Do older feminists respond with intellectual and spiritual generosity when younger ones take those building blocks to challenge or use them to better reflect their commitments and sensibilities? This is the case within feminism at large, and within the various strands articulated by women of color in the United States: womanist/black feminist, *mujerista*/Latina feminist, and Asian/Pacific American feminist.

Monica Coleman, a young African American woman scholar, not long ago posed the question, "Must I be womanist?" as a way of engaging in intergenerational dialogue and thinking critically about the legacy of African American women's scholarship in theology and religious studies, whether womanist or not.[1] Similar conversations have been happening in recent years among other groups of women of color in the academy: What is ours? What needs to change to better reflect who and where we are as a people? In Asian/Pacific American theologies, we have been trying on multiple lenses—marginality, hybridity, and interstitiality, to name a few—in an effort to make theoretical sense of our religious experience, especially as it intersects with race and gender. Along with this generational transition is the cross-pollination across other lines of difference. Whether these differences concern race and ethnicity, sexual orientation, or other categories, in interrogating them we continue the critical task begun by the second wave of feminists and question the ideas of inclusion and exclusion.

Ongoing changes in culture and demographics will continue to push feminism to become more complex and textured so that it will be mindful of differences—in all their varieties—while becoming better able to navigate them. Our sensibilities will be, per force and by habit, more finely tuned so that we can determine when differences matter enough to be taken into account in our moral lives.

At times, then, one facet of identity might well be singled out for treatment, rather than considered in fluid, ever-shifting combinations with other ones: How much do certain facets matter, and when, and how, and why? And as the scope shifts from one difference to many and back again, the challenge is to take into account and keep in focus the human dignity—indeed, the personhood—at the heart of the individuals and communities at stake.

Empire and Structural Violence

From the fields of biblical scholarship, especially Christian Testament and political philosophy, come the language and lenses that are critical of empire. For those who are already familiar with liberation theologies and their emphasis on proclaiming that God sides with the vulnerable, however defined, this will not sound entirely new. For these oppressed peoples, this may offer both encouragement and comfort. But for those who are or have been in power, what the language critical of empire provides is rather like an examination of conscience. Does the power we have come justly? Is it wielded with justice and love for other and self in mind, or, at the very least, with good intentions and in good conscience? Sitting squarely as targets of critical reflection (and, ultimately, critical transformation) are the kinds of pathological, destructive, life-denying power relations that empire itself models, as well as the imbalances and instabilities it creates and perpetuates.

At the risk of oversimplification, the purpose of empire is sovereignty. Likewise, the tendency of empire is to control all it sees—in fact, to seek, hoard, and concentrate all power into itself and to make itself the center of attention. The empire is that entity whose pervasive, encroaching, larger-than-life presence cannot be ignored, not even for lack of trying. Put another way, it is "the man" whom Shug Avery says Celie must get off her eyeball in Alice Walker's *The Color Purple.*[2] It is the master's house—the one that cannot be dismantled and instead remains ever in view despite our best efforts to clear it away to make room for new growth—that writer and activist Audre Lorde discusses in her classic essay.[3] It is the nation or institution that commands that everything in its path be subject to its will and agenda, its sense of memory and time.[4] Like the kudzu vine, it has some worth and limited uses, but it is better known for being ecologically invasive. Difficult to control, it grows over and strangles everything in its path, but remains indifferent to the fact that its very being, action, and "will" are in fact life-denying to others.

Anti-imperial rhetoric in early Christianity and the Christian Scriptures compels us to reflect anew on Jesus and Gospel claims as being countercultural. The kingdom of God and its "underdog" values are presented in sharp contrast to the Roman Empire and all it represents. In our present historical moment, such rereadings of the Bible tap into potent, righteous anger that can spur change in ways that "softer" readings of liberation theology—which may spiritualize or romanticize the suffering of the oppressed if not done carefully—can miss. How, for example, do Jesus's messages and examples of love and mercy challenge the status quo that is blind to its own injustices?

Of course, some adaptation of Christianity's thought and institutional structure was inevitable once the movement had the backing, legitimacy, and endorsement of the empire it had initially critiqued.

Reflecting on the social, religious, and political development of early Christianity in the shadow of the Roman Empire offers valuable lessons for social ethics and ministry. This language critical of empire and its hegemonic discourses is a newer, sharper tool that enables us to understand better how structural violence—the web of systems, institutions, habits, practices, and mindsets that perpetuate injustice and exacerbate misery—develops and operates. With this finer understanding, we can unravel more cleanly and expose more completely the tangles in its web. However, this approach is slower, more delicate work. I think, for example, of the work and writings of Paul Farmer, the renowned physician, medical anthropologist, and public health activist who has devoted his life to providing decent health care to poor communities worldwide and to empowering the poor to take care of themselves.[5] He has acknowledged the role that liberation theology has played in his thinking and praxis about theodicy and structural violence. But imagine what heft and clarity the emphasis on critiquing privilege and dismantling the empire that sustains and enables it would lend to causes and practices like his.

Bringing anti-imperial language to bear on how we think about and address structural violence would, first of all, reveal with great force and power the myriad ways, great and small, that we have failed each other and continue to do so, despite our good intentions—the ways in which we are complicit with the very things that ensure unequal power relations that in turn deny life again and again. It would highlight, too, the many interconnections and relations between us—person to person, community to community—that all need to be changed and made right if the kingdom of God is something we take seriously enough to want to achieve.

We would be reminded in raw, sometimes painfully real ways that, as much as we might value freedom and self-reliance, we are also dependent upon and responsible for one another. Lastly, anti-imperial language feeds the moral imagination and gives us the vocabulary and vision to live in line with the (difficult, but ultimately more fruitful) countercultural demands of the gospel and make way for this alternate kingdom where life is not only possible, but flourishes. It can call us out of our passivity and free us to recognize more readily the dignity and personhood in one another, and in turn to live accordingly.

Personhood

When I say that we are rethinking what it means to be a human person, I am considering this not only in terms of theological anthropology, which is concerned with who we are before God or the divine. Beyond theological considerations, personhood is, at heart, a much more philosophical and relational problem, with multiple aspects: Who are we for ourselves and for each other? Who carries moral weight? Who gets to be a moral agent, and is that always to be expressed as having the autonomy, will, and presence of mind to make our own choices? Who counts as authentically human, and who gets to approve or deny any such claim? The answers to these questions have direct bearing on all manner of things regarding body and nature—such as bioethics, reproductive issues, gender, and sexuality—and, beyond that, implications for fields such as politics, public policy, church polity, human rights, psychology, and law.

This notion of personhood is one that is difficult to treat concisely and succinctly precisely because it is shaped by so many disciplines and cultures while having so many dimensions and possible applications in return. For example, there are shelves upon shelves of scholarship addressing identity in terms of cultural theories of all kinds. As it is, personhood goes beyond historicity, biography, and lived experience to be deconstructed, theorized, configured, and imagined in alternative ways. Going beyond theory to the ever-proliferating cases where technologies are involved, ethics, public policy, and law are especially hard-pressed to keep up with developments before we know reasonably well the ramifications of our new discoveries, practices, skills, and choices. In many instances, we must begin by asking ourselves, Should we do this just because we can? If not, why not? Who will be affected, and how?

In reconsidering personhood, perhaps the fundamental point is that by being embodied and incarnated, we get to be real and disruptive, contingent and imperfect; we are not just a list of attributes and categories, and we are not mere representations. We are, in fact, enfleshed absolutely in history (that is, in a specific context) in order to assert a reality that consciously transcends the abstractions of negotiated identities and identity politics, useful as they may be sometimes. In other words, we are more than the sum of our identities. There is a fine line between a functionally fluid self and one that is fragmented beyond repair. Insistence upon embodiment in the face of erasure is an assertion of our human dignity—a claim for integrity and wholeness. Acknowledging the importance of the body puts relationality at the heart of a workable theo-ethic and makes it possible to hold the universal and the particular in meaningful, fruitful tension. Our being, our very existence, contradicts the tendency toward erasure and negation.

What does feminist Christianity look like, given new ethical insights? It looks like a field ready for an exercise of moral imagination, ready to focus on flesh and embodiment rather than on absence and erasure. Indeed, it is ready to be remixed, and in fact, this is arguably part of its method and process. Feminist Christianity is about bringing history, tradition, and culture into conversation with the aim of addressing the needs of the common good according to the community's commitments, insights, and values. On the level of the individual, it is also about the person's search for virtue and integrity in the midst of competing claims and commitments.

Keeping in mind that persons are constitutive of communities, recognizing personhood makes a sense of the common good possible. The recognition of the common good, in turn, is the ground for discerning what is liberative. If liberation according to Christian tradition is to be complete, it cannot be just an individual release but rather must take into account the larger body; the common good is ultimately nonnegotiable.

Critical theory's deconstructive tendencies—and in this I would include anti-imperial critique—enable us to see behind the structures and formations of our daily living. Critical theory itself has great subversive power in its capacity to challenge norms and habits of thought and action, which makes it a valuable tool for enabling us to imagine otherwise. As long as personhood—critically approached and understood so that it takes bodies and lived experience seriously—remains at the center of our theo-ethical reflection and exploration, and is set in the context of the community of accountability, we should be able to honor experience's demands for liberative truth-telling and criticism's demands for liberative imagination, all toward something not only constructive but also transformative.

With liberative thought from a feminist perspective, we can bring the weight of precedent and moral force to bear on demands for justice. With theory critical of empire, we can bring incisiveness of insight and flexible, supple imagination to the question of what it means to flourish as a person (and as a community) in, through, and despite constructions that tend toward objectification and erasure. A focus on personhood serves a dual purpose, disrupting the rhetoric that negates, erases, and makes invisible while reconciling with worlds beyond the self and inviting constructive imagination that has the power to transform.

Kate M. Ott is a Christian ethicist and activist. Dr. Ott educates and writes curricula for faith communities on issues of sexuality, childhood/adolescence, and moral decision making. Dr. Ott is coauthor of the second edition of *A Time to Speak: Faith Communities and Sexuality Education*. She wrote the "Sexuality Education Curricula for Faith Communities: An Annotated Bibliography." Her current writing project is a book, *Sexuality, Faith, and Family: Talking to Our Children from Toddlers to Teens.*

Searching for an Ethic

Sexuality, Children, and Moral Agency

KATE M. OTT

I have spent many years working with children and adolescents. From my days of volunteering at Children's Hospital in Milwaukee, Wisconsin, to running an afterschool program in Bridgeport, Connecticut, youth and children's ministries have been my passion. My theo-ethical thought was formed simultaneously as I worked on my graduate degrees in feminist studies and ethics, ran a youth group, worked for a juvenile sanctions program, and served as a case manager at a safe home for abused and neglected children. Questions about liberation, salvation, common good, reconciliation, and justice were not abstract theological notions; they were realities of the daily struggle. It became obvious to me that the academic categories and language I had were neither *sufficiently complex* nor *realistically simple* enough to accurately address the challenges these children's perspectives and circumstances posed.

As I look forward to how new feminist Christianities are taking shape, issues involving the lives and perspectives of children have changed my work in feminist ethics and are pushing other feminist ethicists to reevaluate understandings of moral agency, gender/sexuality, and moral development. Many of the children with whom I worked—poor and wealthy; white, Latina, black, and Asian American; from urban neighborhoods and the suburbs—seemed to face a common problem: silence from adults about sexuality and relationships.

It seems, as our cultural, theological, and ethical responses to sexuality have shifted for adults, most Christian churches continue to perpetuate traditional moralisms (for example, no sex until marriage) and restrict sexuality information (abstinence-only education or silence) for children and youth. It is children and youth who are suffering from our silence—from sexual abuse and violence, teen pregnancy, sexually transmitted diseases, poor body image, and growing rates of HIV; those who suffer reproductive and sexual health disparities are most often poor girls of color in the United States and globally.[1] Most urgent in my mind is a new feminist Christian sexual ethical response for children and youth that takes both their moral agency and developing sexuality seriously. Such an ethic would give children and youth greater ownership of their bodies and sexuality, as well as demand greater accountability from adults and our community structures.

Our resistance to tackling the project of sexual ethics for children and adolescents (beyond or instead of "just say no!") may result from two distinct issues in the field of ethics. First, the discipline of ethics does not (often) recognize children and youth as subjects. Thus, we are lacking well-articulated arguments for the moral agency of children. Second, sexual ethics has been and continues to be overly concerned with sexual acts rather than sexual development, especially when it is implemented in church-based sexuality education programs. The feminist sexual ethicist Margaret Farley recently wrote, "We know the dangers as well as ineffectiveness of moralism, and the potential dangers of narrowly construed moral systems and rules. We do not yet know whether an ethic of just love and just sex will transform any young person's understanding or action. Insofar as we care about our children, it is worth a try."[2] It is time! It has long been time—to address sexual ethics for children and youth in *sufficiently complex* and *realistically simple* terms.

Children and Youth as Moral Agents

Feminist Christian ethics has in the past talked about children and youth at least insofar as they were connected to women's issues of reproduction and family. Historically, many of the church fathers and their modern counterparts wrote about children.[3] However, their interest in children was often to prove a theological tenet already in place, such as infant baptism, or to address parental duties. Children were not understood, nor taken to be subjects in and of themselves. In the past fifty years, academic study of children's morality has been the domain of psychology and moral education, often sharing overlap with practical theology. Recent works in practical theology have lifted children and youth to the status of subject rather than object.[4] Yet, ethics has remained relatively silent with the exception of less than a handful of Christian ethicists who are currently doing academic writing on the moral agency of children.

Feminist Christian ethicists Cristina Traina and Jennifer Beste are two examples of scholars engaged in ethical reflection on the moral status of children—as subjects! Another Christian ethicist, John Wall, has contributed significantly to the project of raising children's voices and status in Christian ethics. He has coined the term *childist* as a way to note a preferential option for children. Traina's, Beste's, and Wall's nuanced arguments regarding children's moral agency challenge both historical religious writings on children as well as current psychology and moral education literature.[5] In historical religious writings, children's morality was thought of in a dichotomous way as either angelic (in need of protecting) or devilish (in need of vigilant reform). Those of us who take care of children may agree that they are at times angelic and at others devilish.

However, this theological view compartmentalizes how children interact in the world, and denies the moral complexity of children's actions and our responsibilities as caregivers. Traina and Wall advocate that children be understood as moral agents but not any more or less predetermined as "good" or "evil" than we might consider adults. They argue not for adult control of children's development, but rather conceive of moral agency as an interdependent relationship. In other words, moral agency is not solely determined by our radical individuality (I can do it myself) or super rationality (I reason, therefore I'm moral).

Traina balances claims of individuality and responsibility as well as ability to articulate a coherent moral reason with the intended behavior of the agent. Simply because a child, by virtue of age and ability, is by definition dependent on others and by definition less cognitively astute, she is no less a moral agent. Traina writes, "Children's behavior in situations of dependency is still moral agency even though it is not fully autonomous. Agency is not a zero-sum game; even when others are gravely responsible for the conditions of her behavior, a dependent's action is still her action. Children are neither marionettes nor mere conduits for powerful adults' action."[6] For example, Michelle, at age six, shares her lunch with a friend who forgot his. This is a moral act. And yet, it is born of a combination of examples set for her at home, school, and perhaps church; of her love for her friend; and of her access to food. Additionally, Michelle may not, at age six, be able to provide a fully developed argument for why she chose to share her lunch. Her act is no more or less moral in the absence of a rational explanation or its contingency on role modeling, resources, and a basic sense of duty or love.

This shift in how we understand and define moral agency will have ramifications for adult agency. Our exercising of moral agency may not be as developmentally linear as psychologists and moral education experts would have us believe. It reminds us that "persons are both agents and patients at once, capable of interpreting their social worlds but also in turn always interpreted by those social worlds and by others within them."[7] As children and adults, we will experience differing levels of autonomy and rational capacity throughout our lifetime, but we are all equally moral agents. Our accountability for our actions is not determined by whether or not we have agency, but by growing knowledge and experience of moral requirements to self and others.

For the purposes of sexual ethics for children and youth, these insights are valuable. First, they call us to take the moral agency of children seriously, even, or especially, with regard to their sexuality. Second, they highlight the potential positive and negative effects adults can have on children's exercise of moral agency.

Children and Youth as Sexual Beings

When sexual ethics addresses children, it is usually in one of two ways—preventing sexual abuse or seeking to restrict early sexual behaviors between youth. We rarely spend time talking about the positive formation of our sexuality, from the loving and caring touch we might receive as babies to the naming of all our body parts without shame, or the affirmation of deep friendships in elementary school to our first romantic loves, not to mention the uncontrollable and often jarring bodily changes in between. Breaking the silence about sexuality is the first step; expanding our notion of how our sexuality develops and is understood by us is the second.

Feminist sexual ethics is encountering a shift in how it addresses sexuality. This shift affects how we understand our developing sexuality and biological, cultural, psychological, and environmental influences. Sexuality, and more specifically our current binary structure of sex (male/female), gender identity (masculine/ feminine), and sexual orientation (heterosexual/homosexual), are in question. Many scientists do not believe the human population fits into discreet categories of sexual orientation or gender. From data provided by social science, medical practice, and personal experience, we are aware of a continuum of sex, gender identity, and sexual orientation that need not be either fixed or predetermined, and yet are neither fully the result of choice nor preference.[8]

In the end, the scientific research confirms "a complex array of genetics, prenatal hormones, sociocultural influences, psychosocial factors, or some combination of these" form our orientation and gender identity.[9] When speaking of male and female, there is a wide diversity of chromosomal, hormonal, internal, and external genitalia configurations that do not always line up on one side of the spectrum of male or female. Many individuals, specifically in Christian denominations, use the inconclusiveness of the science to maintain their claims of God-ordained heterosexual, male-dominant relationships. I do not have space or the desire to respond to these heterosexist, and often economically and racially motivated, claims.[10] We may not be equally open to fully embracing multiple sexes and gender identities, but at least we should not immediately seek to shove intersex babies or gender-variant children into one category or another. We may not fully embrace the fact that we are neither "completely heterosexual" nor "completely homosexual" in our attractions, behaviors, or relationships. There is no conclusive data to suggest either nature or nurture is the final cause.

What we do know is that "nature" gives us a wider sexual and gender diversity than we had originally conceived. And, "nurture" seems to matter most with respect to acceptance of individual sense of self and fostering relationships that model love and justice. The acknowledgment of a wide diversity of gender identities, sexual orientations, and sexes adds complexity to children's changing bodies and developing feelings of attraction. It also requires being open to a child discovering her gender and orientation rather than starting with a fixed notion that she needs to struggle against or live into. Thus, we need a sexual ethic that supports children's moral agency to navigate the unknown mix of nature and nurture that would bring them to a place of sexual health lived out in just relationships.

A Sexual Ethic for Children and Youth

More than fifteen years ago, Joan Timmerman, professor of theology at St. Catherine's College in St. Paul, Minnesota, wrote, "The virtue is not in repressing but in cultivating the human capacity to respond sexually.... One does not come into life fully developed; one has an obligation to grow toward full adulthood."[11] Feminist Christian ethics have engaged and altered the face of sexual ethics for adults. It is time we do the same with regard to youth and children. I suggest a developmental sexual ethic that stresses the dynamic and qualitative character of relationships; considers incremental sexual behaviors as valuable (as children become teens) and recognizes them as stages, not absolute "next steps" to more intimate sexual behaviors; and requires ongoing sharing of information, resources, and opportunity.[12]

First, a sexual ethic for children and youth should focus on relationships and their dynamic quality. Relationships, as Traina suggests, are integral to our developing sense of responsibility and accountability for our moral agency.[13] Our ability to negotiate relationships even as they change—because of growing up, growing apart, and growing closer—begins early and is in relation to self, parents, siblings, and friends. How we act, react, and are acted upon in these relationships shape (but do not determine) our understandings of intimacy, sensuality, gender, and orientation. Taking direction from adult sexual ethics, normative criteria for an ethical relationship would include consent, honesty, equality, mutual pleasure, and protection.[14]

Second, incremental sexual behaviors provide valuable opportunities to learn about your sexual self. We can refocus the normative characteristics of sexual ethics to include when to say "yes" to sexual behaviors rather than only focusing on saying "no." Trying on less mature sexual behaviors would also provide youth with the opportunity to explore their attractions and identity. Engagement in sexual behaviors would be tied directly to the ethical dimensions of the relationship (based on the first component), not inevitable building blocks (or bases).

Third, the ethic contains a social-justice component and articulates a moral obligation for adults.[15] Children need ongoing information sharing and building of communication skills in early childhood related to body parts, prevention of sexual abuse, and physical sexual development; and later in childhood, related to protection from sexually transmitted infections, pregnancy prevention, and sexual pleasure. Such an ethic would help children and youth explore their sexuality in a fluid manner, allow them to take responsibility for their own behaviors, and provide them with experience to recognize and feel confident about naming when their sexuality was violated.

The third component of the ethic is perhaps the most important and integral to making the other two components successful. Sexual and reproductive health and relationships are influenced by many factors, not the least of which is injustices such as racism, classism, ableism, and heterosexism. Children are often the most vulnerable in society, doubly and triply affected by social injustices. Leaving them out of our ethical discussions further alienates them and leaves our faith communities with little direction on how to best educate children and youth with regard to sexuality.

Children and youth are our future, the future of feminist Christianity, of feminist ethics, and of our faith communities. We owe them a sexual ethic that is *sufficiently complex* and *realistically simple*. I have had the privilege to walk with youth as they survive and often thrive even in the midst of broken relationships and denial of their agency by adults. If we start doing sexual ethics from the perspectives of children, I am convinced we will better understand the central place of relationships, the imperative for communication, and the openness to development and exploration as a nonlinear, interdependent process. The constantly deepening and changing embodiment of feminist Christianity will be better for it, as will our children.

Part IV

Feminist Liturgical and Artistic Frontiers

Most people meet the Christian religion in liturgy and ritual. Indeed, more rely on their churches for services when they marry or bury than read the tomes and study the texts. So what happens in worship has a deep and far-reaching impact.

Aesthetic challenges to the status quo are among the most powerful because they upset the emotional and spiritual applecart. They replace old, tired, oppressive images with new, fresh, provocative ones. They dislodge the comfortable prayers and rituals from their exalted places and invite new ways of articulating faith and beliefs, new ways of expressing in bodily, textual, and artistic forms the most deeply held truths.

Some of the most creative colleagues have taken the liberty—better, assumed the responsibility—to bring feminist insights to worship. They have faced resistance in their churches though they have managed to incorporate some insights there. It is hard to hide behind words and images that express feminist understandings of the divine; it is impossible to deny the impact of diverse faith perspectives on Christianity when such resources are used in rituals. Pictures and icons do not lie; music is not silent when it comes to naming once and for all the endless ways that diverse communities worship and, thus, knit together the lives of their members.

Exciting and compelling services are now increasingly available via feminist organizations. They are inclusive in both content and reach so that many beyond the parameters of Christianity find such services meaningful and uplifting. Feminist liturgists are in the vanguard of the new ministers who are able to be present to and helpful among the wide variety of people seeking religious challenge and solace well beyond the confines of any one faith.

We learn some of the history of that movement from Jeanette Stokes, who has worked for decades on art and liturgy with magnificent results. Deborah Sokolove contributes another overview in her chapter on the many ways in which worship that was once limited to words is now inclusive of images, art, and music that reflect those sensibilities of contemporary life. Diann L. Neu surveys the various ways in which Eucharist at meals is emerging in communities and their implications for the wider church. Janet Walton describes how feminist groups conduct their worship such that it changes from a spectator experience into a participatory one. Victoria Rue shares the ways in which some feminist Catholic women celebrate a Critical Mass and others are ordained in the Roman Catholic Womenpriests movement. Marjorie Procter-Smith reflects on the impact of feminist artistic and liturgical innovations and where they are leading.

It is safe to say that the churches will never be the same. Neither will the millions of women and men who now can exercise their human right to worship. They can do so both within and beyond Christian churches in welcoming, inclusive, and creative ways commensurate with their theopolitical commitments. There is much more creativity to be explored. But that children will grow up with this new normative experience of innovative worship is one of the signal achievements of feminist Christianity.

Jeanette Stokes is the founding director of the Center for Women and Ministry in the South and an ordained Presbyterian minster. Rev. Stokes is the author of *Hurricane Season: Living Through a Broken Heart,* a memoir about recovering from divorce, and *25 Years in the Garden,* a collection of essays. She writes, paints, dances, gardens, and leads workshops on women, spirituality, creativity, and social justice.

The Feminist Face of God

Art and Liturgy

JEANETTE STOKES

I attended a memorial service recently for a beloved female clergy colleague who died too young of a disease no one could control. Several of her longtime women friends from as far back as her college days were also present. The local pastors led a fairly traditional service and mentioned only the portions of her life with which they were familiar. None of the feminists were invited to participate in the planning of or leadership in the service. Instead, they struggled through the service for their dead friend, cleaning up the language of the hymns and liturgy in their heads as they went along.

Afterward I thought, "This is not the way we do things anymore." Never do I lead a memorial service without searching far and wide to find out who should be included, what multiplicity of voices should be heard. Oh, the service included black, white, and Hispanic leaders, but not the ones who knew her intimately. The speakers represented their categories well, but most did not represent a close connection or personal relationship with our dearly departed friend.

What "we" do now is much more like what we did last December 21. A hundred people (women, men, and children of many ethnic and religious backgrounds) gathered in Durham, North Carolina, for an interfaith celebration. It was the fifteenth year for such an event in December. We sat in a circle with candles in the center. We listened, meditated, sang, and danced in celebration of community, spirit, and change.

How did we get from the staid forms of the Christianity of my childhood to new feminist religious expressions? How did I get there as a Presbyterian clergywoman?

History

I often say I have had only one conversion experience, a conversion to feminism in the early 1970s during college. The new research on women began to sink in, and I stopped giving preferential treatment to men and turned to pay closer attention to women, myself included.

My interest in feminist Christianity began in my seminary days at Duke Divinity School. I noticed that patriarchal religious language predominated, discussions about women and the experience of women were missing from the classrooms, and there was only one woman on the faculty. Women students gathered in empty classrooms and dared to tell one another of our personal images for God: roaring wind, mother's arms, mystery, presence, lover, friend. There was no clear path for women to follow as we critiqued patriarchal Christianity and began to construct new images and practices.

Classmate Heather Murray Elkins combined a background in theater with theological training to produce dramatic pieces performed in the stately university chapel. Her poetic renderings of biblical stories were acted out by dancers who embodied characters in the narratives.[1] I was especially moved by one piece about a tender meeting between Mary and Elizabeth, expectant mothers carrying something of God's promise.

Watching the words become flesh before my eyes touched my imagination, delighted my senses, and moved me more deeply than sermons usually did. With our explorations during seminary I came to understand there were more ways for groups of people to enter God's presence than with hymns, prayers, and sermons. I was not alone in my hunger for expressions of faith that fed the senses. In the 1970s, liturgical arts swept through mainstream North American Protestantism. Liturgical dance, artful banners, parades in and around the church, and dramatic reenactments of lectionary passages joined folk music, which had found a place in churches in the 1960s.

I had visited cathedrals in Europe, where my senses were thrilled by the sights and sounds, lavish expressions of adoration, an extravagant altarpiece of Mary rising toward heaven at the cathedral at Chartres, the flowers, candles, and offerings left to her in the chapels of every church. I also knew the last remnants of the feminine had been left behind by the Protestant Reformation, but I had no real notion of what they might have looked like before. I was hungry for more.

In seminaries around the country, women students tried out new liturgical forms, such as worship services with inclusive language. At Duke, we sat on the stone floor of the chapel instead of in pews and adjusted the language, images, structure, and leadership to make worship less hierarchical and more intimate. We were more interested in exploring God's presence with us than in keeping God "out there."

Theologian Mary E. Hunt has often said, "You can't just add women and stir." When women began to add their voices, images, and experiences to Christian theology and liturgy, everything changed. The forms and the functions were transformed.

When I graduated from seminary in 1977, friends and I founded the Resource Center for Women and Ministry in the South (RCWMS) to support women established in and entering ministry.[2] We wanted to get women together and encourage them as they made their ways through religious structures that were patriarchal in nature and practice. We also wanted to foster the women's movement in the religious community by offering feminist theology to an audience outside the academy. Similar centers were appearing in Boston; New York; Chicago; Berkeley; Washington, D.C.; and elsewhere.

RCWMS began hosting conferences of fifty to a hundred women with feminist theologians as speakers, a wide variety of workshops, and worship. Planning worship with Christian women from different traditions proved to be challenging. The Episcopalians wanted to have communion every time and the Baptists would not hear of it. The participants at these gatherings were not even all Christians, so we reached for more ecumenical and interfaith forms of worship. Silence provided an excellent meeting ground in which we could attend to the sacred mysteries of creation and life. Music and readings from a range of sacred literatures also provided common ground. We found that if we stopped preaching to one another, we got along a lot better.

Artists and Musicians

Over time it became clear that the real priestesses of the women's movement were not the ministers and theologians but the artists, writers, and musicians. Inspiring feminist and womanist artists and writers included singers Holly Near, Ronnie Gilbert, Cris Williamson, Meg Christian, and the women of Sweet Honey in the Rock; novelists Alice Walker and Toni Morrison; poets Marge Piercy, May Sarton, Audre Lorde, and later, Mary Oliver.[3] When Cris Williamson sang, "Lean on me, I am your sister," she described the solidarity women were finding with other women. When Sweet Honey sang, "When we fall on our knees with our faces to the rising sun, then we'll have a little happiness," they offered a vision of solidarity that crossed lines of race, class, and sexual orientation.[4]

These musicians and writers sang and wrote of racism, sexism, and homophobia. They taught us to listen to our ancestors, to trust our own experience, to break the silence, and to tell our secrets. They helped lift the spirits of women, giving us strength and courage.

Visionary artist Meinrad Craighead published *The Mother's Songs: Images of God the Mother*, a book of her writings and images, in 1986.[5] A Catholic mystic and former nun, Meinrad painted visions that came to her in prayer and meditation. Her feminine images of the divine expand our imaginations.

The interweaving of art, theory, and activism is a hallmark of the development of the womanist and feminist movements of the past three decades of the twentieth century. Together we learned that each facet needed the others to offer another perspective on our complex lives.

Women's Spirituality Groups

Thousands of women joined consciousness-raising groups in the United States in the sixties and seventies. In small, nonhierarchical groups, women did everything from looking at their own vaginas to exploring their relationships with authoritarian men to preparing one another to struggle against racism, sexism, and war. Together they honed their political analysis and deepened their self-respect.

In the late 1970s, a new kind of women's group came into being, the women's spirituality group. With the publication of Starhawk's *The Spiral Dance: A Rebirth of the Ancient Religion of the Great Goddess,* small groups of women had a guidebook for creating new rituals tied to the seasons of the year and the cycles of women's lives. Some of these had a Christian focus. Rosemary Radford Ruether's *Woman-Church: Theology and Practice* helped feminists in the church create more of their own rituals.[6]

Miriam Therese Winter (*Defecting in Place: Women Taking Responsibility for Their Own Spiritual Lives*), Teresa Berger (*Dissident Daughters: Feminist Liturgies in Global Context*), and others have documented the efforts of women around the country and throughout the world to develop both groups and practices to meet their own spiritual needs.[7] Some of these groups gathered for liturgies led by clergy, but more often they took seriously the claim to a priesthood of all believers and developed the liturgies and rituals that met the spiritual needs of their communities. They embraced the arts in many forms: music, song, dance, visual arts, and poetry. Many of these women continued to participate in their local congregations but found that their deepest needs for presence, guidance, and forgiveness were being met elsewhere in small, often renegade, groups.

While the focus of this volume is on feminist Christianity, it is important to note that while new liturgical forms were emerging among Christian women, they were also taking shape in other traditions as well, especially in Judaism.

Re-Imagining

The arts are critically important to the expression of faith. Whether through adoration, lament, or hope, expressions of faith in feminist Christian circles have moved away from traditional Christian forms to more eclectic ones. The Re-Imagining Conference held in Minneapolis in 1993 contained many examples of new liturgical forms and feminist artistic expressions.[8] It also caused something of a furor. With heavy sponsorship from the national women's offices of the Presbyterians and United Methodists, the Re-Imagining Conference brought together hundreds of feminist Christians from many denominations and from all corners of the country. The arts were an integral part of the conference. Participants sat at large round tables that were covered with clean white paper each morning of the conference. They were supplied with waxy pastels in vibrant colors and encouraged to make art during the lectures and presentations.

Afterward, conservative Presbyterians and United Methodists protested some of the unorthodox occurrences at the conference. A ritual of milk and honey was called heretical by some conservatives. This practice was no more objectionable than the Moravian Love-feasts of coffee and sweet rolls celebrated on Christmas Eve in churches around the world.

Another criticism centered on a large mural that artist Nancy Chinn created during the conference. In one corner of the mural there was a half-naked woman. That image was captured by conservative women at the conference and displayed on the front of magazines for shock value. Portions of the Sistine Chapel would have been much more shocking had they been isolated from their context and exhibited in a similar way. Conservative church members were shocked and raised a protest that resulted in some national staff losing their jobs. If the artist was trying to say, "God made woman and here she is," she was successful. Some elements in the church responded as if to say, "God made woman, but she is an embarrassment; cover her up!"

A third complaint arose over the use of a Sophia chant. A blessing, based on a traditional Hawaiian chant, was taught to the gathering: "Bless Sophia, dream the vision, share the wisdom, dwelling deep within." Together with gestures, the chant was used repeatedly to bless speakers and participants. Since the Christian trinity has no place for a female person, women have been left to develop relationships with such feminine figures as Mary Magdalene, Mary the mother of Jesus, or Sophia, the embodiment of wisdom in Hebrew Scripture. Attempts to lift up such figures are often met with accusations of heresy.

All over the country, feminist Christians were experimenting with art and liturgy. These groups included the RCWMS; the Women's Alliance for Theology, Ethics and Ritual (WATER) in Silver Spring, Maryland; Holy Ground in Asheville, North Carolina; and Mary and Martha's Place in Atlanta, Georgia.

Creativity and Spirituality

Beginning in the late 1990s, we at the RCWMS turned our attention to programming around creativity and spirituality and developed working definitions of both. Spirituality is the process of opening to the experience of the presence of God. It is about getting closer to God and to ourselves. Creativity is about choices, being allowed to express our own uniqueness by selecting from the variety of options available to us. Picking a yellow shirt over a blue one on a Tuesday morning is a creative decision, as is choosing to paint a red flower instead of a pink one.

Freedom of expression is an important ingredient in any democracy. Encouraging creativity strengthens a society. Totalitarian regimes put a stranglehold on art and culture. They take away people's rights, individuality, and spontaneity. Making art is an empowerment process. Encouraging people to make art, to dance, and to write strengthens democracies and movements for social change within them.

We began offering more workshops on writing, art, and meditation. In 2006 we sponsored a project, Art and the Feminine Divine, to celebrate the many forms and faces of God the Mother, Lover, and Creatrix. The project included a month-long exhibit of work by a hundred artists, displayed in five venues open to the public. The exhibit included pieces in fabric, collage, painting, and sculpture. Musical events, storytelling, and a meditation session were held during the exhibit.

Interfaith Celebrations

In preparation for Art and the Feminine Divine we focused the December 2005 interfaith celebration on the feminine divine. RCWMS had been involved in an annual interfaith celebration of community, spirit, and change since 1995. The service always includes leaders, readings, and music from a wide variety of religious traditions. We made an effort to create a place in which people of any faith or no faith could feel at home. We were sharing a variety of religious expressions, not trying to promote any one. The only thing we were pushing was acceptance and appreciation of the many paths to the holy. The service honored Hanukkah, the winter solstice, Christmas, Kwanzaa, and more. It included a teaching by a Zen priest, a presentation on God as Mother in Hindu tradition, and music by Native American singers.

My favorite picture from that service is of Páola Kipp, a Middle Eastern dancer of Lebanese-Peruvian heritage. In the photograph, translucent gold fabric cascades from her shoulders. When Páola grasped it in her hands and raised her arms, the fabric spread like great diaphanous wings. As she spun around, a drummer in the background was visible through her wings. Together the dancer and the musician created a breathtaking expression of gratitude for all that is beautiful and creative and life-giving. Páola says that when she dances she reconnects with the feminine divine within her: "I feel the power and force of the Feminine as it is manifested in undulating, circling and flowing movements."[9]

Recent Projects

After Art and the Feminine Divine ended, RCWMS continued to sponsor projects that engaged the arts. Some focused on the feminine face of God, others on God's creation. Artist Carole Baker created an interactive exhibit called Mary: The Paper Doll Project. Its life-size paper dolls, each with a different cultural depiction of the Holy Mother, included Our Lady of Lourdes, Byzantine Theotokos, the Virgin of Guadalupe, and Madonna of Soweto. Some were holding the baby Jesus and each wore a robe that could be removed and placed on the other dolls. Visitors to the exhibit were encouraged to interact with the dolls by changing their clothes.[10]

We housed the making of an hour-long documentary, *Meinrad Craighead: Praying with Images,* which traces the artist's life and work.[11] Craighead says of her work, "I draw and paint from my own myth of personal origin."[12] For her, each picture is a realization of this story and is connected to the ancient images of the God Mother in art and mythology. The film traces her journey from her roots in Arkansas, to parts of Europe where she taught and studied, to England where she spent fourteen years as a nun, to New Mexico where she now makes her home, and finally to her last pilgrimage—a visit to the Black Madonna of Montserrat in Spain. Catholicism, ancient mythology, and Native American shamanism all influence Craighead's images, nearly a hundred of which appear in the film.

While environmental artist Bryant Holsenbeck was serving as the artist-in-residence at RCWMS, we decided to capture her on film. Using entirely recycled materials, Holsenbeck creates such wonders as birds made of credit cards, nests of chopsticks, and room-size mandalas of bottle caps. In our fifteen-minute documentary, *Blackbirds, Bottle Caps, and Broken Records: Environmental Artist Bryant Holsenbeck at Work,* the artist points out how much stuff we throw away and inspires people to protect God's creation by embracing full-circle recycling.[13]

Where Am I Now? Where Are We Now?

I am not an evangelist for Christianity. I am an evangelist for finding or creating a community of support and practices that sustains you. For my beloved Presbyterian grandmother, spiritual support came in reading the Bible and praying every day. For me it comes from a weekly yoga class, from painting and walking, from writing every day, and from feminists with whom I share the journey of faith.

As a writer, I am accustomed to having words and images pour out of me. I am interested in many things feminist, Presbyterian; in ministry, spirituality, creativity; in justice and social change. When asked to write about Christianity these days, I freeze up. Having said that, I acknowledge I am a thoroughgoing Christian—soaked in it, professed in it, ordained in it, and in "good standing" with one arm of it.

Instead of being an apologist, trying to explain Christianity to feminists and feminism to Christians, I choose to be a heretic, to remain within the bounds of the Christian faith, to create new forms, and to explore new practices.

I spend a lot of time with women who grew up as practicing Christians and now have found other, more sustaining practices. Many of them have "defected in place" and some of them simply defected. These deeply spiritual and ethical women would rather do yoga or art than attend a church, even a progressive one, on a Sunday morning. Most of the churches in our area are still Christocentric and use patriarchal language. Some of my feminist colleagues have turned in their ordinations. I have no instinct to do that. I still love the religion of my childhood; it is just that when I step into it these days, I tend to freeze. I do not want to say some of the words anymore.

Almost all the gatherings I am part of are interfaith or multifaith. RCWMS's gatherings may include a Protestant woman who attends a local synagogue and teaches Buddhist dharma, an African American who grew up Protestant and is now a Zen priest, Jewish women who practice Buddhism or yoga, and women who have no interest in claiming any particular religious tradition. The faithful, spiritual feminism I see, organize, and participate in can hardly be contained in the label "Christian."

I am tired of the ways Christianity has said to people, not just women, "Believe like this, make art like this, make love like this." I have trouble with traditional Christian theology and practice—from baptism, which we cheerfully say is a sign of welcoming a child into a community of faith, but is really the washing away of the uncleanness of being born of a woman; to communion, which can be seen as sharing the feast of the "kingdom," but manages to steal some of the grace from the Passover feast and from food women have prepared at home for thousands of years.

I do not believe in and I cannot subscribe to a version of Christianity that insists that what Jesus meant was that we were to get together regularly and celebrate his torture and murder at the hand of the state. It is misguided theology. It would be like getting together every January 15 and celebrating the cold-blooded murder of Martin Luther King Jr. and saying how fabulous it was that he was murdered in the name of freedom. But maybe that is what we do, and in so doing we encourage other people to go get themselves killed for what they believe in.

No thoroughgoing feminist would tolerate the language of torture and violence anymore. Christianity has changed because of feminist analysis. One stellar example of a new feminist Christianity is found in the work of Rita Nakashima Brock and Rebecca Parker in *Saving Paradise: How Christianity Traded Love of This World for Crucifixion and Empire.*[14] The authors discovered within the early church a Christian aesthetic that focused on beauty. They found that in the first thousand years or so of Christianity the focus was on this world as paradise. The focus on Jesus's suffering and dying did not come until Charlemagne forced Europeans to convert at sword point. When the Holy Roman Emperor caused suffering in the name of Christ, it became holy to suffer.

Though feminist Christianity is my spiritual home, my life and work have carried me beyond, outside, and around the corner from exclusive Christianity. My perspective is certainly not feminist Judaism, or feminist Buddhism, or even secular feminism, but the weddings, funerals, naming ceremonies, workshops, retreats, and writing I am involved in no longer take an exclusively Christian view. They are much closer to the ground, to the seasons and cycles, to things that my inherited Christianity was trying to squelch.

Do not get me wrong. I actually love Jesus. I just have a really hard time with how the church has so often screwed up his message of liberation and wholeness, his concern for every person, his love of justice, his practice of peace. But I do not think he is the only one or the only way. Christianity is the path my ancestors left me. I am stuck being a Southerner (which I like just fine), being white (which is something of a burden in this country), being female (which is great), and being Christian (which I claim but have no interest in defending), and increasingly interfaith. I do not need or want to be with people of faith who are only like me. Being in a gathering with only Christians is as boring as being in a gathering of only white people, unless the conversation is about how we have used our position to limit ourselves and oppress other people. Feminist Christianity invites so much more than that.

Deborah Sokolove is an artist, a liturgical scholar, and the director of the Henry Luce III Center for the Arts and Religion at Wesley Theological Seminary. Dr. Sokolove is a member of a group that writes liturgies and prayers collaboratively for Seekers Church, a small progressive Christian community in Washington, D.C. Her paintings have been shown locally and nationally in both private and public collections. Her articles on faith, art, and the artist's life appear in numerous publications.

More Than Words

DEBORAH SOKOLOVE

Liturgy—congregational worship—is the heartbeat of Christian life, gathering the body of Christ together to pray, to give thanks, to remember the ancient stories that tell us who we are, and to send us back into the world as bearers of those stories. Congregational worship is also the place where art and faith come together in the most public way, where the Word of God comes to us in words, but also in pictures, in movement, in music, in drama, in poetry, and in all the other ways that human beings communicate with one another. Congregational worship forms us as Christians, giving us patterns of prayer that come back to us in the difficult moments of our lives, songs that stay with us even when other memories fade, images that inform our imaginations and tell us who God is in ways that are beyond the reach of reasoned discourse.

As a liturgical scholar, practicing artist, and director of the Henry Luce III Center for the Arts and Religion at Wesley Theological Seminary in Washington, D.C., I spend my professional life at the intersection of art and worship. As a member of a small ecumenical church founded on feminist principles, I have the privilege of practicing what I study by writing liturgy, designing rituals, and leading congregational worship on a regular basis. As a feminist, I celebrate the changes that feminist scholars, activists, and ministers have already brought to Christian worship, mourn the backward steps, and look toward the future with a mixture of concern and hope.

When I consider the future of feminist Christian liturgical life, I am heartened by the reality that at least some feminist values and practices have already become an accepted and unquestioned part of much mainstream Christian worship. Women preach and preside regularly in many congregations. Ordinary members work collaboratively to design services and create worship visuals. In many places, there is more attention to truth and authenticity than to following the official rubrics. And the language of prayer and song is changing, along with new ways of understanding the divine.

There is, of course, the weight of a tradition that has been patriarchal and hierarchical for so long that many still cannot conceive of any other way to speak of God than as Father and King, or conduct liturgy in any other way than sitting lined up in pews passively listening as if the Word of God were not more than mere words. But neither feminism nor Christian worship is monolithic, and the future of feminist liturgical life looks different among Catholics than among Protestants, and different again in women-only gatherings than in mixed-gender assemblies.

Perhaps the biggest difference that feminism has made in the worship of mainstream Protestant congregations is in the area of leadership. In the late twentieth century, the Episcopal Church, the Evangelical Lutheran Church in America, the Presbyterian Church USA, the United Church of Christ, the United Methodist Church, and many other denominations opened full ordination to women, recognizing that, like men, they are called by God to serve as leaders in all aspects of worship, including preaching and presiding. Today, about half the students in seminaries connected with these denominations are women. But while the question of whether women may preach, teach, lead worship, or act in any other capacity in the church is largely undisputed in many places, some of my women students—even in denominations that officially ordain women—report an ongoing resistance to being called to ordained ministry. Women's ordination is completely closed among Roman Catholic, Eastern Orthodox, and many evangelical Christian churches.

Of course, the simple fact that women are ordained does not necessarily imply that the worship services they design or lead will be feminist in any meaningful sense. As Gail Ramshaw writes in her book *God Beyond Gender,*

> A recent study of ordained ministers, which set out to examine any differences between a feminine and a masculine style of ministry, discovered in fact no clear sex-based distinction; different styles of ministry depended on a wide variety of complex factors. Gender is only one of many factors, and not the sole determinative, in establishing individual behavior.[1]

Indeed, while the women who are currently ordained or moving toward ordained ministry are the beneficiaries of previous generations of feminists, many do not know this history and do not understand themselves as feminists. This is particularly true of many of the younger women I encounter in my classes who associate the term *feminism* with a kind of radicalism that is at odds with their own understanding of Christian discipleship.

As in the secular world, *feminism* for many has become a word that implies male-bashing militancy rather than an egalitarian stance in which women and men are seen as equal members of society, whether in political, private, or religious life. While they agree with Paul's admonition to the Galatians, "There is neither Jew nor Greek, slave nor free, male nor female, for you are all one in Christ Jesus" (Gal. 3:28 NIV), these students do not necessarily associate the word *feminism* with this biblical passage. Nor do they necessarily value the kind of "in the round" worship or the principle of talking back to tradition that Letty Russell wrote of in her 1993 proposal for a new way of doing church.[2] On the other hand, regardless of whether they identify with feminist principles, many of the churches described as "emergent" do seem, in practice, to be less hierarchical in their worship, doing away with the traditional pew arrangement in favor of coffeehouse-style tables and chairs, and offer many possibilities for individuals to be involved in church life.

For many self-described feminists, women's gatherings have often been seen as the only legitimate site of feminist worship. Others, however, have seen mixed-gender congregations as the place where both male and female feminist Christians can best live out their egalitarian ideals and teach a new generation of girls and boys how to treat one another with respect, dignity, and justice. One of the most important tools that such feminists have employed has been what generally is referred to as inclusive or gender-neutral language about both humans and the divine.

This attempt to change the language that we use to speak about the divine, in particular, has met with great resistance, even though theologians have consistently insisted that God is bigger than any earthly categories. Ramshaw notes that as early as the fourth century, Gregory of Nazianzus and other Cappadocian Fathers maintained that the traditional masculine language for God did not mean that God is actually male. Pointing out the difficulty of eradicating a centuries-old habit of thought, she writes,

> The task of degendering the word *God* is massive. Pronouns, designations, doctrinal speech, metaphors, and personifications of the deity must speak more truthfully of a God who according to Christian tradition is beyond gender. We need to whitewash murals that depict God as a male creature. Children's books must be devoid of demeaning portraiture of God. Light streaming from behind a cloud is no profound picture of God, but it is surely more Christian than a drawing of Jupiter.[3]

Ramshaw is not really calling for the wholesale destruction of the masterpieces of Western art. Rather, she is issuing a challenge not only to writers of hymns and prayers but also to artists to find new ways of depicting God that free us to see both male and female as created in God's own image, as we read in Genesis 1:26–28. This is a difficult task, and I am not aware of any artists who have taken it up explicitly.

In her widely influential book on feminist liturgy, *In Her Own Rite: Constructing Feminist Liturgical Tradition,* Marjorie Procter-Smith takes the notion of degendering God another step, saying that it is not enough that the language of worship be gender neutral. Distinguishing between nonsexist, inclusive, and emancipatory language, she writes,

> Non-sexist language seeks to avoid gender-specific terms. Inclusive language seeks to balance gender references. Emancipatory language seeks to transform language use and to challenge stereotypical gender references.[4]

Despite Procter-Smith's cautions, this careful distinction seems to be observed rarely, and any attempt to move away from patriarchal language is generally called "inclusive" regardless of whether it simply calls God a rock or tries, as does Brian Wren's hymn, "Bring Many Names," to expand our descriptive vocabulary to see God as both strong mother and nurturing father.[5]

Hymnody is one of the primary ways that we learn how to speak of the divine. In 1995 the United Church of Christ published the *New Century Hymnal.*[6] In a bold assertion of the importance of inclusive language in worship, the editors not only found many new hymn texts that exemplified their ideals, but also carefully edited many of the old, familiar songs to eliminate any suggestion that God is king, father, or lord. While this effort is commendable, many find the results clunky, inconsistent, or hard to sing, with too many stop consonants that do not allow the music to flow, or too many repetitions of the word *God* as a way to avoid saying "he" or "him." Others wave away the objections, rejoicing in the relative freedom from masculine pronouns as well as in the liberating imagery found in new hymns by Wren, Ruth Duck, and others who have made a conscious effort to give Christians words that everyone can sing with conviction.[7]

The editors of *The Faith We Sing,* the United Methodist Church's 2000 supplement to their 1989 hymnal,[8] made a different choice in response to a different situation. While it does include several excellent hymns that celebrate both God and humans in gender-neutral or multigendered language, it also includes a large number of praise choruses and other songs in which God is addressed or described as exclusively male. That these praise choruses are widely favored by younger people is evidence that inclusive language in worship is not necessarily an important value for them.

This observation was supported in a course I taught recently called "Writing for Worship." As the title suggests, students in the class were to compose prayers, responsive readings, and other elements of a worship service with the exception of a sermon. All of the students were relatively young, and seemed to have given no thought to what inclusive language for God might sound like. When I asked them if they would be willing to address God as anything other than Father or Lord, most of them looked bewildered or shocked, assuming that the only alternative would have to be Mother or Goddess, which were obviously unacceptable to them. It was clear that none of them had ever really thought about even the most obvious gender-neutral possibilities, such as Rock of our Salvation, or even Holy One. The maleness of God was so deeply ingrained in these young students that to suggest that God is bigger than or beyond gender was, quite literally, unthinkable. The good news is that by the end of the term all of them had expanded their vocabulary of the divine into a wide range of images and metaphors.

Language about people that is inclusive of women seems to be generally more accepted than inclusive language about God, both in worship and in ordinary speech. One notable exception is found in the training of Roman Catholic priests. One day I was speaking to a young Dominican about problems of translation and the official Roman Catholic insistence on the phrase "for us men" in the Nicene Creed, even though the passage is clearly intended to refer to all people. Having grown up with that language, and been taught the standard grammatical assertion that *men,* in such instances, includes women, he was honestly bewildered by my objection to such male-centered language. It was only when I pointed out that it was impossible to know with any certainty whether any particular passage applied to men only or to all humans that he began to see the logical inconsistency, if not the matter of justice, implied in making women invisible in the language of worship.

Perhaps the largest impediment to the widespread use of inclusive language in worship is none of these issues, however, but instead the competing value that congregations and individuals need to have prayers and songs that they know without looking at the words. Congregations that consistently use inclusive or even emancipatory language in prayers, sermons, and responsive readings continue to recite the old translations of the Lord's Prayer and the aforementioned Nicene Creed as a way to maintain continuity with the past and with a larger Christian world that sees no reason to change the familiar words. Even in my own small, progressive congregation, which is heavily committed to principles of social justice and the full equality of women and men in all walks of life, we no longer use the *New Century Hymnal* at Christmas because so many people complained of the seemingly arbitrary changes the editors had made to songs such as "Joy to the World" and "Silent Night," which they have known by heart since childhood. As my feminist colleague, New Testament scholar Sharon Ringe, once told me, it is better to change our language about God by adding new words than to try to erase the old ones, especially at times that carry great emotional weight.

Worship is more than words, even the words that we say to or about God. In the past, feminist Christians have looked for new words, new ways to arrange space, new images, new ways to relate to one another and to God. Today, many of these new words and images and arrangements have become part of the common vocabulary of Christian worship, helping us know God and one another in ways that honor the gifts that both women and men bring to the life of the body of Christ. The future is mixed, as it always is, anchored by a tradition that now includes feminist hymns and prayers as well as the creeds and formulations handed on by those who came before, and pulled ever forward by a God that is beyond gender, beyond names, beyond our wildest dreams: a holy Word that is much, much more than words.

Diann L. Neu is cofounder and codirector of WATER, the Women's Alliance for Theology, Ethics and Ritual. She is a feminist liturgist and minister, spiritual director and psychotherapist. Dr. Neu is the author of *Return Blessings: Ecofeminist Liturgies Renewing the Earth* and *Women's Rites: Feminist Liturgies for Life's Journeys.* She writes and designs, leads and celebrates liturgies with faith and justice communities, especially the women-church movement.

Feminist Eucharists at Wisdom's Many Tables

DIANN L. NEU

From generation to generation, Divine Wisdom calls feminist Christians to Her many tables to break bread and do justice. We celebrate feminist Eucharists that proclaim Her wonderful deeds around the world throughout time.

Called to Break Bread and Do Justice

> Wisdom has built Her house....
> She has set Her table....
> "Come eat my bread,
> and drink the wine I have prepared."
>
> PROVERBS 9:1–2, 5

This is Divine Wisdom's invitation to celebrate feminist Eucharists. She gives Her people on every continent daily bread, including *injera* from Africa, tortillas from South America, rye bread from Europe, *mochi* from Asia, *damper* from Australia, cornbread from North

America, and much more. She provides drinks, including water, wine, juice, tea, milk and honey, and many more. She offers a variety of foods from every culture. She calls Her friends from every corner of Earth to gather at diverse tables in Her name. Women-church communities, women's spirituality circles, discipleship of equals, church in the round, and other inclusive communities are all ways of responding to this call of a divine One who looks like us to reimagine and renew Eucharist.[1]

As a feminist Christian, my experience of Eucharist is filled with passion, pain, and promise. Called by Divine Wisdom to break bread and do justice, I have been celebrating feminist Eucharists for more than forty years. The discipleship of equals worldwide affirms my call, and yet the kyriarchal Catholic Church continues to deny it, refuses to bless it, and tries to silence it. My story is similar to many others as we name ourselves church, celebrate Eucharists, and work for systemic change in church and society.

I am influenced by several movements in being called by Divine Wisdom to the practice of feminist Eucharist. My childhood rooted me firmly in Christianity. My ancestors were Catholic, Lutheran, Methodist, and probably Jewish. My adolescent years taught me to critique religious traditions on the basis of experience and conscience. In adulthood I awakened to the exclusive dimensions of the churches, especially the Catholic Church. When my male classmates at the Jesuit School of Theology at Berkeley, California, were ordained in 1980 and the six of us women who were equally called—ready, willing, and able—were not, my feminist colleagues and I protested this action by educating the community of the Graduate Theological Union about feminist ministry. We invited people to wear a daisy to symbolize the varieties of ministries in the community. I still remember who wore a daisy and who did not!

After the kyriarchal ordination of my Jesuit classmates, the community of women and men to which I belonged "ordained" me (called me forth for feminist ministry). We gathered on the rooftop of the building in which we lived for a feminist Eucharist. Overlooking the San Francisco Bay, they each gave me a shell to symbolize my gifts from the Holy Spirit, Divine Wisdom. They blessed me with water and anointed me with oil: symbols of Holy Orders. Together we blessed bread, wine, and food, and shared a meal: symbols of Eucharist. We sang, danced, and talked about the challenges before us. They sent me forth to do justice: to minister with feminist communities worldwide.[2]

I am called forth by my community for feminist ministry in the church of Divine Wisdom. As my colleague Alieda Verhoeven, a Methodist pastor and human rights advocate in Mendoza, Argentina, says, "Jesus taught feminist disciples to fish on the other side of the boat."[3]

More than forty years ago, inspired by the strides made by other feminist Christians, including Lutherans and Episcopalians with their focus on sacramental priesthood, my Catholic colleagues and I imagined ourselves ordained. Hundreds of us trained for priesthood and we proved to ourselves and others that it is only misogynist discrimination that in Catholicism gives men seven sacraments and women six. We moved into women's base communities, created women-church, the discipleship of equals. We set the tables of Divine Wisdom. As Mary E. Hunt, Catholic feminist theologian, says:

> Feminist ministry involves widespread participation, empowerment of all, especially women as religious agents. It means communal responsibility for what was previously reserved to priests, namely, the liturgical, educational, and fiduciary aspects of the community. It is an invitation to form communities of justice-seekers who will engage in the long-term work of social justice from a base of people who share values, support one another, and construct a quality life in the meantime.[4]

Within these communities we began celebrating feminist Eucharists. What brought us to this spiritual justice and ecclesiastical (dis)obedience? Many women like me, and perhaps you, have been breaking bread and doing justice since the 1960s. In the late 1970s when I was in seminary studying for my master of divinity and master of sacred theology, my professors encouraged me to celebrate the traditional Eucharist of the Catholic Church. After all, I had the same education as my male colleagues and I, too, was called. In those days we would gather together in our homes for Eucharist and we would invite a "real" male Catholic priest when we could. One was not easy to find.

One evening the invited priest did not show. We were a community yearning for Eucharist. We looked at one another, paused for a half second, and the group asked me to preside at the Eucharist. I heard the call from the community, paused for a half second, took the bread and wine, and said the official words according to the Pauline tradition, "This is my body. This is my blood."

The next morning I woke up after breaking through this major taboo, and the sun was shining. Yes, I had celebrated the official Eucharist of the Catholic Church. Yet something did not feel right. It was not that I was a woman leading the celebration. It was not that I was not officially ordained. It was not that I was afraid because I had broken a church taboo and could be excommunicated, silenced, or put under interdict.

It was that this eucharistic form did not nourish my spirit or feed my soul. The order of the liturgy did not feel alive. Its focus was death, the death of Jesus. My intuition, or Divine Wisdom, told me that there had to be another way to celebrate Eucharist. Yes, of course, include women's experience of body: "This is my body. This is my monthly blood. This is my life force given for you." Yes, of course, include bodies in pain: "This is my body. The body of Christ has cancer and HIV/AIDS." Yes, of course, include Earth's experience of body: "This is my body. This is my air, water, fire, soil. This is my life shared with you." Yes, of course, include even more. I suspected that the "more" had something to do with the meal. Since that time I have been creating feminist Eucharists that put meals back into Eucharist.

Stories of Feminist Eucharists

> So that bread, our daily bread, the very same bread that has been taken away from our people, will be given back because it is our right, no pleas to God needed, forever and ever.
> Amen.
>
> ALICIA PARTNOY[5]

Feminist Eucharists celebrated at a meal reclaim the eucharistic tradition of the early Christian community. They affirm the centrality of meals to the identity and development of the Christian community. The faithful come together to share community life, hear the word and teachings of the disciples who are women, break bread and share a meal, engage in conversations, and sing and dance. Communities tell stories and create memories at shared meals. We give thanks, claim power, and actualize visions in memory of Jesus and in memory of Divine Wisdom. The word *companion* comes from the Latin *cum,* meaning "with," and *panis,* meaning "bread." Companions are those with whom we break bread, share meals, and do justice.

Since 1983, the Women's Alliance for Theology, Ethics and Ritual (WATER) has celebrated feminist Eucharists in homes and in public places.[6] In several conferences I have worked on as liturgy or conference coordinator, the planning committee has included a feminist Eucharist at a meal as the high point of the gathering.[7] I remember Chicago, 1983, "Woman Church Speaks: From Generation to Generation," when three women dressed as mimes reached for bread and the lights went out, symbolizing that women do not look like Jesus and therefore cannot be ordained and cannot celebrate Eucharist. These mimes were invited to the community table to share a meal, thus transforming our eucharistic consciousness to include a meal with an inclusive community. I remember Cincinnati, 1987, "Women-Church: Claiming Our Power," when 3,200 participants made the eucharistic bread together, baked it at the seminary, and then blessed it, broke it, and ate it at our eucharistic meal. I remember Berkeley. I remember Washington, D.C. I remember de Tiltenberg, the Netherlands. I remember Crystal City. I remember Cuba. I remember Boston. I remember Ghana. I remember Chicago, 2007, "Celebrating Catholic Feminist Ministries: A Women-Church Forum," when feminist ministers on every continent blessed many breads, drinks, and foods.

Looking at forty years of uncovering stories around feminist Eucharists, I question: Why feminist Eucharist? Or ecofeminist Eucharist? What is there about Eucharist that keeps feminist communities celebrating it? What does feminist Eucharist at a meal look like in these communities? How does celebrating feminist Eucharists make a difference for the world?

Experiencing Feminist Eucharists at Meals

> I should like a great lake of finest ale for all the people
> I should like a table of the choicest foods for the family of heaven.
> Let the ale be made from the fruits of faith, and the food be for giving love.
> I should welcome the poor to my feast, for they are God's children.
> I should welcome the sick to my feast for they are God's joy.
> Let the poor sit with Divine Wisdom at the highest place and the sick dance with the angels.
> Bless the poor, bless the sick, bless our human race.
> Bless our food, bless our drink, all homes, O God embrace.
>
> ST. BRIGIT'S TABLE GRACE, FIFTH CENTURY

Feminist Eucharists take a variety of forms. Many feminist Christians are celebrating Eucharists at meals in the tradition of the early Christian community. We are reclaiming graces and meals as Eucharist and we invite Christian communities to make these practices their own. I offer two stories of feminist Eucharists as models for ones you and your community may want to create and celebrate. The first is a table grace that we prayed in my house. The second is a Eucharist at a banquet that was created for and celebrated at the conference "Celebrating Catholic Feminist Ministries: A Women-Church Forum."

A Story of a Table Grace

It was Friday night. Everyone was tired. The children had been in school all week. The adults had been working. Three households were dining together. One woman began the meal by lighting the candles and inviting everyone to hold hands.

> Blessed are you, Gracious and Loving Holy One, Divine Wisdom, for gathering us together to share bread, drink, and food at the end of a very busy week. Bless us and bless our food. Bless all the hungry of the world, especially the children, that they may have food and peace. Let us each share what we are thankful for tonight. I give thanks for....[8]

Everyone shared food. The children sang and played games. The adults talked about politics, theology, work, family, and their search for meaning. It was a typical Shabbat, the main meal of the week presided over by women on Friday night in Jewish households.

Grace before or after a meal is common practice for Christians. It is derived from one of the most standard features in all early Christian meals and banquets, the *beracha* or blessing over food and drink, in continuation with Jewish meal custom. Feminist Christians invite communities to claim these graces and meals as Eucharist.

A Story of the Eucharistic Banquet of Divine Wisdom

It was an amazing event. As three hundred people entered the banquet room, dancers blessed them with flowing scarves representing the Spirit of Divine Wisdom among us. A women's music group performed with piano, violin, guitar, flute, and singing. The community sang "We are gathering at Wisdom's tables" and sat at thirty round tables set with decorative cloths and festive foods.[9] Several women rose to begin the meal, saying, "Welcome to this 'Eucharistic Banquet of Divine Wisdom' celebrating feminist ministers who have been breaking bread and doing justice as women-church for twenty-five years and twenty centuries. *Buenas noches, Mujer-Iglesia! Wănshang hăo nüshìjiàotáng! Guten Abend, Frauen-kirche! Femme-Eglise, bonsoir!* Good evening, Women-Church!"

Many women spoke words of welcome in many different languages: *Bienvenue* ... *Huānyíng* ... *Willkommen* ... *Fáilte* ... *Benvenuto* ... *Oideyasu* ... *Bienvenida* ... *Mabuhay.* A Mexican American woman proclaimed Proverbs 9:1–3, 5–6, in Spanish and English, Wisdom's call to a feminist Eucharist:

> Wisdom has built Her house. She has put up Her seven pillars.... She has set Her table. She has sent out Her [feminist] ministers to proclaim from the highest places in the town.... "Come eat my bread, and drink the wine I have prepared. Leave immaturity, and live. Walk in the way of Wisdom."

An elder, wise woman lit a candle and said, "Let us welcome into our hearts the light of wisdom among us." A young woman lit a candle and proclaimed, "Let us welcome into our hearts the light of youth among us." Each table community lit a candle and prayed, "Let us welcome the light of community among us."

Twelve feminist ministers symbolizing the twelve tribes of Israel and representing the continents of South America, Africa, Europe, Australia, Asia, and North America sat together at a round table with a centerpiece of flowers shaped like the globe and unique place settings representing each continent. Two women representing each continent stood facing the gathering and blessed bread or drink in turn in a language of one of the countries from their continent. The table communities responded to each blessing by singing to the tune of the traditional African American spiritual "Amen": "We give thanks. *Arigato. Gracias. Merci. Xièxie.*"

Representing South America and holding tortillas, women prayed in Spanish:

> Blessed are You, Divine Wisdom, for giving us these tortillas representing feminist ministers in Central and South America. With them we celebrate the beauty and power of the discipleship of equals who live in the best of struggles from Argentina and Chile to Mexico and Nicaragua, from Brazil to the Caribbean, all throughout Central and South America. Feminist ministers in Central and South America, we bless these tortillas in solidarity with you.

Representing Africa and holding *injera*, women prayed in Zulu, blessing the *injera* in solidarity with feminist ministers all across Africa. Representing Europe and holding multigrain bread, women prayed in German, blessing the bread in solidarity with feminist ministers throughout Europe. One woman at each table was invited to hold a basket of many more breads and everyone extended their hands in blessing, saying together:

> Blessed are you, Divine Wisdom, Spirit of Sustenance, for you bring forth many grains from Earth. We take, bless, break, and eat these breads, acknowledging the beauty and power of our diversity as we celebrate feminist ministers and feminist ministries.

Representing Australia and holding a glass of apple juice, women blessed the juice in English, in solidarity with feminist ministers from the South Pacific Islands, Australia, and New Zealand. Representing Asia and holding a pot of water and tea, women blessed in Japanese in solidarity with feminist ministers from Asia. Representing North America and holding wine, women blessed in French in solidarity with feminist ministers from the Arctic Ocean and all throughout Canada and the United States.

The table communities were invited to raise their glasses, extend their hands, and bless these drinks together, praying:

> Blessed are you, Divine Wisdom, Holy One of Struggle, for you call us to live in the best of struggles. We take, bless, and drink these drinks in solidarity with all who are called to feminist ministry.

We blessed our food as a symbol of the diversity and common life that we shared, praying together:

> Blessed are you, Divine Wisdom, Embracing Diversity, for you toss together our distinctive personalities. Empower us to respect one another and share our diverse gifts as we celebrate feminist ministers and feminist ministries.

We talked at tables about the wonderful events and challenges that had happened during three full days of being together for the conference "Celebrating Catholic Feminist Ministries: A Women-Church Forum." We sent one another forth dancing and singing, "Ring us 'round O ancient circle, / Great Wisdom dancing free, / Beauty, strength and Holy Wisdom, / Blessing you and blessing me."[10] We danced late into the night to music played by a women's swing band.

Celebrating the Eucharist at a meal or banquet was common for the early Christian community. It was derived from the Greco-Roman meal practice of the time. This "Banquet of Divine Wisdom" reclaimed early Christian worship within the space and time of women-church. Feminist Christians are reclaiming these meals as Eucharist. We invite Christian communities to put the full meal back into Eucharist.[11]

Women at Meals in Early Christian Communities

> May the blessing of God go before you.
> May Her grace and peace abound.
> May Her Spirit live within you.
> May Her love wrap you 'round.
> May Her blessing remain with you always.
> May you walk on holy ground.
>
> MIRIAM THERESE WINTER[12]

First-century Christians, including women, gathered for their meetings at meals in the dining rooms of people's homes, in dining rooms at rented locations (Luke 24:28–30), at graveyards (Acts of Thecla 25), or at the homes of the poor and sick, for example, Simon the leper (Mark 14:3). Research shows that these meals were highly stylized banquets that functioned throughout the Greco-Roman world and in Judaism and early Christianity.[13] These meals were about much more than eating. They became a model for worship and organization. For Christians, they provided a place for the formation and transmission of Jesus traditions, for the reading of early Christian documents like letters and gospels, for telling and composing stories, for singing hymns or songs, for discussion and speeches, for drama, performance, and dance.

The ancient symposium or banquet model for the early Christian meal and for Greco-Roman meals in general suggests a two-part structure to the meal: the *deiphon* (order of supper) at which the food was consumed; and the *symposium*, an occasion for conversation, singing, music, and various types of performance.[14] The social dynamics of Greco-Roman meals included the values of community (*koinonia*), equality (*isonomia*), friendship (*philia*), and generosity (*charis*).[15]

Research shows that women were producers and transmitters of Christian tradition.[16] In the words of New Testament scholars Carolyn Osiek and Margaret MacDonald, "Women participated in all the activities of the house church in the first generations of the Christian era and the house church was the center for worship, hospitality, patronage, education, communication, social services, evangelization, and mission."[17]

What was Eucharist like in the early Christian community? A new paradigm emphasizes that the early Christian ritual meal developed out of the ancient symposium or banquet tradition. Early Christians gathered for a ritual meal because that is what groups did, not what Jesus commanded them to do.[18] Ignatius in the early first century used *Eucharist* to refer to a ritual meal that must have been a full meal, not a token meal of bread and wine only (Epistle to

Dare we believe there is power here not yet evident on the
surface of things?[23]

Feminists Renewing Eucharist

Together, woman, let us, you and me,
cook a huge dinner for all the hungry of the world.
Woman, good friend,
let us dream together of a new tomorrow.

ESEARIO SOSA RODRÍGUEZ[24]

Feminist eucharistic communities are emerging everywhere, dining together in the struggle, and renewing Eucharist. The occasions are many: women in traditional religious communities gathering at motherhouses or in local communities; women coming together at national and international meetings; women of diverse backgrounds and traditions gathering in each other's homes; women gathering for shared retreats and workshops; women and men gathering in inclusive communities; women, children, and men breaking bread and sharing a meal at the family table. Universally, these communities claim Jesus and the early Christian movement as heritage and life source.

What Are the Implications of Celebrating Eucharist at a Meal?

For the church community, feminist Eucharists at meals in the banquet traditions of the early Christian community put the full meal back together with breaking the bread. Feminist Eucharists invite the church to remember and reclaim the table traditions of the early Christian community.

For families and communities, feminist Eucharists reclaim the home, the dining room table, as a sacred place. Feminist Eucharists reunite spirituality and daily life. They invite families and communities to remember and reclaim the table traditions of the early Christian community, which have roots in the Jewish meal traditions of the Seder and Passover.

For Catholic women, celebrating Eucharist at a meal is the only option to actualize our baptismal call to priesthood since ordination remains closed to us.

For all Christians, celebrating Eucharist is a way to express and celebrate our feminist faith in community. This is a must if our faith is to survive and flourish.

How Do Feminist Eucharists Renew Eucharist?

Feminist Eucharists redesign relationships. Women are leaders in community eucharistic meal communities; therefore, relationships within the eucharistic community (assembly) become inclusive.

Feminist Eucharists uncover the leadership roles of women. Catholic women have been celebrating Eucharist publicly in our communities since the 1960s. In the 1970s we used the language "women of the church," and formed a coalition of the leadership of Catholic women's organizations named Women of the Church Coalition, which in 1983 became the Women-Church Convergence (W-CC). In the 1980s Elisabeth Schüssler Fiorenza spoke of the "*ekklēsia* of women," which I translated into "women-church." We proclaimed "We are church" and called ourselves women-church. In the 1990s women-church communities emerged and more women in rural areas and in city centers were called by Divine Wisdom and their communities to celebrate Eucharists. In the twenty-first century, women are sharing Eucharists at meals we create and celebrate with our communities.

Feminist Eucharists reveal that women's holy discontent with Eucharist leads to the transformation of the Eucharist. A company of women who gather regularly for feminist Eucharists tells the story of Jesus anew as they search for the living and life-giving Divine Holy One. Called by Divine Wisdom to holy discontent, we are using our gifts to reenvision Eucharist for women, the church, the interfaith community, and the world.

Feminist Eucharists challenge participants to put into practice the themes of the Eucharist. The following "Commissioning for Feminist Ministry" offers this challenge:

> Take feminist Eucharists
> To the city streets and country roads of the world!
> Let us go forth in all directions of the universe to bless and
>   to embrace,
>   To forgive and to heal,
>   To welcome and to sanctify.
> Let us go forth to the homeless and to the hospitable,
>   To the hungry and to the full,
>   To the thirsty and to the justice-seekers.
> Let us go forth to the elderly and to those who seek wisdom,
>   To the exiled and to those who understand freedom,
>   To the hopeless and to those who see visions.
> Let us go forth to church leaders who are blind to the needs
>   of their people,
>   To government officials who are deaf to the cries of
>   the poor,
>   To world leaders who are numb to the movements
>   for peace.
> Let us go forth to the women and to the men of every race
>   and place,
>   To the young and to the old of every neighborhood,
>   To the next generations and to their children of
>   every nation.
> Let us go forth in the name of Divine Wisdom,
>   The God of love and liberation,
>   The Goddess of power and justice.
> Let us go forth to break bread, share meals, and do justice!
> Let us go forth to renew Eucharist!
> Let us go forth to transform the world![25]

Janet Walton is professor of worship at Union Theological Seminary in New York City. Dr. Walton focuses her research and teaching on ritual traditions and practices in religious communities, with particular interest in artistic dimensions, feminist perspectives, and commitments to justice. Her books include *Art and Worship: A Vital Connection; Sacred Sound and Social Change,* coedited with Lawrence Hoffman; *Women at Worship: Interpretations of North American Diversity,* coedited with Marjorie Procter-Smith; and *Feminist Liturgy: A Matter of Justice.*

The Road Is Made by Walking

JANET WALTON

War, ever more of it; health care suspiciously limited for women and poor people; girls with no access to school; human trafficking and sexual violence too rarely prosecuted; people without jobs, potable water, and food: these are urgent concerns. The numbers are growing. Nothing is new. Tonight a group of women gathers for liturgy. The planners shape a ritual from feelings of despair and disempowerment. It is a time when we feel our dreams slipping into oblivion.

Feminist Liturgy: Claiming and Practicing

Feminist liturgy intends to shore up belief in possibilities in such a moment. It provides a space where everything matters: our dashed hopes, sadness, determination, joys, and small successes. We count on our liturgies to meet our day-to-day, year-after-year human concerns and public responsibilities with long-term hope bolstered by beliefs in one another and in a living God. On any one day we do not know what will happen ahead of time, that is, what the structure of the liturgy will be or what texts, textures, objects, sounds, or movements will engage our focus. However, we can be certain that whatever we use, whether it is the inner workings of an old radio to spark our understanding of how resistors work (in a liturgy about resistance) or photos taken after Hurricane Katrina by one of our members (in a liturgy about death and birth), we know we will experience unpredictable connections that will open a window for some fresh air and courage. We are sure that we will leave with determination to keep on taking necessary steps, sometimes small, sometimes big, to live justly. Feminist liturgy is a time to claim our possibilities and practice believing in them.

For years now—decades, really—women have been working to create liturgical experiences that deal with the world as they see it and that will, at the same time, uplift and inspire them. The future of feminist Christianity, as experienced in feminist liturgy, will not be in the center of Christianity but rather in many spaces along its edges. Feminist Christians do not rest in the certainty that exists in the center of Christian institutions (it has limited them); rather, we live in a different kind of certainty that is dynamic. We look backward and forward at the same time. We are leaving behind a model of life and liturgy steeped in kyriarchy,[1] where women have been told what to think and feel and do, where our participation is restricted simply because we are female. We are leaving behind everything in which gender, class, race, sexuality, or abilities determines who anyone is and can be. However, leaving behind deeply ingrained attitudes is not a one-time commitment. It takes years, even a lifetime, to learn how to resist images of inferiority and limited expectations and to discover God in consistently unfolding metaphors.

We go forward as a community with responsibilities to each other. We desire to be subjects of our liturgical actions, not objects or mere viewers. We do not prize one model of liturgy but rather multiple experiences with a variety that matches our human desires and the world's needs in the moment. Each liturgy has some characteristics in common: doing rather than watching, speaking in our own names, paying attention to spaces and to what is "in between."

Doing Rather Than Watching

Most inherited ritual forms focus on presentations and cognitive interactions. A few leaders speak. They assume responsibility for what happens. They create the ambience, choose the texts, write the prayers, select the music, preach to the community, and bless each person. Everyone else watches and listens.

Feminist liturgy, from its earliest stages in the 1970s, adopted a different pattern. While a few people prepare the structure for the liturgy (usually not the same people), everyone comes expecting to contribute to it. There are no mere spectators. Over many years of gathering month after month, the New York Women's Liturgy Group has learned that *doing* rather than *watching* can be exhilarating despite its unrelenting demands. We are practicing another way of living:

> ... enjoying the freedom of self-determination, setting our own limits, trusting self-approval;
>
> ... not expecting protection, but risking and getting around barriers;
>
> ... being prepared for opposition, and learning to live with fear;
>
> ... and having the courage to walk away from places that are secure but deadening.[2]

Doing implies interaction and communal exploration, listening, looking, moving, and responding. It is active, embodied, and sensual, not passive or primarily in our minds. "The road is made by walking."[3] At times we use processions, an inherited form, changed to meet our own needs. On Passion Sunday we carried posters of women who have risked their reputations and political careers to reverse injustices in the world. We walked to feel their power and our own power in our bodies. This expression of solidarity helps us remember our authority when we need to link arm in arm with many others to express publicly our resistance to injustice.

At times, doing is inspired by ritual objects. An ice sculpture was a focus for a liturgy on rage.[4] With ice picks, we chipped away at it until it cracked and melted. The ice was hard to break. It was cold on our hands. It gave way only from the constant chipping of each person. We reflected: We will not be frozen by inaction. We will work together to discover how to express our rage and use it for every struggle. We poured the melted water over primroses, not to resolve or dissolve our rage but rather to find ways to nourish ourselves in the midst of it with beauty found in nature and in ourselves. Feminist Christianity requires a lifetime of resistance, persistence, and imagination.

Speaking in Our Own Names

Brazilian theologian Ivone Gebara defines resistance "as an internal and external movement that invites women … not to accept a predetermination of their being," not to be submissive to others' desires, and not to obey and repeat.[5] This movement is within each person and it is also public, social, and collective. Resistance pries open a door shut tight by others with authority and power. The kyriarchal stronghold that feminists breathe is all around us. To resist is to embrace a process that moves from awareness to taking a stand and staying in the struggle. There are costs and rewards.

During a liturgy intended to gird us with hope, one of our members shared a story of resistance. This woman had lived temporarily in a city-owned shelter. There, she was identified only by a number, though all the people did know each other's names. When she accepted a job as a counselor for persons living with HIV/AIDS, she noticed the same dehumanizing attitudes. Spend as little time as possible with each one, she was told; they will die soon. She did not obey. She treated them with particularity and respect. She was rebuffed by the supervisor: that was not the practice in this agency. Her resistance and her persistence honored her clients, who are often marginalized in many venues, and she honored herself, too. Acting from her own experience and convictions, she did not give in. She spoke up in her own name, regardless of the cost, even at a job she needed desperately.

Not to be submissive to others' orders and expectations is difficult for many women. Many women are trained from an early age to sacrifice themselves, both their minds and their bodies, for the needs of others. Equally problematic is the stance that suggests women's bodies exist for the pleasure of men. Sexual harassment and violence, an egregious reality for many woman and girls, fall into this category.

Some years ago artist Elizabeth Schell planned a feminist liturgy to explore abuse and its relationship to Christian faith. She chose a biblical text from the book of Judges that recounted the story of an unnamed woman, a concubine, who was gang-raped. After a night of abuse, the men left her body on the doorstep of the host who had offered the concubine to them for their pleasure. Schell made a twelve-foot soft sculpture of a women's body. On it were names of people who were broken, sacrificed, and violated and also images of the earth as susceptible to abuse as well. The sculpture was beautiful, with vibrant colors and striking shapes.[6]

When the community gathered for liturgy at the door of the chapel we listened to the story of Judges. As we entered the main room, we saw the sculpture in twelve pieces placed all over the floor. We felt the brokenness of this body, of a woman and of our earth. It was not easy. We took time, generous amounts of time, for silence, for speaking, and for action. Breaking silence about abuse requires the support of one another. We tied the pieces together as an act of commitment, personal and collective, to remember and to speak out. It was a liturgy of justice and freedom.

In feminist liturgies in the New York Women's Liturgy Group we remind ourselves month to month about what it takes to claim what is true. Drawing from deep within ourselves, we rehearse speaking in our own names. In so doing we know God in the mystery of where we are living.

Feminist Christianity is not for women only. It extends to all who are defined by what others say about them, and to all whose voices are stifled by external and internal forces.

The season is Advent. The days are short. We depend more and more on generated lights. An artist created a lighted sculpture from five hundred syringes that she melted and stretched into a small sphere and wired with a lightbulb.[7] She called it *A Point of Light.* She works with a harm-reduction community that intends to reduce the impact of drug-related harm on injection drug users. She says about the artwork:

> I created this point of light to re-imagine/re-configure/re-fashion these very contested/criminalized objects (and symbolically their users) into something beautiful, light-generating, light capturing.[8]

To take in the complexity and beauty of *A Point of Light,* we looked at the piece in total darkness. The darkness was necessary. More often than not, doors are shut to drug users; they are marginalized by laws, by their addictions, and by stigma. This piece of sculpture invited them and us to see through drug addicts' eyes, to glimpse for a short time what it feels like to depend on something that, though as life-preserving for them as daily food, is prohibited in society. This sculpture symbolized darkness pierced by light. For a moment, people who lurk in the shadows of society were a point of light for everyone. Their struggles were visible. The care, respect, and determination of an artist opened the door. Drug users and their allies were in the same movement to honor each other as human and particular and important. Professor Elaine Scarry describes the action of seeing something so beautiful as a "radical decentering ... what happens, happens in our bodies ... we find that we are standing in a different relation to the world than we were a moment before."[9]

No one explained the meanings of *A Point of Light* to us. There was not one interpretation. Each person responded to it from her own context and experience. Listening to each other opened multiple layers of meanings that exist in the spaces between the object and our lived realities.

Paying Attention to Spaces

Feminist liturgy is not rooted in soil created from dogmas that each person must believe and confess. It is dynamic and fluid. It develops in varied spaces where faith meets justice, personal and global. The words we use about ourselves, others, and God were the first step in a new direction. Decades later it continues to be an ongoing challenge.

Writers and editors Casey Miller and Kate Swift published a small book, *Words and Women,* in 1977. In the midst of an editing project about sex education they saw something they had not noticed before: "The way English is used to make the simplest points can either acknowledge women's full humanity or relegate the female half of the species to secondary status."[10] They were discovering something others had pointed to years earlier. But now the civil rights movements of the 1960s provided a new momentum for a larger, continuous discussion of language. Words determined possibilities: "Language is not merely a means of communication; it is also an expression of shared assumptions. Language transmits implicit values and behavioral models to all those people who use it."[11]

Throughout the intervening years there has been sustained feminist attention to how language works in inclusive or expansive or emancipatory ways. Whatever the description, the goal is the same: to name people accurately and, in so doing, to prevent limiting them, and instead to cherish each one.

Though the awareness about language began with attention to sexist language, very soon it included attention to similar misuse of words that demeaned people of different ethnicities, sexual identities, races, or limited physical and mental abilities. The task of educating people about language is far from over. Although some churches have committed themselves to it, most have not. It is still common for leaders of worship to use male-biased language (*man* rather than *human beings*). It still remains acceptable to hear only male pronouns when talking about women and men. We still hear adjectives describing people negatively, as if to be poor or deaf or yellow, black, or an addict defines a person's possibilities. What seems so obvious—inclusive, nonjudgmental language—continues to be resisted vehemently.

Feminist Christians bring the same critique to language used for God that is also awash in maleness, as if God could be described adequately as Father or even by any one image. More often than not we encounter images and language in our churches that perpetuate an understanding that God is male. This is idolatry in its most formative expression.

As feminist Christians we thought that much of what we were learning and cherishing would be received by congregations and incorporated into worship with gratitude. Some of it is and will be. But for the most part, from what we have seen from the struggle to incorporate expansive and emancipatory language, the center of Christianity is fixed and certain and fearful. It is not a welcoming space for listening, speaking, and acting in our own names in response to day-to-day realities.

Honesty in variation, anticipation in uncertainty, hope in what is ongoing, shared responsibility for each other, God living in the mystery of all of life—all these describe more adequately and fully what feminist Christians believe and what feminist liturgies embody. Our future is made by walking—on the edges, in the gaps, into the openings—where resistance and persistence, imagination and action meet and embody a living God. Our future as feminist Christians is good, beautiful, hard, and demanding. Because it is true for us, there is no going back.

Victoria Rue is a theater writer/director, professor, and Roman Catholic woman priest. Dr. Rue works as a spiritual care counselor with VNA/Hospice in Salinas, California. She is the author of *Acting Religious: Theatre as Pedagogy in Religious Studies*. She is an activist working for the transformation of the Roman Catholic Church as a woman and also as a lesbian. Her website is www.victoriarue.com.

This Is My Body

VICTORIA RUE

The future builds on the past. Visions of the future of feminist Christian theology can be found, for me, within my past experiences and reflections on feminist theater and liturgy.

The Past

I cut my feminist teeth on feminist theater, which also happened to be my first experience of feminism. In 1974, I came out as a lesbian. For the first time in my life I felt the beauty of my own body. One of my most memorable learning moments occurred during a rehearsal of *Lady Lazarus*, a play I adapted and directed using the poetry of Sylvia Plath. It was produced in Los Angeles by the Mark Taper Forum, and featured Tyne Daly, Madge Sinclair, and Barra Grant. The year was 1976. The rehearsals were all about discovering ways to "make seeable" Plath's complex relationships to daily life, memory, birth, and family.

At one rehearsal, all three actresses were on their backs on the floor, having finished warm-ups. We were about to begin an exploration of Plath's long birthing poem. One of the actresses had just come from an unusual yoga class. She offered, "Let's do an experiment; stay on your backs, spread your legs apart; now, let's see if we can breathe through our vaginas." I remember we all exploded in laughter. Breathe through what? Our vaginas? This was a word we barely spoke, let alone breathing through it! *The Vagina Monologues* was still two decades away.[1] However, once our shock and laughter faded, we decided to take on the challenge. It proved to be the basis for a scene that we created collaboratively about birthing.

This story illustrates the bedrock of feminist theater and some of its key ideas. Feminist theater is all about bodies both in pain and joy, particularly women's bodies. It is also about women's experiences and relationships. Both feminist plays and the collaborative process of creating them help build community. Feminist liturgy shares these same qualities.

Fast-forward to 1994. I completed my doctorate in feminist theology and feminist theater and wrote a play about women and cancer that brought all my research and methods together. In the play, *CancerBodies,* women's spiritualities were reflected in their approaches to healing and in their relationships to their bodies.[2] The collaborative process of creating the play with actresses and a woman who had cancer built community inside the larger community of women's health.

The entire project was thrilling to me. I needed to continue this work. I wanted to create a similar nexus of feminist theology and theater, but to add liturgy using the form of the Catholic Mass. Working with Sister Monica Kaufer, we founded and created a feminist, inclusive Eucharist/Mass with twelve other women and hundreds of witnesses on the former site of the Oakland Cathedral in California. We called ourselves "A Critical Mass: Women Celebrating the Eucharist."[3] The site for our Eucharist was an inner-city park, the exact spot where the cathedral collapsed in the Loma Prieta earthquake of 1989.

We celebrated "A Critical Mass" publicly in this park, also known as "the snake pit," for six years. The park was inhabited by the homeless people of Oakland, and was known for drug selling and using. Before each Mass, we scrubbed and cleaned the park and fed the homeless. We put up flags of many colors along the entire perimeter of the park so that cars and people passing by would see something new was happening in this place of pain and poverty.

Our "Critical Mass," as we celebrated it, used gesture, silence, and the arts, keeping elements of the tradition and balancing it with "something new." As a Roman Catholic community we believed that by our baptism we are all members of the "priesthood of all believers," thus we were all priests, all leaders of the liturgy. There was no single presider at our Eucharists; we all were presiders.

The Mass opened with a spiral dance that charted the entire perimeter of the park. Once everyone spiraled into layers of circles at the park's center point, we sang "This Is Holy Ground."[4] We continued with the sign of the cross, done in silence. This gesture traced the cross and the four directions on our bodies and ended with our arms open wide, taking in the community and the wider world. This was followed by a silent gestural invocation to the Spirit based on the prayer, "Come Holy Spirit, fill the hearts of your faithful, enkindle in us the fire of Your Love, send forth Your Spirit, and renew the face of the earth."

Readings were not only from the Hebrew and Christian Bibles, but also from contemporary women writers. The readings were enacted or done in mime, or with puppets. Different kinds of breads and several pitchers of wine and grape juice were danced around the park by joyous women who placed them on a card table covered with cloths of colors from all over the world. We stood in a large circle, sometimes many circles, around the round table.

At the consecration, not only were the traditional words spoken by all, but they were also embedded within an improvised story that opened up our imaginations through specific details of color, sound, and texture:

> It was evening. Women, men, and children were gathered in an upper room in Jerusalem. It was Passover. You could

> hear the excited voices of many families in other buildings. It was a warm evening. The smells of the food from this gathering and from others around were in the air. There were many conversations going on. A child cried. Other children laughed and scampered under the tables. For a moment everything became still. Then Jesus took the bread, blessed it, broke it and gave it to the people gathered, saying, "Take this and eat it, this is my body."

At each Eucharist, the consecration was both different and the same because of the improvised storytelling.

Following each consecration, we enacted it as both a feminist interpretation and a testament to the mystical body of Christ. Turning to one other, taking one another's hands, and looking directly at one another, we would say, "This is my body. This is my blood." For this was how we understood Eucharist. It was an incarnation of the Holy in the Christian community, humanity itself, and in fact, all of life.

Our theology had to be wide since some of us believed that the bread and wine were the body and blood of Jesus, while others believed that the function of the substances was to point to the mystical body of Christ shared in community. But we all agreed on one point—a liturgy based on blood violently spilled was not our focus. We focused rather on the daily life of compassion and good works that our brother Jesus had enacted in the world.

The Priesthood

After six years of this joyous and visionary celebration, I began to see that most Catholics supported the idea of a priesthood of all believers and our creative methods to embody it. But they were not ready to transform their own parish life, or to stand up to the hierarchy and claim their church. At least not yet. There seemed to be several interim steps that were still needed, married priests being one. Another interim step would be gender inclusivity. Many women and men believe, as I do, that the ordination of women will help lead to the myriad changes long overdue in the Roman Catholic Church, which affect women's lives globally. With other women, I took that step, and was ordained a priest in 2005 on the St. Lawrence Seaway by three Roman Catholic women bishops. Since then, many have asked questions: Why claim being Roman Catholic? Why have women bishops? Why try to make relevant the problematic idea of apostolic succession? Why be ordained at all? Good questions, all. Since the Vatican does not recognize the seventy women priests ordained in the United States, and the thirty in Europe, and those who are to come through the Roman Catholic Womenpriests movement, we are illegal entities. This is exactly where I want to be. I do not want to be in the first batch of Vatican-approved women priests who will no doubt be cut from the same kyriarchal cloth as the men. Rather, as illegal women priests we have the freedom, the mandate, and the urgency to model a wider vision where the people take back their church. Hence our liturgies have many leaders. Our communities are powered by the decisions of all of those within the community. We do not want to just "add women and stir." We do not want to pour women into cassocks. As illegal women priests we must be conscious agents of change working to advocate justice and systemic change in our church.

Much of what we dreamed and enacted in "A Critical Mass" I have tried to incorporate into the Eucharists in which I now participate as a woman priest: gestures as prayer rather than words, alternative readings and the use of theater, shared homilies, the eucharistic prayer divided into many voices, saying to each other "this is my body, this is my blood" as a testament to the mystical body, offering each other the bread and wine. All of this is consciously done to decenter the role of priest and to involve as many people as possible in leadership.

One woman remarked that when she comes to our liturgies it is hard to tell who is the priest since everyone seems to be creating the liturgical experience. This is my goal: to empower, enable, and get out of the way. Yes, liturgy always will need leaders. But leaders do not have to be priests. The divide between clergy and laity, between first-

and second-class church citizens needs to fade away and ultimately be erased. As an illegal woman priest, this is part of my mission. Perhaps that is what I had in mind when I wrote the poem below, the year before I was ordained a priest.

When I am priest
    Eve and Lilith will be friends
    and Bible verses denigrating women, men and other
        creatures
    will be understood as historical relics
    and never used against us again
When I am priest
    sexualities will be celebrated
    the human body and mother earth will be seen as sacred
    and living in right relationship with all beings and with
        the planet,
    a discipleship of equals
When I am priest
    the definition of what it means to be family
    will be opened wide to the fresh air of all committed
        relationships
    no matter the gender
When I am priest
    there will be many others ordained as well:
    ordained to feed the hungry
    ordained to minister to the sick
    ordained to teach
    ordained to be artists in residence in each church
        community
    ordained to offer spiritual direction and counseling
    ordained to build houses for all
    ordained to be peacekeepers in our world
    ordained to build bridges to other religious
        denominations

When I am priest
there will be no kyriarchy
but only circles of voices seeking mutuality and
collaboration
there will be no Pope or infallibility
When I am priest
the Roman Catholic "world" will be comprised of four
geographic sectors
the Vatican will be only one of four
each sector will convene a college of cardinals and bishops
as well as
a college of the laity
each sector will gather four times a year
and the four sectors will meet as a body once a year
When I am priest
the stocks, property, jewels, and gold of the Vatican
will be given to the world's poor
When I am priest
the lion will lay down with the lamb
swords will be turned into plowshares
and the fields of the world
will abundantly feed the peoples of the world
When I am priest
When we are all priests
When there are no more priests
When we are....

The Future

The joy and the pain of the human body. Relationship. The everyday lived experience of women, children, and men—of all ethnicities and sexualities. Collaboration. Community. These are the feminist elements of my past. And these are the feminist elements of the future as I see it.

So what is the future of feminist liturgy and the arts? More silence. More music. More gesture. More circles. Fewer boundaries and borders. More mystery. More blending of Christian faiths, ecumenically. More blending of all faiths and the beauty of each vision. We must get beyond polarization and impasse.[5] We must get past barriers of ideology into the heart—not to exclude the head, but to remember the heart, for that is where we all meet. Not Jew or Greek, female or male, gay or straight ... but in the experience of the heart, we are all sisters and brothers of the divine.

A feminist approach to liturgy and the arts demands an unlocking of hermetically sealed positions that idolize, on the one hand, the impossible view of religions as objective or neutral, and on the other, a pristine belief that religions are untouched by social and political contexts. Instead, a feminist approach to liturgy and the arts is disruptive, questioning, shifting, and complex.

Provocative and messy, like life, the arts, particularly theater, situate religions and faiths into contexts with faces.[6] Challenging and unsettling, the arts inspire creative interpretations and points of view that lead to new visions. And for me, this is exactly the breath of new life that is needed in a feminist approach to liturgy and the arts.

Marjorie Procter-Smith is the LeVan Professor of Christian Worship at Perkins School of Theology, Southern Methodist University. Dr. Procter-Smith is the author of *In Her Own Rite: Constructing Feminist Liturgical Tradition; Praying With Our Eyes Open: Engendering Feminist Prayer;* and *The Church in Her House: A Feminist Emancipatory Prayer Book for Christian Communities.*

"The Ones Who've Gone Before Us"

The Future of Feminist Artistic and Liturgical Life

Marjorie Procter-Smith

Feminist Christianity is the embodied belief that the Christian tradition contains within it, alongside the story of repression and denial of women, the power of transformation that is essential to making the world a place where women can live and thrive. Feminist Christian liturgical and artistic life affirms that belief when it claims women's ritual and creative agency in the world.

Without memory, we have no future. Without seeing our past, we cannot envision our future. This we have learned, painfully, again and again. The story of women's contributions to Christianity has been forgotten, lost, distorted, and belittled, and has had to be searched out, reconstructed, reinterpreted, and defended against those who say women made no significant contribution.

So before turning to an exploration of feminist artistic and liturgical life, I offer some memories as a context for envisioning the future of feminist Christian life. This is the recent past generation of the feminist liturgical movement, speaking to the next and future generations.

The year was 1974. Women were just beginning to make our presence felt in theological schools and seminaries across the country, no longer now just a handful, no longer just preparing for subservient "women's ministries" in childcare, education, and missions, but in noticeable numbers and entering programs for church leaders. The women's movement in society had its echo in the halls of theological schools and on the floors of church conferences and conventions. Women in Christian communities were beginning to (re)discover our voices, and to claim our liturgical and artistic authority.

Songs for Struggle

I was a student in seminary during this time. As far as we knew, we were part of something new, something not seen before in the history of the church, something the male religious and academic leaders had not experienced before. We coped with being "the first" by organizing into groups to hear each other—Nelle Morton called it "hearing one another into speech"[1]—to learn from each other, and to support each other. We coped with being "the first" by studying harder, reading more, and asking questions—"Where were the women?"—to find what we could of our hidden and erased history. And for the sake of our souls, we sang. We sang songs we taught each other by ear, songs we sang from mimeographed song sheets, songs that circulated among us and our friends like good news.

We sang rousing songs to keep our spirits up:

> Well, we might come in a-fightin' 'cause there's lots that
>   needs a-rightin',
> we've learned a lot from livin' never taught to us in schools.
> If they say come in like a man, well they must not
>   understand:
> When we enter in the game, we're gonna change the god-
>   damned rules!
>
> Carolyn McDade, 1973[2]

Oh well, let's keep our eyes on the broad horizon
and move, sisters, move …

Carolyn McDade, 1975[3]

We are women, and we are proud about it,
we are loud about it, as together we stand.
We are women, we have a song to sing,
and we will shout about it through the land!

Doris J. Ellzey, 1974[4]

We sang plaintive songs that gave expression to our longings and hopes:

We are gathered here together in the presence of the Spirit
The Spirit that keeps breaking in our lives.
Well, we don't have all the answers, but we sure do have the
 questions,
We know that to create is to survive.
We're traveling on a road we've never seen before;
And oh, it's hard to know which way to go.
But somewhere there's a promise 'bout some distant shore
That those who seek will someday know.

Doris J. Ellzey, 1974[5]

There are times, we reach the edge of an opening, a coming
 through,
And we know the situation calls for something new.
There are times we cannot see what lies ahead, but still we
 know
We have a course that's clear, a path to follow,
And we must go (and we must go …)
And the ones who've gone before us
will show us the way.

> And the ones who follow after
> will welcome the new day.
> And the ones who've gone before us
> will join in the chorus when we do,
> When we make it through.
>
> DORIS J. ELLZEY, 1975[6]

We sang witty songs to refute the common charge that feminists had no sense of humor and to share a laugh at the foolishness of the world and especially the church:

> Oh, when the church runs out of men, they might give you an
> inch;
> But they'll forget you soon again when they're in a pinch.
> The only thing that bothers me is that I didn't know;
> I got my foot inside the door, that's how I broke my toe!
>
> ANONYMOUS

We particularly enjoyed performing a choral reading, "A Collage of Concerns," written by Reverend Tilda Nordberg of the United Church of Christ for the UCC Women's Liberation Task Force in the 1970s. The instructions recommend six readers and a bell ringer, to ring a bell at the repetition of the words *man* and *men*, or male referents to God. We made a small adjustment in these directions: we all carried pot lids and wooden spoons, and performed it thus:

> I believe in God the *Father* [banging of pot lids].... An ad in the *Christian Century* to recruit people for the ministry: *MEN WANTED* [banging of pot lids].... *Father* love [pot lids banging] is reigning o'er us, *brother* love [bang] binds *man* [bang] to *man* [bang].... Rise up, O *men* [bang] of God.[7]

This piece of performance art was a fine combination of irony, fury, and humor. I cannot say with certainty what effect its performance had on our audiences, but I can say that we who performed it found it deeply cathartic.

We shared these songs, our stories, these litanies, and choral readings, whenever and wherever we could. We shared them at Grailville's Seminary Quarter for Women in rural Ohio, and we sang them at feminist coffeeshops, and we shared them at YWCA meetings and women's society banquets. They were our common project, aimed at helping us and other women survive, celebrate, and share our common struggle.

In the process of working to recover and reform our identities as women in Christian tradition and practice, we sought the voices and visions of women artists and poets. Our imaginations had been constrained by the lack of history we could call our own. We were appalled and pained by the pervasive negative and exploitative images of women found in the larger culture and by the passive and bloodless images of women found in the church. The massive installation piece by artist Judy Chicago, *The Dinner Party,* a reimagining of the Last Supper as a feast to which women of history and memory were invited, became a feminist pilgrimage destination. The installation itself invited ritual interpretation, as visitors entered through a long passageway hung with massive textile banners bearing a poetic introduction to the work, then moved into the presence of a vast triangular table set with elaborately detailed ceramic plates representing individual women.[8] We were able to envision women, not at the margins of a central ritual act of the Christian tradition, but as honored guests and as creators of culture.

Our search for imaginative nourishment took us into the 1980s. The visionary paintings of Meinrad Craighead, especially as found in her book *The Mother's Songs: Images of God the Mother,* accompanied by Craighead's own poetic commentary, opened up the possibility of experiencing God as a woman in imaginative visual terms.[9] Drawing on her own life in a Catholic religious order and on personal mystical experiences, Craighead provided evocative artwork for Miriam Therese Winter's books of feminist prayer, *WomanPrayer, WomanSong: Resources for Ritual; WomanWisdom; WomanWitness;* and *WomanWord,* combining visual and verbal art in a feminist liturgical context.[10]

From the sharing of these songs, the performing of these litanies, the time spent together hearing one another's stories, the seeking out of feminist artists, and the cultivation of our own imaginations, we sought to create forms for worship and art that could nourish, inform, and encourage us and other women, especially the women coming after us. We formed the basis of the feminist liturgical movement, a process of reform that leaped the bounds of women's gatherings to inform the development of new hymn collections, worship resources, and biblical translations. We sought nothing less than the complete transformation of the Christianity we saw around us into something vigorous and viable for women's lives.

The feminist liturgical movement was, therefore, first and foremost a grassroots movement. Across the United States women were gathering in groups within and outside of established churches to "hear one another into speech" and to claim their ritual authority to create the worship their hearts sought. These groups were as diverse as the women who formed and sustained them, and some of these groups, with roots in the seventies and eighties, continue into the present. Our search for common ground among women placed denominational ties and traditional religious loyalties in the background, as we first explored what connected us with one another. But we also explored our roots in the traditions and religions that had brought us to that point. For some, those traditions remained vital, although in need of deep transformation. For others, to retain old loyalties was to be disloyal to our truest selves, and some women found they must separate, often painfully, from their past religious communities.

The movement also generated an academic movement, as feminist scholars of religion, sacred texts, and sacred rituals began to raise questions about the tradition and to seek the missing parts of the stories. The feminist liturgical movement itself became a subject of academic study, and all these new lessons were shared back with the grassroots movement that gave them birth.[11]

The great strengths of this nascent movement were the passion and creativity that we poured into the work. We were blazing a new path, we were imagining a form of Christianity with women at the center, and we were inventing as we went. We claimed all the freedom to explore that we possibly could, and drew freely from reconstructed matriarchal practices and symbols, even as we knew such practices were themselves largely reinvented.

But we learned our limitations as well. Because we were predominantly white, Anglo, middle class, and well-educated, our imaginations were too limited to incorporate other experiences and perspectives. Women of color, women of different classes and education levels, women with different abilities and commitments rightly challenged us and broadened the vision of feminist liturgical and artistic life, and taught us that liturgical and artistic reform and revolution is an ongoing process.

Next Steps

What, then, are the challenges for the next and future generations? First, it is important to our collective memory to preserve and honor the work of the past. In order to construct my remembrance of early feminist liturgical songs and rituals, I pulled out an old file folder full of mimeographed song sheets. As far as I know, many, perhaps most, of the songs and prayers and rituals I collected there and elsewhere have never been published and are at risk of being lost forever. In part, the energy and rage we experienced in the seventies and eighties grew from our recognition that much of our past had been lost. Even so notable and substantial a project as *The Woman's Bible,* published in 1898 by Elizabeth Cady Stanton and a partly anonymous revising committee, had to be resurrected and reprinted by feminist presses in the twentieth century and reincorporated into the history of biblical interpretation by feminist biblical scholars. We might wonder how modern biblical studies might have differed if the work of *The Woman's Bible* had been recognized as part of the history of biblical interpretation all along. And we might, therefore, also wonder what songs, prayers, liturgical texts, and religious rituals, arising out of women's complex and varied religious struggles and hopes, have been lost forever. What would our present liturgical practices look like, sound like, if these memories had not been lost? We must make every effort to preserve and pass on our history as creators of liturgy and art.

Second, it will be important for the next and future generations to claim their own ritual and artistic authority. It is to be hoped that this authority can be shaped and informed by the work of earlier generations of feminists of all kinds, but the future must be grown in its own soil, out of its own unique struggles and passions. What these are, or what they might be, is not for my generation to determine. We have done what we could, and however flawed it might be, we offer it to the next generation in the hope that future feminists will develop, improve, and expand it for blessing and strengthening those who come after. Undoubtedly, new forms of worship, new artistic approaches, new voices and passions, will give their own stamp to the work as they emerge. It is worth noting that much of current liturgical change and experimentation is influenced by conservative, male-dominated Christian traditions. Within the contemporary worship context, the issues of inclusivity and emancipatory language and leadership must be reiterated, and old struggles we thought were perhaps resolved must be fought again. In the excitement of new models of worship and ritual, it is easy to lose gains made in previous contexts.

Third, next and future feminist Christians will be challenged to continue the work done within existing religious institutions, in churches both locally and nationally, and in institutions of theological education. To shift the theological landscape requires massive effort on every front. While separate institutions for worship and study that are for women only serve as important and necessary sites to engender and nourish feminist imagination and courage, taking the work to the larger context is essential. Much of the work of the early 1970s is at risk of being lost, and some is undoubtedly already lost because it was kept within women's groups, albeit often for very good reasons. But it is often the case that what we do to survive in the short run is the opposite of what we need to do to survive in the long run. Disseminating our work, seeing it into print and in other widely available media, is the best remedy against loss and the best defense against those who charge that the concerns of feminist Christians are marginal.

Disseminating our work, of course, will mean challenging the status quo in churches at all levels and in theological education. This is inevitably a thankless, painful, arduous task, involving as it does dealing with those who view our work and our passions and our commitments as threats to the church. It is a task that requires patience to listen to and hear the concerns of those who differ, candor about what is at stake for all of us and for the church, and the courage to learn, change, grow, and persist. We can take considerable comfort from the fact that women and men, working diligently within the church, have brought about significant changes in many places: new prayers, liturgies, and rituals are now found in official denominational resources that reflect feminist concerns about language for God and for human beings and our mutual interconnections with the creatures of Earth. There are more women hymn writers represented in denominational hymnals and songbooks than ever before, and more hymns that bring a new voice and new perspective to congregational song. New prayers name new concerns and reflect struggles and petitions long omitted from public prayer. And these changes are, indeed, the fruit of the feminist liturgical movement. Those who labored hard for many decades to bring about these changes, modest though they may seem to us, deserve our thanks and praise.

Finally, it is essential that all of those of us who work in feminist liturgical and artistic fields bear in mind that it is in the nature of liturgy and art that they work on us, collectively and individually, at a slow and incremental pace. We must think of the long-term effects of generations of Christians, both men and women, praying and singing and seeing images of women as well as men as generators of tradition, as bearers of Good News, as courageous in the struggle for human dignity and the survival of this good Earth and all its denizens.

Part V

Feminist Ministerial Challenges

Ministers are the faces of feminist Christianity. To the people in the pews as well as to all who need pastoral accompaniment in their everyday lives, especially in marginal situations, feminist ministers are a welcome group. The lack of women ministers in the first millennia plus of Christianity was a serious problem that is only now being remedied. Gender alone means little without structural and attitudinal changes. But feminist ministers with the full panoply of antiracist, antiviolence, gender-inclusive, sex-positive, environment- and animal-embracing views are a boon to the whole community.

Ministers in virtually every denomination are being shaped by feminism to one degree or another. Most seminaries, graduate schools, and other training programs now reflect the impact of feminist scholarship and practice. In some denominations, the number of women approaches or exceeds that of the men entering the field, a shift that is reflected in the growing, if slowly, percentage of women in leadership. A complex mosaic emerges as feminist men and women shape the ministry of the future and deal with the backlash against their efforts.

Even those who reject women's leadership, who recoil at the notion of women preaching or presiding at sacramental worship, have had to deal with the reality of feminist Christianity. It is perplexing to imagine just how patriarchal holdouts make sense of the vital, exuberant, talented feminist colleagues they encounter. Whether in their own denominations or in wider ecumenical circles, feminist ministers are a rich resource for the whole community.

We explore this new reality thanks to Barbara Brown Zikmund's thoughtful look at the field as it shifts. Eunjoo Mary Kim explores the power of preaching a new word. Cynthia Lapp makes the changes very concrete through her Mennonite experience and the history of that church as women have gradually taken on leadership in their own ways. Eleanor Moody-Shepherd offers an overview of how African American women are living out the impact of womanist Christianity in one local (New York City) community. Mary E. Hunt explores the difficult terrain for feminist Catholic women in ministry and community. Finally, Meg A. Riley lays out signs of hope as feminism takes hold, especially among younger colleagues, and signs of dismay as the push-back against gains made by feminists gathers momentum even in the most progressive of denominations.

Ministry is a constant in Christianity. As feminists take on more and more responsibility and leadership, matters of language and images, preaching and counseling become increasingly differentiated to meet the pastoral needs of increasingly diverse communities. The real test is how structures change, how the very models of church that feminists create reflect the values of inclusivity and equality, mutuality and justice. That remains to be seen.

Barbara Brown Zikmund is actively retired in Washington, D.C. Ordained in the United Church of Christ, the Reverend Zikmund did interim ministry in several churches in Michigan and then spent thirty years in administration and teaching in theological schools: Chicago Theological Seminary, Pacific School of Religion, and Hartford Seminary, where she was the president. Dr. Zikmund is a church historian who specializes in the history of the United Church of Christ and the history of women in the church in the United States.

Women in Ministry in a Postfeminist Era

BARBARA BROWN ZIKMUND

Although I grew up in a progressive Protestant denomination where women had been ordained for more than one hundred years, I never met a woman minister until I was in high school. My Roman Catholic friends had a place in their system for women (nuns) who felt some kind of call to Christian vocation, but my options seemed extremely limited. I could become a missionary or a director of Christian education—spreading Christianity in some distant country or supporting the needs of children and youth in local congregations. Becoming a pastor did not seem to be an option. Although I did not know what my "call" was or where it was leading me, in high school I thought a lot about ministry.

For me and many people, ministry was male. Yet, in the 1950s there were not enough young men to meet the need for clergy in post–World War II suburbia. Denominations that had no formal prohibition against women clergy began encouraging young women to seek ordination, and denominations that prohibited the ordination of women were challenged to change. In my high-school youth fellowship I began to imagine the idea that God might be calling me to some form of ministry.

The 1960s expanded my horizons. I went to seminary and became one of three women preparing for ordained ministry in my class. A handful of male classmates and professors took me seriously, but many people did not. I read Betty Friedan's *The Feminine Mystique;* I absorbed Valerie Saving Goldstein's analysis of classic theology; I discovered Mary Daly; I watched Roman Catholic women religious reshape their communities; and I celebrated the dramatic vision of the Second Vatican Council. Slowly I became a feminist. Yet, I was not an ideological feminist; I was a pragmatic feminist. Right after college I married a man preparing to be a college professor. When I finished my seminary degree, I went on to get a doctorate, hoping that a PhD would give me more credibility in campus ministry. I had a baby and wrestled with nature-nurture issues and gender identity. My father died and I helped my mother reconstruct her life as an independent widow. In 1964 I was ordained, and after a few years serving local congregations I embarked upon thirty years of teaching and administration in theological education.

During my career—preaching, teaching, giving speeches, mentoring faculty and students, doing research, and writing books about the church and women—I have thought a lot about women in ministry. What is the future of women and ministry? I wish to lift up three things that I believe are shaping the future of feminism in the church:

1. During the past fifty years definitions of ministry and the meaning of ordination have changed, precisely because of the increasing numbers of women in church leadership.
2. The language of "feminism" is fading, but feminist values have infiltrated our society and are supported by most women and men—even when they eschew all connections with "feminism."

3. Formal leadership patterns in the institutional church (from the *magisterium* of Roman Catholicism to the celebrity clergy of megachurches) are less and less important to religious people in American society. New forms of church are emerging.

Ministry and Ordination

All Christians are called to ministry by their baptism. Yet, for thousands of years the church has also formally "set apart" (by prayer and laying on of hands) certain persons to be clergy (priests, ministers, spiritual guides, and liturgical leaders). Historical evidence suggests that these men (today we would say persons) were selected and charged to protect the purity of the faith and to pass on the heritage of Christianity. It has only been in the past several centuries that the issue of women's ordination has surfaced.

As a student of church history I have always wondered about the emergence of women's ordination. Why did the idea become so significant in the United States? History holds some clues. During the struggle for political independence, Americans were very suspicious of all hierarchical forms of governance. The new United States of America had escaped monarchy and replaced it with a democratic republic. Religious groups also began to claim religious independence from hierarchical bishops and elders. Roman Catholics and Anglicans in colonial America did not completely sever relationships with the Vatican or Canterbury, but they insisted on policies suited to their new setting. Some more radical Protestant movements actually rejected all formal titles and credentials related to religious leadership, even ordination itself. They quoted the prophet Joel's writing that God promises to "pour out my spirit on all flesh; your sons and your daughters shall prophesy" (Joel 2:28; Acts 2:17).[1]

In early America women and men worked to spread Christianity. Female evangelists were called "female laborers." When critics quoted the words of the apostle Paul suggesting that "women were to be silent in the churches" and not "rule" (1 Cor. 14:34), the female laborers came up with a creative response. They accepted Paul's prohibition of women "ruling" in the church, but insisted that the apostle never prohibited women from praying aloud, singing, witnessing, exhorting, and preaching *in public*. Inside the churches women did need to keep silent, allowing men to carry out their governance roles. Men were ordained to institutional headship and ecclesiastical responsibility, but women were never prohibited from doing the important things. One male leader rejoiced, "As long as women did not try to rob men of their rightful authority in the church, [women] could help [men] save souls."[2]

By the mid-twentieth century, however, denying women institutional headship was questioned. From the mid-1950s to the 1980s numerous denominations granted equal status and ordination to women. Soon large numbers of women were attending theological schools. By the 1990s, when I became part of a big research project on women clergy, surveying more than five thousand women clergy in fifteen Protestant denominations, we specifically asked the women "whether they thought that women clergy were changing the meaning of ordination."[3]

Many respondents said that was impossible. Yet, a significant number of women clergy were more likely than men to believe that women were changing the meaning of ordination—63 percent answered "yes." A Church of the Brethren clergywoman from California told us, "I think women in ministry are changing the understanding of power in relation to ordination. Rather than something conferred upon them, women are using ordination as a means to claim their power and gifts and use them in service with others. I think it is a subtle shift from power over [others] to power claimed and shared."[4]

During recent decades the ordination issue has become much more than a question of the status of women's leadership in the churches. It involves the basic ways Christians understand gender in church and society. It is not about taking power from men and giving it to women; it is about how people on all sides of the issue understand the relationship of their faith to modern culture. Denominational rules about women's ordination give symbolic messages to the world, pointing to (or away from) the "broad liberal agenda associated with modernity and religious accommodation to the spirit of the age."[5]

Some observers believe that the dramatic increase of women clergy during the past thirty years will force churches to become more egalitarian. Others look at the same data and predict a conservative backlash, because the ordination of women is so closely aligned with the modern liberal agenda. A third group laments that Protestant ministry is becoming a "pink-collar" enclave. It may be easier and easier for women to become ordained clergy, but it will not make any difference because women are simply becoming part of a devalued vocation that keeps dying denominational systems alive. A fourth opinion about the impact of women clergy celebrates the increasing numbers of ordained Protestant women, but remains cynical. There may be more women clergy, but they will increasingly be crowded into lower- and midlevel positions, and their impact will be little more than a token. Finally, there is a fifth response to women clergy that is upbeat and optimistic, arguing that clergywomen are reinventing the meaning of ordination for the whole church.

This final group points out that clergywomen are challenging the assumption that ordained ministry is only for ecclesiastically paid, full-time, lifelong male pastors of local congregations or churches. In many cases women are stretching the rationale for ordination and creating new forms of ministry. Women have less and less interest in breaking down barriers to get into a vocation shaped and still dominated by male perspectives. Instead, women are reinventing ministry for the future, refusing old definitions, and reshaping understandings of ordained persons.

The Future of Feminism

I was (and still am) a first-generation feminist. I grew up naïve and ignorant about feminist issues. I had what Betty Friedan called "the problem with no name" and I did not even know that I had a problem. Yet, as my consciousness was raised I found feminist ideas liberating. I can remember the moment when I "got it," and ceased using exclusively masculine pronouns and male metaphors to speak about people and God. I rejected words such as *brotherhood* and *mankind.* And even though Jesus told his disciples to pray, "Our Father," I was convinced that it was important to find feminine ways to speak about and pray to God.

At first when women spoke up about sexist language, we were told that we were being picky and that there were biblical and theological mandates requiring masculine language. Sometimes male clergy, committed laity, and Scripture scholars got defensive. Yet, slowly things changed. Feminists helped everyone see how new language patterns could expand biblical understanding and enliven worship practices. Often secular educators and media experts got the point before the churches did. Voices of authority, which had been almost exclusively white and male in my childhood, began to come from women and persons of color. As we enter the twenty-first century, many younger women and men do not even notice these changes because for them it has always been that way.

Language is only one expression of feminism, yet it reflects what has happened to Christian thinking. In a recent class, I created two small discussion groups (one all male and one all female) and asked students to respond to a brief essay about the theological importance of inclusive language. Most of the women did not like the question and did not think that inclusive language was very important. The male group, however, was not so sure. They appreciated the legacy of feminism. They wanted to relate ideas of equality and gender to their ministry. Female students resisted the conversation, insisting that they were not feminists.

Conservative evangelical Mary Kassian's recent book, titled *The Feminist ~~Mystique~~ Mistake: The Radical Impact of Feminism on Church and Culture,* laments the impact of feminism on Christianity.[6] The author argues that feminism started with a social and political agenda to obtain equal rights for women. Then it moved to encourage women to celebrate and be proud of the differences between men and women—emphasizing female strengths. Finally, in a third phase it has raised and reinterpreted spirituality and creation. Kassian writes, "Feminists are becoming difficult to identify, not because they do not exist, but because their philosophy has been integrated into mainstream society so thoroughly that it is virtually indistinguishable from the mainstream." She continues,

> We are entering into an era in which feminist precepts are largely accepted by default. This has profound implications for the evangelical church ... because those who adopt feminist philosophy—even unwittingly—are placing themselves on the side of a divide that will lead them far away from the Christianity of the Bible. Feminism is a watershed issue. It is to the evangelical church of the new millennium what liberalism was to the church in decades past.
>
> Feminism has failed miserably, and ironically it has exacerbated the very problem it set out to resolve. Instead of promoting a healthy self-identity for women or contributing to a greater harmony between the sexes, it has resulted in increased gender confusion, increased conflict and a profound destruction of morality and family. It has left in its wake a mass of dysfunctional relationships and shattered lives. People of this culture no longer know what it means to be a man or a woman or how to make life work.[7]

Kassian concludes her book by challenging faithful biblical Christians to reclaim the biblical message that men and women are created for different roles and responsibilities. She writes that feminism, by denying the complementary natures of men and women, has rejected the goodness and wisdom of God's plan for creation. Feminism has tried to name the world and formulate interpretations and boundaries that are independent of God the Creator. When feminists do that, according to Kassian, they are exchanging "the truth of God for a lie" and worshiping and serving "created things rather than the God who created them."[8]

I do not agree. I find Kassian's attack on feminism sad. I know that feminist arrogance exists, but I read the Bible very differently. I believe that the good news of Christianity opens windows and gives everyone equal access to divine love and fullness of life. Even the apostle Paul, who often gets trapped in gender stereotypes, writes that in Christ Jesus there is "neither male nor female" (Gal. 3:28). Therefore, whether we use the word *feminism* or not, we have been shaped by its message of liberation and egalitarian discipleship. Kassian asserts that feminism now dominates much of our culture. I agree. Our task now is not to deny its liberating insights, but to commit ourselves to promoting its values and potential.

What Will Become of the Church?

In my theology I believe that it is impossible to be a Christian alone. Individuals may offer private prayers, engage in solitary meditation, and make personal sacrifices, but being a Christian is communal. We gather around water and bind ourselves together in baptism; we meet each other at the Eucharist altar or around the communion table; we anoint and forgive each other in times of weakness; and we witness to each other in moments of commitment. If people say that they are good Christians but have no relationship to the church (to the community of the faithful), their Christianity is flawed.

I am also a church historian. I love the history of the church. I stand in wonder at the incredible ways in which the church has survived through the centuries. I find its history both awful and awesome. As I look ahead I am convinced that the dramatic increase in the numbers of ordained clergywomen and the creative leadership of women in theological education are reshaping the Christian church.

Yet, when I think about feminist ministry in the twenty-first century, my somewhat conventional ecclesiology begins to unravel. In my research about clergywomen and women leaders in theological education, there are many women who have "made it" by being as good as the boys, but there are also others who are seeing ministry in new ways and redefining the church. I don't begrudge those women who have succeeded in roles dominated by males for centuries. I take my hat off to them. At the same time, I am most excited when I meet or hear about women who are stepping out to challenge longstanding theological and ecclesial traditions, and even leaving the church (as we know it) behind. They are women who are breaking down the male hegemony of church leadership and the exclusivist claims of Christianity—imagining new ways to be faithful in any spiritual community that liberates (Christian, Jewish, Muslim, Buddhist, Hindu, indigenous, and others).

Female leaders in ministry are incredibly patient. When female presidents and deans in theological education were asked how they handle situations where people resist their leadership, their responses were inspiring. One told us:

> I say to them I recognize that there are passages in scripture that would cause you to question me, but I read that differently. However, I understand how you are reading it, and I don't want to shake that for you. I firmly believe that God is using me in ways beyond my imagination, and I imagine that's true for you—that I am way beyond your imagination of what women should be doing.... When my role is questioned I don't back off from it, but I don't debate them either.[9]

Feminist Ministry in a Postfeminist World

What will feminist ministry look like in the twenty-first century? I am not sure. However, I am convinced that women are pushing all Christians to 1) challenge longstanding sacred assumptions about ordination; 2) overcome fears of feminism; and 3) envision new types of faith communities (whether called church or not called church). In postfeminist Christianity there may not be any ordination. What is called ordination will affirm the ministry of all Christians, healing the artificial chasm between clergy and laity. In a postfeminist world the word *feminism* will fade, as issues once so important to feminists are mainstreamed into modern society and recast to embrace womanist, *mujerista,* and neopagan world views. And finally, in a postfeminist world the church will not be an institution or a building. The church will live wherever communities of faithful, humble women and men focus upon human need, honor the mysteries of life and death, and commit themselves to work toward a better world. This postfeminist world links compassion and responsibility. Will it actually come to pass? Yes and no. I may not live to witness such dramatic changes, but I celebrate the ways in which women's lives today point toward such a future.

Eunjoo Mary Kim is associate professor of homiletics and director of the Doctor of Ministry program at Iliff School of Theology in Denver, Colorado, and is an ordained Presbyterian minister. Dr. Kim has written numerous articles and has published three books, *Preaching the Presence of God: A Homiletic from the Asian American Perspective; Women Preaching: Theology and Practice Through the Ages;* and *Preaching in an Age of Globalization.*

Asian American Women and Renewal of Preaching

EUNJOO MARY KIM

The Asian American Church in Transition

I still remember the summer of 1991, when I was admitted to the PhD program in the field of preaching at the Princeton Theological Seminary. A renowned preaching professor of a Presbyterian seminary in Korea visited me and said in regret, "My denomination, which is one of the largest Protestant denominations in Korea, does not ordain women to be ministers. Women in the master of divinity program are only half a percent of the student body. Who, then, is going to learn preaching from a woman? Girl, you stepped out of your place!" Ironically, the professor's denomination began to ordain women as ministers of the Word and Sacrament just five years later, the same year I graduated from the doctoral program, was ordained, and became associate pastor of a Korean American church. If only the professor had eyes to see just five years ahead! Ten years later, in 2006, his seminary invited me to preach in its chapel, and the

Korean Association of Homiletics invited me as the keynote speaker to give its members, who were all male at that time, a lecture on how to teach preaching at its annual conference.

As my personal anecdotes illustrate, the Korean church has gone through many changes toward egalitarianism in its leadership structure during the past twenty years. Today, a great number of female ministers are serving the Korean church as local pastors and in other areas of the ministry. While numerous factors have played a role in changing the leadership structure of the Korean church, the sociocultural reality that Asian countries in general have been changing into more democratic and egalitarian societies, rather than remaining in their traditional patriarchal cultures, has played a major role in transforming the leadership of Korean and other Asian churches.

Just as Asian churches are following the trend of egalitarianism, so are Asian American churches.[1] This is because churches in Asia have a crucial impact on Asian American churches. The history of Asian American communities is relatively short, compared with that of European American communities. Most Asian American churches are composed of first-generation immigrants, who grew to adulthood in their native countries in Asia, and "first-and-a-half" generation immigrants, who only spent their childhood there. Although they live in the United States, they still keep strong cultural and religious bonds between their immigrant communities and their native countries and desire that their offspring inherit their Asian identity. Asian American churches have contributed to preserving Asian cultural DNA by teaching their children their native languages and unique histories, celebrating Asian cultural events, and nurturing their spiritual lives by calling ministers from their motherlands to be their religious leaders. In addition to this double-identity consciousness, the advancement of communication technology and transportation has allowed Asian American Christians to keep close relationships with churches in their native countries, which are regarded as role models as well as the religious roots of their immigrant churches.

Asian American churches, particularly those that belong to mainstream liberal denominations in the United States, have also been influenced by the denominational trend toward egalitarian leadership. It has only been since the middle of the twentieth century that mainstream churches in the United States have gradually enhanced women's leadership roles by ordaining them to be ministers of the Word and Sacrament. These days, mainstream churches have a growing number of female clergy serving local churches as ministers of the Word and Sacrament or working in the fields of various specialized ministries. Currently, about fifteen Protestant denominations allow women to be ordained pastors. Among them, the Presbyterian Church (USA) has about 30 percent of active (non-retired) clergy as women.[2] In the United Methodist Church, 23 percent of clergy is female.[3] The Evangelical Lutheran Church in America reported that the percentage of its ordained clergywomen doubled from 1991 to 2003, to 16 percent.[4]

Because of the impact of the churches both in Asia and in the United States, Asian American churches are changing toward an egalitarian leadership, though somewhat slowly. Twenty years ago, I was told that one of my Korean schoolmates who studied with me at Princeton became the pastor of a Korean American Presbyterian church in Long Island, and after his installation service he announced to his congregation and the Long Island Presbytery that as long as he was the pastor, his church would never ordain women to be elders or ministers, because women's ordination was against Korean tradition and culture. However, such bravado is simply history. In the case of the Presbyterian Church (USA), the number of Asian American clergywomen was nineteen in 2001, but by 2008, the number had more than quadrupled to eighty-seven.[5] Recently, I was invited to the Korean American Worship and Music Conference to preach four sermons on baptism and to lead preaching workshops. I was surprised by this invitation because I knew that most Korean and other

Asian American Christians had difficulty imagining a woman preaching and teaching about preaching. Such an invitation is still pretty untraditional among many Asian American churches. When I participated in that conference, I was amazed by the fact that many female church leaders attended the conference, and that they had a strong interest in learning about the ministry of preaching.

The old way of a gender-specific ministry based on a sexist mentality and a patriarchal system, sanctioned by traditional Asian culture and practiced by Asian and Asian American churches for a long time, should not be the standard for the present and future of the Asian American church. One of my most memorable experiences as a preacher occurred after I preached a Sunday morning sermon. A seven-year-old girl came to me and said, "Pastor, I want to be a preacher like you. Would you tell me what I should do from now on to be a good preacher?" She must now be in her early twenties, and I wonder about her childhood dream. Has her church continued to witness that God's grace in Christ appears equally in both women and men and is actualized by grace-gifts in their lives? Have her family, church, and larger society supported and encouraged her to fulfill her childhood dream?

Asian American Women Seeking a New Paradigm of Preaching

The history of women's ordination to the Word and Sacrament shows us that women in liberal Protestant churches have gained the right to preach, not without cost, but as the fruit of our foresisters' long and strenuous struggle against patriarchy within the church. Female leaders in Quaker, Congregationalist, Unitarian Universalist, and Freewill Baptist churches were among the earliest in the United States to fight against the sexist mentality in public and against the misogynous, male-centered hierarchy of the institutionalized church, even at the cost of their lives.[6] In the history of Asian churches, we find female church leaders who were itinerant preachers or evangelists without any support from their denominations or local churches, in danger of physical violence and social ostracism.[7] Their dedicated lives as preachers paved the way to women's ordination in the Word and Sacrament.

Nowadays, most mainstream churches in the United States share the privilege of preaching with women by inviting them to stand behind the pulpit on a regular basis as ordained pastors. The more women become involved in leadership roles, however, the more they feel that the traditional patriarchal leadership model based on hierarchical clericalism does not work for their ministry, because their experiences as church leaders are different from those of their male colleagues. For example, Asian American congregations consciously or unconsciously see in female pastors traditional feminine images of leadership such as mother, caregiver, conversation partner, or counselor, rather than masculine images of authoritarian ruler or autonomous decision maker, and do not grant female pastors the same authority and power that has automatically been given to male pastors based on their gender. Thus, female pastors need to use a different process to build up their leadership, with a different understanding of pastoral authority from the traditional one.

These experiences challenge clergywomen to rethink the concept of pastoral leadership in a new way and to seek to practice their leadership in more effective ways, particularly in relation to preaching. Actually, preaching represents individual pastors' distinctive leadership styles. It is the most important medium of communication between the pastor and the congregation. Through preaching, pastors regularly communicate spiritual and pastoral issues and concerns in public and provide theological and ecclesiastical directions to their community of faith on a personal and corporate level. Therefore, the search for a new preaching paradigm is one of the most urgent tasks for female pastors.

In the search for a new paradigm of preaching, it is important to note that Asian women's personhood is communal and that their traditional leadership style is to seek communal support and collaborative participation of the members. I agree with Boyung Lee, an Asian American Christian educator, when she says,

> Asian and Asian North American women take communal support for one another very seriously. Rather than abandoning communal personhood based on hierarchical patriarchy and then embracing the Western autonomous self as an alternative personhood, many Asian and Asian North American women seek a communal personhood that respects their being and experiences as women.[8]

The significance of communal personhood in the leadership of Asian and Asian American women gives insight into a new leadership model for the ministry of preaching.[9] While the traditional concept of pastoral leadership is hierarchical, with the pastor as leader and laity as followers, leadership rooted in communal personhood pursues a shared ministry. That is, rather than working alone to set a goal and accomplish it as their individual duty, pastors understand their leadership as communal and collaborative and encourage their members to participate in their ministry. Such leadership aims to create and nurture the environment of a shared ministry and equip the members of the church to fully participate in various parts of the ministry, including preaching. This new leadership model requires pastors to have the ability and skill to call forth their members and train them to actively participate in the ministry, as well as to have enough openness to share the ministry with the laity by creating a proper space for them to participate in the ministry, based on their talents and interests.

The leadership model of a shared ministry is not a new concept in the Christian church. In fact, the Christian church was first formed by means of a shared ministry. The Acts, the Pauline letters, and the pastoral Epistles in the New Testament provide historical evidence that the origin of the Christian ministry was a ministry shared between traveling apostles and local church members across gender, race, and social status. Such metaphors as the body whose parts have different functions (Rom. 12:4ff; 1 Cor. 12:12ff) and household utensils made for different purposes (2 Tim. 2:20–22) illumine that the primitive church understood the ministry of the church to be the collaborative work of all the members based on the variety of gifts of the Spirit granted to them. Church history also shows that the leadership of the early church was shared by the members through dynamic interaction between the clergy and the laity acting in a wide variety of roles, such as apostles, deacons, teachers, prophets, and priests, regardless of their gender, race, or social status. Preaching was also practiced as a shared ministry, as witness to the risen Christ, by the members.[10]

However, since the church was institutionalized under the Roman Empire, church leadership has belonged only to the clergy. Through the process of institutionalization, the church created hierarchical leadership positions and limited those positions to educated male clergy. The clergy-oriented ministry changed the concept of preaching from bearing witness to the risen Christ to giving instruction in moral guidelines, and considered preaching one of the most authoritative, male-centered practices of the Christian ministry. This shift to clericalism excluded women and laymen from the ministry and degraded their roles from preachers to passive recipients.

While most contemporary churches are still accustomed to the traditional model of clergy-oriented leadership, the movement of feminist theology has raised a prophetic voice against it. In her book *Church in the Round: Feminist Interpretation of the Church*, Letty Russell regrets clerical privilege and the exclusion of women from church leadership and proposes roundtable leadership as a way to revive the practice of shared ministry.[11] According to Russell, roundtable leadership presupposes that leadership is "the gifts of the Spirit among all those who share new life in Christ" and that power and authority are "something to be multiplied and shared rather than accumulated at the top."[12] Thus, in roundtable leadership,

> there are never too many leaders, for power is not understood as a zero-sum game that requires competition and

> hoarding in order to "win." Rather, power and leadership gifts multiply as they are shared and more and more persons become partners in communities of faith and struggle.[13]

Preaching as Shared Ministry

If we consider preaching as a way to the roundtable or shared ministry, how can preaching be practiced in an actual ministerial setting? Preaching as a shared ministry means a collaborative ministry between the pastor and the congregation. It can be practiced in a wide range of ways, from inviting the congregation to Bible study focused on preaching texts, to performing preaching as a group project, to evaluating it with the congregation. Designing a sermon as a dialogue with preaching partners rather than as a monologue by the pastor, or as an embodied performance including congregation members talented in singing, drama, dancing, or other arts, are just a couple ideas for shared preaching. For the effective practice of shared preaching, it is useful to organize a sermon formation and feedback committee, whose role is not only to participate in preparing, performing, and evaluating preaching but also to recruit participants who are interested in sharing their experiences of God's grace with others through preaching.

The practice of preaching as a shared ministry may be a great challenge for pastors who are used to conventional preaching. However, the new paradigm of preaching as a shared ministry renews preaching's nature and function. Preaching as a shared ministry is a communal calling, a calling to an interdependent and collaborative partnership with others to give witness to the grace of God beyond race, gender, and class barriers. This communal and egalitarian paradigm of preaching is grounded in the understanding that pastoral authority is not equivalent to control over the congregation, but is relational, in that God has granted authority to people in manifold ways "as abundant commodity" or as a gift to be shared with others to build up the body of Christ (cf. Eph. 4:7–12).[14]

The new paradigm of preaching as a shared ministry encourages people to participate in discerning the grace of God and to allow God's abundant authority to be shared with others. By sharing preaching with others, pastors make it possible for congregations to discern together what God is doing in the world "to make and keep human life human."[15] Eventually, preaching as a shared ministry brings forth the transformation of the community of faith by praying, studying, discerning, and witnessing the Word together.

Cynthia Lapp is pastor at Hyattsville Mennonite Church in Maryland. She studied music at Eastern Mennonite University and theology at Wesley Theological Seminary. Music is a central mode of her ministry. Social justice concerns shape her work in the broader community as well as in Mennonite circles.

Balancing Power and Humility

Feminist Values in Mennonite Ministry

CYNTHIA LAPP

Feminism is a Mennonite value. This statement would surprise some people and horrify others. The denominational leaders certainly would never admit it. Though it is not named, feminism has become integral to how Mennonite Church USA does business. With a long-term denominational goal of being antiracist and affirming women in leadership roles at all levels, the principles of feminism are present. While I may claim that feminism influences the church, the work of feminists is not finished, and in many parts of the church the work has barely begun.

When I was a girl in the 1960s and 1970s, I delighted in watching my father preach and my mother lead congregational singing in our local Mennonite church. If I imagined myself in one of these roles, it was as the song leader, not the preacher. But thank goodness history and the Spirit are not limited by the small imaginations of children.

My mother, Nancy, was raised in a conservative Mennonite church but became a strong feminist fighting against the prescribed roles of women in the church. She was derogatively called a "women's libber." She was told she was not a good model of a pastor's wife. She persistently struggled to make her voice heard, to have her gifts used and her womanly body acknowledged in liturgical language. After graduating from seminary in 1987, she was ordained for her work as a minister.

While the motto of the congregation where I grew up was "Every member a minister," I did not imagine myself a minister. While my mother was a model for me, I did not imagine myself a minister. While my feminist friends pushed me to consider ministry, I could not imagine myself a minister. I graduated from seminary, I led music, planned worship, and preached occasionally, but I did not imagine myself a minister. I lost my mother to cancer and I began to imagine that ministry was a possibility. Fifteen years after my mother was ordained, with my third child at my breast, I too was ordained into ministry.

Men of my father's generation could know that they wanted to be pastors. The church affirmed their call to ministry while they studied in college. For me, and for many women, the trail to ministry is more circuitous. Try out this career, find a partner, try out that career, go to school, have a child, listen to the voices of those around, and then—find your own voice. I do not want to discount a long and winding road to ministry. It may be a frustrating mystery, but the wisdom and patience, compassion and humility gained in wandering the labyrinth toward feminist ministry is a gift to the individual minister and the people whom we serve. I am grateful that the meandering way to ministry is not the only path available to women today. Today young women in high school and college envision themselves (and can practice) pursuing the pulpit.

It is not any wonder that for women the path to ministry has been circuitous in the Mennonite Church. The 1995 *Confession of Faith in a Mennonite Perspective* explicitly calls for the ordination of women and men.[1] Every year since 1996 there have been more women than men studying at Associated Mennonite Biblical Seminary in

Elkhart, Indiana. Yet it was not until 2007 that women were ordained in the Lancaster Mennonite Conference, the largest conference in Mennonite Church USA. This came only after a local bishop, Linford King, contradicted the decision of his fellow bishops and ordained Elizabeth Nissley and Janet Brenneman.

Of course, we must never assume that someone is a feminist just because she is a woman. Emma Richards was ordained in the Mennonite Church in 1972. (This was the second ordination of a woman; the first woman, Anne Allebach, was ordained sixty-two years earlier in 1910.) Emma approached her work as a pastor carefully. She went to seminary and was a missionary with her husband. On the one hand, she says, "I tried to preach well-prepared expository sermons, keeping Jesus central in sermons and worship. This included … using inclusive, nonsexist language, following guidelines of the National Council of Teachers of English, to avoid the awkward and ridiculous church language of the 1970s." On the other hand, she says, "In keeping Jesus central I found it easier to avoid faddish emphases that whirled around church and society, [including] do your own thing, women's lib and the civil rights movement, liberation theology and activist forms of justice."[2]

Even though Emma was a pioneer, she did not publicly make the connections between liberation theology, feminism, and her faith and work. In her mind, her woman's body in the pulpit was controversy enough; she chose not to challenge the institution with her words as well.

Though I maintain that the church affirms feminist values, the use of the term *feminist* is rare in public discourse. As a people historically committed to peace, Mennonites try not to rock the boat on issues that cause controversy. The use of terms that are controversial in "the world" is considered divisive in and of itself. Unfortunately, *feminism* has been one of those words. Even with the principles of feminism at work, we fear using the term *feminist* in the church to prevent conflict and to avoid being discounted. It is a contradiction.

One example of this phenomenon: In 1999 two books were published about Mennonite women leaders.[3] There was an implicit acknowledgment in these books that feminism was part of what it meant to be a woman in ministry. And yet at a retreat that celebrated the publication of the two books, Mennonite women spoke of the "F word" and were reluctant to name themselves as feminists even among other women church leaders.[4]

My mother's struggle in the church, Emma's approach to ministry, and the reluctance to identify as feminist all illustrate one of the conundrums that Mennonite women face. In an odd and bothersome way, in the Mennonite world humility is what gives a person power in the church. We are emulators of a humble Jesus. Leaders do not want to appear as if they have all the answers. Many pastors, rather than pushing their own ideas, wait for cues from the congregation or even the larger denomination. While "humility theology" as lived out in early Anabaptism has not been practiced for decades, the remnants are still present. We still look for a leader who is not proud or flashy, who is willing to suffer, and who carries power carefully.[5]

This kind of power might be described as an approach to team building and a feminist style of leading. It is a way to increase involvement and equalize participation in the local church. Giving everyone a voice can be done at the local level and was even done at the denominational level when formulating the 1995 *Confession of Faith in a Mennonite Perspective*. Local congregations discussed the proposed confession and reported their conversations back to the committee of theologians, who took their comments into account when writing the final draft.

This kind of shared theology and leadership is a gift. It is integral to how we have historically been church. The congregation reads and interprets the Bible together. The pastor does not have the final word on interpretation. In many congregations, the people are invited to respond with their own understandings and insights after the sermon is preached.

But there is another side. If not examined carefully, this humility can be a denial of the power a person does have, the power that is inherent in the position of pastor. Leaders can lead with a false humility that barely disguises the hubris just below the surface. Pastors may deny the power that has been vested in them by the congregation, the local conference, and the denomination. When we are not aware of the power we possess, it is easy to abuse that authority.

For women, this is a double bind. We are already taught, especially in church, that to be humble is our lot. It has been the role of the woman to serve and take care of others. We have been trained to see what others need and want. We are trained to anticipate the needs of others almost before they know them. So what does it mean for women who have been trained in servility to "rise above" their place and become "humble" leaders?

Women sometimes have trouble claiming their power without attempting to deny it or relinquish it at the same time. It is a good thing that women are stereotypically good at juggling. As feminist Mennonite ministers, we are challenged to juggle the power we have, the power we are calling forth in other people, and the power of the Spirit. As we juggle power, we stand with those who live in humility as enforced by the powerful: poor people, those with disabilities, immigrants, LGBTQ folks, other women. We work to eradicate racism, colonialism, heterosexism, ageism, all "isms"—all the while keeping a watchful eye, albeit humbly, on those who believe they hold the institutional power.

I can trace the path from angry, idealistic feminist to "humble" pastor in my own case. As a college student I headed up the Student Women's Association to help women find their voices as feminists. At age twenty-five I was asked to share my spiritual journey in a Sunday school class. I have little recollection of the occasion, but have been reminded of it several times over the years by the fathers of young sons in the congregation. I apparently began my story by saying, "I hate men." In a few years I moderated my feelings somewhat and married a man. Eric, my husband, and I were asked to tell of our spiritual journeys together, and the men, who had been so shocked some years earlier at my "hate" statement, waited with baited breath to see what I would say now that I was married.

Imagine my shock and surprise when ten years later I was asked to be the pastor of this same congregation, a group that includes women and men, boys and girls. Given my propensity to speak so boldly, it is only with humility that I can pastor this congregation where I made such a declaration. Men in the congregation have been gracious and forgiving of the youthful indiscretions in my speech.

On the other hand, I wonder whether my truth speaking is also a gift. In the Mennonite context it is unusual for a woman to be so forthcoming with feminism, to state unequivocally the struggle with men, male language, and issues of power. It certainly caught people's attention and it has not prevented me from being a leader in the congregation.

This, then, is one more thing for feminists to juggle: truth telling. I have been in situations where there is potential for great conflict. One of the things that helps diffuse the heat is to speak the truth with humility. As a feminist I speak the truth as I understand it, but I do not cloak it in mighty theology or proof texts from the Bible. I do not try to force other people to believe as I do or deny the experiences of other people. When we do not hide our own questions or processes, when we lead with humility and respect for mystery, the respect is often returned.

So what is a feminist minister to do? How can feminists encourage all women to recognize their own leadership, to step out and speak out, even while remaining humble? We need to find our voices as women. It is no longer enough for feminists to speak out only on behalf of women. We have done that work well. Now we are called to speak out and act with those who live in enforced humbleness—other women, the abused, immigrants, LGBTQ people, children; unfortunately, the list is long. And yet, in the Mennonite context, we are heard best when we speak softly and humbly.

As a Mennonite feminist minister, I aim to model the way in which I imagine the church can work. I want to be part of a model that sees connection and relationship between those in power and those who are imagined to be without power. Doing this humbly is a long and slow process. If I do not toot my own horn or seek publicity, how do I spread the word?

For Mennonites, Jesus is the model. He lived a humble, local life, and yet his refusal to support the power systems of his day is known and reproduced the world over. His ministry and leadership have inspired many to overthrow their enforced humility and live in chosen humility. As feminists, we remind the church of this great lesson, not just for women but for all whose voices are silenced and marginalized.

While we need to stay vigilant and faithful, we can also look around and see the signs of change. I grew up with my father as a minister and my mother as the song leader. Now I am the lead pastor, with a man as the associate pastor who is in charge of music. He came to the congregation precisely because he wanted to work with a woman lead pastor. Now after worship services the young girls of the congregation go to the front of the church, stand behind the pulpit, and pretend to be the preacher. My youngest son wants to be a preacher, not so he can lord it over others, but because he likes a good metaphor for how the Spirit works.

The Spirit is indeed at work. As feminist ministers, we are in good company as we work with Her and with each other.

Eleanor Moody-Shepherd is vice president of academic affairs, academic dean, and professor of women's studies at New York Theological Seminary. The Rev. Dr. Moody-Shepherd is a clergywoman who pastors a church that is part of the Presbyterian Church USA. She mentors women in the academy and the church. She is engaged in struggle against all of the "isms" that continue to divide and leave scars on bodies and souls.

Our Voices

Loud and Clear

ELEANOR MOODY-SHEPHERD

This is a dynamic time for African American women in the black church and in the academy of religion. Women in both of these communities continue to engage in conscientization, resistance, persistence, struggle, and self-definition.[1] The tumultuous periods of the 1960s, 1970s, and 1980s laid a foundation for the development of womanist thought that opened a prism through which black women could view and place their issues at the center of analysis and actions.[2] While womanist theory was developed and articulated by women in the academy, it quickly became a powerful force for change in the churches and in other areas of women's work and experiences. It is important to note that this self-identification as womanist is still primarily the language of the academy. Most of the women in the black church still do not fully identify with womanist theology even while they are using the language and strategies developed by womanist scholars and practitioners. In fact, most of them just make the claim that they are women called by God to ministry.

This essay focuses on the voices and observations of black women who are practicing ministry in the church and are affiliated with seminaries in the New York City metropolitan area. Women make up about 50 percent of the enrollment in the seminaries and more than 70 percent of the membership in local congregations. Some of the seminaries have heard the voices of women in the church and are offering more intentional curricula that help women debunk the traditional patriarchal reading of history and the Bible.

It is important to note that this essay is not an attempt at objectivity but an attempt to share observations and interpretations of these women through a particular set of lenses—lenses that were developed in the social location that theologian Jacquelyn Grant identifies as the "underside of history."[3] Dr. Grant's analysis of black women's position in society describes this social location as having a multidimensional character of racism, classism, and sexism. These women are still functioning in this space and are still struggling and speaking out of this painful location. They have recognized a new category of oppression, or perhaps they are including other people who are oppressed in a nontraditional way by heterosexism.[4] Heterosexism historically has been associated with opposition to homosexuals or same-sex-loving people. Women are reporting that they, too, are being oppressed by the hegemony of heterosexism. Their claim is that women who are heads of household, single, or divorced live their lives under clouds of suspicion; loaded questions of morality swirl around their every action. Their sexuality is held hostage by codes of abstinence and the "good girl" syndrome, the double standard by which the church and community expect women in the ministry to live their lives. Women are expected to live chastely until marriage, while men are free of such restrictions.

During the last decade women have taken some important strides and opened some portals in the sexist hierarchal structures in the traditional black churches. Several women have been consecrated bishops in the African Methodist Episcopal and African Methodist Episcopal Zion denominations. More recently, there was a highly publicized call of a woman, Rev. Dr. Leslie D. Callahan, to a historic black Baptist congregation in Philadelphia. Rev. Dr. Callahan's call is important because she is in the academy and now has realized her dream. She has always known that she had a call to pastoral leadership in the church, but the road to this call was littered with disappointment and tears. She reports that the church was the primary reason she went to seminary and graduate school. She and a growing number of women are ministering in both the academy and the church.

Rev. Dr. Callahan also represents a small number of women who have scaled the heights and ascended to the area in the church where women have been historically excluded. She and the women who are in these places are cognizant of the fact that they left behind many women who are still struggling against sexism in the church. These "left behind" women, and other women who are both participants and observers, must be cautious and avoid the trap that antiracist activist and writer Tim Wise identifies as "enlightened exceptionalism."[5] Wise describes this "ism" as existing when an organization holds negative stereotypes of a group and yet carves out acceptable spaces for individuals. There are still too many black women who have the distinction of being "the first" and "the only" one in their isolated and rarified position: isolated because many of us are surrounded by traditional power brokers who still have control of the decision-making process. This is not an attempt to minimize our achievements, but a reminder that we must always remain vigilant and remember we are still important to the development and empowerment of the women who are still struggling for recognition and agency in the church and other areas in the community.

Some of the women who are engaged in the struggle for voice and agency in the church are analyzing the ways that their foremothers used their gifts and achieved their goals through the periods of enslavement, Reconstruction, Jim Crow, and the tumultuous struggles in the fifties, sixties, and seventies. Their biographies or autobiographies are being mined for strategies and clues to be used to help us negotiate and continue to fight oppression that black women have faced since the beginning of this fledgling democracy. The published works of womanist scholars have made the life and work of many of the foremothers more accessible to women in the church and the academy. Harriet Ross Tubman, Isabella Baumfree (Sojourner Truth), Jarena Lee, Nannie Helen Burroughs, Mary McCloud Bethume-Cookman, Anna Julia Cooper, Ella Baker, Septima Clark, Pauli Murray, Fannie Lou Hamer, and Audre Lorde are a few of the women whose voices and legacies are instructive for this generation. Cheryl Townsend Gilkes posits that women's self-understanding is embedded in their "prophetic narratives."[6] She identifies prophetic narrative as the call to remember, retell, and relive stories that highlight the development of character, civility, and a sense of community.

Those of us who are connected with the church and the academy are in a strategic position to engage and observe women scholars from traditional African American religious traditions who can and do share their common concerns. For the first time, it is in seminary that they come into contact with women from different races, classes, cultures, sexual orientations, religious affiliations, and theological perspectives. They are in enviable positions because they are able to talk together in safe spaces, and share their stories of triumph, defeat, joys, sadness, and empowerment. Equally as important to the sharing of their stories is that they can share worship experiences and gather in spaces outside of their own communities.

Audre Lorde's work is particularly instructive. She reminds us how difficult it is for women who are seeking to gain agency and office in a world where they have been silenced by the church and a patriarchal culture that taught women through explicit and implicit language and misogynistic behavior that it was "not their place" to speak in the pulpit or perform cultic functions such as administer the sacrament of the Lord's Supper and baptism. Lorde, who was one of the early black feminist scholars, made the seminal statement "The master's tools will never dismantle the master's house."[7] This truism speaks to the fact that most women in the black church have only experienced the patriarchal culture operative in the church. Therefore, they *only* have the "master's tool" as their model.

Black women are not monolithic, nor do they adhere to their religious tradition as a solid, unified whole. Lorde's "theory of difference" helps us understand that the category of women itself is full of subdivision.[8] There are three categories of women who represent many of the women in the church and the academy identified in this essay: 1) women who have been influenced by ecclesiastical dogma and doctrine that hold that women are not called to ordained ministry;[9] 2) women who have also been influenced by ecclesiastical dogma and doctrine that hold that women are not called to ordained ministry, but who reject these foundational teachings and systems of oppression; and 3) women who are the proverbial "church hoppers," who have been members of several traditional black denominations and some mainstream, predominantly white, denominations.

The first category is women who have been steeped in their tradition to such an extent that their minds have been *colonized* by the patriarchal ideology and culture in society.[10] Delores Williams, a first-wave womanist theologian, suggests that these women have internalized their oppression and understand this teaching and practice as normative.[11] Mary is one of my mentees who is a member of one of these more conservative religious traditions. She represents a growing number of women who are enrolled in seminary and are being influenced by the curriculum and fellowship with women from more progressive denominations. She feels that the most powerful aspect of her church is that it is more than a spiritual center. It is an extended family network with members throughout the United States and congregations around the globe. Mary's mother expressed concern when she entered seminary, and she became even more alarmed when Mary accepted an invitation from one of her more progressive classmates to attend a women's retreat. This was a life-changing event for both Mary and her mother. For the first time, Mary actually saw women who had agency in the church. After attending this event, she admits to experiencing dissonance in the community where she had previously accepted her role without question. Friends at the seminary are asking her when she is going to leave her denomination and join a church where she could declare her call to ministry. Prior to these experiences she had never thought about leaving her spiritual family. For the first time she is waiting to hear a word from the Lord regarding her future in the church.

The second category is women who are in traditions where women are excluded or marginalized in the church. The patriarchal structure is supported and maintained by traditional gate-keepers. The gate-keepers are the women in the congregation who have internalized the notion that women are not called to ordained ministry. Women make up 70 percent, and sometimes 80 percent, of the membership in some of the churches. Nevertheless, in spite of these barriers, some are breaking through the "blood-stained ceiling"[12] and are being ordained to function with full agency. The question is whether they have access to office. Few are called to serve as pastors. The women who are called to the pastorate usually serve small churches that cannot support a full-salaried pastor. They are not alone on their journey, for they have developed supportive networks in the seminary classrooms and women's centers where their issues are at the center of analysis and culture. These courageous women are taking a stand by staying in their tradition and waging war against the hegemony of the sexist structures in the church. This group is what Rev. Dr. Katherine Henderson, president of Auburn Theological Seminary and a Presbyterian minister, calls "God's troublemakers." According to Henderson, these women leaders seem to employ a different kind of calibration and sense of proportion, realizing that the important thing is to start somewhere, trusting that through hard work and collaboration their impact will eventually grow.[13]

Debra is one of those pesky troublemakers who relocated to the South and became active in the local ministerial association. Some of the ministers attempted to exclude her from joining the session for ministers. She made trouble and was admitted to this bastion of male dominance. The disgruntled brothers attempted to put her in her place by quoting Scripture from the Roman Empire's household codes, found in the New Testament.[14] These bullies did not know that Debra had taken courses in seminary that equipped her to "rightly divine" the Word. She quickly debunked the oppressive interpretations that have held women hostage and robbed them of the power to declare and exercise their call. She called me at the seminary immediately after the session to report gleefully that she had roundly won that skirmish with the group of sexist pulpit bullies. Debra said that she understands that she has not won the war and destroyed the sexist ways in which these pastors think and function. She is prepared to continue the struggle.

The third category is those women who have been the proverbial "church hoppers." Many of them describe themselves as ecumenists because they have been members of most of the black church traditions, and some predominantly white mainstream ones. Even though they have not given up on Jesus, they have given up on the traditional church. They seem to feel that they have been betrayed by the female pastors of the churches they attended. They thought that they would have more satisfactory spiritual experiences in churches that are being led by women. Unfortunately, only the gender had changed. These women pastors are still using the "master's tools." Many of these disgruntled women are echoing the sentiment of Fannie Lou Hamer, a Mississippi sharecropper and an inspirational figure to many involved in the struggle for civil rights, who declared she was "sick and tired of being sick and tired" and organized a movement.[15] They are on the brink of planning and organizing a movement to develop space where they can worship and recover their sacred selves.

Finally, the Bible is central to the spiritual development of all of these women. Traditionally, they have been taught to hear and read the Bible through a patriarchal lens and interpretation. Women in the Bible were seen as either saints or sinners; therefore, the women in the church could not identify with them. The stories of powerful biblical women have been "hidden in plain sight." Renita Weems, a first-wave Hebrew Scriptures scholar, argues that the Bible has been adopted by black women through generations by their ancestors as the medium for experiencing and knowing the will of God. She also posits that the status of the Bible as an authoritative text within the Christian community is seen as binding upon our existence. The Bible has been used to both oppress and inspire women and other marginalized people.[16] Therefore, the women who are the subject of this essay have learned to approach the task of reading and interpreting Scripture with a new hermeneutical lens and are equipped with new interpretative skills. Armed with these new tools, they are able to locate biblical women who have made major contributions to salvation history. They are being empowered by the ability of these biblical women to create their own space, exercise power, and claim voice, agency, and office in the Jewish and Christian religious traditions.[17]

I am not sure whether any of the women from this study have worked out all of the details for the new ways they plan to live their lives as Christian women. I suggest, however, that there is a not-so-quiet revolution being waged by them and other women within the black religious community. They are working in their own context to make systemic changes in the relationship between men and women in the church, where they may all sit at the table and celebrate God's gifts together.

Mary E. Hunt is cofounder and codirector of WATER, the Women's Alliance for Theology, Ethics and Ritual. She is a Catholic feminist theologian active in the women-church movement. Dr. Hunt lectures and writes on theology and ethics with particular attention to liberation issues. She is editor of *A Guide for Women in Religion: Making Your Way from A to Z* (Palgrave), among many other publications.

New Feminist Catholics

Community and Ministry

MARY E. HUNT

The implosion of the Roman Catholic hierarchy over the epidemic of priest pedophilia and episcopal cover-ups means that Catholic women face many new challenges.[1] The clerics who have long excluded and demeaned women are now undergoing rigorous scrutiny. Feminists have long had ideological differences with Roman Catholic officials. Now, sadly, it is clear that some of those who oppose women's full rights as members of the Catholic community—many more than once thought—have engaged in criminal behavior or have covered up the criminal behavior of others. It is hard to overestimate how devastating this is for Catholics. As a consequence, feminist work for social and ecclesial change is being taken more seriously than ever as the kyriarchy collapses.

Catholic feminist theologian Elisabeth Schüssler Fiorenza coined the term *kyriarchy* (from *kyrios*, Greek for "lord") to describe literally the "structures of lordship" that underlie the Roman Catholic Church and other oppressive social structures.[2] Kyriarchy is the interweaving of sexism, racism, classism, heterosexism, colonialism, ageism, ableism, and other forms of prejudice and discrimination that form the backdrop of systems that oppress most people and privilege a few. Women, people of color, and same-sex-loving people are marginalized within the Roman Catholic community by structures—not just by people with certain attitudes, but by laws and customs. All that is changing.

The way forward is fraught and vexed lest women fall into the trap of cleaning up after those who have wreaked havoc on the lives, spirits, and bodies of millions of people. I am not naïve about how long it will take for the corrupt Roman Catholic kyriarchy to crumble. But the reality is that many leaders, including Pope Benedict XVI himself, have been involved in one way or another in a systemic and widespread problem. Some blame priestly celibacy, others mistakenly say homosexuality is the problem, and still others implicate the so-called lax sexual mores of the day. But what is obvious to those with eyes to see is that the entire ministerial and ecclesial structure of Roman Catholicism is exclusively male, rigidly hierarchical, suffused with secrecy and deception, and rewarding of duplicity. The system "works" because of the collusion of those schooled in obedience to law and authority, who adhere to codes of behavior that preserve the priesthood and the institutional church at the expense of children. This is the context in which Catholic women will develop and exercise our ministry in the decades and generations to come.

Catholic Women Are Church

Many Catholic women are studying theology and developing innovative ministries. Some are being ordained in the Roman Catholic Womenpriest movement. Others are engaging in ministries in the kyriarchal church system as lay ministers. Progressive feminist women are part of the women-church movement of base communities without clergy. Still others are getting ordained in more welcoming Christian denominations, but retaining their Catholic identities. Thus, Catholic women are taking on greater leadership in a variety of settings. But without substantive structural change, that is, more emphasis on small communities and egalitarian models of ministerial leadership, some women could end up acting like their male predecessors.

As a feminist theologian and longtime participant in the women-church movement, I am struck by how so many of the issues we have been raising for decades in Catholic circles—a male-only priesthood, a hierarchal model of church, celibacy as a requirement for priesthood, lack of democratic practices, objectification of and disregard for women, unhealthy teachings and practices with regard to sexuality, to name just a few—are coming into mainstream conversation. Now, more than ever before, the possibility of actualizing needed changes is upon us as the kyriarchal institution loses credibility with each successive sordid revelation of abuse and cover-up. It is not the way we would have wanted change to come, as the human price is incalculable. But it is incumbent upon feminists to make sure the same mistakes are not repeated.

When I say that Catholic women are church, I mean *ekklēsia*, which in classical Greek meant not a religious body as we know it now, but a political body, an assembly of those called forth to make decisions. As democractic practices have developed, the *ekklēsia* is all of us—what Elisabeth Schüssler Fiorenza has so helpfully called a "discipleship of equals."[3] By "church" I mean a vision for common life, both political and religious, that is forged by participation and by commitments. "Church" as the building on the corner where Father presides and people go on Sunday to fill up their sacramental tanks is gradually being replaced by house churches, small communities, and other settings where people think, pray, and celebrate as agents of their own spirituality. Feminists are in the vanguard of this movement.

The Roman Catholic Church is but one expression of Catholic Christianity. Orthodox Catholics, Old Catholics, Women-Church Catholics, and other such groups exist even though the term *Catholic* is often used synonymously, albeit in error, with *Roman Catholic.* The Roman model of church is hierarchical and dualistic. Its structure is top-down, with a small group of ordained clergymen making decisions for the vast remainder of the community, which is referred to as *laity*. Since no women have yet been validly and licitly ordained as priests according to the rubrics of the Roman Catholic Church, all women, including nuns or sisters, are lay. Likewise, most men, including men who belong to religious congregations as brothers (not priests), are also laity.

The lines of clerical power are so tightly drawn that even women in religious congregations, nuns or sisters as they are usually called, are not autonomous. They do not always have the final say on the leaders they elect, the use of their own property, or the ways in which they conduct their daily life and ministry. All of that is regulated by the male authorities from the Vatican.

At this writing, the Vatican has initiated an Apostolic Visitation of active women's religious congregations in the United States.[4] This is a grand-jury-like investigation of women's communities with inquiries into the women's modes of work and prayer and their adherence to kyriarchal teaching. No one expects the report to be laudatory. Mercy Sister Theresa Kane, in a conference with the National Coalition of American Nuns, observed, "Regarding the present interrogation, I think the male hierarchy is truly impotent, incapable of equality, co-responsibility in adult behavior.... In the church today, we are experiencing a dictatorial mindset and spiritual violence."[5]

In the 2010 U.S. political wrangle over health care, the nuns and the Catholic bishops found themselves on opposite sides. The bishops contended that the pending legislation could possibly include funding for abortion. The nuns, following the lead of the Catholic Health Association, read it more realistically to realize it did not. Any hint that it might allow abortion funding was more than mitigated by the fact that millions of uninsured people would receive benefits. The legislation passed. The bishops are licking their wounds. Catholics, and, hopefully, political leaders, realized that the bishops are not the only voices or votes of this large faith community. I hope that in the future the nuns will put their weight on the side of women's reproductive justice, but this was a step in the right direction to exercise their own agency.

There are many women in informal leadership in Roman Catholicism. Women function as members of marriage tribunals (where annulments are decided); as campus, hospital, and hospice ministers; as chancellors and vicars for religious in diocesan bureaucracies; as well as in parish ministry. But ultimate decisions on most fronts are still reserved for the all-male clergy. For example, in 1999, Francis Cardinal Law, then archbishop of Boston, forbade the group Massachusetts Women-Church to meet on church property because they favored the ordination of women. The women had no say in the matter; they had nowhere to appeal the decision.

Roots of Women's Struggle

Feminist scholars point to the active participation of women in the early Christian period. But it requires some imagination to piece together the strands of the narrative, because patriarchal influences probably kept women's participation marginal and news of it even more so. The witness of the women who gathered at the foot of the cross—including Mary the mother of Jesus and Mary Magdalene—is essential to the founding narrative of Christianity. Nonetheless, as kyriarchal Catholicism emerged, patriarchal customs dictated that women were not permitted to lead once a clerical priesthood developed.

Medieval women in religious communities, including Hildegard of Bingen and Julian of Norwich, were notable exceptions to the usual patriarchal pattern. They were intellectual and spiritual leaders whose scholarship and creativity influenced groups of women with whom they lived, as well as the Christian community as a whole. The Beguines were thirteenth- and fourteenth-century women focused on spirituality who lived alone or in small groups in Belgium and the Netherlands. They, too, exerted a kind of spiritual leadership, but it differed from that of the nuns in that the Beguines were not under vows of poverty, chastity, or obedience, and they were responsible for their own livelihood.

Catholic Nuns

There are now about sixty thousand nuns in the United States, down from a high of several hundred thousand in the 1960s. Their median age is about seventy-two, so major changes are ahead as groups shrink and disappear. Nuns (women who live contemplative lives in monasteries), sisters (women members of congregations who live active lives of service), or women religious (members of canonical religious orders), as they are known virtually interchangeably, took seriously the Second Vatican Council mandate to update their often medieval practices. Many changed from religious habits to clothes more typical of secular women. Convents emptied as women began to live in houses and apartments alone or in small groups. Some went to graduate school and moved into professions such as college teaching, law, theology, medicine, and social work, fields well beyond the previous scope of nursing, support for priests, and school teaching. Other women trained in pastoral ministry just like priests. They became pastoral associates, associate pastors, or coordinators in parishes that lacked a resident priest as the number of priests waned.

The nuns are process-oriented in their decision making, experimenting with consensus rather than fiat in the ways they handle their internal business. They include members, not only leaders, in decisions about where each one lives and works. They maintain close ties using technology and periodic meetings to replace the common daily life they shared in convents when they lived together in large groups. Whole communities embrace ecological living with style, turning their vast properties into models of green life.[6] Driving hybrid vehicles, raising alpacas, and other earth-friendly practices form essential parts of contemporary religious life in many groups.

Feminist Theologians

Prior to the mid-twentieth century, women's contributions to theology had been mostly from mystics and spiritual writers. However, with the rise of the women's movement, women's intellectual and scholarly leadership have made an enormous feminist contribution to Catholic life. Feminist theology reflects the lives and practices of people who take the well-being of women and children as a serious priority.

By the late 1960s, empowered by the Second Vatican Council (1962–1965) and emboldened by the women's movements, Mary Daly wrote *The Church and the Second Sex.*[7] Following Simone de Beauvoir, she argued that women were second-class citizens in their own church. No women had cast votes at Vatican II; some were official observers, but none had any decision-making power.[8] A few years later, Daly wrote her most famous book, *Beyond God the Father: Toward a Philosophy of Women's Liberation*, in which she argued that male hierarchy in the world is a direct result of a male-centered understanding of the divine.[9]

An avalanche of feminist scholarship followed. Catholic feminist theologian Elisabeth Schüssler Fiorenza laid the biblical foundation for new Catholic thinking about women in her landmark book *In Memory of Her: A Feminist Theological Reconstruction of Christian Origins.*[10] She contended that patriarchal power was so strong that even if women had been involved in early Christian communities, it would take "imaginative reconstruction" to know about them. Elisabeth cofounded (with Judith Plaskow) the *Journal of Feminist Studies in Religion*, which is the premier vehicle for scholarly publishing in the field.[11] Elisabeth's active participation in the women-church movement, and her insistence on feminist ministry rather than ordained clericalism, are important exertions of intellectual leadership.

Catholic feminist scholar Rosemary Radford Ruether trained as a scholar of the patristic period, in which the early church "fathers" did foundational work, but soon turned her considerable knowledge to contemporary ethical issues, beginning with birth control. She has written dozens of books, including works on feminist systematic theology, feminist studies of church history, the women-church movement, encyclopedias, and other resources for understanding the development of women's roles in world religions.[12]

Ada María Isasi-Díaz and María Pilar Aquino have provided insightful intellectual leadership from Latina feminist Catholic perspectives.[13] They have contributed *mujerista* and *feminista* approaches, respectively, with emphases on the role of local base communities in doing theology. They insist on the importance of daily life (*lo cotidiano*) as the starting point for theological reflection.

I have offered a lesbian feminist Catholic perspective, writing on friendship and women's struggles for justice as important focal points for theology.[14] Sandra Schneiders specializes in theological analysis of women in religious communities.[15]

All of these women, and many more, are feminist scholar-activists who combine rigorous intellectual work with concrete applications to contemporary life. They are critical of a kyriarchal church and are involved in creating new feminist forms of ministry and community.

Women-church

One such innovation is the women-church movement, a network of local groups, house churches, and women's organizations committed to developing a "discipleship of equals."[16] Women-church is an outgrowth of both the refusal by the Roman Catholic kyriarchal church to ordain women and the deeply felt need by Catholic women to act publicly as moral and religious agents despite exclusion from official church positions. In fact, their very exclusion has highlighted how inadequate church structures are for men as well as women, in that they are antithetical to gospel values of inclusivity and equality. So women-church aims to be an egalitarian form of community without rank or office, with full democratic participation.

The Women-Church Convergence is a coalition of more than thirty Catholic-rooted feminist groups that meets twice a year for networking, education, and activism.[17] Local organizations and ministries take shape in a variety of forms but always with women acting as agents of their own spiritual and political lives, whether as a house church or a national group.

The first large gathering of women-church was held in Chicago, Illinois, in 1983, at a conference titled "From Generation to Generation: Woman Church Speaks." Women celebrated the Eucharist, strategized about myriad issues, and protested against U.S. involvement in El Salvador. A second gathering, "Women-Church: Claiming Our Power," was held in Cincinnati, Ohio, in 1987. There, women made clear that they were not tinkering with the Roman Catholic Church, but that they were "women-church," the regularly convoked assembly of those who seek to live out equality and justice in continuity with the Jesus movement. The power women claimed was not an elitist share of the pie, but a commitment to transform structures of inequality, to create new structures and institutions that are egalitarian, participatory, and democratic.

The third time this "*ekklēsia* of women" came together in plenary form was in Albuquerque, New Mexico, in 1993, as "Women-Church: Weavers of Change." There women confronted the contradictions and challenges of racism and classism among women, discovering that it is not easy to make change, especially among ourselves.

The meeting held in Chicago, Illinois, in 2007, marked the twenty-fifth anniversary of the beginning of the movement with a conference titled "Celebrating Catholic Feminist Ministries: A Women-Church Forum." The feminist ministries were identified as political, community-building, feminist theologies, spiritualities for justice, and gender/racial justice, with women sharing their successes and challenges in each.

More than two decades after women-church began, the movement is mature enough to let the needs of the world, not the failings of the institutional church, guide it. Women-church has never been a reform movement trying to change a recalcitrant kyriarchal church. It has always been a constructive feminist force that tries to embody what it envisions. Members keep the justice focus sharp by prodding one another to explore hard issues including racism, reproductive choice, homosexuality, and economic justice. They have never been in lock-step agreement. But women-church has long been a forum for expressing a variety of views, finding ways to work together, making public its shared values, and celebrating the Eucharist as a source and symbol of common struggle.

Women-church is "catholic" in the most ancient and enduring sense of that word—from the Latin *catholicus*, "universal," and the Greek *katholikós*, "according to the whole." While not "Roman" in focus, the women-church movement is a good example of how women can and will lead differently.

There are no priests of women-church, even though the Roman Catholic Womenpriests group is an official member of the Women-Church Convergence. Rather, there is an acknowledgment of the priesthood of all baptized Catholics as articulated at the Second Vatican Council. There are many ways of worshiping in women-church, including, but not exclusively, the Eucharist.

Leadership in house churches tends to rotate among participants. Empowering lots of people to be involved is a goal in women-church. Still, there is much work to do to train future leaders, to recognize their ministries both within the movement and beyond (for example, to obtain state licensure to officiate at marriages without being ordained), and to instill in women themselves a sense of their own power. Women-church is a good model for the whole church.

Non-ordination of Women

The non-ordination of women is a major issue in Catholic circles, because ordination seems to be an obvious route to leadership for women.[18] It would be if women wanted to lead in the kyriarchal structures that currently exist, hence my worry that adding women to this model will result in more of the same problems and abuses. But the way is still barred and many women understand the dangers of being co-opted into such a system. Thus, for Catholic women ordination is but one of many routes to leadership, and perhaps not the most effective one.

The movement for women's ordination in Catholicism began in the middle part of the twentieth century when Mary B. Lynch and her friends raised the question as women in other Christian churches were being ordained. In 1975, when the first Women's Ordination Conference (WOC) was held in Cleveland, Ohio, women answered with a resounding commitment to new models of ministry.[19] An organization by the same name emerged from the meeting to foster conversation, training, and strategizing on how to achieve this goal.[20] WOC sponsored a second conference held in Baltimore, Maryland, in 1978, where further discussion of the issue included international voices.

Some women prepared for ordination in precisely the same way as men, including all of the practical training such as Clinical Pastoral Education, internships, practicums in churches, courses on preaching, and celebrating the sacraments. When women were refused ordination, it was clearly because of gender and not because of any lack of preparation. In fact, in many instances, women proved to be better students than men, getting higher grades and better evaluations on their pastoral work. Nonetheless, they could not be ordained—more precisely, they could not test their vocations—because they were biologically female.

Bishops responded to the growing shortage of priests in the U.S. by importing ordained men, "male-order priests" as I have come to think of them, from developing countries, including the Philippines, India, and several African countries.[21] Meanwhile, many well-trained women work in parishes, but always as pastoral associates. They are rarely if ever pastors in charge of the business aspects of parish administration. They are not allowed to celebrate the Eucharist or hear confessions, although many do so without permission or discussion.

The Women's Ordination Conference, and later an international coalition of such groups called Women's Ordination Worldwide, held in tension those who still wanted to be ordained in the kyriarchal system and women-church groups that favored a nonclerical approach to church in general. WOC long had a subgroup named Rapport that met with bishops about actually defying the Vatican and ordaining women.

In 2002, a group called Roman Catholic Womenpriests found several bishops to ordain a small group of women on a boat on the Danube (to finesse the question of jurisdiction).[22] The group eventually had women bishops ordained by male bishops. The women bishops have subsequently ordained all of the other Roman Catholic Womenpriests around the world in a series of ceremonies.

The Roman Catholic Womenpriests claim apostolic succession based on the fact that the original ordaining bishops were in good standing, although their names have never been revealed. They admit that their ordinations are not licit because canon law requires an ordained person to be *vir*, that is, male. But Womenpriests argue that their ecclesial disobedience is a way to change the law.

These women undertake a variety of ministries, including hospice work and leadership of small communities. The Vatican claims that the Womenpriests have excommunicated themselves by engaging in a sacrament that is prohibited to them. Only the Vatican can lift the censure. As the Vatican's influence wanes, the women's credibility grows.

Co-optation of Women

One regrettable dimension of kyriarchy is the degree to which, absent critical analysis, those who are oppressed can easily become oppressors. Three examples make this clear in the case of Catholic women. First, the National Council of Catholic Women (NCCW) was founded in 1920 with the goal of giving women a "common voice and an instrument for united action."[23] The group has become a mouthpiece for the U.S. Catholic Bishops. In February 2009, the NCCW ran a full-page ad against abortion in the *New York Times,* which they admitted was "written at the request and direction of all the Bishops."[24] Why can't the NCCW set its own agenda?

Second, it is increasingly common to find women functioning as official spokespersons for Roman Catholic clergy. Many dioceses have spokeswomen who convey the will and wishes of the male leaders. The United States Conference of Catholic Bishops has long had a woman as its director of media relations, as well as a woman who speaks for its Secretariat for Pro-Life Activities. These women are not to be confused with decision makers.

A third example is the Vatican's 2009 announcement of "visitation" of U.S. women's religious congregations. This is expected to be an investigation of why there are not more nuns and probably an occasion to tell the more progressive ones to return to pre–Vatican II habits and customs. The visitation is under the auspices of Cardinal Franc Rode, who heads the Vatican office on women religious. But it will be carried out by Mother Mary Clare Millea, ASCJ, who was appointed apostolic visitator by the Vatican, with Sister Eva-Maria Ackerman, FSGM, as the spokesperson. Women are investigating women. Feminist Catholics have lots of work to do.

Strategies for Change

Change is coming in Catholicism, and it is coming fast. There is widespread rejection, or *non recepcionis*, of kyriarchal teaching and practice. This *non recepcionis* happens when the faith community does not receive a teaching promulgated by those in authority. It is not an angry, bitter response of the disenfranchised, although it can appear that way. Rather, it is a legitimate and responsible way of participating in the governance of the community. "For a law or rule to be an effective guide for the believing community it must be accepted by that community," as James Coriden argues.[25] He goes on to say, "The reception of canonical rules by the communities regulated by them is an ancient and honored part of the Catholic tradition. The users really do confirm their laws by their own practice, as Gratian said.... The doctrine deserves to be restored to a prominent place in canonical teaching and interpretation."[26] The whole community, and not simply a few clerics, ought to be making the laws.

The Vatican does not appear to care what feminists think, despite the soaring rhetoric on conscience from Vatican II: "Humans perceive and acknowledge the imperatives of the divine law through the mediation of conscience. In all activity a person is bound to follow her/his conscience in order that she/he may come to God, the end and purpose of life."[27] This ought to be a guiding principle in organizing a community. Acceptance or reception of canon law, or lack of reception, does not imply governance by focus groups or exit polls, as conservatives would argue. It is the legitimate exercise of baptismally conferred responsibility. Feminists can and must say, "thanks, but no thanks" to policies and practices that exclude rather than include. New models of church include and welcome all without exception.

When asked if they need clergy, many Catholics respond in the negative, but all agree that they want ministers—people who pay attention to and respond to the needs of a community. Catholics need many kinds of ministers, but not clerics who are elevated above the rest in their status or decision-making or sacramental power. Catholics need leaders, but not hierarchs—people who will take on and carry out tasks for the community—who are animators, who are facilitators, who chronicle and communicate. The heart of the clerical problem is not a few rotten apples in the bushel, as the bishops have suggested in the pedophile cases, but a clerical structure that needs to be replaced.

Feminists are replacing hierarchy with shared ministry, which includes shared responsibility for the sacramental life of the community, for its economic dimensions, and for the solidarity of our Christian commitment, whether in education, political work, or caring for those who are poor, sick, disabled, young, or old. I suggest it is time to use new language—to leave aside the differences between clergy and lay, and instead speak of ourselves simply as "baptized Catholics," with the implication that all baptized people are priests according to the sacrament. It is time to leave aside distinctions such as "nuns and lay women" or "the sisters and the laity," because all women and non-ordained men are laity. We are socialized to a fundamentally flawed logic and the linguistic missteps that go with it. Such distinctions have no place in a discipleship of equals. Now that there is a growing cohort of baptized Catholic women and men trained in theology and canon law, we cannot be lied to nor defrauded by the hierarchy.

Baptized Catholics have the power to transform a seemingly intractable institution into a cooperative community. We are exercising this power in a variety of ways with slow but sure results. Power is meant to be shared, not feared. Catholic people do not seek to turn the tables on our beleaguered clergy. We seek to open the tables to all who wish to participate—even bishops—on an equal footing. This is the opposite of excommunication and interdict. This is an end to clericalism and the start of a church based on shared ministries.

Concrete Ways to Be Church Now

To be Catholic is to be part of a process, a two-millennia-long process of living out the challenges of ultimate meaning and value, of life and death, in the company of those who commit to love and justice, equality and mutuality after the fashion of the Jesus movement. Our feminist base communities, religious communities, and regional groups need to be models of democracy with full participation and committed, rotating, nonhierarchal leadership, welcoming and empowering all, especially those who are marginalized. We must recognize that priestly ministry is a function of baptism, not of ordination. Our communities can pool their talents and resources, connect with similar groups of both Christian and other faiths, and unleash what Catholic moral theologian Daniel C. Maguire calls the "renewable moral energy of religion" for global good.[28]

To go from a kyriarchy to a discipleship of equals will not happen overnight. It will require that Catholics take their time, talent, and money out of kyriarchal institutions and put them into new models of community. It will require that Catholics refuse to cooperate in their own oppression using nonviolent but determined efforts to change ecclesial structures. One easy way to do this is to stop inviting ordained male priests to preside at the Eucharist that rightly belongs to the whole community.

The move toward a discipleship of equals involves making common cause with those who seek a just world on the myriad fronts of social change where Catholics' energies are needed—for example, on reproductive justice. Many feminists who hold views in conflict with those of the kyriarchal church say simply, "this is what a Catholic looks like" when asked if we are *really* Catholic. We do so grounded in a spirituality of generosity and gratitude, in a practice of hospitality and solidarity, lest we replicate the flawed model that has oppressed Catholic feminists too often. This is how new feminist Catholics join other feminist Christians, and indeed all who are committed to using love and justice to remake the world.

Meg A. Riley is senior minister of the Church of the Larger Fellowship and has served the Unitarian Universalist movement. The Reverend Riley is the founding president of Faith in Public Life: A Resource Center for Justice and the Common Good. She has served on dozens of committees and boards, including the Interfaith Alliance, Americans United for Separation of Church and State, Interfaith Worker Justice, and the Religious Coalition for Reproductive Choice.

Signs of Hope, Signs of Dismay

MEG A. RILEY

In the late 1980s, fresh out of seminary, I had an instructional dream. "Embrace the best pharaoh," I was told. I took this as a sign to go ahead and take that job at the denominational headquarters of the Unitarian Universalist Association. The president at the time was a handsome, young, bearded man, a gifted speaker, a visionary for justice—the best pharaoh I could find. After all, what are denominations, really? They're a strange compartmentalization of the holy, a brand name for the nameless. To my astonishment, I remained at the Unitarian Universalist Association (UUA) for more than twenty years, serving in a variety of capacities.

What I have learned both reinforces and contrasts with what I have learned in dozens of interfaith settings. I have pretty much seen it all by now. So, I share my signs of hope and signs of dismay, with the thought that they have relevance beyond my small universe.

Signs of Hope

Here are three things over the past years that have made me hopeful about our visions and about our life together as engendered beings.

The Numbers

When my daughter was three years old, she astonished us when we were driving by the local fire station. "Stop the car!" she demanded. When asked why, she said, "I want to go see how many women are really in there to fight fires!"

We had been giving her the liberal line, of course: women do anything they want to, everything they want to. We had always carefully said "firefighters," never "firemen." Still, she was puzzled by the disconnection she was already experiencing between our rhetoric and how things looked from two-and-a-half feet high. Like good liberals, we demurred and hedged, saying we were in too much of a rush to count the women firefighters. Really, we were too scared about what she would learn in the counting process.

In moderate and liberal religions where women are ordained, there are high numbers of brilliant women ministers. Within the UUA, the number of ordained women surpassed the number of ordained men more than a decade ago. No search committee of any size church would consider only male candidates for ministry, although the largest churches still tilt pretty overwhelmingly toward choosing men. While the UUA has yet to elect a female president, women have been at every other level of leadership for decades. Other denominations with saner election systems have done even that.

The Development of Our Vision

There is an ever-evolving vision of who "we" are. When I ask young adults whether they identify as feminists, predictably, they begin their answers by informing me as to why "my" feminism is inadequate—inadequate to embody transgender equality, racism, global consciousness. I am thrilled to hear them. This critique is exactly what feminism is, and always has been, for me. I do not claim that I understood what I know now about any of these things three decades ago when I embraced the label "feminist." Needing to qualify it even then, I was a "radical feminist." But these young adults, demanding that we continue to evolve, continue to gain consciousness, and broaden our vision, give me hope for a feminist future.

Our movement toward multiculturalism is not smooth or easy, and we UUs are still predominantly Euro-American. Still, we are drawing people of other cultures who share our social values about gender and sexual orientation, and who are looking for a home that can affirm their religious belief in the inherent worth and dignity of every person.

The UUA stands fully for women's rights in the statements we pass at our general assemblies. Whether it's marriage equality, reproductive health, transgender equality, comprehensive sexuality education—we are there on the social issues. For us, LGBTQ rights and women's equality are comfortable resting places, even as we wrestle with issues of economic justice and immigration that some other denominations understand much better than we do. We do not split hairs the way Methodists, Presbyterians, and other liberal Protestants do when they say that gays should not be discriminated against in the secular world, but here in our church we cannot hire them as ministers. Or that you can be gay but you need to be celibate.

In all of the denominations' LGBTQ caucuses, work for transgender equality is growing, though it has a long way to go! The young, as usual, lead the way, and I am confident that this work can only move forward. The UUA, United Church of Christ (UCC), and others have ordained openly transgender people for some time now, and the leadership emerging there is beginning to gain critical mass to have impact.

Women have been on the cutting edge of insisting that our faith be less exclusively U.S. based and that we think about global religious values. A UU conference on international women's issues in 2009 drew far more participants than anyone expected. Even in a bad budget year, women still came from across the country to reflect together on international women's issues.

Strong Leadership

The vital question for any movement is this: Are there compelling leaders with grounded theology, communication skills, and vision? The answer within communities of faith is a resounding yes. The passion for justice fueling current seminarians is strong. Increasingly, younger people are attending seminary and taking the helm of our congregations. This is good. These are people who were raised by feminist parents. In a way they take feminism for granted because it is what they have seen all their lives.

The UUA sponsors an interfaith outreach program called "Standing on the Side of Love: Harnessing Love's Power to Stop Oppression."[1] We have created materials for people of all faiths to use in their local communities as they respond to instances of exclusion, oppression, or violence. Local leaders are grabbing hold of these resources and using them for issues ranging from marriage equality to supporting families torn apart by bad immigration policy. Using love as a framework is not only theologically grounded, but it is also a much more family-friendly way to engage in public debate. We are not arguing intellectually about what is fair. We are talking about what it means to be a loving culture.

So, these are very real signs of hope. Still, being a critical thinker, I always see things to be concerned about as well.

Signs of Dismay

Here are four things that have made me wonder, over the past years, about our vision and about our life together as gendered beings.

Growing Complacency

Sometimes the absence of overt or pernicious discrimination against women lulls us to sleep. We act as if we "took care of" sexism back in the 1970s, just as racism crumbled irrevocably in Selma, Alabama, in 1963. We forget that every movement for justice takes place moment after moment, day after day, year after year. One woman minister said to me, "I took a few years off [in the early 1980s] to get married and have a few kids, and when I came back, it was as if the women's movement was déclassé."

For Catholic feminists, the blatant sexist discrimination in ordination practices keeps the relevance of feminism focused and visible. For Protestants, with that blatancy lifted, the soft, blurry lines of sexism make it much harder to name and resist. I have, for instance, talked with ministers (women and men) who don't believe that women or children in their congregation are physically or sexually abused! It is as if our espoused equality of genders would render impossible any kind of power imbalance among our members. I have also had gay male leaders, numerous times, presume that they understand sexism because they have suffered from it, too. Yes, they really have. But no, that does not mean that they have a clue what it is to be female in this culture.

Losing Ground to Hierarchy

Somehow, we appear to have decided without ever talking about it that hierarchy actually is a good thing and that those visions of coleadership and mutuality from the 1970s are too time-consuming and don't work.

For instance, many UU congregations and institutional bodies are turning to "policy governance" as a guiding tool for how to work effectively (key word: *effectively*). "Policy governance" comes from the corporate world, and it works to tell people their roles and responsibilities in a clear and specific way. I am not opposed to it. But I am, honestly, appalled by the absolute lack of conversation about the theological assumptions about this or any other governance structure. I am not an enemy of functional hierarchies, and there are countless occasions when I have longed for *someone* to be in charge and tell a floundering group what to do. But I also know that corporations are in no way my source of spiritual revelation, and indeed are the source of much of the pain and suffering in the world.

So what I wonder about in this move to policy governance is: Where are people talking about how it impacts historically marginalized people, including women? Where is the conversation about how it reflects or doesn't reflect our espoused theology? Where is the outcry that these conversations are *not* happening? Where is the conversation about models of leadership that come from other places, including from historically marginalized people—women, communities of color, young people? Why are we not beginning by looking to their wisdom?

Another hierarchical movement afoot in the UUA is the desire by the senior ministers of large churches—remember, the ones that are still predominantly male—to have more hierarchical structure *within* the congregation, where the senior minister is boss and can hire and fire all others. Traditionally, within our polity, all ministers are called by their congregation, and serve as covenanted with that congregation. Over the years this has led to some triangulation in churches and serious problems when the various ministers do not get along. However, it has also led to some thriving ministries, where the leadership is mutually supportive. The move to short-circuit the covenantal process and install a more corporate model breaks my heart. I do not know where this desire will lead, but I hope that the covenantal model will not be surrendered without a serious fight. If it is, women (more often than not serving in non-senior roles in the largest churches) will lose a great deal of autonomy and power.

Silencing Ourselves

Many of us, myself included, are still (again?) publicly protecting leaders who engage in sexist behavior, fearful that we will only do damage to the larger movement (ourselves?) if we call them out. Many stories are not in this anthology for that reason, not only from my denomination but from every other, as well as from interfaith movements!

Women tell these stories to each other. We laugh, we cry, and we rage about them. We find each other; we learn whom we can trust; we create subcultures on the margins of organizations driven by predominantly male egomaniacs. We meet at the bar outside the hall where the "spiritual leader" gathers thousands. We talk from bathroom stall to bathroom stall.

I remember, some time ago, calling a queer leader in another denomination to describe an atrocious encounter I had with several of his folks about homophobia. Did he want me, I asked, to name this experience publicly? As an outsider, I could do so. Sadly, he told me that the people I named were "some of the best" and that for me to describe publicly what they had done (over the edge of atrocious, believe me!) would only set back his LGBTQ caucus's bid for respect. So, out of respect for his hard work, I held my tongue publicly. One more story for the late-night café.

Recently, when a woman colleague challenged a male leader about an overtly sexist decision he had made, she was told by him that "no one under sixty really cares about that anymore." She has not publicly named his behavior to find out if that is true; she needs her job and is not sure that support is there for her. Even if she did not need her job, she needs for his ministry to be a success. We are a small group; we do not want to fight publicly. She waited for the outcry that his obvious, public sexist move would bring up. Not a peep. Is it that no one is watching? Are we all too busy? Do we all presume it is someone else's problem?

Of course, this lack of calling out is not limited to sexism—feminism is inseparable from racism, homophobia, ableism, and other forms of oppression. But how do we hold one another accountable? Where are the accountability mechanisms? In the UUA, there are at least denominational offices in place related to racial diversity and LGBTQ equality. We have someone in the Washington, D.C., office doing advocacy for women's equality. We have a staff person who handles lapses of what we euphemistically call "right relationship," which is to say sexually inappropriate behavior by ministers. But for decades there has not been a staff person specifically addressing the spiritual needs of women within the denomination. Even the volunteer committees have been dismantled over the years.

Losing Urgency

There is a lack of depth, focus, or momentum of feminist theology and praxis within Unitarian Universalism.

Our religious movement has some urgency about gender roles for our young people. Almost all of our congregations use the curriculum "Our Whole Lives," which we cocreated with the United Church of Christ to explicitly address gender equality, self-esteem, body image, and other specific issues for children and youth.[2]

There are congregations of all mainstream denominations that are committed to self-study and to welcoming people of all sexual orientations, and to a lesser degree, people of all gender orientations, into their midst. These churches create teen drop-in centers, engage in legislative advocacy, and create communities where gay, lesbian, and straight people mingle easily. The UUA's work for marriage equality on both a state and a federal level is probably the most consistent and compelling work I have seen our ministers engage in, because it touches them where they live. This work is always done in interfaith coalitions that include Protestants, Jews, and progressive Catholics and evangelicals. Some ministers even engage in all-options pregnancy counseling for women, and support local or statewide reproductive health organizations.

But little of this activism includes deep reflection about the theological values at work in either sexism or antisexism. Work for marriage equality, for instance, does not often ground itself in theological reflection about what holy partnership looks like, and how marriage has affected women throughout history. Rather, it begins and ends with the liberal premise "Equal is equal."

I have been told by women ministers that they do not preach about feminism at all because they are labeled as "strident" if they do so. One Jungian told me, "I figure I am already representing the mother to my parishioners—if I talk feminism, they will hear me as the scolding mother and I will lose them!"

Of course, social justice work in all congregations tends more to social service—soup kitchens and after-school tutoring—than it does to deep analysis. Still, I see churches of many denominations focusing intentionally on immigration, peace, homelessness, and many other issues without ever explicitly analyzing what these have to do with women.

It is a deep privilege for me to be in a position of leadership in the religious world at this time. There is no other time in history I can imagine where so much has been created and handed down to feminist leaders. I only hope we are worthy of this inheritance! Mary Daly's death made me realize that I have not been explicit enough with the young adults I mentor about how much feminist theology called me into my life of faith and has nurtured me during these past twenty-five years. Many of them have never read her works or have only heard criticisms about her.

There is much to be said about how we can learn from one another and how, together, we might be a stronger force for transformation than any of us can be in our own congregations, communities, or denominations. It has been the company of beloved friends, colleagues, mentors, and even challengers of all faiths that has made my work so rich and energizing all these years. May the coming years bring equal opportunity for creativity, vision, and movement toward that beloved circle of equality and mutuality that we all desire.

Conclusion

Strengthening Our Resolve, Moving Ever Forward

New feminist Christianity is having an important impact on both the Christian churches and the world at large. It is a way of talking about how women's (and some men's) lives have changed because they refuse to tolerate the limits of kyriarchal oppression and have instead committed to actualize justice and equality in social and ecclesial life. Much work remains to be done. We conclude with a few suggestions, aware that more will emerge from the reading of this text.

Theology is imaginative activity. Many more feminist Christian theological visions need to be formulated and articulated. Womanist and Native American visions, for example, need to be added to the collection here. An international volume similar to this one is warranted in order to see the big picture. Children's stories and drawings are an untapped source for feminist theological reflection. Interreligious work lies ahead with feminist Buddhists, feminist Jews, feminist Muslims, and others engaging in direct conversation with feminist Christians. We may well be the last generation that does any theological work within a single religious tradition. In fact, we hope we are.

Scriptural work is still in its early stages despite the remarkable depth and breadth of the current offerings. Again, womanist perspectives are crucial. Feminist bibliodrama needs exploration. Latina feminists' Bible study methods remain to be tried in settings other than Latin America so that many communities of believers can interact creatively with texts. Postcolonial feminist scholars have their hands full as they train their insights on work that has profoundly shaped the Christian tradition as oppressive.

Ethical work is similarly sketchy thus far in feminist Christianity. Despite the widespread use of feminist theo-ethical reflection (for example, on abortion), huge swaths of ethical terrain remain almost untouched. Feminist work on economics and the environment are two areas that beg attention. Good sexuality beyond the gender binaries remains a moral mystery. Health care, employment, and housing are all topics that feminists address in the marketplace but few tackle in the academy. Animal well-being is a feminist topic for which feminist theological reflection is still wanting. And there is never enough work on violence to eradicate it.

The liturgical and artistic doors are only beginning to open in feminist Christianity. While the work done by scholars and specialists is impressive, precious little of it has filtered into the pews. This is largely due to active resistance by those who understand, quite rightly, that what people do is far more important than what they say, that how people pray says a great deal about them. So there is strategic work to do here, as in every area of feminist Christianity, in spreading the word, integrating the achievements, and sharing the wealth of ideas.

Feminist ministers and ministry students are one large audience for this book. They have their work cut out for them as the backlash against gains made by pioneers and early practitioners grows. It is not easy to be a feminist today, to use the "F word" without apology. Nor is it always as important to name a feminist starting point as it is to live out a feminist vision of accompaniment and solidarity in ministry. Still, structural changes are necessary to incorporate feminist values of inclusivity and mutuality in churches, communities, and the broader world. Until that is done, we will insist on naming the feminist sources of inspiration and action.

This unfinished agenda is the challenge we pass on to future scholars, ministers, and activists who will make new feminist Christianity a part of history and replace it with their own voices and views.

NOTES

Introduction

1. Elizabeth Cady Stanton and the Revising Committee, *The Woman's Bible* (New York: European Publishing, 1895, 1898; reprint, Seattle: Seattle Coalition Task Force on Women and Religion, 1977).
2. Valerie Saiving, "The Human Situation: A Feminine View," in *Womanspirit Rising: A Feminist Reader in Religion*, ed. Carol P. Christ and Judith Plaskow (San Francisco: HarperSanFrancisco, 1979), 25–42.
3. Simone de Beauvoir, *The Second Sex*, trans. H. M. Parshley (London: Jonathan Cape, 1953); and Betty Friedan, *The Feminine Mystique* (London: W. W. Norton, 1963).
4. Mary Daly, *The Church and the Second Sex* (New York: Harper & Row, 1968; Boston: Beacon Press, 1985).
5. Rosemary Radford Ruether, "Male Chauvinist Theology and the Anger of Women," *Cross Currents* 21 (1971): 173–85.
6. Elisabeth Schüssler Fiorenza, *Der vergessene Partner: Grundlagen, Tatsachen und der Möglichkeiten beruflichen Mitarbeit der Frau in der Heilssorge der Kirche* (Düsseldorf, Ger.: Patmos, 1964).
7. Nelle Morton, *The Journey Is Home* (Boston: Beacon Press, 1985); Anne McGrew Bennett, *From Woman-Pain to Woman-Vision: Writings in Feminist Theology*, ed. Mary E. Hunt (Minneapolis: Fortress Press, 1989); Pauli Murray, *Pauli Murray: The Autobiography of a Black Activist, Feminist, Lawyer, Priest, and Poet* (Knoxville, Tenn.: University of Tennessee Press, 1989); and Pauli Murray, *Song in a Weary Throat: An American Pilgrimage* (New York: Harper & Row, 1987).
8. Katie Cannon, *Katie's Canon: Womanism and the Soul of the Black Community* (New York: Continuum, 1995); and Delores S. Williams, *Sisters in the Wilderness: The Challenge of Womanist God-Talk* (Maryknoll, N.Y.: Orbis Books, 1993).
9. See Patricia Beattie Jung, Mary E. Hunt, and Radhika Balakrishnan, eds., *Good Sex: Feminist Perspectives from the World's Religions* (New Brunswick, N.J.: Rutgers University Press, 2005).
10. Resource Center for Women and Ministry in the South, www.rcwms.org.
11. FaithTrust Institute, www.faithtrustinstitute.org.
12. Women's Alliance for Theology, Ethics and Ritual (WATER); www.hers.com/water.

Part I Feminist Theological Visions

A Postcolonial Feminist Vision for Christianity

Kwok Pui-lan

1. "Table C. Status of Global Mission, Presence, and Activities, AD 1800–2025," *International Bulletin of Missionary Research* 32, no. 1 (2008): 30.
2. See Isabel Apawo Phiri, Beverley Haddad, and Madipioane Masenya, eds., *African Women, HIV/AIDS and Faith Communities* (Pietermaritzburg, S. Afr.: Cluster Publications, 2003); the websites www.ecclesiaofwomen.ning.com and www.conspirando.cl; and María Pilar Aquino and Maria Jóse Rosado-Nunes, eds., *Feminist Intercultural Theology: Latina Exploration for a Just World* (Maryknoll, N.Y.: Orbis Books, 2007).
3. Ivone Gebara, "A Feminist Theology of Liberation: A Latin American Perspective with a View toward the Future," in *Toward a New Heaven and a New Earth: Essays in Honor of Elisabeth Schüssler Fiorenza,* ed. Fernando F. Segovia (Maryknoll, N.Y.: Orbis Books, 2003), 255.
4. Mercy Amba Oduyoye, "Ecclesiology in African Women's Perspective," in *On Being Church: African Women's Voices and Visions,* ed. Isabel Apawo Phiri and Sarojini Nadar (Geneva: World Council of Churches, 2005), 155.
5. Ibid., 152.
6. See Letty M. Russell, *Church in the Round: Feminist Interpretation of the Church* (Louisville: Westminster John Knox Press, 1993), and *Just Hospitality: God's Welcome in a World of Difference,* ed. J. Shannon Clarkson and Kate M. Ott (Louisville: Westminster John Knox Press, 2009).
7. Carmelita Usog, "Women's Spirituality for Justice," in *Ecclesia of Women in Asia: Gathering the Voices of the Silenced,* ed. Evelyn Monteiro and Antoinette Gutzler (Delhi: ISPCK, 2005), 239.
8. "Many Americans Mix Multiple Faiths: Eastern, New Age Beliefs Widespread," Pew Forum on Religion and Public Life, www.pewforum.org/docs/?DocID=490.
9. Thich Nhat Hanh, *Touching Peace: Practicing the Art of Mindful Living,* rev. ed. (Berkeley: Parallax Press, 2009), 1.
10. See www.catherineofsiena.net.

Feminist Theology in Theological Education

Rosemary Radford Ruether

1. Rosemary Radford Ruether, "Male Chauvinist Theology and the Anger of Women," *Cross Currents* 21 (1971): 173–85.
2. Toni Morrison, "What the Black Woman Thinks about Women's Lib," *New York Times Magazine,* August 22, 1971.
3. Chung Hyun Kyung, *Struggle to Be the Sun Again: Introducing Asian Women's Theology* (Maryknoll, N.Y.: Orbis Books, 1990).
4. Sarah Moore Grimké, "Letter II: Woman Subject Only to God," Newburyport, July 17, 1837, in *Letters on the Equality of the Sexes and the Condition of Woman* (Boston: I. Knapp, 1838), 10.

Notes

Latina Feminist Theology: Charting Future Discourse

NANCY PINEDA-MADRID

1. Ada María Isasi-Díaz, "Toward an Understanding of *Feminismo Hispano* in the U.S.A," in *Women's Consciousness, Women's Conscience: A Reader in Feminist Ethics,* ed. Barbara Hilkert Andolsen, Christine E. Gudorf, and Mary D. Pellauer (Minneapolis: Winston Press, 1985), 51–61; Ada María Isasi-Díaz and Yolanda Tarango, *Hispanic Women: Prophetic Voice in the Church* (Minneapolis: Fortress Press, 1988); María Pilar Aquino, ed., *Aportes para una teología desde la mujer* (Madrid: Biblia y Fe, 1988); María Pilar Aquino, *Our Cry for Life: Feminist Theology from Latin America* (Maryknoll, N.Y.: Orbis Books, 1993).
2. For a discussion of her work and contribution, see Michelle A. González, *Sor Juana: Beauty and Justice in the Americas* (Maryknoll, N.Y.: Orbis Books, 2003); Michelle A. González, "Sor Juana Ines de la Cruz," in *Empire and the Christian Tradition: New Readings of Classical Theologians,* ed. Kwok Pui-lan, Don H. Compier, and Joerg Rieger (Minneapolis: Fortress Press, 2007), 229–42. For an extended discussion, see Nancy Pineda-Madrid, "Latina Theology," in *Liberation Theologies in the United States: An Introduction,* ed. Stacey M. Floyd-Thomas and Anthony B. Pinn (New York: New York University Press, 2010), 61–85.
3. For an extended discussion of this term, see Michelle A. González, "Rethinking Latina Feminist Theologian," in *Rethinking Latino(a) Religion and Identity,* ed. Miguel A. De la Torre and Gastón Espinosa (Cleveland: Pilgrim Press, 2006), 176–99.
4. Ada María Isasi-Díaz, La Lucha *Continues:* Mujerista *Theology* (Maryknoll, N.Y.: Orbis Books, 2004); Ada María Isasi-Díaz, Mujerista *Theology: A Theology for the Twenty-First Century* (Maryknoll, N.Y.: Orbis Books, 1996); Ada María Isasi-Díaz, "Praxis: The Heart of *Mujerista* Theology," *Journal of Hispanic/Latino Theology* 1, no. 1 (November 1993): 44–55; Ada María Isasi-Díaz, "*Mujeristas*: A Name of Our Own," in *Yearning to Breathe Free: Liberation Theologies in the U.S.,* ed. Mar Peter-Raoul, Linda Rennie Forcey, and Robert Fredrick Hunter Jr. (Maryknoll, N.Y.: Orbis Books, 1990), 121–28.
5. Rosemary Radford Ruether defines *patriarchy* as "the 'rule of the father,' … [and] refers to systems of legal, social, economic, and political relations that validate and enforce the sovereignty of male heads of families over dependent persons in the household. In classical patriarchal systems … dependent persons included wives, unmarried daughters, dependent sons, and slaves, male and female." Rosemary Radford Ruether, *Women Healing Earth: Third World Women on Ecology, Feminism, and Religion* (London: SCM Press, 1996), 205–6.
6. Elisabeth Schüssler Fiorenza distinguishes kyriarchy from patriarchy. *Kyriarchy* is "the Greek word for the domination of elite propertied men over women and other men, whereas *patriarchy* is generally understood in feminist discourses in terms of the western sex/gender system which posits a man/woman opposition." Elisabeth Schüssler Fiorenza, *Bread Not Stone: The Challenge of Feminist Biblical Interpretation* (Boston: Beacon Press, 1984), 211. More specifically, Schüssler Fiorenza clarifies that the "neologism *kyriarchy-kyriocentrism* (from Greek *kyrios* meaning lord, master, father, husband) seeks to express this interstructuring of

domination and to replace the commonly used term *patriarchy,* which is often understood in terms of binary gender dualism. I have introduced this neologism as an analytic category in order to be able to articulate a more comprehensive systematic analysis, to underscore the complex interstructuring of domination, and to locate sexism and misogyny in the political matrix or, better, patrix of a broader range of oppressions." Elisabeth Schüssler Fiorenza, *Rhetoric and Ethic: The Politics of Biblical Studies* (Minneapolis: Fortress Press, 1999), 5. See also Elisabeth Schüssler Fiorenza, *But She Said: Feminist Practices of Biblical Interpretation* (Boston: Beacon Press, 1992), 114–18, 122–25; and *Jesus—Miriam's Child, Sophia's Prophet: Critical Issues in Feminist Christology* (New York: Continuum, 1994), 36.

7. Nancy Pineda-Madrid, "Holy Guadalupe … Shameful Malinche? Excavating the Problem of 'Female Dualism,' Doing Theological Spade Work," *Listening: Journal of Religion and Culture* 44, no. 2 (Spring 2009): 71–87.
8. Berta Esperanza Hernández-Truyol, "Culture and Economic Violence," in *The Latino Condition: A Critical Reader,* ed. Richard Delgado and Jean Stefancic (New York: New York University Press, 1998), 536.
9. Alvina E. Quintana, *Home Girls: Chicana Literary Voices* (Philadelphia: Temple University Press, 1996), 101.
10. Cherríe Moraga, *The Last Generation: Prose and Poetry* (Boston: South End Press, 1993), 158.
11. *Feminicide* refers to the killing of girls and women by men in an exceptionally brutal manner, on a massive scale, and with impunity for the perpetrators. These characteristics, namely, brutality, massive scale, and impunity, distinguish feminicide from femicide. *Femicide* refers to the killing of any female because she is female, but this term does not necessarily signify the characteristics that distinguish feminicide. Both terms refer to the extermination of females. For a further discussion of terms, see Diana E. H. Russell, "Defining Femicide and Related Concepts," in *Femicide in Global Perspective,* ed. Diana E. H. Russell and Roberta A. Harmes (New York: Teachers College Press, 2001), 12–25; Johanna Ikonen, "Feminicide: The Case in Mexico and Guatemala," background paper for European Parliament, April 19, 2006 (www.europarl.europa.eu/meetdocs/2004_2009/documents/fd/droi20060419_h_backgroundnote_/droi20060419_h_backgroundnote_en.pdf); Monica A. Maher, "Daring to Dream: Faith and Feminicide in Latin America," in *Weep Not for Your Children: Essays on Religion and Violence,* ed. Lisa Isherwood and Rosemary Radford Ruether (Oakville, Conn.: Equinox, 2008), 187–213.
12. In June 2008, María Pilar Aquino convened a group of U.S. Latina, Latin American, and Caribbean feminist theologians in San José, Costa Rica. Each of these scholars has contributed a chapter to "Ruptured Bodies, Sacred Lives: Women's Sexuality and Human Dignity" (forthcoming), which addresses the question of women and violence.
13. Julia Preston, "Latino Leaders Use Churches in Census Bid," *New York Times,* December 22, 2009.
14. Steven Greenhouse, "Low-Wage Workers Are Often Cheated, Study Says," *New York Times,* September 1, 2009.

15. Hector Avalos, ed., *Introduction to U.S. Latina and Latino Religious Experience* (Boston: Brill Academic, 2004).
16. Pew Hispanic Center, *U.S. Population Projections: 2005–2050*, February 11, 2008, www.pewhispanic.org/reports/report.php?ReportID=85; Pew Hispanic Center, "A Statistical Portrait of Hispanics at Mid-Decade," table 3, "Detailed Hispanic Origin: 2005," August 29, 2006, www.pewhispanic.org/files/other/middecade/Table-3.pdf; Pew Hispanic Center, "Religion and Demography," in *Changing Faiths: Latinos and the Transformation of American Religion*, April 25, 2007, www.pewhispanic.org/files/reports/75.1.pdf, 7.
17. Some of the fruits of these conversations are reflected in the following works: Anthony Pinn and Benjamín Valentín, eds., *The Ties That Bind: African-American and Hispanic American/Latino/a Theologies in Dialogue* (New York: Continuum, 2001); María Pilar Aquino and María José Rosado-Nunes, eds., *Feminist Intercultural Theology: Latina Explorations for a Just World* (Maryknoll, N.Y.: Orbis Books, 2007).
18. Aquino and Rosado-Nunes, eds., *Feminist Intercultural Theology.*
19. Raúl Fornet-Betancourt, *La Interculturalidad a Prueba* (Aachen, Ger.: Verlagsgruppe Mainz in Aachen, 2006), 22.

Crossing Borders: Feminist Christianity in Latin America

WANDA DEIFELT

1. Ivone Gebara, *As Incômodas Filhas de Eva na Igreja da América Latina* (São Paulo: Paulinas, 1989).
2. An example of this is Sociedade de Teologia e Ciências da Religião's (SOTER) annual conference dedicated to feminist theology. SOTER, *Gênero e Teologia: Interpelações e Perspectivas* (São Paulo/Belo Horizonte: Paulinas/Loyola/SOTER, 2003).
3. Nelson Kirst, ed., *Rethinking Luther's Theology in the Context of the Third World* (Third World Lutheran Theological Educators Conference, São Leopoldo, Brazil, September 5–11, 1988), 148.
4. For a comprehensive account of the creation of the first chair in feminist theology in Latin America, see Wanda Deifelt, "Feminist Theology: A Key for Women's Citizenship in the Church," in *Toward a New Heaven and a New Earth: Essays in Honor of Elisabeth Schüssler Fiorenza*, ed. Fernando F. Segovia (Maryknoll, N.Y.: Orbis Books, 2003), 244–46.
5. Lucia Weiler, Raquel Pena Pinto, Sandra Maira Pires, eds., *Teologia Feminista: Tecendo Fios de Ternura e Esperança* (Porto Alegre, Brazil: ESTEF, 2008).
6. Sandra Duarte de Souza, org., *Gênero e Religião no Brasil: Ensaios Feministas* (São Bernardo do Campo, Brazil: Universidade Metodista de São Paulo, 2006).
7. José Trasferetti, org., *Teologia e Sexualidade: Um Ensaio Contra a Exclusão Moral* (Campinas, Brazil: Editora Átomo, 2004).
8. Ivone Gebara, *Longing for Running Water: Ecofeminism and Liberation* (Minneapolis: Fortress Press, 1999); Maricel Mena López, *Cuestión de Piel: De las Sabidurías Hegemónicas a las Emergentes* (Cali, Colombia: Sello Editorial Javeriano, 2008); Vicenta Mamani Bernabé, *Mujer Aymara Migrante* (Cochabamba, Bolivia: Editorial Verbo Divino, 2007).

9. For instance, the first woman to enter the Lutheran Seminary in São Leopoldo, Brazil, was Eve Wysk in 1952, but she and several others who entered seminary did not graduate. It was Elisabeth Dietschi, who started her studies in 1966 and graduated in 1970, who completed all of the training and was able to work as pastor, albeit in Germany, not in Brazil.
10. Sibyla Baeske, org., *Mulheres Desafiam as Igrejas Cristãs* (Petrópolis, Brazil: Vozes, 2001).
11. Lutheran World Federation, *Churches Say "No" to Violence against Women: Action Plan for the Churches* (Geneva: LWF, 2002).
12. The website for Las Dignas, in El Salvador, is www.lasdignas.org.
13. The website for Colectivo Con-spirando, in Chile, is www.conspirando.cl.
14. The website for SOS Corpo, in Brazil, is www.soscorpo.org.br.
15. The website for Iniciativa de Mujeres por la Paz, in Colombia, is www.mujeresporlapaz.org.

Analysis, Interconnectedness, and Peacebuilding for a Just World

María Pilar Aquino

1. Letty M. Russell, *Human Liberation in a Feminist Perspective—A Theology* (Philadelphia: Westminster Press, 1974), 62, 107, 131, 133.
2. Rosemary Radford Ruether, *Sexism and God-Talk: Toward a Feminist Theology*, 10th anniv. ed. (Boston: Beacon Press, 1993), 254–55.
3. Rosemary Radford Ruether, *Women and Redemption: A Theological History* (Minneapolis: Fortress Press, 1998), 274.
4. Elisabeth Schüssler Fiorenza, *Discipleship of Equals: A Critical Feminist Ekklesialogy of Liberation* (New York: Crossroad, 1993), 12.
5. Elisabeth Schüssler Fiorenza, *Rhetoric and Ethic: The Politics of Biblical Studies* (Minneapolis: Fortress Press, 1999), 53.
6. Elisabeth Schüssler Fiorenza, "Feminist Theology as a Critical Theology of Liberation," *Theological Studies* 36, no. 4 (December 1975): 617.
7. Ignacio Ellacuría, "Liberación," in *Conceptos Fundamentales del Cristianismo*, ed. Casiano Floristán and Juan José Tamayo (Madrid: Trotta, 1993), 702.
8. Russell, *Human Liberation*, 107.
9. Ibid., 110–11.
10. Second General Conference of Latin American Bishops, *The Church in the Present-Day Transformation of Latin America in the Light of the Council: Conclusions II*, Document on "Peace," 2nd ed. (Washington, D.C.: United States Catholic Conference, 1973), 59. I have modified the sexist language of this document to make it inclusive of women.
11. Marie M. Fortune, *Sexual Violence: The Sin Revisited* (Cleveland: Pilgrim Press, 2005). See also other illustrative works on this: Elisabeth Schüssler Fiorenza and M. Shawn Copeland, eds., *Violence against Women* (London: SCM Press, 1994); Mary John Mananzan, Mercy Amba Oduyoye, Elsa Tamez, et al., eds., *Women Resisting Violence: Spirituality for Life* (Maryknoll, N.Y.: Orbis Books, 1996); Carol J. Adams and Marie Fortune, eds., *Violence against Women and Children: A Christian Theological Sourcebook* (New York: Continuum, 1998); Nantawan

Boonprasat Lewis and Marie M. Fortune, eds., *Remembering Conquest: Feminist/Womanist Perspectives on Religion, Colonization, and Sexual Violence* (Binghamton, N.Y.: Haworth Pastoral Press, 1999); Traci C. West, *Wounds of the Spirit: Black Women, Violence, and Resistance Ethics* (New York: New York University Press, 1999); Elizabeth A. Castelli and Janet R. Jakobsen, eds., *Interventions: Activists and Academics Respond to Violence* (New York: Palgrave Macmillan, 2004); Regina Soares Jurkewicz, *Desvelando a política do silêncio: Abuso sexual de mulheres por padres no Brasil*, Cuadernos Católicas Pelo Direito de Decidir, no. 12 (São Paulo, Brazil: Católicas Pelo Direito de Decidir, 2005); Daniel C. Maguire and Sa'diyya Shaikh, eds., *Violence against Women in Contemporary World Religion: Roots and Cures* (Cleveland: Pilgrim Press, 2007); Joy A. Schroeder, *Dinah's Lament: The Biblical Legacy of Sexual Violence in Christian Interpretation* (Minneapolis: Fortress Press, 2007); Lisa Isherwood and Rosemary Radford Ruether, eds., *Weep Not for Your Children: Essays on Religion and Violence* (London: Equinox, 2008).

12. For a consistent approach to feminist systemic analysis for transformation, see Elisabeth Schüssler Fiorenza, *Jesus—Miriam's Child, Sophia's Prophet: Critical Issues in Feminist Christology* (New York: Continuum, 1994), 3–24; *Rhetoric and Ethic: The Politics of Biblical Studies* (Minneapolis: Fortress Press, 1999), 48–55; *Wisdom Ways: Introducing Feminist Biblical Interpretation* (Maryknoll, N.Y.: Orbis Books, 2001), 165–94. For a consistent approach to feminist systemic analysis in connection to environmental justice, see Rosemary Radford Ruether, *New Woman, New Earth: Sexist Ideologies and Human Liberation*, reprint ed. (Boston: Beacon Press, 1995); *Women Healing Earth: Third World Women on Ecology, Feminism, and Religion* (Maryknoll, N.Y.: Orbis Books, 2000); *Integrating Ecofeminism, Globalization, and World Religions* (Lanham, Md.: Rowman & Littlefield, 2005).
13. See Miguel Hidalgo, "América Latina y el Caribe 2008: Una Región en Erupción," *Revista Pasos* 138 (July–August 2008): 1–10; Samir Amin, "¿Debacle Financiera, Crisis Sistémica? Respuestas Ilusorias y Respuestas Necesarias," *Revista Pasos* 139 (September–October 2008): 7–9.
14. Russell, *Human Liberation*, 51.
15. Lisa Schirch, *Strategic Peacebuilding: A Vision and Framework for Peace with Justice* (Intercourse, Penn.: Good Books, 2004), 13. See also Lisa Schirch, *Ritual and Symbol in Peacebuilding* (Bloomfield, Conn.: Kumarian Press, 2005).
16. John Paul Lederach, *Building Peace: Sustainable Reconciliation in Divided Societies* (Washington, D.C.: United States Institute of Peace, 1997), 77.
17. John Paul Lederach, *Conflict Transformation: Clear Articulation of the Guiding Principles by a Pioneer in the Field* (Intercourse, Penn.: Good Books, 2003), 5. See also John Paul Lederach's pioneer book, *Building Peace*, and his other influential books: *The Journey toward Reconciliation* (Scottdale, Penn.: Herald Press, 1999) and *The Moral Imagination: The Art and Soul of Building Peace* (New York: Oxford University Press, 2005). See also John Paul Lederach and Janice Moomaw Jenner, eds., *Into the Eye of the Storm: A Handbook of International Peacebuilding* (San Francisco: Jossey-Bass, 2002) and John Paul Lederach, Reina Neufeldt, and Hal Culbertson, *Reflective Peacebuilding: A Planning, Monitoring, and Learning Toolkit*

(Notre Dame, Ind.: Joan B. Kroc Institute for International Peace Studies of the University of Notre Dame and Catholic Relief Services, 2007).

18. Amnesty International, *Amnesty International Report 2006: The State of the World's Human Rights* (London: Amnesty International Publications, 2006). Available at www.amnesty.org/en/library/info/POL10/001/2006.

Race, Class, Gender, Sexuality: Integrating the Diverse Politics of Identity into Our Theology

W. Anne Joh

1. Frantz Fanon, *The Wretched of the Earth*, trans. Richard Philcox (New York: Grove Press, 1968).
2. Nami Kim, "The 'Indigestible Asian': The Unifying Term 'Asian' in Theological Discourse," in *Off the Menu: Asian and Asian North American Women's Religion and Theology*, ed. Rita Nakashima Brock, Jung Ha Kim, Kwok Pui-lan, and Seung Ai Yang (Louisville: Westminster John Knox Press, 2009), 23–43.
3. See Judith Butler, *Gender Trouble: Feminism and the Subversion of Identity* (New York: Routledge, 2006).
4. See M. Jacqui Alexander and Chandra Talpade Mohanty, *Feminist Genealogies, Colonial Legacies, Democratic Futures* (New York: Routledge, 1996).
5. For an excellent critique of colonialism, race, gender, and sexuality, see Anne McClintock, *Imperial Leather: Race, Gender and Sexuality in the Colonial Contest* (New York: Routledge, 1995).
6. See Bonnie Honig, *Democracy and the Foreigner* (Princeton, N.J.: Princeton University Press, 2001).
7. See M. Jacqui Alexander, *Pedagogies of Crossing: Meditations on Feminism, Sexual Politics, Memory, and the Sacred* (Durham, N.C.: Duke University Press, 2005).
8. See Gary Y. Okihiro, *Common Ground: Reimagining American History* (Princeton, N.J.: Princeton University Press, 2001).
9. See Khyati Y. Joshi, *New Roots in America's Sacred Ground: Religion, Race, and Ethnicity in Indian America* (New York: Routledge, 2006).
10. For an excellent discussion on white supremacy, heteronormativity, and racialization of religion and sexuality, see Jasbir Puar, *Terrorist Assemblages: Homonationalism in Queer Times* (Durham, N.C.: Duke University Press, 2007).
11. See Gayatri Chakravorty Spivak, *A Critique of Postcolonial Reason: Toward a History of the Vanishing Present* (Cambridge, Mass.: Harvard University Press, 1999).
12. See Judith Butler, *Precarious Life: The Powers of Mourning and Violence* (New York: Verso, 2004).
13. See Edward Said, *Orientalism* (New York: Vintage Books, 1978), *Musical Elaborations* (New York: Columbia University Press, 1991), and *Music at the Limits* (New York: Columbia University Press, 2008).
14. Gayatri Chakravorty Spivak, *Other Asias* (Malden, Mass.: Blackwell, 2007), 57.
15. For an excellent theological work that critiques the "logic of One" and offers a theology of multiplicity, see Laurel Schneider, *Beyond Monotheism: A Theology of Multiplicity* (New York: Routledge, 2008).

Notes

Why We Need Evangelical Feminists

LETHA DAWSON SCANZONI

1. For more detailed, descriptive, and historical explanations of evangelicalism in general, as well as how it has related to feminism, see the discussions in Donald W. Dayton, *Discovering an Evangelical Heritage* (New York: Harper & Row, 1976); Nancy A. Hardesty, *Women Called to Witness,* 2nd ed. (Knoxville, Tenn.: University of Tennessee Press, 1999); Janette Hassey, *No Time for Silence: Evangelical Women in Public Ministry around the Turn of the Century* (Grand Rapids, Mich.: Zondervan, Academie Books, 1986); Sally K. Gallagher, *Evangelical Identity & Gendered Family Life* (New Brunswick, N.J.: Rutgers University Press, 2003); George M. Marsden, *Fundamentalism and American Culture,* 2nd ed. (New York: Oxford University Press, 2006); George M. Marsden, ed., *Evangelicalism and Modern America* (Grand Rapids, Mich.: Wm. B. Eerdmans, 1984); Letha Dawson Scanzoni and Susan Setta, "Women in Evangelical, Holiness, and Pentecostal Traditions," in *Women & Religion in America: A Documentary History,* vol. 3, *1900–1968,* ed. Rosemary Radford Ruether and Rosemary Skinner Keller (San Francisco: Harper & Row, 1986), 223–65.
2. Gallagher, *Evangelical Identity & Gendered Family Life,* 4.
3. Hardesty, *Women Called to Witness,* x–xi.
4. See the section on "Religious Revivalism in the 1820s" in Alice S. Rossi, ed., *The Feminist Papers* (New York: Columbia University Press, 1973), 254–8.
5. Letha Scanzoni, "The Feminists and the Bible," *Christianity Today,* Feb. 2, 1973, 10–15.
6. Hassey, *No Time for Silence.*
7. Betty A. DeBerg, *Ungodly Women: Gender and the First Wave of American Fundamentalism* (Minneapolis: Fortress Press, 1990), 141.
8. Julie Ingersoll, *Evangelical Christian Women: War Stories in the Gender Battles* (New York: New York University Press, 2003), 50.
9. See Virginia Hearn, ed., *Our Struggle to Serve: The Stories of 15 Evangelical Women* (Waco, Tex.: Word Books, 1979).
10. *All We're Meant to Be: A Biblical Approach to Women's Liberation* (Waco, Tex.: Word Books, 1974). Subsequent editions were published by Abingdon in 1986 (with a new subtitle, *Biblical Feminism for Today*) and in a greatly expanded and updated edition by Wm. B. Eerdmans in 1992.
11. Richard Bledsoe, review of *All We're Meant to Be,* in the *Cambridge Fish* (Winter 1975–1976): 7.
12. *Daughters of Sarah* magazine ceased publication in 1996, although a collection of articles from its twenty-one years of existence was published in 2001 under the title *Wisdom of Daughters: Two Decades of the Voice of Christian Feminism,* ed. Reta Halteman Finger and Kari Sandhaas (Philadelphia: Innisfree Press, 2001).
13. J. Victor Baldridge, *Sociology: A Critical Approach to Power, Conflict, and Change* (New York: Wiley, 1975); Letha Dawson Scanzoni, "Marching On," speech delivered for the EWC Organization Day, Pasadena, Calif., June 17, 1978. See also an expansion of this approach in L. D. Scanzoni's two articles, "Biblical Feminism as a Social Movement" in the tenth anniversary issue of *Daughters of Sarah*

(November–December 1984) and "Reflections on Two Decades of Christian Feminism," in the twentieth anniversary issue of *Daughters of Sarah* (Fall 1994).

14. See S. Sue Horner, "Trying to Be God in the World: The Story of the Evangelical Women's Caucus and the Crisis over Homosexuality," in *Gender, Ethnicity & Religion*, ed. Rosemary Radford Ruether (Minneapolis: Fortress Press, 2002), 99–124; Ingersoll, *Evangelical Christian Women*, 41–42; Pamela Cochran, *Evangelical Feminism: A History* (New York: New York University Press, 2005); also see the fall 2005 and winter 2006 issues of *Christian Feminism Today* for a review and critiques of Cochran's book, including some corrections of factual inaccuracies in telling EWC's story.
15. "The Top 50 Books That Have Shaped Evangelicals: Landmark Titles That Changed the Way We Think, Talk, Witness, Worship, and Live," *Christianity Today*, October 2006, www.christianitytoday.com/ct/2006/october/23.51.html.
16. Sally K. Gallagher, "The Marginalization of Evangelical Feminism," *Sociology of Religion* 65, no. 3 (Fall 2004): 215–237.
17. Anne Graham Lotz, video interview by Sally Quinn, "Anne Graham Lotz on 'Breaking Lots of Glass Ceilings,'" www.washingtonpost.com/wp-dyn/content/video/2009/12/15/VI2009121504587.html.
18. Council on Biblical Manhood and Womanhood (CBMW), "About Us," www.cbmw.org.
19. J. Ligon Duncan and Randy Stinson, "Preface," in *Recovering Biblical Manhood and Womanhood: A Response to Evangelical Feminism*, 2nd ed., ed. John Piper and Wayne Grudem (Wheaton, Ill.: Crossway Books, 2006), ix.
20. See Mary A. Kassian, *The Feminist Gospel: The Movement to Unite Feminism with the Church* (Wheaton, Ill.: Crossway Books, 1992), and her second edition of the book under a new title, *The Feminist ~~Mystique~~ Mistake: The Radical Impact of Feminism on Church and Culture* (Wheaton, Ill.: Crossway Books, 2005).
21. See Molly Worthen's article on Mark Driscoll, "Who Would Jesus Smack Down?" *New York Times*, January 11, 2009; and Brandon O'Brien, "A Jesus for Real Men: What the New Masculinity Movement Gets Right and Wrong," *Christianity Today*, April 2008, www.christianitytoday.com/ct/2008/april/27.48.html. See also Stephen B. Clark, *Man and Woman in Christ* (Ann Arbor, Mich.: Servant Books, 1980). Clark seems to think that "feminine" qualities are contagious and can be caught, even from a man's wife. He writes that "the heavy emphasis on always having the married couple together tends to 'feminize' the men, both in their personality traits and in their ability to take a concern for the larger society" (622). Clark believes that "if men are going to develop manly character, they must be freed from the dominant social pattern of spending most of their time with women" (641).
22. Russell Moore, presentation at the 57th annual meeting of the Evangelical Theological Society on November 17, 2005, at Valley Forge, Penn.
23. "Feminism in Your Church and Home with Russell Moore, Randy Stinson, and C.J. Mahaney," audio interview, May 1, 2007, http://resources.christianity.com/default/mrki.aspx.
24. For example, see the four-minute video that was produced to promote the book *Radical Womanhood: Feminine Faith in a Feminist World* (Chicago: Moody, 2008), at www.radicalwomanhood.com. One book from the antifeminist or complementarian side that avoids the disdainful tone that is so common in many of the other

books is *Jesus and the Feminists: Who Do They Say That He Is?* by Margaret Elizabeth Kostenberger (Wheaton, Ill.: Crossway Books, 2008). Kostenberger attempts a more analytical and respectful approach through a summary of the three waves of feminism, followed by a typology of religious feminists, whom she locates in one of three categories: radical feminists, reformist feminists, and evangelical feminists. In the acknowledgments, she thanks her dissertation mentor, "who represented an opposing viewpoint" to her own and thereby helped sharpen her thinking on the topic.

25. See the Radical Womanhood website at www.radicalwomanhood.com.
26. See the True Woman website at www.truewoman.com. You can watch a conference video with Mary Kassian's speech "You've Come a Long Way, Baby," which begins with a recording of Helen Reddy singing "I Am Woman" and then goes on to ridicule and disparage feminism. The speech reveals a nostalgic yearning for a *Leave It to Beaver* world as she invites her audience to remember the 1950s. The picture she paints is of a middle-class, white, privileged world where (white) married women could stay home, care for the children, and bake cookies while husbands supported a suburban lifestyle on a single-earner living wage—a time when feminists weren't questioning the assumed traditional social order.
27. See "Comparison of 1925, 1963 and 2000 Baptist Faith and Message," Section XVIII, "The Family," www.sbc.net/bfm/bfmcomparison.asp.
28. Although I was asked to contribute this essay from the standpoint of an evangelical feminist, and I have no problem with applying the term (in its historic sense) to myself personally, I recognize that some of my closest EEWC friends now shy away from this designation either because they do not wish to be identified with the widespread negative image of "evangelicals" that is so common today or because they have been personally wounded by churches or organizations that fit this negative image. The Evangelical & Ecumenical Women's Caucus, though retaining its official title and honoring its history, is increasingly becoming known by the name of its publication, *Christian Feminism Today*, or is referred to as EEWC–Christian Feminism Today.
29. The August 2009 post for *72-27*, an intergenerational Christian feminist blog that I coauthor with Kimberly George, discusses the impact of religion for good or ill on women's status in a society (www.eewc.com/72-27/2009/08). This archived post also contains links to third-wave secular feminist blogs, such as Feministing, in which young women, writing in the community forum discussion section of the Feministing website, have discussed whether or not they can have both their faith and their feminism and, if so, how.

Part II Feminist Scriptural Insights

Where Are You Really From? An Asian American Feminist Biblical Scholar Reflects on Her Guild

Gale A. Yee

1. Mia Tuan, *Forever Foreigners or Honorary Whites: The Asian Ethnic Experience Today* (New Brunswick, N.J.: Rutgers University Press, 1998); Frank H. Wu,

"The Perpetual Foreigner: Yellow Peril in the Pacific Century," in *Yellow: Race in America Beyond Black and White* (New York: Basic Books, 2002), 79–129.

2. Gale A. Yee, "The Author/Text/Reader and Power: Suggestions for a Critical Framework in Biblical Studies," in *Reading from This Place: Social Location and Biblical Interpretation*, vol. 1, *Social Location and Biblical Interpretation in the United States*, ed. Fernando F. Segovia and Mary Ann Tolbert (Minneapolis: Fortress Press, 1995), 109–18.
3. Patricia Hill Collins, "Toward a New Vision: Race, Class, and Gender as Categories of Analysis and Connection," in *Social Class and Stratification: Classic Statements and Theoretical Debates*, ed. Rhonda F. Levine (Lanham, Md.: Rowman & Littlefield, 1998), 231–48.
4. See the articles by J. Cheryl Exum on feminist criticism, Danna Nolan Fewell on deconstructive criticism, and Gale A. Yee on ideological criticism in *Judges and Method: New Approaches in Biblical Studies*, 2nd ed., ed. Gale A. Yee (Minneapolis: Fortress Press, 2007).
5. See, for example, Alice Bach, ed., *Biblical Glamour and Hollywood Glitz*, Semeia 74 (1996); Alice Bach, *Religion, Politics, Media in the Broadband Era* (Sheffield, U.K.: Sheffield Phoenix Press, 2004); J. Cheryl Exum, *Plotted, Shot, and Painted: Cultural Representations of Biblical Women* (Sheffield, U.K.: Sheffield Academic Press, 1996).
6. See Deryn Guest, Robert E. Goss, Mona West, and Thomas Bohache, eds., *The Queer Bible Commentary* (London: SCM Press, 2006); and Deryn Guest, *When Deborah Met Jael: Lesbian Biblical Hermeneutics* (Louisville: Westminster John Knox Press, 2005).
7. See Musa Dube, *Postcolonial Feminist Interpretation of the Bible* (St. Louis: Chalice Press, 2000); Gale A. Yee, *Poor Banished Children of Eve: Woman as Evil in the Hebrew Bible* (Minneapolis: Fortress Press, 2003), 111–58; Gale A. Yee, "Postcolonial Biblical Criticism," in *Cambridge Methods in Biblical Interpretation: The Book of Exodus*, ed. Thomas B. Dozeman (New York: Cambridge University Press, 2010), 193–233.
8. For example, see Marion Ann Taylor and Heather E. Weir, eds., *Let Her Speak for Herself: Nineteenth-Century Women Writing on Women in Genesis* (Waco, Tex.: Baylor University Press, 2006); and Christiana de Groot and Marion Ann Taylor, eds., *Recovering Nineteenth-Century Women Interpreters of the Bible* (Atlanta: Society of Biblical Literature, 2007).
9. See Caroline Vander Stichele and Todd Penner, eds., *Her Master's Tools? Feminist and Postcolonial Engagements of Historical-Critical Discourse*, Global Perspectives in Biblical Scholarship (Atlanta: Society of Biblical Literature, 2005).
10. Randall C. Bailey, Tat-siong Benny Liew, and Fernando F. Segovia, eds., *They Were All Together in One Place? Toward Minority Biblical Criticism*, Semeia Studies 57 (Atlanta: Society of Biblical Literature, 2009).
11. Elisabeth Schüssler Fiorenza, *But She Said: Feminist Practices of Biblical Interpretation* (Boston: Beacon Press, 1992), 73–76.
12. Athalya Brenner, *I Am … Biblical Women Tell Their Own Stories* (Minneapolis: Fortress Press, 2005), x–xi. Brenner has made tentative movements in this direction in "Age and Ageism in the Hebrew Bible, in an Autobiographical Perspective," in *Autobiographical Biblical Criticism: Between Text and Self*, ed. Ingrid Rosa

Kitzberger (Leiden, Neth.: Deo, 2002), 105–13; and "Wide Gaps, Narrow Escapes: I Am Known as Rahab the Broad," in *First Person: Essays in Biblical Autobiography,* ed. Philip R. Davies (New York: Sheffield Academic Press, 2002), 47–58.

13. Eleanor Ferris Beach, *The Jezebel Letters: Religion and Politics in Ninth-Century Israel* (Minneapolis: Fortress Press, 2005). See also Suzanne Shaw, "Letters to the Editor of Genesis," in *First Person: Essays in Biblical Autobiography,* ed. Philip R. Davies (New York: Sheffield Academic Press, 2002), 25–46, and Yairah Amit, "I Delilah: A Victim of Interpretation," in *First Person,* ed. Davies, 59–76, for similar retellings.

Critical Feminist Biblical Studies: Remembering the Struggles, Envisioning the Future

ELISABETH SCHÜSSLER FIORENZA

1. See my book *Wisdom Ways: Introducing Feminist Biblical Interpretation* (Maryknoll, N.Y.: Orbis Books, 2001); see also María Pilar Aquino and Elisabeth Schüssler Fiorenza, eds., *In the Power of Wisdom (Concilium)* (London: SCM Press, 2000).
2. See my article "Invitation to Dance: In the Open House of Wisdom: Feminist Study of the Bible," in *Engaging the Bible: Critical Readings from Contemporary Women,* eds. Choi Hee An and Katheryn Pfisterer Darr (Minneapolis: Fortress Press, 2006), 81–104.
3. Among many works, see, for example, María Pilar Aquino, Daisy L. Machado, and Jeanette Rodrigues, eds., *A Reader in Latina Feminist Theology, Religion and Justice* (Austin: University of Texas Press, 2002); María Pilar Aquino and Maria José Rosado-Nunes, eds., *Feminist Intercultural Theology: Latina Explorations for a Just World* (Maryknoll, N.Y.: Orbis Books, 2007); Marcella Althaus-Reid, *From Feminist Theology to Indecent Theology: Readings on Poverty, Sexual Identity and God* (London: SCM Press, 2005); Katie Geneva Cannon, *Katie's Canon: Womanism and the Soul of the Black Community* (New York: Continuum, 1995); Katie Geneva Cannon, "Womanist Perspectival Discourse and Canon Formation," *Journal of Feminist Studies in Religion* 9, nos. 1–2 (Spring/Fall 1993): 29–37; Ann Braude, *Transforming the Faiths of Our Fathers: Women Who Changed American Religion,* 1st ed. (New York: Palgrave Macmillan, 2004); Ada María Isasi-Díaz, En La Lucha / *In the Struggle: Elaborating a* Mujerista *Theology* (Minneapolis: Fortress Press, 2004); Hedwig Meyer-Wilmes, *Rebellion on the Borders* (Kampen, Neth.: Kok Pharos, 1995); Stephanie Y. Mitchem, *Introducing Womanist Theology* (Maryknoll, N.Y.: Orbis Books, 2002); Anne Pattel-Gray, *Aboriginal Spirituality: Past, Present, Future* (Blackburn, Australia: HarperCollins Religious, 1996); Kwok Pui-lan, *Introducing Asian Feminist Theology* (Sheffield, U.K.: Academic Press, 2000).
4. I have introduced the neologism *kyriarchy* instead of *hierarchy. Kyriarchy* is derived from the Greek words *kyrios,* which means, "lord, slavemaster," and *archein,* which means, "to rule, dominate." For kyriarchal analysis as intersectional analysis, see my introduction to *Prejudice and Christian Beginnings,* ed. Laura Nasrallah and Elisabeth Schüssler Fiorenza (Minneapolis: Fortress Press, 2009); see also my book *But She Said: Feminist Practices of Biblical Interpretation* (Boston: Beacon Press, 1992).

5. See, for instance, among many others, Alicia Suskin Ostriker, *Feminist Revision and the Bible* (Oxford, U.K.: Blackwell, 1993); Elisabeth Schüssler Fiorenza, ed., *Searching the Scriptures: A Feminist Introduction* (New York: Crossroad, 1993); Elisabeth Schüssler Fiorenza, ed., *Searching the Scriptures: A Feminist Commentary* (New York: Crossroad, 1994); Renita Weems, *Battered Love: Marriage, Sex, and Violence in the Hebrew Prophets* (Minneapolis: Fortress Press, 1995); Alice Bach, ed., *Wo/men in the Hebrew Bible* (New York: Routledge, 1999); Phyllis Bird, ed., *Reading the Bible as Women: Perspectives from Africa, Asia and Latin America,* Semeia 78 (Atlanta: Society of Biblical Literature, 1997); Kwok Pui-lan, *Discovering the Bible in the Non-Biblical World* (Maryknoll, N.Y.: Orbis Books, 1995); Shelly Matthews, Cynthia Briggs Kittredge, and Melanie Johnson-DeBaufre, eds., *Walk in the Ways of Wisdom: Essays in Honor of Elisabeth Schüssler Fiorenza* (Harrisburg, Penn.: Trinity Press International, 2003); Holly Hearon, ed., *Distant Voices Drawing Near: Essays in Honor of Antoinette Clark Wire* (Collegeville, Minn.: Liturgical Press, 2004); Caroline Vander Stichele and Todd Penner, eds., *Her Master's Tools? Feminist and Postcolonial Engagements of Historical-Critical Discourse* (Atlanta: Society of Biblical Literature, 2005); Kathleen O'Brien Wicker, Althea Spencer Miller, and Musa W. Dube, eds., *Feminist New Testament Studies: Global and Future Perspectives* (New York: Palgrave Macmillan, 2005), 43–62; Elsa Tamez, *Struggles for Power in Early Christianity* (Maryknoll, N.Y.: Orbis Books, 2007).
6. Wilda C. Gafney, *Daughters of Miriam: Women Prophets in Ancient Israel* (Minneapolis: Fortress Press, 2009).
7. In order to indicate the brokenness and inadequacy of human language to name the Divine, I have switched in my book *Jesus—Miriam's Child, Sophia's Prophet: Critical Issues in Feminist Christology* (New York: Continuum, 1994) from the Orthodox Jewish writing of "G-d," which I had adopted in *But She Said* and *Discipleship of Equals* to this writing of "G*d," which seeks to avoid the conservative malestream association that the writing of G-d has for Jewish feminists. Since the*logy means speaking about G*d, I write "the*logy" also in this broken form.
8. See, for instance, Susan Haskins, *Mary Magdalen: Myth and Metaphor* (New York: Harcourt, 1993); Karen L. King, *The Gospel of Mary of Magdala: Jesus and the First Woman Apostle* (Santa Rosa, Calif.: Polebridge, 2003); Holly Hearon, *The Mary Magdalene Tradition: Witness and Counter-Witness in Early Christian Communities* (Collegeville, Minn.: Liturgical Press, 2004); Jane Schaberg, *The Resurrection of Mary Magdalene: Legends, Apocrypha and the Christian Testament* (New York: Continuum, 2002).
9. See my book *In Memory of Her: A Feminist Reconstruction of Christian Origins,* 10th anniv. ed. (New York: Crossroad Publishers, 1994).
10. See my article "'What She Has Done Will Be Told … ': Reflections on Writing Feminist History," in *Distant Voices Drawing Near: Essays in Honor of Antoinette Clark Wire,* ed. Holly E. Hearon (Collegeville, Minn.: Liturgical Press, 2004), 3–18.
11. See my article "Discipleship of Equals: Memory and Vision," *Journal of the European Society in Theological Research* 16 (2008): 67–90.
12. See my books *The Power of the Word: Scripture and the Rhetoric of Empire* (Minneapolis: Fortress Press, 2007) and *Democratizing Biblical Studies: Toward an Emancipatory Educational Space* (Louisville: Westminster John Knox Press, 2009).

13. Elizabeth A. Castelli, "The Ekklesia of Women and/as Utopian Space: Locating the Work of Elisabeth Schüssler Fiorenza in Feminist Utopian Thought," in *On the Cutting Edge: The Study of Women in Biblical Worlds,* ed. Jane Schaberg, Alice Bach, and Esther Fuchs (New York: Continuum, 2004), 36–52.
14. For realizing the practices of the *ekklēsia* of wo/men, see Mary E. Hunt, "Feminist Catholic Theology and Practice: From Kyriarchy to Discipleship of Equals," in *Toward a New Heaven and a New Earth: Essays in Honor of Elisabeth Schüssler Fiorenza,* ed. Fernando F. Segovia (Maryknoll, N.Y.: Orbis Books, 2003), 459–72; and Marjorie Procter-Smith, "Feminist Ritual Strategies: the Ekklēsia Gynaikōn at Work," in *Toward a New Heaven and a New Earth,* 498–515.
15. See also my book *Discipleship of Equals: A Critical Feminist Ekklesia-logy of Liberation* (New York: Crossroad, 1993); Mary Ann Beavis, *Jesus & Utopia: Looking for the Kingdom of God in the Roman World* (Minneapolis: Fortress Press, 2006), and her article "Christian Origins, Egalitarianism, and Utopia," *Journal of Feminist Studies in Religion* 23, no. 2 (2007): 27–49.
16. For documentation, see my books *Jesus—Miriam's Child, Sophia's Prophet: Critical Issues in Feminist Christology* (New York: Continuum, 1994) and *Jesus and the Politics of Interpretation,* reprint ed. (New York: Continuum, 2001).
17. Rosemary Radford Ruether, *Faith and Fratricide: The Theological Roots of Anti-Semitism* (New York: Seabury Press, 1974).

Inclusivity and Distinctions: The Future of Dalit Feminist Biblical Studies

SUREKHA NELAVALA

1. Indian Christian theology was developed mostly by caste Christians under the influence of the Christian missionaries who supported Hindu-Christian dialogue. It emerged as a result of indigenization of the Gospels in the Indian context. Indian Christian theology, in its urge to balance the standards of systematic theology from the West and its dialogue with Hindu philosophy, has turned out to be highly metaphysical and philosophical. It denies the importance of physical and social reality. For more discussion on a Dalit view of Indian Christian theology, see Arvind P. Nirmal, "Doing Theology from a Dalit Perspective," in *A Reader in Dalit Theology,* ed. Arvind P. Nirmal and V. Devasahayam (Madras, India: Gurukul, 1997), 139–145; and for a concise reading on Indian Christian theology, see Robin Boyd, *An Introduction to Indian Christian Theology* (Edinburgh, U.K.: University of Edinburgh, 1969).
2. Nirmal, "Doing Theology from a Dalit Perspective," 139–145.
3. V. Devasahayam, "Doing Dalit Theology: Basic Assumptions," in *Frontiers of Dalit Theology,* ed. V. Devasahayam (Madras, India: Gurukul, 1997), 270–82.
4. For a discussion about the generalized term *women's experience,* see Pamela Dickey Young, *Feminist Theology/Christian Theology: In Search of Method* (Minneapolis: Fortress Press, 1990), 49–69; and Chris Weedon, *Feminist Practice and Poststructuralist Theory* (Oxford, U.K.: Blackwell, 1987), 74–86. See also, for a discussion on the subjective experience of knowledge, universal female experience, and

personal politics, Judith Grant, *Fundamental Feminism* (New York: Routledge, 1993), 40–45.

5. Although all untouchables can be categorized as Dalits, in reality Dalits are divided into subcastes where each one claims a higher status than the other. Which subcaste dominates in a particular region depends mostly on the local population.
6. See Anupama Rao, "Introduction: Caste, Gender and Indian Feminism," in *Gender and Caste,* ed. Anupama Rao (Delhi: Kali for Women, 2003), 1, 5.
7. See, for example, Stephen Butterfield, *Black Autobiography in America* (Amherst, Mass.: University of Massachusetts Press, 1974); John W. Blassingame, ed., *Slave Testimony: Two Centuries of Letters, Speeches, Interviews and Autobiographies* (Baton Rouge: Louisiana State University Press, 1977); Margo Culley, ed., *American Women's Autobiography: Feasts of Memory* (Madison: University of Wisconsin Press, 1992).
8. M. B. Tappan, "Domination, Subordination and Dialogical Self: Identity Development and the Politics of 'Ideological Becoming,'" *Culture and Psychology* 11 (2005): 47–75.
9. Rao, "Introduction," 13.

The Future of Feminist Scripture Studies

Shelly Matthews

1. Melanie Johnson-DeBaufre has compellingly argued that many sayings in the Q tradition, which have been traditionally read as Jesus focused, are more properly understood as sayings focused on the *basileia* of God. Such a reading makes possible the acknowledgment of alliance, rather than division, between Jesus believers and other Jews. See *Jesus Among Her Children: Q, Eschatology, and the Construction of Christian Origins* (Cambridge, Mass.: Harvard University Press, 2005).
2. See Elisabeth Schüssler Fiorenza, "Missionaries, Apostles, Coworkers: Romans 16 and the Reconstruction of Women's Early Christian History," *Word and World* 6, no. 4 (1986): 420–33.
3. Antoinette Wire, *Corinthian Women Prophets: A Reconstruction through Paul's Rhetoric* (Minneapolis: Augsburg Fortress Press, 1995).
4. Clarice Martin, "The *Haustafeln* (Household Codes) in African American Biblical Interpretation: 'Free Slaves' and 'Subordinate Women,'" in *Stony the Road We Trod: African American Biblical Interpretation,* ed. Cain Hope Felder (Minneapolis: Fortress Press, 1991), 206–31; Linda Maloney, "The Pastoral Epistles," in *Searching the Scriptures: A Feminist Commentary,* ed. Elisabeth Schüssler Fiorenza and Shelly Matthews (New York: Crossroad, 1994), 361–80.
5. Of the many feminist scholars who have cautioned against reading a "feminist" Jesus as standing against a "hopelessly patriarchal" Judaism, see Katharina von Kellenbach, *Anti-Judaism in Feminist Religious Writing* (Atlanta: Scholars Press, 1994).
6. Gay L. Byron, *Symbolic Blackness and Ethnic Difference in Early Christian Literature* (New York: Routledge, 2002).
7. Jennifer Glancy, *Slavery in Early Christianity* (New York: Oxford University Press, 2002).

8. Jane Schaberg, *The Resurrection of Mary Magdalene: Legends, Aprocrypha and the Christian Testament* (New York: Continuum, 2002).
9. For one accounting of the popularity of the Thecla cult in antiquity, see Elizabeth Castelli, *Martyrdom and Memory: Early Christian Culture Making* (New York: Columbia University Press, 2004). See also Shelly Matthews, "Thinking of Thecla: Issues in Feminist Historiography," *Journal of Feminist Studies in Religion* 17, no. 2 (2001): 39–55.
10. For an English translation of this excerpt from Philo's *Special Laws,* see Ross Shepard Kraemer, ed., *Women's Religions in the Greco-Roman World* (New York: Oxford University Press, 2004), 32–33.
11. Elisabeth Schüssler Fiorenza, *Wisdom Ways: Introducing Feminist Biblical Interpretations* (Maryknoll, N.Y.: Orbis Books), 71–73.
12. Though the household codes of Colossians, Ephesians, and 1 Peter exhort both the submission of wives *and* slaves in the patriarchal household, my biblically fundamental students seem to have no difficulty in making distinctions between the ethical relevance of these two types of exhortation. Few, if any, would argue in defense of biblical support for the institution of slavery, but this generally does not prevent them from regarding exhortations concerning wives' submission as sacrosanct.

Part III Feminist Ethical Agendas

What Does Antiracist Feminist Christian Social Ethics Look Like?

TRACI C. WEST

1. See S. Karthic Ramakrishnan, *Democracy in Immigrant America: Changing Demographics and Political Participation* (Palo Alto, Calif.: Stanford University Press, 2005); Ronald Schmidt Sr., Yvette M. Alex-Assensoh, Andrew L. Aoki, and Rodney E. Hero, *Newcomers, Outsiders, and Insiders: Immigrants and American Racial Politics in the Early Twentieth Century* (Ann Arbor, Mich.: University of Michigan Press, 2009).
2. Pioneering white feminist Christian social ethicist Beverly Harrison articulates this need nicely: "When I first developed this hermeneutic of suspicion that women's wisdom had been omitted, I still did not realize that my understanding of women's lives and experience was obscured by my location in white, middle strata, 'old line' Protestantism." *Justice in the Making: Feminist Social Ethics* (Louisville: Westminster John Knox Press, 2004), 7.
3. The very title of the first womanist theology book captures this dichotomy. Black theologian Jacqueline Grant wrote *White Women's Christ and Black Women's Jesus: Feminist Christology and Womanist Response* (Atlanta: Scholar's Press, 1989). Though the framework of this text is consistent with the title, Grant acknowledges that black women share sexist oppression with "White women and other Third World women" and that poverty is shared among "poor Blacks and Whites, and other Third World peoples, especially women" (216–17).
4. For examples of discussions about the growth and variety of womanist thought, see Monica Coleman, "Must I Be Womanist?" *Journal of Feminist Studies in Religion* 22, no. 1 (Spring 2006): 85–96; Stacey M. Floyd-Thomas, ed., *Deeper Shades of Purple: Womanism in Religion and Society* (New York: New York University Press, 2006).

5. See Amnesty International, *Maze of Injustice: The Failure to Protect Indigenous Women from Violence in the USA* (New York: Amnesty International, 2007). Available at www.amnestyusa.org/women/maze/report.pdf.
6. See, for example, Sylvanna Falcón, "'National Security' and the Violation of Women: Militarized Border Rape at the US-Mexico Border," in *Color of Violence: The Incite! Anthology,* ed. Incite! Women of Color Against Violence (Cambridge, Mass.: South End Press, 2006), 119–29.
7. See critiques in Amy-Jill Levine, *The Misunderstood Jew: The Church and the Scandal of the Jewish Jesus* (New York: HarperCollins, 2006).
8. After more than a decade of struggle by civil and gay rights activists, in 2009 President Barack Obama signed the law (Public Law No. 111-84) that made it a federal crime to assault an individual on the basis of sexual orientation, gender identity, or disability.
9. At the time of this publication, the struggle for passage of the Employment Non-Discrimination Act (ENDA) S.1584/H 3017, a federal law to bar employment discrimination on the basis of sexual orientation or gender identity, remains unsuccessful.
10. See my lengthier discussion of this topic in "Naming the Problem: Black Clergy, U.S. Politics, and Marriage Equality" in *Our Family Values: Same-sex Marriage and Religion,* ed. Traci C. West (Westport, Conn.: Praeger, 2006), 177–90.
11. Cara Mia DiMassa and Jessica Garrison, "Why Gays, Blacks Are Divided on Prop. 8," *Los Angeles Times,* November 8, 2008.
12. For an extremely well-argued analysis of these dynamics, see Irene Monroe, "Between a Rock and a Hard Place: Struggling with the Black Church's Heterosexism and the White Queer Community's Racism," in *Out of the Shadows and Into the Light: Christianity and Homosexuality,* ed. Miguel A. De La Torre (St. Louis: Chalice Press, 2009), 39–58.
13. Jessica Garrison, "Black Clergy Both Attack, Defend Prop. 8," *Los Angeles Times,* October 22, 2008.

Trans-forming Feminist Christianity

VIRGINIA RAMEY MOLLENKOTT

1. Gerard Manley Hopkins, "Pied Beauty," *Gerard Manley Hopkins,* ed. W. H. Gardner (Baltimore: Penguin, 1952), 30–31.
2. Christopher A. Shelley, *Transpeople: Repudiation, Trauma, Healing* (Toronto: University of Toronto Press, 2008), 54.
3. Edward Tripp, *Crowell's Handbook of Classical Mythology* (New York: Thomas Y. Crowell, 1970), 301.
4. Shelley, *Transpeople,* 181, 183.
5. Virginia R. Mollenkott, *Omnigender: A Trans-religious Approach* was first published by Pilgrim Press in 2001, and as of 2007 is available in a revised and updated edition.
6. Cheryl Chase, "Hermaphrodites with Attitude: Mapping the Emergence of Intersex Political Activism," in *The Transgender Studies Reader*, ed. Susan Stryker and Stephen Whittle (New York: Routledge, 2006), 312–13.

7. Gayle Rubin, "Of Catamites and Kings: Reflections on Butch, Gender, and Boundaries," in *The Transgender Studies Reader,* 476–77.
8. For a Southern Baptist perspective on my evangelicalism, see Trish Hawley, *Desperate for Authenticity: An Evangelical Critique of the Feminist Theology of Virginia Ramey Mollenkott* (forthcoming from the University Press of America). For my own description of how I was radicalized by the Bible and Milton's hermeneutics, see *Transforming the Faiths of Our Fathers: Women Who Changed American Religion,* ed. Ann Braude (New York: Palgrave/Macmillian, 2004), 55–72.
9. H. Southam, as quoted in Shelley, *Transpeople,* 111.
10. Lewis Gannett, "A Double Standard in Lincoln Studies," *The Gay and Lesbian Review* (November–December 2009): 22–24.
11. Ibid., 24.
12. Theodore W. Jennings Jr., *Plato or Paul? The Origins of Western Homophobia* (Cleveland: Pilgrim Press, 2009), 88–89.
13. Ibid., 220.
14. Ibid., 223. Jennings does not use the term *transphobia* directly, but he is very clear about the classical meaning of *effeminate* as "soft" or "self-indulgent" (not homosexual); he shows that Plato, Philo, Josephus, and Chrysostum sometimes conflated transgenderism with homosexuality; and he demonstrates that Roman edicts against homosexuality showed "a horror of the transgendering or feminization of the male."
15. Among these scholarly works, I strongly recommend *The Queer Bible Commentary,* ed. Deryn Guest, Robert E. Goss, Mona West, and Thomas Bohache (London: SCM Press, 2006); Dale Martin's *Sex and the Single Savior: Gender and Sexuality in Biblical Interpretation* (Louisville: Westminster John Knox Press, 2006); my own book *Omnigender: A Trans-religious Approach* (Cleveland: Pilgrim Press, 2001); and Theodore W. Jennings Jr.'s trilogy: *Jacob's Wound: Homoerotic Narrative in the Literature of Ancient Israel* (London: Continuum, 2005); *The Man Jesus Loved: Homoerotic Narratives from the New Testament* (Cleveland: Pilgrim Press, 2003); and *Plato or Paul? The Origins of Western Homophobia* (Cleveland: Pilgrim Press, 2009).
16. Candace West and Don H. Zimmerman, "Doing Gender," in *The Gendered Society Reader,* 2nd ed., ed. Michael E. Kimmel and Amy Aronson (New York: Oxford University Press, 2004), 162.
17. Julia Ward Howe, *The Hermaphrodite,* ed. Gary Williams (Lincoln: University of Nebraska Press, 2004), 195–96. The novel consists of sections that have been pieced together by Gary Williams, with the help of many Julia Ward Howe scholars. This is its first publication.
18. Marie Cartier, "The Butch Woman Inside James Dean," in *Trans/formations,* ed. Lisa Isherwood and Marcella Althaus-Reid (London: SCM Press, 2009), 108, 110.
19. Michelle Ann Abate, *Tomboys: A Literary and Cultural History* (Philadelphia: Temple University Press, 2008), 155, 163.
20. Ibid., 159.
21. As quoted in Shelley, *Transpeople,* 203.
22. B. K. Hipsher, "God Is a Many-Gendered Thing," in *Trans/formations,* ed. Isherwood and Althaus-Reid, 103. Emphasis mine.
23. Lisa M. Diamond, *Sexual Fluidity: Understanding Women's Love and Desire* (Cambridge, Mass.: Harvard University Press, 2008), 11.

24. Ibid., 11.
25. Ibid., 201.
26. Ibid., 246.
27. Chase, "Hermaphrodites with Attitude," 301.
28. Ibid., 300.
29. Mollenkott, *Omnigender*, 47.
30. Hipsher, "God Is a Many-Gendered Thing," 99.

Seeking Justice and Healing: Violence against Women as an Agenda for Feminist Christianity

MARIE M. FORTUNE

1. Audre Lorde, *Sister Outsider: Essays and Speeches* (Freedom, Calif.: Crossing Press, 1984), 40–41.
2. In 1977, I founded the Prevention of Sexual Violence Project, which became the Center for the Prevention of Sexual and Domestic Violence, and later became the FaithTrust Institute. See the institute's website at www.faithtrustinstitute.org.
3. I tried to address this problem by establishing the *Journal on Religion and Abuse* in 2000, published originally by Haworth Press. Its subtitle was *Advocacy, Pastoral Care and Prevention.* We wanted this journal to bridge the academy and the faith communities and support research and writing that was both scholarly and practical to be of use in the classroom and the congregation. *JORA* was sustained until 2008, when we concluded that we simply did not have adequate material to maintain its publication. Unfortunately, without a journal like this, the issues of sexual and domestic violence are once again easily lost in both the academy and the church.
4. Rita Nakashima Brock and Rebecca Ann Parker, *Proverbs of Ashes: Violence, Redemptive Suffering, and the Search for What Saves Us* (Boston: Beacon Press, 2001).
5. Rita Nakashima Brock and Rebecca Ann Parker, "A Witness for/from Life: Writing Feminist Theology as an Act of Resisting Violence" (presentation at the American Academy of Religion Annual Meeting, Denver, November 17, 2001).
6. Maimonides, Mishnah Torah, *Book One: Knowledge: Repentance*, ed. Philip Birnbaum (New York: Hebrew Publishing, 1944), 2.9.
7. Ibid., 2.1.
8. It appears in Shakespeare's *King Lear*, act 4, scene 7.

Feminist Theo-ethics in Remix Culture

RACHEL A. R. BUNDANG

1. Monica Coleman, "Must I Be Womanist?" *Journal of Feminist Studies in Religion* 22, no. 1 (Spring 2006): 85–96.
2. Alice Walker, *The Color Purple* (New York: Harcourt Brace Jovanovich, 1982).
3. Audre Lorde, "The Master's Tools Will Never Dismantle the Master's House," in *Sister Outsider: Essays and Speeches* (Berkeley: Crossing Press, 1984), 110–113.

4. See Jon Sobrino and Felix Wilfred, eds., *Globalization and Its Victims* (London: SCM Press, 2001).
5. See, for example, Paul Farmer, *Partner to the Poor: A Paul Farmer Reader*, ed. Haun Saussy (Berkeley: University of California Press, 2010).

Searching for an Ethic: Sexuality, Children, and Moral Agency

KATE M. OTT

1. For specific data on each of these issues and the resultant health disparities, see the "Publications" section of the Guttmacher Institute website, at www.guttmacher.org. Their work includes policy reviews, national and international statistics, and policy briefs.
2. Margaret Farley, *Just Love: A Framework for Christian Sexual Ethics* (New York: Continuum, 2006), 235.
3. See Marcia J. Bunge, ed., *The Child in Christian Thought* (Grand Rapids, Mich.: Eerdmans, 2001).
4. On children, see Joyce Ann Mercer, *Welcoming Children: A Practical Theology of Childhood* (Atlanta: Chalice Press, 2005); Bonnie Miller-McLemore, *Let the Children Come: Reimagining Childhood from a Christian Perspective* (San Francisco: Jossey-Bass, 2003); and Karen M. Yust, *Real Kids, Real Faith: Practices for Nurturing Children's Spiritual Lives* (San Francisco: Jossey-Bass, 2004). On young adults, see Robert C. Dykstra, Alan Coles, and Donald Capp, eds., *Losers, Loners, and Rebels: The Spiritual Struggles of Boys* (Louisville: Westminster John Knox Press, 2007), and Evelyn Parker, ed., *The Sacred Selves of Adolescent Girls: Hard Stories of Race, Class, and Gender* (Cleveland: Pilgrim Press, 2006).
5. Cristina L. H. Traina, "Children and Moral Agency," *Journal of the Society of Christian Ethics* 29, no. 1 (2009): 19–37; Jennifer Beste, "Children Speak: Second Graders' Experience of Sin, Forgiveness, and Moral Agency in the Sacrament of Reconciliation" (presentation at the Society of Christian Ethics Annual Meeting, San Jose, January 8, 2010); and John Wall, "Childhood Studies, Hermeneutics, and Theological Ethics," *Journal of Religion* 86, no. 4 (October 2006): 523–48.
6. Traina, "Children and Moral Agency," 24.
7. Wall, "Childhood Studies, Hermeneutics, and Theological Ethics," 540.
8. Groundbreaking work in this area has only become part of religious discourse in the past ten to fifteen years and is still under great dispute. See Virginia Ramey Mollenkott, *Omnigender: A Trans-religious Approach* (Cleveland: Pilgrim Press, 2001).
9. See review of the prevalence and science of sexual orientation and gender identity in Timothy Palmer and Debra W. Haffner, *A Time to Seek: A Study Guide on Sexual and Gender Diversity* (Westport, Conn.: Religious Institute, 2007). For discussion of sexual behaviors and attraction related to sexual self-identity, see Edward O. Laumann, et al., *The Social Organization of Sexuality: Sexual Practices in the United States* (Chicago: University of Chicago Press, 1994). See also Louis Diamant and Richard D. McAnulty, eds., *The Psychology of Sexual Orientation, Behavior, and Identity: A Handbook* (Santa Barbara, Calif.: Greenwood Press, 1995).
10. See, for example, Marvin Ellison, *Erotic Justice: A Liberating Ethic of Sexuality* (Louisville: Westminster John Knox Press, 1996); Kelly Brown Douglas, *Sexuality*

and the Black Church: A Womanist Perspective (Maryknoll, N.Y.: Orbis Books, 1999); and Patricia Beattie Jung, Mary E. Hunt, and Radhika Balakrishnan, eds., *Good Sex: Feminist Perspectives from the World's Religions* (Rutgers, N.J.: Rutgers University Press, 2001).

11. Joan Timmerman, "Sex, Sacred or Profane?" in *Dialogue About Catholic Sexual Teaching,* vol. 8, *Readings in Moral Theology,* ed. Charles E. Curran and Richard A. McCormick (New York: Paulist Press, 1993), 53.
12. See Kate M. Ott, "Re-Thinking Adolescent Sexual Ethics: A Social Justice Obligation to Adolescent Sexual Health," *Journal of Lutheran Ethics* 7, no. 2 (2007): http://archive.elca.org/jle/article.asp?k=697.
13. See Traina, "Children and Moral Agency."
14. These normative criteria are put forward in "An Open Letter to Religious Leaders on Adolescent Sexuality," Religious Institute on Sexual Morality, Justice, and Healing (2007), available at www.religiousinstitute.org/resources/open-letters.
15. Farley, *Just Love,* 228.

Part IV Feminist Liturgical and Artistic Frontiers

The Feminist Face of God: Art and Liturgy

JEANETTE STOKES

1. See www.depts.drew.edu/tsfac/helkins for more information about the work of Heather Murray Elkins.
2. See www.rcwms.org for information on the programs and publications of the RCWMS.
3. Many of the musicians and writers cited have their own websites. To purchase feminist music, visit the women-owned distribution company Ladyslipper at www.ladyslipper.org. Holly Near's website is www.hollynear.com; Ronnie Gilbert's, www.ronniegilbert.com; Cris Williamson's, www.criswilliamson.com; and Sweet Honey in the Rock's, www.sweethoney.com. Alice Walker's website is www.alicewalkersgarden.com; see especially *The Color Purple* (New York: Harcourt Brace Jovanovich, 1982) and *In Search of our Mothers' Gardens: Womanist Prose* (San Diego: Harcourt Brace Jovanovich, 1983). For Toni Morrison, see especially *Beloved* (New York: Alfred A. Knopf, 1987). Marge Piercy's website is www.margepiercy.com; see especially *The Moon Is Always Female* (New York: Alfred A. Knopf, 1980). May Sarton, *Journal of a Solitude: Reflections during One Year* (New York: W. W. Norton, 1977). Audre Lorde, *Sister Outsider: Essays and Speeches* (Berkeley: Crossing Press, 1984). Mary Oliver, *New and Selected Poems* (Boston: Beacon Press, 1992).
4. "Lean on me, I am your sister," is a line in "Sister" by Cris Williamson on the album *The Changer and the Changed* (Wolf Moon Records, 1975). Sweet Honey in the Rock, "Let Us Break Bread Together" on *Sweet Honey in the Rock* (Flying Fish, 1976).
5. Meinrad Craighead, *The Mother's Songs: Images of God the Mother* (Mahwah, N.J.: Paulist Press, 1986). See www.meinradcraighead.com. Much of *The Mother's Songs* is reprinted in *Meinrad Craighead: Crow Mother and the Dog God—A Retrospective* (San Francisco: Pomegranate, 2003).

6. Starhawk, *The Spiral Dance: A Rebirth of the Ancient Religion of the Great Goddess* (San Francisco: HarperSanFrancisco, 1979); Rosemary Radford Ruether, *Woman-Church: Theology and Practice* (San Francisco: Harper & Row, 1985).
7. Miriam Therese Winter, *Defecting in Place: Women Taking Responsibility for Their Own Spiritual Lives* (New York: Crossroad, 1995); Teresa Berger, *Dissident Daughters: Feminist Liturgies in Global Context* (Louisville: Westminster John Knox Press, 2001).
8. For more information about the Re-Imagining Conference, see Nancy J. Berneking and Pamela Carter Joern, eds., *Re-Membering and Re-Imagining* (Cleveland: Pilgrim Press, 1995).
9. Personal statement by Layla (Páola) Kipp, bulletin for the Interfaith Celebration sponsored by the Resource Center for Women and Ministry in the South (RCWMS) and Stone Circles, December 18, 2005.
10. See www.carolebakerartist.com for more information about the work of artist Carole Baker.
11. See www.meinradproject.org for more information about the one-hour documentary *Meinrad Craighead: Praying with Images,* produced by Amy Kellum, RCWMS, and Minnow Media (Durham, N.C.: Resource Center for Women & Ministry in the South, 2009). DVDs may be ordered through that website or by contacting RCWMS at www.rcwms.org or rcwmsnc@aol.com.
12. Meinrad Craighead, *Crow Mother and the Dog God: A Retrospective* (San Francisco: Pomegranate Communications, 2003), 32.
13. See www.bryantholsenbeck.com for more information about artist Bryant Holsenbeck. To order a DVD of the documentary *Blackbirds, Bottle Caps, and Broken Records: Environmental Artist Bryant Holsenbeck at Work*, directed by Margaret Morales (Durham, N.C.: Resource Center for Women & Ministry in the South, 2009), contact RCWMS at www.rcwms.org or rswmsnc@aol.com.
14. Rita Nakashima Brock and Rebecca Ann Parker, *Saving Paradise: How Christianity Traded Love of This World for Crucifixion and Empire* (Boston: Beacon Press, 2008). For more information about the book, see www.savingparadise.net.

More Than Words

Deborah Sokolove

1. Gail Ramshaw, *God Beyond Gender: Feminist Christian God-Language* (Minneapolis: Fortress Press, 1995), 125.
2. Letty M. Russell, *Church in the Round: Feminist Interpretation of the Church* (Louisville: Westminster John Knox Press, 1993), 21.
3. Ramshaw, *God Beyond Gender,* 21.
4. Marjorie Procter-Smith, *In Her Own Rite: Constructing Feminist Liturgical Tradition* (Nashville: Abingdon Press, 1990), 63.
5. Brian Wren, "Bring Many Names," in *The New Century Hymnal,* United Church of Christ (Cleveland: Pilgrim Press, 1995), 11.
6. United Church of Christ, *The New Century Hymnal* (Cleveland: Pilgrim Press, 1995).

7. See, for example, the following hymns by Ruth Duck found in *The New Century Hymnal:* "Colorful Creator" #30; "To God Compose a Song of Joy" #36; and "My Heart Sings Out with Joyful Praise" #106, among others.
8. United Methodist Church, *The Faith We Sing* (Nashville: Abingdon Press, 2000).

Feminist Eucharists at Wisdom's Many Tables

DIANN L. NEU

1. See Rosemary Radford Ruether, *Women-Church: Theology and Practice* (San Francisco: Harper & Row, 1986); Diann L. Neu and Mary E. Hunt, *Women-Church Sourcebook* (Silver Spring, Md.: WATERworks Press, 1993); Elisabeth Schüssler Fiorenza, *Discipleship of Equals: A Critical Feminist Ekklesia-logy of Liberation* (New York: Crossroad, 1993); and Letty Russell, *Church in the Round: Feminist Interpretation of the Church* (Louisville: Westminster John Knox Press, 1993).
2. A description of this liturgy is in my thesis, "Feminist Liturgies: Claiming Ourselves Church" (Graduate Theological Union, 1981).
3. Alieda Verhoeven, a Dutch Methodist pastor who ministered in Argentina, in seminar at Bossey, Switzerland, January 2001.
4. Mary E. Hunt, "Feminist Ministry," *WATERwheel* 8, no. 3 (Fall 1995): 2.
5. Alicia Partnoy, *The Little School: Tales of Disappearance and Survival in Argentina,* trans. Alicia Partnoy with Lois Athey and Sandra Braunstein (Pittsburgh: Cleis Press, 1986), 86. On January 12, 1977, Alicia Partnoy was disappeared in Argentina. The military held her for five months without charge and without her family knowing her whereabouts. She was "re-appeared" and held in prison for another two and a half years before going into exile. Her prose poem "Bread" concludes with this defiant parody of the Lord's Prayer.
6. WATER, the Women's Alliance for Theology, Ethics and Ritual, was founded in 1983 when Mary E. Hunt and Diann L. Neu gathered thirteen women from diverse religious backgrounds to talk about what religious feminists needed. They called for an alliance focusing on theology, ethics, and ritual.
7. These include: "Women's Gifts/Changing Church," 1980, Berkeley, California; "Women Moving Church," 1981, Washington, D.C.; "Woman Church Speaks: From Generation to Generation," 1983, Chicago, Illinois; "Women Church: Claiming Our Power," 1987, Cincinnati, Ohio; "Women of Fire: A Pentecost Celebration," 1989, De Tiltenberg, the Netherlands; "Women and the Gospel Traditions," 1989, Lincoln, Nebraska; Re-Imagining, 1993, Minneapolis, Minnesota; "Breaking Bread/Doing Justice," 1995, Crystal City, Virginia; "A Shared Garden," 1999, Cuba; "A Women-Church Harvest Eucharist," 2000, Boston, Massachusetts; "Going Forth from This Holy Place," 2001, Accra, Ghana; "Called to Be a Healing Community," 2001, Colorado Springs, Colorado; "Breaking Bread/Blessing Ministries," 2002, Orlando, Florida; "Easter Vigil: Renew the Earth," 2003, Washington, D.C.; "Celebrating Catholic Feminist Ministries: A Women-Church Forum," 2007, Chicago, Illinois; "Gathered at Sophia's Table," 2010, Silver Spring, Maryland; and many more. This list reads like the synods of the church! And women talk about them this way.
8. Table grace from a dinner at the Hunt-Neu house in 2010.
9. "Wisdom's Table" adapted from the spiritual "Jacob's Ladder."

10. Colleen Fulmer, "Dancing Sophia's Circle," *Dancing Sophia's Circle* CD (Loretto Spirituality Network, 1994).
11. Section adapted from Diann L. Neu, "Eucharistic Banquet of Divine Wisdom" from the conference "Celebrating Catholic Feminist Ministries: A Women-Church Forum," *WATERwheel* 18, no. 4 (2007): 3–4.
12. Miriam Therese Winter, "Blessing Song," *Songlines* (New York: Crossroad, 1996), 21; recorded on the album *Womansong* (Medical Mission Sisters, 1987).
13. See Hal Taussig, *In the Beginning Was the Meal: Social Experimentation & Early Christian Identity* (Minneapolis: Fortress Press, 2009); Dennis Smith, *From Symposium to Eucharist: The Banquet in the Early Christian World* (Minneapolis: Fortress Press, 2003); Hal Taussig and Dennis E. Smith, *Many Tables: The Eucharist in the New Testament and Liturgy Today* (Philadelphia: Trinity Press International, 1990); Kathleen E. Corley, *Private Women, Public Meals: Social Conflict in the Synoptic Tradition* (Peabody, Mass.: Hendrickson, 1993); Angela Standhartinger, "Women in Early Christian Meal Gatherings: Discourse and Reality," Meals in the Greco-Roman World: A Seminar of the Society of Biblical Literature (Philadelphia, 2005), www.philipharland.com/meals/AngelaStandhartingerWomeninMeals.pdf; and Ellen B. Aitken, "Remembering and Remembered Women in Greco-Roman Meals," Meals in the Greco-Roman World: A Seminar of the Society of Biblical Literature (Philadelphia, 2005), www.philipharland.com/meals/Aitken,_Remembering_Women.pdf.
14. Smith, *From Symposium to Eucharist*; Matthias Klinghardt, *Gemeinschaftsmahl und Mahlgemeinschaft: Soziologie und Liturgie Frühchristlicher Mahlfeiern* (Tübingen, Ger.: Francke Verlag, 1996).
15. Klinghardt, *Gemeinschaftsmahl und Mahlgemeinschaft*, 153.
16. See Corley, *Private Women, Public Meals* and "Women and Greco-Roman Meals," Meals in the Greco-Roman World: A Seminar of the Society of Biblical Literature (Philadelphia, 2002), http://www.philipharland.com/meals/2002%20Corley%20Paper.pdf; and Angela Standhartinger, "Women in Early Christian Meal Gatherings: Discourse and Reality."
17. Carolyn Osiek and Margaret Y. MacDonald, *A Woman's Place: House Churches in Earliest Christianity*, with Janet H. Tulloch (Minneapolis: Fortress Press, 2005), 9.
18. Dennis E. Smith, "Response to Andrew McGowan's Article on 'Rethinking Eucharistic Origins,'" Meals in the Greco-Roman World: A Seminar of the Society of Biblical Literature (San Diego, 2007), www.philipharland.com/meals/2007%20Smith%20Response%20to%20McGowan.pdf.
19. Ibid., 2.
20. Miriam Therese Winter, *eucharist with a small e* (Maryknoll, N.Y.: Orbis Books, 2005).
21. Caroline Walker Bynum, *Fragmentation and Redemption: Essays on Gender and the Human Body in Medieval Religion* (New York: Zion Books, 1991), 222–235.
22. Tissa Balasuriya, *The Eucharist and Human Liberation* (Maryknoll, N.Y.: Orbis Books, 1978), 22.
23. Mary Collins, "Is the Eucharist Still a Source of Meaning for Women?" in *Living in the Meantime: Concerning the Transformation of Religious Life*, ed. Paul J. Philibert (New York: Paulist Press, 1994), 185–197.

24. Esario Sosa Rodríguez, "Soñemos Juntos el Amancer (New Dawn)," in *Companera* 21 (mimeographed newsletter, Movimiento Cristiano CALEB, Caracas, November–December 1987), 2.
25. Diann L. Neu, "Commissioning for Feminist Ministry," from "A Feminist Eucharist: Honoring Women Who Break Bread and Do Justice," Women's Ordination Worldwide (WOW), Ottawa, Canada, 2005; *WATERwheel* 17, no. 2 (2005): 3–4.

The Road Is Made by Walking

JANET WALTON

1. *Kyriarchy* is a word coined by Elisabeth Schüssler Fiorenza to express power over others, instead of the more typical word *patriarchy. Kyriarchy* includes all structures of domination. Elisabeth Schüssler Fiorenza first used this term in *But She Said: Feminist Practices of Biblical Interpretation* (Boston: Beacon Press, 1992).
2. Text by Patricia Malarcher, member of the New York Women's Liturgy Group, written for the Advent liturgy "Women Expecting … An Advent Experience." See note 3 below.
3. Taken from the "Walker" chant, with text by Antonia Machado, translated by Ada María Isasi-Díaz, and set to music by Annette Covatta. It was composed for an Advent liturgy of the New York Women's Liturgy Group titled "Women Expecting … An Advent Experience."
4. Diane Harwood, a member of the New York Women's Liturgy Group, made this ice sculpture for a liturgy to provide an object that would hold our outrage during the hearings to name Clarence Thomas a justice on the U.S. Supreme Court.
5. Ivone Gebara, "Spirituality of Resistance: A Latin American Perspective" (lecture given in Matanzas, Cuba, May 2008). Ivone Gebara is a friend and a teacher. These words are hers and these insights come from ideas she has shared with us.
6. Elizabeth Schell created this sculpture while she was a master of divinity student at Union Theological Seminary.
7. Erica Poellot, a student at Union Theological Seminary, created this ritual object as an assignment in a course on worship and the arts.
8. Erica Poellot, personal conversation.
9. Elaine Scarry, *On Beauty and Being Just* (Princeton, N.J.: Princeton University Press, 1999), 111–12.
10. Casey Miller and Kate Smith, *Words and Women: New Language in New Times* (Garden City, N.Y.: Anchor Books, 1977), x.
11. Ibid., xi.

This Is My Body

VICTORIA RUE

1. Eve Ensler, *The Vagina Monologues* (New York: Villard, 1998).
2. Victoria Rue, "CancerBodies: Women Speaking the Unspeakable—Feminist Theatre Enacts Feminist Theology" (doctoral dissertation, Graduate Theological Union, 1993).

3. See Kaye Ashe, "Women Celebrating Eucharist: Path to Transformation," www.cta-usa.org/res_ashe.html.
4. Christopher Beatty and Geron Davis, "This Is Holy Ground." See www.redsal.com/church15.htm.
5. See the group Engaging Impasse: Circles of Contemplation and Dialogue, at www.engagingimpasse.org/welcome.html.
6. Victoria Rue, *Acting Religious: Theatre as Pedagogy in Religious Studies* (Cleveland: Pilgrim Press, 2005), 154.

"The Ones Who've Gone Before Us": The Future of Feminist Artistic and Liturgical Life

Marjorie Procter-Smith

1. Nelle Morton, *The Journey Is Home* (Boston: Beacon Press, 1985), 127.
2. "We Might Come in a-Fightin'," words and music by Carolyn McDade, on *Honor Thy Womanself* (McDade Music, 1973), and included in the nine-CD *Long Road of Music* set covering the first two decades of Carolyn's work. How we loved to shout out the line, "Change the goddamned rules!" and how that line always brought about spontaneous laughter and applause from the audience!
3. "Move, Sisters, Move," words and music by Carolyn McDade, on *Leave the Breads a-Burning* (Surtsey, 1975), and included in the nine-CD *Long Road of Music* set.
4. "We Are Women," by Doris J. Ellzey, 1974.
5. "We Are Gathered," by Doris J. Ellzey, 1974.
6. "The Ones Who've Gone Before Us," by Doris J. Ellzey, 1975.
7. See Tilda Norberg, *Gathered Together: Creating Personal Liturgies for Healing and Transformation* (Nashville: Upper Room Books, 2007).
8. Judy Chicago, *The Dinner Party: From Creation to Preservation* (London: Merrill, 2007).
9. Meinrad Craighead, *The Mother's Songs: Images of God the Mother* (New York: Paulist Press, 1986).
10. Miriam Therese Winter, *WomanPrayer, WomanSong: Resources for Ritual* (Oak Park, Ill.: Meyer Stone Books, 1987); *WomanWisdom: A Feminist Lectionary and Psalter*, vol. 1, *Women of the Hebrew Scriptures* (New York: Crossroad, 1991); *WomanWitness: A Feminist Lectionary and Psalter*, vol. 2, *Women of the Hebrew Scriptures* (New York: Crossroad, 1992); *WomanWord: A Feminist Lectionary and Psalter—Women of the New Testament* (New York: Crossroad, 1990).
11. For some examples of this scholarly work, see Teresa Berger, *Women's Ways of Worship: Gender Analysis and Liturgical History* (New York: Pueblo Press, 1999); Ruth Duck and Patricia Wilson Kastner, *Praising God: The Trinity in Christian Worship* (Louisville: Westminster John Knox Press, 1999); Heather Murray Elkins, *Worshiping Women: Re-forming God's People for Praise* (Nashville: Abingdon Press, 1994); Marjorie Procter-Smith, *In Her Own Rite: Constructing Feminist Liturgical Tradition* (Akron, Ohio: OSL, 2000) and *Praying with Our Eyes Open: Engendering Feminist Liturgical Prayer* (Nashville: Abingdon Press, 1995); Elizabeth J. Smith, *Bearing Fruit in Due Season: Feminist Hermeneutics and the Bible in Worship* (New

York: Pueblo Press, 1999); Janet Walton, *Feminist Liturgy: A Matter of Justice* (Collegeville, Minn.: Liturgical Press, 2000); Janet Walton and Marjorie Procter-Smith, eds., *Women at Worship: Interpretations of North American Diversity* (Louisville: Westminster John Knox Press, 1993); Susan J. White, *A History of Women in Christian Worship* (Cleveland: Pilgrim Press, 2003).

Part V Feminist Ministerial Challenges

Women in Ministry in a Postfeminist Era

Barbara Brown Zikmund

1. Elizabeth Nordbeck and Lowell H. Zuck, eds., *The Living Theological Heritage of the United Church of Christ*, vol. 4, *Consolidation and Expansion* (Cleveland: Pilgrim Press, 1999), 67–81.
2. Catherine Brekus, *Strangers and Pilgrims: Female Preaching in America, 1740–1845* (Chapel Hill, N.C.: University of North Carolina, 1998), 136, 217–19.
3. Barbara Brown Zikmund, Adair T. Lummis, and Patricia Mei Yin Chang, *Clergy Women: An Uphill Calling* (Louisville: Westminster John Knox Press, 1998), 106–8.
4. Ibid.
5. Mark Chaves, *Ordaining Women: Culture and Conflict in Religious Organizations* (Cambridge, Mass.: Harvard University Press, 1997), 191–92.
6. Mary Kassian, *The Feminist ~~Mystique~~ Mistake: The Radical Impact of Feminism on Church and Culture*, rev. ed. (Wheaton, Ill.: Crossway Books, 2005); originally published in 1992 as *The Feminist Gospel: The Movement to Unite Feminism with the Church.*
7. Ibid., 299.
8. Ibid., 296.
9. This quotation is from a 2009 research project on female chief executive officers and female chief academic officers in theological schools that are part of the Association of Theological Schools (ATS) in the United States and Canada (interviewee #36). The project interviewed 59 of the 63 female presidents and deans serving in 252 schools. A complete report of this research appears in *Theological Education* (the journal of the ATS) in 2010.

Asian American Women and Renewal of Preaching

Eunjoo Mary Kim

1. The term "Asian American church" is used strategically. See note 9.
2. "Celebrating Turning Points in Women's Ordination," October 23, 2006, www.pcusa.org/pcnews/2006/06538.htm.
3. www.gcsrw.org.
4. www.elca.org.
5. "Asian Clergy Women 2008," released from the General Assembly of the Presbyterian Church (USA) by a personal contact.
6. Eunjoo Mary Kim, *Women Preaching: Theology and Practice through the Ages* (Cleveland: Pilgrim Press, 2004), 79–117.

7. Ibid., 118–156.
8. Boyung Lee, "Re-Creating Our Mother's Dishes," in *Off the Menu: Asian and Asian North American Women's Religion & Theology*, ed. Rita Nakashima Brock, Jung Ha Kim, Kwok Pui-lan, and Seung Ai Yang (Louisville: Westminster John Knox Press, 2007), 299.
9. The term "Asian American women" in this essay is used strategically, rather than in essentialism, to represent those who have been victimized by patriarchal culture and the hierarchical system based on gender discrimination largely prevailing in Asian and Asian American communities. Considering socioeconomic, religiocultural, and linguistic plurality among those communities, I admit that the use of the term "Asian American women" is in danger of generalizing Asian American women's distinctive experiences. However, it is unavoidable for its usefulness when it is used strategically. Using the term strategically means that it is used "with the acknowledgement of 'the unavoidable usefulness of something that is very dangerous.'" Nami Kim, "The 'Indigestible' Asian," in *Off the Menu: Asian and Asian North American Women's Religion & Theology*, 37.
10. Kim, "'Indigestible' Asian," 34–35.
11. Russell, *Church in the Round: Feminist Interpretation of the Church* (Louisville: Westminster John Knox Press, 1993), 63.
12. Ibid., 64, 57.
13. Ibid., 56.
14. Celia Allison Hahn, *Growing in Authority, Relinquishing Control: A New Approach to Faithful Leadership* (Bethesda: Alban Institute, 1994), 27.
15. Paul Louis Lehmann, *The Transfiguration of Politics* (New York: Harper & Row, 1975), 7.

Balancing Power and Humility: Feminist Values in Mennonite Ministry
CYNTHIA LAPP

1. *Confession of Faith in a Mennonite Perspective* (Scottdale, Penn.: Herald Press, 1995). Adopted by the delegates of Mennonite Church General Assembly, and by the General Conference Mennonite Church Triennial Session, July 28, 1995, Wichita, Kansas. Mennonite Church USA, formed by the merger of these two groups, has adopted this confession as its statement of faith.
2. Emma Sommers Richards, "Emma Sommers Richards, Pioneer Pastor," in *She Has Done a Good Thing: Mennonite Women Leaders Tell Their Stories*, ed. Mary Swartley and Rhoda Keener (Scottdale, Penn.: Herald Press, 1999), 62–63.
3. Swartley and Keener, eds., *She Has Done a Good Thing*; Louise Stoltzfus, *Quiet Shouts: Stories of Lancaster Women Leaders* (Scottdale, Penn.: Herald Press, 1999). While these books celebrate the leadership of women in the Mennonite Church, in 2009 Mennonite Church USA commissioned an audit of women in leadership to understand why the numbers of women in church and denominational leadership seem to be stagnating. See Joanna Shenk, "Survey: More Women in Leadership but Still Not Enough," *The Mennonite*, March 9, 2010, www.themennonite.org/issues/13-3/articles/Survey_more_women_in_leadership_but_still_not_enough.

4. This retreat was held in October 1999, at Laurelville Mennonite Church Center in Mt. Pleasant, Pennsylvania.
5. For a fuller picture of humility in Anabaptist history, see Theron F. Schlabach, "Humility," *Global Anabaptist Mennonite Encyclopedia Online* (1989), www.gameo.org/encyclopedia/contents/H854ME.html.

Our Voices: Loud and Clear

ELEANOR MOODY-SHEPHERD

1. According to Brazilian educator and philosopher Paulo Freire, conscientization is the process through which people come to a self-awareness that helps them shape their own personal and social history and learn their own potential for action in shaping their world. I am indebted to Letty Russell for this reference. Paulo Freire, *Pedagogy of the Oppressed* (New York: Seabury Press, 1973).
2. *Womanist* is derived from the sense of the word as it is used in the African American community. Alice Walker suggests: "Womanist from womanism. A black feminist or feminist of color. A woman who loves other women, sexually and/or nonsexually. Appreciates and prefers women's culture, women's emotional flexibility and women's strength. Committed to the survival and wholeness of entire people, male and female. Loves struggle, loves the folk; loves herself regardless. Women is to feminist as purple is to lavender." Alice Walker, *In Search of Our Mothers' Gardens: Womanist Prose* (San Diego: Harcourt Brace Jovanovich, 1983), xi–xii.
3. Jacquelyn Grant, *White Women's Christ and Black Women's Jesus: Feminist Christology and Womanist Response* (Boston: South End Press, 1984), 3.
4. Angela Bauer defines heterosexism as the privileging and absolutizing of heterosexuality and, by implication, male-female "power relations" (domination and submission) in all aspects of individual life. This is systemic "oppression and marginalization" of persons or groups due to their real or perceived same-sex orientation and preference. See Angela Bauer, "Heterosexism in Biblical Interpretation," in *Dictionary of Feminist Theologies*, ed. Letty M. Russell and J. Shannon Clarkson (Louisville: Westminster John Knox Press, 1996), 141–42.
5. Tim Wise, *Between Barack and a Hard Place: Racism and White Denial in the Age of Obama* (San Francisco: City Lights Books, 2009), 23.
6. Cheryl Townsend Gilkes, "Keeping Faith with the People: Reflections on Ethic, Leadership, and the African American Women's Historical Experience," in *The Stones That the Builders Rejected: The Development of Ethical Leadership from the Black Church Tradition*, ed. Walker Fluker (Harrisburg, Penn.: Trinity Press, 1998), 81.
7. Audre Lorde, "The Master's Tools Will Never Dismantle the Master's House," in *Sister Outsider: Essays and Speeches* (Trumansburg, N.Y.: Crossing Press, 1984), 110–113.
8. Ibid., 2.
9. By *call*, I mean the sense of being set aside or "called" by God to the ministry. Ordination is the process by which a preacher's ministry is officially legitimated by a religious tradition. It is a credentialing process that enables a person to participate

fully in the tradition, to acquire certain rights, and to assume certain responsibilities denied to an unordained minister. It provides authorization for a minister to pastor a church and to ascend to higher positions in a religious organization's hierarchy. Historically, for many preaching women, ordination was a major step toward attaining recognition and acceptance in the polity. Ordination might be viewed as another level in women's struggle to preach; it allowed them to preach with authorization. See Bettye Collier-Thomas, *Daughters of Thunder: Black Preachers and Their Sermons, 1850–1979* (San Francisco: Jossey-Bass, 1998), 18.

10. *Patriarchy* means the "rule of the father," in reference to systems of legal, social, economic, and political relations that validate and enforce the sovereignty of male heads of families over dependent persons in the household. The exclusion of women from public and cultural offices and from higher education, and the preparation of men only for such offices, accounts for the almost exclusively male elite formation of public culture under patriarchy and the definition of women from the male point of view. See *Dictionary of Feminist Theologies*, ed. Letty M. Russell and J. Shannon Clarkson (Louisville: Westminster John Knox Press, 1996), 205–6.
11. Delores S. Williams, *Sister in the Wilderness: The Challenge of Womanist God-Talk* (Maryknoll, N.Y.: Orbis Press, 1993), 241.
12. The "blood-stained ceiling" is an artificial barrier derived from a patriarchal reading of the Bible that prevents women from claiming agency and office in the church and society. I first used the term in the title of my doctoral dissertation, "Breaking through the Blood-stained Ceiling: The Implications of Womanist Biblical Hermeneutics for the Empowerment of African-American Women in the Church" (Teachers College, Columbia University, 2000). It is now widely used in scholarship.
13. Katherine Rhodes Henderson, *God's Troublemakers: How Women of Faith Are Changing the World* (New York: Continuum, 2006), 73.
14. Clarice J. Martin, "The *Haustaflen* (Household Codes) in African American Biblical Interpretation: 'Free Slaves' and 'Subordinate Women,'" in *Stony the Road We Trod: African American Biblical Interpretation*, ed. Cain Hope Felder (Minneapolis: Fortress Press, 1991), 209.
15. Bettina Aptheker, *Women's Legacy: Essays on Race, Sex, and Class in American History* (Amherst, Mass.: University of Massachusetts Press, 1982), 150–51.
16. Renita Weems, "African-American Women and the Bible," in *Stony the Road We Trod*, 63.
17. Agency is very important because it is the capacity, condition, or state of acting or exerting power. Very often, women are placed in roles that are without the capacity to exercise power. See *Merriam-Webster's Collegiate Dictionary*, 9th ed., s.v. "agency."

New Feminist Catholics: Community and Ministry

Mary E. Hunt

1. Mary E. Hunt, "Father Does Not Know Best: How to Fix the Catholic Church," April 5, 2010, www.religiondispatches.org/archive/religionandtheology/2417/father_does_not_know_best%3A_how_to_fix_the_catholic_church.

2. Elisabeth Schüssler Fiorenza, *But She Said: Feminist Practices of Biblical Interpretation* (Boston: Beacon Press, 1992), 7–8; *Wisdom Way: Introducing Feminist Biblical Interpretation* (Maryknoll, N.Y.: Orbis Books, 2001), 118–124, 211.
3. Elisabeth Schüssler Fiorenza, *Discipleship of Equals: A Critical Feminist Ekklesia-logy of Liberation* (New York: Crossroad, 1993).
4. Mary E. Hunt, "American Nuns Under the Vatican Microscope," August 17, 2009, www.religiondispatches.org/archive/religionandtheology/1766/american_nuns_under_the_vatican_ microscope. See also Sandra Schneiders's five-part essay "Religious Life as Prophetic Life Form," January 4–8, 2010, www.ncronline.org/news/women/religious-life-prophetic-life-form.
5. See Thomas C. Fox, "Mercy Sister Theresa Kane Criticizes Church Hierarchy," September 29, 2009, www.ncronline.org/news/mercy-sister-theresa-kane-criticizes-church-hierarchy?page=2.
6. Sarah McFarland Taylor, *Green Sisters: A Spiritual Ecology* (Cambridge, Mass.: Harvard University Press, 2007).
7. Mary Daly, *The Church and the Second Sex* (Boston: Beacon Press, 1968).
8. Carmel McEnroy, *Guests in Their Own House: The Women of Vatican II* (New York: Crossroad, 1996).
9. Mary Daly, *Beyond God the Father: Toward a Philosophy of Women's Liberation* (Boston: Beacon Press, 1973).
10. Elisabeth Schüssler Fiorenza, *In Memory of Her: A Feminist Theological Reconstruction of Christian Origins* (New York: Crossroad, 1983).
11. *Journal of Feminist Studies in Religion*, www.fsrinc.org/jfsr.
12. Rosemary Radford Ruether, *Women-Church: Theology and Practice of Feminist Liturgical Communities* (San Francisco: Harper & Row, 1985); *Sexism and God-Talk: Toward a Feminist Theology* (Boston: Beacon Press, 1993); *Catholic the Vatican: A Vision for Progressive Catholicism* (New York: New Press, 2008).
13. Ada María Isasi-Díaz, En la Lucha *(In the Struggle)—Elaborating a* Mujerista *Theology: A Hispanic Women's Liberation Theology* (Minneapolis: Fortress Press, 1993); Mujerista *Theology* (Maryknoll, N.Y.: Orbis Books, 1996); La Lucha *Continues:* Mujerista *Theology* (Maryknoll, N.Y.: Orbis Books, 2004). María Pilar Aquino, *Our Cry for Life: Feminist Theology from Latin America* (Maryknoll, N.Y.: Orbis Books, 1993).
14. Mary E. Hunt, *Fierce Tenderness: Toward a Feminist Theology of Friendship* (New York: Crossroad, 1992).
15. Sandra M. Schneiders, *New Wineskins: Re-Imagining Religious Life Today* (New York: Paulist Press, 1986); *Beyond Patching: Faith and Feminism in the Catholic Church* (New York: Paulist Press, 1991); *Finding the Treasure: Locating Catholic Religious Life in a New Ecclesial and Cultural Context* (New York: Paulist Press, 2000); *Selling All: Commitment, Consecrated Celibacy, and Community in Catholic Religious Life* (New York: Paulist Press, 2001).
16. *Encyclopedia of Women and Religion in North America*, ed. Rosemary Skinner Keller and Rosemary Radford Ruether (Bloomington, Ind.: Indiana University Press, 2006), s.v. "Women-Church."
17. Women-Church Convergence, www.women-churchconvergence.org.

18. See "The Non-Ordination of Women and the Politics of Power," ed. Elisabeth Schüssler Fiorenza and Hermann Haring, special issue, *Concilium* 3 (1999).
19. Anne Marie Gardiner, ed., *Women and Catholic Priesthood: An Expanded Vision, Proceedings of the Detroit Ordination Conference* (New York: Paulist Press, 1976).
20. Women's Ordination Conference, www.womensordination.org.
21. Laurie Goodstein wrote a three-part series on these "divine recruits" in the *New York Times*, December 28–30, 2009: www.nytimes.com/2008/12/28/us/28priest.html; www.nytimes.com/2008/12/29/us/29priest.html; www.nytimes.com/2008/12/30/us/30priest.html.
22. Roman Catholic WomenPriests, www.romancatholicwomenpriests.org.
23. "History of NCCW," http://home.catholicweb.com/NCCW/index.cfm/NewsItem?ID=115198&From=Home.
24. *New York Times*, February 13, 2009, A9.
25. James A. Coriden, "The Canonical Doctrine of Reception," in *The Jurist: Studies in Church Law and Ministry*, vol. L, no. 1 (Washington, D.C.: Catholic University of America / Department of Canon Law, 1990), 58.
26. Coriden, "Canonical Doctrine," 82.
27. Pope Paul VI, "Declaration on Religious Freedom / *Dignitatis humanae*: On the Right of the Person and of Communities to Social and Civil Freedom in Matters Religious" (December 7, 1965), www.vatican.va/archive/hist_councils/ii_vatican_council/documents/vat-ii_decl_19651207_dignitatis-humanae_en.html, par. 3.
28. Daniel C. Maguire, *Sacred Energies: When the World's Religions Sit Down to Talk about the Future of Human Life and the Plight of this Planet* (Minneapolis: Fortress Press, 2000).

Signs of Hope, Signs of Dismay

MEG A. RILEY

1. See www.standingonthesideoflove.org.
2. See www.uua.org/religiouseducation/curricula/ourwhole.

Suggestions for Further Reading

Part I Feminist Theological Visions

Adams, Carol, ed. *Ecofeminism and the Sacred.* New York: Continuum, 1993.

Adler, Rachel. *Engendering Judaism: An Inclusive Theology and Ethics.* Boston: Beacon Press, 1999.

Allen, Paula Gunn. *Grandmothers of the Light: A Medicine Woman's Sourcebook.* Boston: Beacon Press, 1991.

———. *The Sacred Hoop: Recovering the Feminine in American Indian Traditions.* Boston: Beacon Press, 1986.

Althaus-Reid, Marcella. *From Feminist Theology to Indecent Theology.* London: SCM Press, 2004.

Amoah, Elizabeth, ed. *Where God Reigns.* Accra, Ghana: Circle of Concerned African Women Theologians, 1997.

Aquino, María Pilar, ed. *Aportes para una teología desde la mujer.* Madrid: Biblia y Fe, 1988.

———. *Our Cry for Life: Feminist Theology from Latin America.* Maryknoll, N.Y.: Orbis Books, 1993.

———, Daisy L. Machado, and Jeanette Rodrigues, eds. *A Reader in Latina Feminist Theology, Religion and Justice.* Austin: University of Texas Press, 2002.

Aquino, María Pilar, and Maria Jóse Rosado-Nunes, eds. *Feminist Intercultural Theology: Latina Exploration for a Just World.* Maryknoll, N.Y.: Orbis Books, 2007.

Baker-Fletcher, Karen. *Sisters of Dust, Sisters of Spirit: Womanist Wordings on God and Creation.* Minneapolis: Fortress Press, 1998.

Beavis, Mary Ann, with Elaine Guillemin and Barbara Pell, eds. *Feminist Theology with a Canadian Accent: Canadian Perspectives on Contextual Feminist Theology.* Ottawa: Novalis, 2008.

Bennett, Anne McGrew. *From Woman-Pain to Woman-Vision: Writings in Feminist Theology.* Edited by Mary E. Hunt. Minneapolis: Fortress Press, 1989.

Berneking, Nancy J., and Pamela Carter Joern, eds. *Re-Membering and Re-Imagining.* Cleveland: Pilgrim Press, 1995.

Boucher, Sandy. *Turning the Wheel: American Women Creating the New Buddhism.* Exp. ed. Boston: Beacon Press, 1993.

Brock, Rita Nakashima. *Journeys by Heart: A Christology of Erotic Power.* New York: Crossroad, 1988.

Brock, Rita Nakashima, Claudia Camp, and Serene Jones, eds. *Setting the Table: Women in Theological Conversation.* St. Louis: Chalice Press, 1995.

Brock, Rita Nakashima, and Rebecca Ann Parker. *Proverbs of Ashes: Violence, Redemptive Suffering, and the Search for What Saves Us.* Boston: Beacon Press, 2001.

———. *Saving Paradise: How Christianity Traded Love of This World for Crucifixion and Empire.* Boston: Beacon Press, 2008.

Brock, Rita Nakashima, and Susan Brooks Thistlethwaite. *Casting Stones: Prostitution and Liberation in Asia and the United States.* Minneapolis: Fortress Press, 1996.

Brubaker, Pamela K., Rebecca Todd Peters, and Laura A. Stivers, eds. *Justice in a Global Economy: Strategies for Home, Community, and World.* Louisville: Westminster John Knox Press, 2006.

Cannon, Katie. *Katie's Canon: Womanism and the Soul of the Black Community.* New York: Continuum, 1995.

Castelli, Elizabeth A., ed. *Women, Gender, Religion: A Reader.* With Rosamond C. Rodman. New York: Palgrave, 2001.

Christ, Carol. *Laughter of Aphrodite: Reflections on a Journey to the Goddess.* San Francisco: HarperSanFrancisco, 1988.

———. *The Rebirth of the Goddess: Finding Meaning in Feminist Spirituality.* Reading, Mass.: Addison-Wesley, 1997.

———, and Judith Plaskow, eds. *Womanspirit Rising: A Feminist Reader in Religion.* San Francisco: Harper & Row, 1979.

Chung Hyun Kyung. *Struggle to Be the Sun Again: Introducing Asian Women's Theology.* Maryknoll, N.Y.: Orbis Books, 1990.

Cochran, Pamela. *Evangelical Feminism: A History*. New York: New York University Press, 2005.

Coleman, Monica A. *Making a Way Out of No Way: A Womanist Theology*. Minneapolis: Fortress Press, 2008.

Daly, Mary. *Beyond God the Father: Toward a Philosophy of Women's Liberation.* Boston: Beacon Press, 1973.

———. *The Church and the Second Sex.* Boston: Beacon Press, 1985.

———, and Jane Caputi. *Websters' First New Intergalactic Wickedary of the English Language.* Boston: Beacon Press, 1987.

Deifelt, Wanda. "Feminist Theology: A Key for Women's Citizenship in the Church." In *Toward a New Heaven and a New Earth: Essays in Honor of Elisabeth Schüssler Fiorenza,* edited by Fernando F. Segovia, 237–48. Maryknoll, N.Y.: Orbis Books, 2003.

Eaton, Heather. *Introducing Ecofeminist Theologies.* New York: T & T Clark International, 2005.

———, and Lois Ann Lorentzen. *Ecofeminism and Globalization: Exploring Culture, Context, and Religion.* Lanham, Md.: Rowman & Littlefield, 2003.

Eiesland, Nancy. *The Disabled God: Toward a Liberatory Theology of Disability.* Nashville: Abingdon Press, 1994.

Fabella, Virginia, and Mercy Amba Oduyoye. *With Passion and Compassion: Third World Women Doing Theology.* Maryknoll, N.Y.: Orbis Books, 1988.

Fabella, Virginia, and Sun Ai Lee Park. *We Dare to Dream: Doing Theology as Asian Women.* Seoul: Asian Women's Resource Center, 1989.

Falk, Marcia. *The Book of Blessings: New Jewish Prayers for Daily Life, the Sabbath, and the New Moon Festival.* Boston: Beacon Press, 1999.

Finger, Reta Halteman, and Kari Sandhaas, eds. *Wisdom of Daughters: Two Decades of the Voice of Christian Feminism.* Philadelphia: Innisfree Press, 2001.

Floyd-Thomas, Stacey M., ed. *Deeper Shades of Purple: Womanism in Religion and Society.* New York: New York University Press, 2006.

Gebara, Ivone. *Longing for Running Water: Ecofeminism and Liberation.* Minneapolis: Fortress Press, 1999.

———. *Out of the Depths: Women's Experience of Evil and Salvation.* Minneapolis: Fortress Press, 2002.

González, Michelle A. *Sor Juana: Beauty and Justice in the Americas.* Maryknoll, N.Y.: Orbis Books, 2003.

Gottlieb, Lynn. *She Who Dwells Within: A Feminist Vision of a Renewed Judaism.* New York: HarperOne, 1995.

Grant, Jacquelyn. *White Women's Christ and Black Women's Jesus: Feminist Christology and Womanist Response.* Boston: South End Press, 1989.

Gross, Rita. *Buddhism after Patriarchy: A Feminist History, Analysis, and Reconstruction of Buddhism.* Albany: State University of New York Press, 1993.

Gudorf, Christine. *Body, Sex, and Pleasure: Reconstructing Christian Sexual Ethics.* Cleveland: Pilgrim Press, 1994.

Hayes, Diana L. *Hagar's Daughters: Womanist Ways of Being in the World.* Mahwah, N.J.: Paulist Press, 1996.

Heyward, Carter. *Our Passion for Justice: Images of Power, Sexuality and Liberation.* Cleveland: Pilgrim Press, 1984.

———. *A Priest Forever.* New York: Harper & Row, 1976.

———. *The Redemption of God: A Theology of Mutual Relation.* Lanham, Md.: University Press of America, 1982.

Hunt, Mary E. *Fierce Tenderness: A Feminist Theology of Friendship.* New York: Crossroad, 1991.

Ingersoll, Julie. *Evangelical Christian Women: War Stories in the Gender Battles.* New York: New York University Press, 2003.

Isasi-Díaz, Ada María. En la Lucha / *In the Struggle—Elaborating a* Mujerista *Theology: A Hispanic Women's Liberation Theology.* Minneapolis: Fortress Press, 1993.

———. La Lucha *Continues:* Mujerista *Theology.* Maryknoll, N.Y.: Orbis Books, 2004.

———. Mujerista *Theology.* Maryknoll, N.Y.: Orbis Books, 1996.

———, and Yolanda Tarango. *Hispanic Women: Prophetic Voice in the Church.* Minneapolis: Fortress Press, 1988.

Isherwood, Lisa, and Elizabeth Stuart. *Introducing Body Theology.* Sheffield, U.K.: Sheffield Academic Press, 1998.

Jarl, Ann-Cathrin. *In Justice: Women and Global Economics.* Minneapolis: Fortress Press, 2003.

Jay, Nancy. *Throughout Your Generations Forever: Sacrifice, Religion, and Patriarchy.* Chicago: University of Chicago Press, 1992.

Johnson, Elizabeth A. *Women, Earth, and Creator Spirit.* Mahwah, N.J.: Paulist Press, 1993.

Joshi, Khyati Y. *New Roots in America's Sacred Ground: Religion, Race, and Ethnicity in Indian America.* New York: Routledge, 2006.

Jung, Patricia Beattie, Mary E. Hunt, and Radhika Balakrishnan, eds. *Good Sex: Feminist Perspectives from the World's Religions.* New Brunswick, N.J.: Rutgers University Press, 2001.

Kanyoro, Musimbi R. A., and Nyambura J. Njoroge, eds. *Groaning in Faith: African Women in the Household of God.* Nairobi, Kenya: Acton, 1996.

Kassian, Mary A. *The Feminist Gospel: The Movement to Unite Feminism with the Church.* Wheaton, Ill.: Crossway Books, 1992. 2nd ed., *The Feminist ~~Mystique~~ Mistake: The Radical Impact of Feminism on Church and Culture.* Wheaton, Ill.: Crossway Books, 2005.

Katoppo, Marianne. *Compassionate and Free: An Asian Woman's Theology.* Geneva: World Council of Churches, 1979.

Keller, Catherine. *God and Power: Counter-Apocalyptic Journeys.* Minneapolis: Fortress Press, 2005.

King, Ursula, ed. *Feminist Theology from the Third World: A Reader.* Maryknoll, N.Y.: Orbis Books, 1994.

Kwok Pui-lan. *Introducing Asian Feminist Theology.* Sheffield, U.K.: Sheffield Academic Press, 2000.

———, Don H. Compier, and Joerg Rieger, eds. *Empire and the Christian Tradition: New Readings of Classical Theologians.* Minneapolis: Fortress Press, 2007.

Mananzan, Mary John. *Women in Asia: Status and Image.* Singapore: Christian Conference of Asia, 1979.

———, Mercy Amba Oduyoye, Elsa Tamez, J. Shannon Clarkson, Mary C. Grey, and Letty M. Russell, eds. *Women Resisting Violence: Spirituality for Life.* Maryknoll, N.Y.: Orbis Books, 1996.

Mar, Peter-Raoul, Linda Rennie Forcey, and Robert Fredrick Hunter Jr., eds. *Yearning to Breathe Free: Liberation Theologies in the U.S.* Maryknoll, N.Y.: Orbis Books, 1990.

McFague, Sallie. *The Body of God: An Ecological Theology.* Minneapolis: Fortress Press, 1993.

———. *Life Abundant: Rethinking Theology and Economy for a Planet in Peril.* Minneapolis: Fortress Press, 2001.

———. *A New Climate for Theology: God, the World, and Global Warming.* Minneapolis: Fortress Press, 2008.

———. *Super, Natural Christians: How We Should Love Nature.* Minneapolis: Fortress Press, 1997.

Mitchem, Stephanie Y. *Introducing Womanist Theology.* Maryknoll, N.Y.: Orbis Books, 2002.

Moltmann-Wendel, Elisabeth. *I Am My Body: A Theology of Embodiment.* New York: Continuum, 1995.

Monteiro, Evelyn, and Antoinette Gutzler, eds. *Ecclesia of Women in Asia: Gathering the Voices of the Silenced.* Delhi: ISPCK, 2005.

Morton, Nelle. *The Journey Is Home.* Boston: Beacon Press, 1985.

Murray, Pauli. *Pauli Murray: The Autobiography of a Black Activist, Feminist, Lawyer, Priest, and Poet.* Knoxville, Tenn.: University of Tennessee Press, 1989.

———. *Song in a Weary Throat: An American Pilgrimage.* New York: Harper & Row, 1987.

Nelson, Julie A. *Economics for Humans.* Chicago: University of Chicago Press, 2006.

Oduyoye, Mercy Amba. *Daughters of Anowa: African Women & Patriarchy.* Maryknoll, N.Y.: Orbis Books, 1995.

———, and Musimbi Kanyoro. *The Will to Rise: Women, Tradition and the Church in Africa.* Maryknoll, N.Y.: Orbis Books, 1992.

Plaskow, Judith. *The Coming of Lilith: Essays on Feminism, Judaism, and Sexual Ethics, 1972–2003.* Edited by Donna Berman. Boston: Beacon Press, 2005.

———. *Standing Again at Sinai: Judaism from a Feminist Perspective.* San Francisco: Harper & Row, 1990.

———, and Carol P. Christ. *Weaving the Visions: New Patterns in Feminist Spirituality.* San Francisco: HarperSanFrancisco, 1989.

Ress, Mary Judith. *Ecofeminism in Latin America.* Maryknoll, N.Y.: Orbis Books, 2006.

Ronan, Marian. *Tracing the Sign of the Cross: Sexuality, Mourning, and the Future of American Catholicism.* New York: Columbia University Press, 2009.

Ruether, Rosemary Radford. *Catholic ≠ the Vatican: A Vision for Progressive Catholicism.* New York: New Press, 2008.

———. *Gaia and God: An Ecofeminist Theology of Earth Healing.* San Francisco: Harper & Row, 1992.

———, ed. *Gender, Ethnicity, & Religion.* Minneapolis: Fortress Press, 2002.

———. *Goddesses and the Divine Feminine: A Western Religious History.* Berkeley: University of California Press, 2005.

———. *Integrating Ecofeminism, Globalization, and World Religions.* Lanham, Md.: Rowman & Littlefield, 2005.

———. *New Women, New Earth: Sexist Ideologies and Human Liberation.* New York: Seabury Press, 1975.

———. *Sexism and God-Talk: Toward a Feminist Theology.* Boston: Beacon Press, 1993.

———. *Women and Redemption: A Theological History.* Minneapolis: Fortress Press, 1998.

———. *Women-Church: Theology & Practice.* San Francisco: Harper & Row, 1985.

———, ed. *Women Healing Earth: Third World Women on Ecology, Feminism, and Religion.* Maryknoll, N.Y.: Orbis Books, 1996.

Russell, Letty M. *Church in the Round: Feminist Interpretation of the Church.* Louisville: Westminster John Knox Press, 1993.

———. *Human Liberation in a Feminist Perspective: A Theology*. Philadelphia: Westminster John Knox Press, 1974.

———, and Shannon Clarkson, eds. *Dictionary of Feminist Theologies.* Louisville: Westminster John Knox Press, 1996.

Scanzoni, Letha Dawson. *All We're Meant to Be: A Biblical Approach to Women's Liberation*. Waco, Tex.: Word Books, 1974.

Schneider, Laurel C. *Beyond Monotheism: A Theology of Multiplicity.* New York: Routledge, 2008.

Schüssler Fiorenza, Elisabeth. *In Memory of Her: A Feminist Theological Reconstruction of Christian Origins*. 10th anniv. ed. New York: Crossroad, 1994.

Shiva, Vandana. *Earth Democracy: Justice, Sustainability, and Peace.* Cambridge, Mass.: South End Press, 2005.

Soelle, Dorothy. *Strength of the Weak: Toward a Christian Feminist Identity.* Philadelphia: Westminster Press, 1984.

Starhawk. *The Spiral Dance: A Rebirth of the Ancient Religion of the Great Goddess.* San Francisco: Harper & Row, 1979.

Taylor, Sarah McFarland. *Green Sisters: A Spiritual Ecology.* Cambridge, Mass.: Harvard University Press, 2007.

Trible, Phyllis. *God and the Rhetoric of Sexuality*. Philadelphia: Fortress Press, 1978.

———. *Texts of Terror: Literary-Feminist Readings of Biblical Narratives*. Philadelphia: Fortress Press, 1984.

Williams, Delores S. *Sisters in the Wilderness: The Challenge of Womanist God-Talk.* Maryknoll, N.Y.: Orbis Books, 1993.

Young, Pamela Dickey. *Feminist Theology/Christian Theology: In Search of Method.* Minneapolis: Fortress Press, 1990.

Part II Feminist Scriptural Insights

Bach, Alice, ed. *Biblical Glamour and Hollywood Glitz*. Semeia Studies 74. Atlanta: Society of Biblical Literature, 1996.

———. *Religion, Politics, Media in the Broadband Era*. Sheffield, U.K.: Sheffield Phoenix Press, 2004.

———, ed. *Women in the Hebrew Bible*. New York: Routledge, 1999.

Bailey, Randall C., Tat-siong Benny Liew, and Fernando F. Segovia, eds. *They Were All Together in One Place? Toward Minority Biblical Criticism.* Semeia Studies 57. Atlanta: Society of Biblical Literature, 2009.

Beach, Eleanor Ferris. *The Jezebel Letters: Religion and Politics in Ninth-Century Israel.* Minneapolis: Augsburg Fortress, 2005.

Beavis, Mary Ann. *Jesus & Utopia: Looking for the Kingdom of God in the Roman World.* Minneapolis: Fortress Press, 2006.

Bird, Phyllis, ed. *Reading the Bible as Women: Perspectives from Africa, Asia, and Latin America*. Semeia Studies 78. Atlanta: Society of Biblical Literature, 1997.

Brenner, Athalya. *I Am ... : Biblical Women Tell Their Own Stories*. Minneapolis: Fortress Press, 2005.

———, and Carole Fontaine, eds. *A Feminist Companion to Reading the Bible: Approaches, Methods and Strategies*. Sheffield, U.K.: Sheffield Academic Press, 1997.

Brooten, Bernadette J. *Women Leaders in the Ancient Synagogue: Inscriptional Evidence and Background Issues*. Chico, Calif.: Scholars Press, 1982.

Byron, Gay. *Symbolic Blackness and Ethnic Difference in Early Christian Literature*. New York: Routledge, 2002.

Cady, Susan, Hal Taussig, and Marian Ronan. *Sophia: The Future of Feminist Spirituality*. San Francisco: Harper & Row, 1986.

Castelli, Elizabeth. *Martyrdom and Memory: Early Christian Culture Making*. New York: Columbia University Press, 2004.

Choi Hee An and Katheryn Pfisterer Darr, eds. *Engaging the Bible: Critical Readings from Contemporary Women*. Minneapolis: Fortress Press, 2006.

Cole, Susan, Marian Ronan, and Hal Taussig. *Wisdom's Feast: Sophia in Study and Celebration*. San Francisco: Harper & Row, 1989.

De Groot, Christiana, and Marion Ann Taylor, eds. *Recovering Nineteenth-Century Women Interpreters of the Bible*. Atlanta: Society of Biblical Literature, 2007.

Dube, Musa W. *Postcolonial Feminist Interpretation of the Bible*. St. Louis: Chalice Press, 2000.

Exum, J. Cheryl. *Plotted, Shot, and Painted: Cultural Representations of Biblical Women*. Sheffield, U.K.: Sheffield Academic Press, 1996.

Gafney, Wilda C. *Daughters of Miriam: Women Prophets in Ancient Israel*. Minneapolis: Fortress Press, 2009.

Glancy, Jennifer A. *Slavery in Early Christianity*. New York: Oxford University Press, 2002.

Guest, Deryn, Robert E. Goss, Mona West, and Thomas Bohache, eds. *The Queer Bible Commentary*. London: SCM Press, 2006.

———. *When Deborah Met Jael: Lesbian Biblical Hermeneutics*. Louisville: Westminster John Knox Press, 2005.

Haskins, Susan. *Mary Magdalen: Myth and Metaphor*. New York: Harcourt, 1993.

Hearon, Holly E., ed. *Distant Voices Drawing Near: Essays in Honor of Antoinette Clark Wire*. Collegeville, Minn.: Liturgical Press, 2004.

———. *The Mary Magdalene Tradition: Witness and Counter-Witness in Early Christian Communities*. Collegeville, Minn.: Liturgical Press, 2004.

Jensen, Anne. *God's Self-confident Daughters: Early Christianity and the Liberation of Women*. Translated by O. C. Dean Jr. Louisville: Westminster John Knox Press, 1996.

Johnson, Luke Timothy. *The Writings of the New Testament: An Interpretation*. Rev. ed. Minneapolis: Fortress Press, 1999.

Johnson-DeBaufre, Melanie. *Jesus Among Her Children: Q, Eschatology, and the Construction of Christian Origins*. Cambridge, Mass.: Harvard University Press, 2005.

King, Karen L. *The Gospel of Mary of Magdala: Jesus and the First Woman Apostle.* Santa Rosa, Calif.: Polebridge, 2003.

Kitzberger, Ingrid Rosa. *Autobiographical Biblical Criticism: Between Text and Self.* Leiden, Neth.: Deo, 2002.

Kraemer, Ross S. *Her Share of the Blessings: Women's Religions Among Pagans, Jews, and Christians in the Greco-Roman World.* New York: Oxford University Press, 1992.

———, ed. *Women's Religions in the Greco-Roman World: A Sourcebook.* New York: Oxford University Press, 2004.

Kwok Pui-lan. *Discovering the Bible in the Non-biblical World.* Maryknoll, N.Y.: Orbis Books, 1994.

———. *Introducing Asian Feminist Theology.* Cleveland: Pilgrim Press, 2000.

Martin, Dale. *Sex and the Single Savior: Gender and Sexuality in Biblical Interpretation.* Louisville: Westminster John Knox Press, 2006.

Matthews, Shelly. "Thinking of Thecla: Issues in Feminist Historiography." *Journal of Feminist Studies in Religion* 17, no. 2 (2001): 39–55.

———, Cynthia Briggs Kittredge, and Melanie Johnson-DeBaufre, eds. *Walk in the Ways of Wisdom: Essays in Honor of Elisabeth Schüssler Fiorenza.* Harrisburg, Penn.: Trinity Press International, 2003.

Nasrallah, Laura, and Elisabeth Schüssler Fiorenza, eds. *Prejudice and Christian Beginnings: Investigating Race, Gender, and Ethnicity in Early Christian Studies.* Minneapolis: Fortress Press, 2009.

Newsom, Carol A., and Sharon H. Ringe, eds. *Women's Bible Commentary.* Louisville: Westminster John Knox Press, 1998.

Ostriker, Alicia Suskin. *Feminist Revision and the Bible.* Oxford: Blackwell, 1993.

Schaberg, Jane. *The Resurrection of Mary Magdalene: Legends, Aprocrypha and the Christian Testament.* New York: Continuum, 2002.

———, Alice Bach, and Esther Fuchs, eds. *On the Cutting Edge—The Study of Women in Biblical Worlds: Essays in Honor of Elisabeth Schüssler Fiorenza.* New York: Continuum, 2003.

Schüssler Fiorenza, Elisabeth. *Bread Not Stone: The Challenge of Feminist Biblical Interpretation.* Boston: Beacon Press, 1984.

———. *But She Said: Feminist Practices of Biblical Interpretation.* Boston: Beacon Press, 1992.

———. *Democratizing Biblical Studies: Toward an Emancipatory Educational Space.* Louisville: Westminster John Knox Press, 2009.

———. *Discipleship of Equals: A Critical Feminist Ekklesia-logy of Liberation.* New York: Crossroad, 1993.

———. *In Memory of Her: A Feminist Theological Reconstruction of Christian Origins.* 10th anniv. ed. New York: Crossroad, 1994.

———. *Jesus—Miriam's Child, Sophia's Prophet: Critical Issues in Feminist Christology.* New York: Crossroad, 1999.

———. *The Power of the Word: Scripture and the Rhetoric of Empire.* Minneapolis: Fortress Press, 2007.

———. *Rhetoric and Ethic: The Politics of Biblical Studies.* Minneapolis: Fortress Press, 1999.

———, ed. *Searching the Scriptures: A Feminist Introduction.* 2 vols. New York: Crossroad, 1993–94.

———. *Wisdom Ways: Introducing Feminist Biblical Interpretation.* Maryknoll, N.Y.: Orbis Books, 2001.

Segovia, Fernando F., and Mary Ann Tolbert, eds. *Reading from This Place: Social Location and Biblical Interpretation.* Vol. 1, *Social Location and Biblical Interpretation in the United States.* Minneapolis: Fortress Press, 1995.

Stanton, Elizabeth Cady, and the Revising Committee. *The Woman's Bible.* Reprint, Seattle: Seattle Coalition Task Force on Women and Religion, 1977.

Tamez, Elsa. *Struggles for Power in Early Christianity: A Study of the First Letter to Timothy.* Maryknoll, N.Y.: Orbis Books, 2007.

Taylor, Marion Ann, and Heather E. Weir, eds. *Let Her Speak for Herself: Nineteenth-Century Women Writing on Women in Genesis.* Waco, Tex.: Baylor University Press, 2006.

Trible, Phyllis. *Texts of Terror: Literary-Feminist Readings of Biblical Narratives.* Philadelphia: Fortress Press, 1984.

Vander Stichele, Caroline, and Todd Penner, eds. *Her Master's Tools? Feminist and Postcolonial Engagements of Historical-Critical Discourse.* Global Perspectives on Biblical Scholarship 9. Atlanta: Society of Biblical Literature, 2005.

Von Kellenbach, Katharina. *Anti-Judaism in Feminist Religious Writing.* Atlanta: Scholars Press, 1994.

Wainwright, Elaine M. *Women Healing/Healing Women: The Genderization of Healing in Early Christianity.* Oakville, Conn.: Equinox, 2006.

Weems, Renita. *Battered Love: Marriage, Sex, and Violence in the Hebrew Prophets.* Minneapolis: Fortress Press, 1995.

Wicker, Kathleen O'Brien, Althea Spencer Miller, and Musa W. Dube, eds. *Feminist New Testament Studies: Global and Future Perspectives.* New York: Palgrave Macmillan, 2005.

Wire, Antoinette. *Corinthian Women Prophets: A Reconstruction through Paul's Rhetoric.* Minneapolis: Augsburg Fortress, 1995.

Yee, Gale A., ed. *Judges and Method: New Approaches in Biblical Studies.* 2nd ed. Minneapolis: Fortress Press, 2007.

———. *Poor Banished Children of Eve: Woman as Evil in the Hebrew Bible.* Minneapolis: Fortress Press, 2003.

Part III Feminist Ethical Agendas

Adams, Carol J. *Woman-Battering.* Creative Pastoral Care and Counseling. Minneapolis: Augsburg Fortress, 1997.

———, and Marie M. Fortune, eds. *Violence against Women and Children: A Christian Theological Sourcebook.* New York: Continuum, 1998.

Suggestions for Further Reading

Albrecht, Elizabeth Soto. *Family Violence: Reclaiming a Theology of Nonviolence.* Maryknoll, N.Y.: Orbis Books, 2008.

Alexander, M. Jacqui, and Chandra Talpade Mohanty. *Feminist Genealogies, Colonial Legacies, Democratic Futures.* New York: Routledge, 1996.

Andolsen, Barbara Hilkert, Christine E. Gudorf, and Mary D. Pellauer, eds. *Women's Consciousness, Women's Conscience: A Reader in Feminist Ethics.* Minneapolis: Winston Press, 1985.

Boonprasat Lewis, Nantawan, and Marie M. Fortune, eds. *Remembering Conquest: Feminist/Womanist Perspectives on Religion, Colonization, and Sexual Violence.* Binghamton, N.Y.: Haworth Pastoral Press, 1999.

Bounds, Elizabeth M., et al., eds. *Justice in the Making: Feminist Social Ethics.* Louisville: Westminster John Knox Press, 2004.

Bunge, Marcia J., ed. *The Child in Christian Thought.* Grand Rapids, Mich.: Eerdmans, 2001.

Butler, Judith. *Gender Trouble: Feminism and the Subversion of Identity.* New York: Routledge, 2006.

Castelli, Elizabeth A., and Janet R. Jakobsen, eds. *Interventions: Activists and Academics Respond to Violence.* New York: Palgrave Macmillan, 2004.

Cooper-White, Pamela. *The Cry of Tamar: Violence against Women and the Church's Response.* Minneapolis: Fortress Press, 1995.

Douglas, Kelly Brown. *Sexuality and the Black Church: A Womanist Perspective.* Maryknoll, N.Y.: Orbis Books, 1999.

Eugene, Toinette M. *Balm for Gilead: Pastoral Care for African American Families Experiencing Abuse.* Nashville: Abingdon Press, 1998.

Farley, Margaret. *Just Love: A Framework for Christian Sexual Ethics.* New York: Continuum, 2006.

Fortune, Marie M. *Is Nothing Sacred? When Sex Invades the Pastoral Relationship.* San Francisco: Harper & Row, 1989.

———. *Keeping the Faith: Guidance for Christian Women Facing Abuse.* San Francisco: HarperSanFrancisco, 1987.

———. *Love Does No Harm: Sexual Ethics for the Rest of Us.* New York: Continuum, 1998.

———. *Sexual Violence: The Sin Revisited.* Cleveland: Pilgrim Press, 2005.

———. *Sexual Violence: The Unmentionable Sin.* New York: Pilgrim Press, 1983.

Harrison, Beverly Wildung. *Our Right to Choose: Toward a New Ethic of Abortion.* Boston: Beacon Press, 1983.

Isherwood, Lisa, and Rosemary Radford Ruether, eds. *Weep Not for Your Children: Essays on Religion and Violence.* Oakville, Conn.: Equinox, 2008.

Jennings, Theodore W., Jr. *Jacob's Wound: Homoerotic Narrative in the Literature of Ancient Israel.* London: Continuum, 2005.

———. *The Man Jesus Loved: Homoerotic Narratives from the New Testament.* Cleveland: Pilgrim Press, 2003.

———. *Plato or Paul? The Origins of Western Homophobia.* Cleveland: Pilgrim Press, 2009.

Kroeger, Catherine, and James R. Beck. *Women, Abuse, and the Bible: How Scripture Can Be Used to Hurt or Heal.* Grand Rapids, Mich.: Baker, 1996.

Lorde, Audre. *Sister Outsider: Essays and Speeches.* Berkeley: Crossing Press, 1984.

Maguire, Daniel C., and Sa'Diyya Shaikh. *Violence against Women in Contemporary World Religion: Roots and Cures.* Cleveland: Pilgrim Press, 2007.

Mananzan, Mary John, Mercy Amba Oduyoye, Elsa Tamez, et al., eds. *Women Resisting Violence: Spirituality for Life.* Maryknoll, N.Y.: Orbis Books, 1996.

Miles, Al. *Domestic Violence: What Every Pastor Needs to Know.* Minneapolis: Augsburg Fortress, 2000.

Mollenkott, Virginia Ramey. *Omnigender: A Trans-religious Approach.* Cleveland: Pilgrim Press, 2001.

———. *Sensuous Spirituality: Out from Fundamentalism.* New York: Crossroad, 1992.

Nason-Clark, Nancy. *The Battered Wife: How Christians Confront Family Violence.* Louisville: Westminster John Knox Press, 1997.

Ott, Kate M. "Re-thinking Adolescent Sexual Ethics: A Social Justice Obligation to Adolescent Sexual Health." *Journal of Lutheran Ethics* 7, no. 2 (2007): http://archive.elca.org/jle/article.asp?k=697.

Parker, Evelyn, ed. *The Sacred Selves of Adolescent Girls: Hard Stories of Race, Class, and Gender.* Cleveland: Pilgrim Press, 2006.

Phiri, Isabel Apawo, Beverley Haddad, and Madipioane Masenya, eds. *African Women, HIV/AIDS and Faith Communities.* Pietermaritzburg, S. Afr.: Cluster, 2003.

Poling, James Newton. *The Abuse of Power: A Theological Problem.* Nashville: Abingdon Press, 1991.

Robb, Carol S. *Equal Value: An Ethical Approach to Economics and Sex.* Boston: Beacon Press, 1995.

Scanzoni, Letha Dawson, and Virginia Ramey Mollenkott. *Is the Homosexual My Neighbor? A Positive Christian Response.* Rev., updated ed. New York: HarperOne, 1994.

Schroeder, Joy A. *Dinah's Lament: The Biblical Legacy of Sexual Violence in Christian Interpretation.* Minneapolis: Fortress Press, 2007.

Schüssler Fiorenza, Elisabeth, and M. Shawn Copeland, eds. *Violence Against Women.* London: SCM Press, 1994.

Townes, Emilie M. *In a Blaze of Glory: Womanist Spirituality as Social Witness.* Nashville: Abingdon Press, 1995.

———, ed. *A Troubling in My Soul: Womanist Perspectives on Evil & Suffering.* Maryknoll, N.Y.: Orbis Books, 1993.

Vigen, Aana Marie. *Women, Ethics, and Inequality in U.S. Healthcare: "To Count among the Living."* New York: Palgrave Macmillan, 2006.

West, Traci C. *Wounds of the Spirit: Black Women, Violence, and Resistance Ethics.* New York: New York University Press, 1999.

Part IV Feminist Liturgical and Artistic Frontiers

Aldredge-Clanton, Jann. *Praying with Christ-Sophia: Services for Healing and Renewal.* Mystic, Conn.: Twenty-Third, 1996.

Anderson, Virginia Cobb. *Prayers of Our Hearts in Word and Action.* New York: Crossroad, 1991.

Balasuriya, Tissa. *The Eucharist and Human Liberation.* Maryknoll, N.Y.: Orbis Books, 1978.

Beben, Mary, and Bridget Mary Meehan. *Walking the Prophetic Journey: Eucharistic Liturgies for 21st Century Small Faith Communities.* Boulder, Colo.: WovenWord Press, 1998.

Bell, Catherine. *Ritual: Perspectives and Dimensions.* New York: Oxford University Press, 1997.

Berger, Teresa. *Dissident Daughters: Feminist Liturgies in Global Context.* Louisville: Westminster John Knox Press, 2001.

———, ed. *Women's Ways of Worship: Gender Analysis and Liturgical History.* Collegeville, Minn.: Liturgical Press, 1999.

Bieler, Andrea, and Luise Schottroff. *The Eucharist: Bodies, Bread, and Resurrection.* Minneapolis: Fortress Press, 2007.

Black, Kathy. *Culturally-Conscious Worship.* St. Louis: Chalice Press, 2000.

———. *Worship Across Cultures: A Handbook.* Nashville: Abingdon Press, 1998.

Bohler, Carolyn Jane. *God the* What? *What Our Metaphors for God Reveal about Our Beliefs in God.* Woodstock, Vt.: SkyLight Paths, 2008.

Bowe, Barbara, Kathleen Hughes, Sharon Karam, and Carolyn Osiek, eds. *Silent Voices, Sacred Lives: Women's Readings for the Liturgical Year.* New York: Paulist Press, 1992.

Brock, Rita Nakashima, and Rebecca Ann Parker. *Saving Paradise: How Christianity Traded Love of This World for Crucifixion and Empire.* Boston: Beacon Press, 2008.

Butler, Becky, ed. *Ceremonies of the Heart: Celebrating Lesbian Unions.* Seattle: Seal Press, 1990.

Bynum, Caroline Walker. *Fragmentation and Redemption: Essays on Gender and the Human Body in Medieval Religion.* New York: Zion Books, 1991.

Carnes, Robin Deen, and Sally Craig. *Sacred Circles: A Guide to Creating Your Own Women's Spirituality Group.* San Francisco: HarperCollins, 1998.

Caron, Charlotte. *To Make and Make Again: Feminist Ritual Thealogy.* New York: Crossroad, 1993.

Cherry, Kittredge, and Zalmon Sherwood, eds. *Equal Rites: Lesbian and Gay Worship, Ceremonies, and Celebrations.* Louisville: Westminister John Knox Press, 1995.

Clark, Linda, Marian Ronan, and Eleanor Walker. *Image-breaking/Image-building: A Handbook for Creative Worship with Women of Christian Tradition.* New York: Pilgrim Press, 1981.

Collins, Mary, and David Power, eds. *Blessing and Power.* Edinburgh, U.K.: T. and T. Clark, 1985.

———. *Can We Always Celebrate the Eucharist?* New York: Seabury Press, 1982.

Con-spirando. *Cuaderno de ritos.* Santiago, Chile: Colectivo Con-spirando, 1995.

Corley, Kathleen E. *Maranatha: Women's Funerary Rituals and Christian Origins.* Minneapolis: Fortress Press, 2010.

———. *Private Women, Public Meals: Social Conflict in the Synoptic Tradition.* Peabody, Mass.: Hendrickson, 1993.

———. "Salome and Jesus at Table in the Gospel of Thomas." *Semeia* 86 (2001): 85–97.

———. *Women and the Historical Jesus: Feminist Myths of Christian Origins.* Santa Rosa, Calif.: Polebridge Press, 2002.

Craighead, Meinrad. *Meinrad Craighead: Crow Mother and the Dog God: A Retrospective.* San Francisco: Pomegranate, 2003.

———. *Meinrad Craighead: Praying with Images.* Produced by Amy Kellum, RCWMS, and Minnow Media. Durham, N.C.: Resource Center for Women & Ministry in the South, 2009.

———. *The Mother's Songs: Images of God the Mother.* Mahwah, N.J.: Paulist Press, 1986.

Dierks, Shelia Durkin. *WomenEucharist.* Boulder, Colo.: WovenWord Press, 1997.

Duck, Ruth, ed. *Bread for the Journey: Resources for Worship.* New York: Pilgrim Press, 1981.

———. *Finding Words for Worship: A Guide for Leaders.* Louisville: Westminster John Knox Press, 1995.

———, ed. *Flames of the Spirit: Resources for Worship.* New York: Pilgrim Press, 1985.

———, and Maren C. Tirabassi, eds. *Touch Holiness: Resources for Worship.* New York: Pilgrim Press, 1985.

Duck, Ruth, and Patricia Wilson-Kastner. *Praising God: The Trinity in Christian Worship.* Louisville: Westminster John Knox Press, 1999.

Eiker, Diane, and Sapphire Eiker, eds. *Keep Simple Ceremonies.* Portland, Maine: Astarte Shell Press, 1993.

Elkins, Heather Murray. *Worshiping Women: Re-forming God's People for Praise.* Nashville: Abingdon Press, 1994.

Ensler, Eve. *The Vagina Monologues.* New York: Villard, 1998.

Froehle, Virginia Ann. *Called into Her Presence: Praying with Feminine Images of God.* Notre Dame, Ind.: Ave Maria Press, 1992.

Furlong, Monica, ed. *Women Pray: Voices through the Ages, from Many Faiths, Cultures, and Traditions.* Woodstock, Vt.: SkyLight Paths, 2001.

Gjerding, Iben, and Katherine Kinnamon, eds. *No Longer Strangers: A Resource for Women and Worship.* Geneva: World Council of Churches, 1984.

Goudey, June Christine. *The Feast of Our Lives: Re-imaging Communion.* Cleveland: Pilgrim Press, 2002.

Grinnan, Jeanne Brinkman, Mary Rose McCarthy, Barbara S. Mitrano, and Rosalie Muschal-Reinhardt. *Sisters of the Thirteen Moons: Rituals Celebrating Women's Lives.* Webster, N.Y.: Prism Collective, 1997.

Haydock, Kathy McFaul, and the Women of Weavers. *We Are Sisters: Prayer and Ritual for Women's Spirituality and Empowerment.* Seattle: Intercommunity Peace & Justice Center, 1996.

Henderson, J. Frank, ed. *Remembering the Women: Women's Stories from Scripture for Sundays and Festivals.* Chicago: Liturgy Training, 1999.

Henry, Kathleen M. *The Book of Ours: Liturgies for Feminist People.* Jamaica Plain, Mass.: Alabaster Jar Liturgical Arts, 1993.

Holsenbeck, Bryant. *Blackbirds, Bottle Caps, and Broken Records: Environmental Artist Bryant Holsenbeck at Work.* Directed by Margaret Morales. Durham, N.C.: Resource Center for Women & Ministry in the South, 2009.

Howard, Julie. *We Are the Circle: Celebrating the Feminine in Song and Ritual.* Collegeville, Minn.: Liturgical Press, 1993.

Imber-Black, Evan, and Janine Roberts. *Rituals for Our Times: Celebrating, Healing, and Changing Our Lives and Our Relationships.* New York: HarperCollins, 1992.

Inclusive-Language Lectionary Committee, ed. *An Inclusive-Language Lectionary: Readings for Years A–C.* Atlanta: Cooperative Publication Association / John Knox Press, 1985–1987.

Jackson, Christal M., ed. *Women of Color Pray: Voices of Strength, Faith, Healing, Hope and Courage.* Woodstock, Vt.: SkyLight Paths, 2005.

Katsuno-Ishii, Lynda, and Edna J. Orteza, eds. *Of Rolling Waters and Roaring Wind: A Celebration of the Woman Song.* Geneva: WCC Publications, 2000.

Kirk, Martha Ann. *Celebrations of Biblical Women's Stories: Tears, Milk and Honey.* Kansas City, Mo.: Sheed and Ward, 1987.

Klinghardt, Matthias. *Gemeinschaftsmahl und Mahlgemeinschaft: Soziologie und Liturgie Frühchristlicher Mahlfeiern.* Tübingen, Ger.: Francke Verlag, 1996.

Klug, Lyn, ed. *Soul Weavings: A Gathering of Women's Prayers.* Minneapolis: Fortress Press, 1996.

Knie, Ute, and Herta Leistner. *Lass horen deine stimme: Werkstattbuch feministische liturgie.* Gutersloh, Ger.: Gutersloher Verlagshaus, 1999.

Leister, Herta. *Lass spuren deine kraft: Feministische liturgie.* Gutersloh, Ger.: Gutersloher Verlagshaus, 1997.

Ling, Coralie. "Creative Rituals: Celebrating Women's Experiences in an Australian Feminist Context." DMin diss., San Francisco Theological Seminary, 1998.

Mananzan, Mary John, ed. *Women and Religion: A Collection of Essays, Personal Histories, and Contextualized Liturgies.* 2nd ed. Manila, Phil.: Institute of Women's Studies, St. Scholastica College, 1992.

Martensen, Jean, ed. *Sing Out New Visions: Prayers, Poems and Reflections by Women.* Minneapolis: Fortress Press, 1998.

McEwan, Dorothea, Pat Pinsent, Ianthe Pratt, and Veronica Seddon, eds. *Making Liturgy: Creating Rituals for Worship and Life.* Cleveland: Pilgrim Press, 2002.

Mitchell, Rosemary Catalano, and Gail Anderson Ricciuti. *Birthings and Blessings: Liberating Worship Services for the Inclusive Church.* New York: Crossroad, 1991.

Morley, Janet. *All Desires Known: Inclusive Prayers for Worship and Meditation*. 3rd ed. Harrisburg, Penn.: Morehouse, 2006.

Muschal-Reinhardt, Rosalie, Barbara S. Mitrano, Mary Rose McCarthy, and Jeanne Brinkman Grinnan. *Rituals for Women Coping with Breast Cancer.* Webster, N.Y.: Prism Collective, 2000.

Neu, Diann L. "Feminist Liturgies: Claiming Ourselves Church." MDiv and STM thesis, Jesuit School of Theology at Berkeley, Calif., 1980.

———. *Feministischen Liturgien*. Silver Spring, Md.: WATERworks Press, 2001.

———. *Gathered at Sophia's Table.* Silver Spring, Md.: WATERworks Press, 2001.

———. *Liturgia: Un jardin compartido*. Silver Spring, Md.: WATERworks Press, 1995.

———. *Peace Liturgies*. Silver Spring, Md.: WATERworks Press, 2001.

———. *Return Blessings: Ecofeminist Liturgies Renewing the Earth.* Cleveland: Pilgrim Press, 2002.

———. *Seasons of Compassion: Resources for Companions of Those Needing Healing.* Silver Spring, Md.: WATERworks Press, 2009.

———. *Seasons of Healing: Journaling and Resources.* Silver Spring, Md.: WATERworks Press, 2008.

———. *Seasons of Survival: Prayers and Rituals for Women with Cancer.* Silver Spring, Md.: WATERworks Press, 2007.

———. *Women and the Gospel Traditions: Feminist Celebrations*. Silver Spring, Md.: WATERworks Press, 1989.

———. *Women-Church Celebrations: Feminist Liturgies for the Lenten Season*. Silver Spring, Md.: WATERworks Press, 1985.

———. *Women's Rites: Feminist Liturgies for Life's Journey.* Cleveland: Pilgrim Press, 2003.

———, Tobie Hofman, Barbara Cullom, and Mindy Shapiro. *Miriam's Sisters Rejoice*. Silver Spring, Md.: WATERworks Press, 1988.

Neu, Diann L., and Mary E. Hunt. *Women-Church Sourcebook.* Silver Spring, Md.: WATERworks Press, 1993.

———. *Women of Fire: A Pentecost Event*. Silver Spring, Md.: WATERworks Press, 1990.

Neu, Diann L., and Ronnie Levin. *A Seder of the Sisters of Sarah: A Holy Thursday and Passover Seder*. Silver Spring, Md.: WATERworks Press, 1986.

Neu, Diann L., Jessica Weissman, and Barbara Cullom. *Together at Freedom's Table.* Silver Spring, Md.: WATERworks Press, 1991.

Northup, Lesley A. *Ritualizing Women: Patterns of Spirituality*. Cleveland: Pilgrim Press, 1997.

———, ed. *Women and Religious Ritual.* Washington, D.C.: Pastoral Press, 1993.

Osiek, Carolyn, and Margaret Y. MacDonald. *A Woman's Place: House Church in Earliest Christianity*. With Janet H. Tulloch. Minneapolis: Fortress Press, 2005.

Philibert, Paul J., ed. *Living in the Meantime: Concerning the Transformation of Religious Life*. New York: Paulist Press, 1994.

Procter-Smith, Marjorie. *The Church in Her House: A Feminist Emancipatory Prayer Book for Christian Communities.* Cleveland: Pilgrim Press, 2008.

———. *In Her Own Rite: Constructing Feminist Liturgical Tradition.* Nashville: Abingdon Press, 1990. Reprint, Akron, Ohio: OSL, 2000.

———. *Praying with Our Eyes Open: Engendering Feminist Liturgical Prayer.* Nashville: Abingdon Press, 1995.

———, and Janet R. Walton, eds. *Women at Worship: Interpretations of North American Diversity.* Louisville: Westminster John Knox Press, 1993.

Ramshaw, Gail. *God Beyond Gender: Feminist Christian God-Language.* Minneapolis: Fortress Press, 1995.

Ricciuti, Gail Anderson, and Rosemary Catalano Mitchell. *Birthings and Blessings II: More Liberating Worship Services for the Inclusive Church.* New York: Crossroad, 1993.

Richardson, Jan L. *Night Visions: Searching the Shadows of Advent and Christmas.* Cleveland: United Church Press, 1998.

———. *Sacred Journeys: A Woman's Book of Daily Prayer.* Nashville: Upper Room Books, 1995.

Rienstra, Marchiene Vroon. *Swallow's Nest: A Feminist Reading of the Psalms.* Grand Rapids, Mich.: William B. Eerdmans, 1992.

Roberts, Elizabeth, and Elias Amidon, eds. *Earth Prayers.* San Francisco: HarperSanFrancisco, 1991.

———. *Life Prayers.* San Francisco: HarperSanFrancisco, 1996.

———. *Prayers for a Thousand Years.* San Francisco: HarperSanFrancisco, 1999.

Roberts, Wendy. *Celebrating Her: Feminist Ritualizing Comes of Age.* Cleveland: Pilgrim Press, 1998.

Rose, Margaret, Jeanne Person, Abagail Nelson, and Jenny Te Paa, eds. *Lifting Women's Voices: Prayers to Change the World.* Harrisburg, Penn.: Morehouse, 2009.

Ross, Susan A. *Extravagant Affections: A Feminist Sacramental Theology.* New York: Continuum, 1998.

Rue, Victoria. *Acting Religious: Theatre as Pedagogy in Religious Studies.* Cleveland: Pilgrim Press, 2005.

Ruether, Rosemary Radford. *Women-Church: Theology and Practice.* San Francisco: Harper & Row, 1985.

Rupp, Joyce, and Macrina Wiederkehr. *The Circle of Life: The Heart's Journey Through the Seasons.* Notre Dame, Ind.: Sorin Books, 2005.

Russell, Letty. *Church in the Round: Feminist Interpretation of the Church.* Louisville: Westminster John Knox Press, 1993.

Schaffran, Janet, and Pat Kozak. *More Than Words: Prayer and Ritual for Inclusive Communities.* Oak Park, Ill.: Meyer Stone Books, 1986.

Schmitt, Mary Kathleen Speegle. *Seasons of the Feminine Divine: Christian Feminist Prayers for the Liturgical Cycle.* New York: Crossroad, 1993.

———. *Seasons of the Feminine Divine: Cycle A, Christian Feminist Prayers for the Liturgical Cycle.* New York: Crossroad, 1995.

———. *Seasons of the Feminine Divine: Cycle C, Christian Feminist Prayers for the Liturgical Cycle*. New York: Crossroad, 1994.

Schüssler Fiorenza, Elisabeth. *Discipleship of Equals: A Critical Feminist Ekklesia-logy of Liberation*. New York: Crossroad, 1993.

———. *Sharing Her Word*. Boston: Beacon Press, 1998.

Sears, Marge. *Life-Cycle Celebrations for Women*. Mystic, Conn.: Twenty-Third, 1989.

Sewell, Marilyn, ed. *Claiming the Spirit Within: A Sourcebook of Women's Poetry*. Boston: Beacon Press, 1996.

———. *Cries of the Spirit*. Boston: Beacon Press, 1991.

Smith, Dennis. *From Symposium to Eucharist: The Banquet in the Early Christian World*. Minneapolis: Fortress Press, 2003.

St. Hilda's Community. *The New Women Included*. London: SPCK, 1996.

———. *Women Included: A Book of Services and Prayers*. London: SPCK, 1991.

Stanton, Elizabeth Cady, and the Revising Committee. *The Woman's Bible*. Reprint, Seattle: Seattle Coalition Task Force on Women and Religion, 1977.

Starhawk. *The Spiral Dance: A Rebirth of the Ancient Religion of the Great Goddess*. 20th anniv. ed. San Francisco: HarperCollins, 1999.

Stuart, Elizabeth, ed. *Daring to Speak Love's Name: A Gay and Lesbian Prayer Book*. London: Hamish Hamilton, 1992.

Swidler, Arlene, ed. *Sistercelebrations: Nine Worship Experiences*. Philadelphia: Fortress Press, 1974.

Taussig, Hal. *In the Beginning Was the Meal: Social Experimentation and Early Christian Identity*. Minneapolis: Fortress Press, 2009.

———, and Dennis E. Smith. *Many Tables: The Eucharist in the New Testament and Liturgy Today*. Philadelphia: Trinity Press International, 1990.

United Church of Christ. *The New Century Hymnal*. Cleveland: Pilgrim Press, 1995.

United Methodist Church. *The Faith We Sing*. Nashville: Abingdon Press, 2000.

Walker, Barbara G. *Women's Rituals: A Sourcebook*. San Francisco: Harper & Row, 1990.

Walton, Janet R. *Feminist Liturgy: A Matter of Justice*. Collegeville, Minn.: Liturgical Press, 2000.

Ward, Hannah, and Jennifer Wild, eds. *Human Rites: Worship Resources for an Age of Change*. London: Mowbray, 1995.

———, and Janet Morley, eds. *Celebrating Women*. London: SPCK, 1995.

Webster, Linda. *Womancircle Rituals: Celebrating Life, Sparking Connections*. Austin, Tex.: Women's Spirituality Group, First Unitarian Church, 1988.

Winter, Miriam Therese. *eucharist with a small e*. Maryknoll, N.Y.: Orbis Books, 2005.

———. *WomanPrayer, WomanSong: Resources for Ritual*. Oak Park, Ill.: Meyer Stone Books, 1987.

———. *WomanWisdom—A Feminist Lectionary and Psalter: Women of the Hebrew Scriptures, Part One*. New York: Crossroad, 1991.

———. *WomanWitness—A Feminist Lectionary and Psalter: Women of the Hebrew Scriptures, Part Two*. New York: Crossroad, 1992.

———. *WomanWord—A Feminist Lectionary and Psalter: Women of the New Testament.* New York: Crossroad, 1990.

———, Adair Lummis, and Allison Stokes. *Defecting in Place: Women Claiming Responsibility for Their Own Spiritual Lives.* New York: Crossroad, 1995.

Women's Ordination Conference. *Liberating Liturgies.* Fairfax, Va.: Women's Ordination Conference, 1989.

World Council of Churches. *Prayers & Poems, Songs & Stories: Ecumenical Decade 1988–1998.* Geneva: WCC Publications, 1988.

Women Musicians and Their Music

Boyce-Tillman, June. www.impulse-music.co.uk/boycet.htm.
Brown, Monica. www.emmausproductions.com.
Duck, Ruth. www.ruthduckhymnist.net.
Fulmer, Colleen. www.CatholicMusic.us.
Gilbert, Ronnie. www.ronniegilbert.com.
Kealoha, Anna. www.thedance/book/songerth.htm.
Libana. www.libana.com.
McDade, Carolyn. www.carolynmcdademusic.com.
Middleton, Julie Forest. www.emeraldearth.net.
Near, Holly. www.hollynear.com.
Novotka, Jan. www.jannovotka.com.
Re-Imagining Community. www.pilgrimpress.com.
Sherman, Kathy. www.ministryofhearts.org.
Silvestro, Marsie. www.ladyslipper.org.
Sweet Honey in the Rock. www.sweethoney.com.
Wendelborn, Betty. www.muzique.infi.net.nz.
Williamson, Cris. www.criswilliamson.com.
Winter, Miriam Therese. www.mtwinter.hartsem.edu.

Part V Feminist Ministerial Challenges

Aquino, María Pilar. *Our Cry for Life: Feminist Theology from Latin America.* Maryknoll, N.Y.: Orbis Books, 1993.

Berneking, Nancy J., and Pamela Carter Joern, eds. *Re-Membering and Re-Imagining.* Cleveland: Pilgrim Press, 1995.

Braude, Ann, ed. *Transforming the Faiths of Our Fathers: Women Who Changed American Religion.* New York: Palgrave, 2004.

Brekus, Catherine. *Strangers and Pilgrims: Female Preaching in America, 1740–1845.* Chapel Hill, N.C.: University of North Carolina, 1998.

Brock, Rita Nakashima, Jung Ha Kim, Kwok Pui-lan, and Seung Ai Yang, eds. *Off the Menu: Asian and Asian North American Women's Religion & Theology.* Louisville: Westminster John Knox Press, 2007.

Collier-Thomas, Bettye. *Daughters of Thunder: Black Preachers and Their Sermons, 1850–1979.* San Francisco: Jossey-Bass, 1998.

Cooper-White, Pamela. *Many Voices: Pastoral Psychotherapy in Relational and Theological Perspective.* Minneapolis: Fortress Press, 2007.

———. *Shared Wisdom: Use of the Self in Pastoral Care and Counseling.* Minneapolis: Fortress Press, 2004.

Daly, Mary. *Beyond God the Father: Toward a Philosophy of Women's Liberation.* Boston: Beacon Press, 1973.

———. *The Church and the Second Sex.* Boston: Beacon Press, 1968.

DeBerg, Betty A. *Ungodly Women: Gender and the First Wave of American Fundamentalism.* Minneapolis: Fortress Press, 1990.

Fiedler, Maureen, ed. *Breaking Through the Stained Glass Ceiling: Women Religious Leaders in Their Own Words.* New York: Seabury Books, 2010.

Gallagher, Sally K. *Evangelical Identity & Gendered Family Life.* New Brunswick, N.J.: Rutgers University Press, 2003.

Gardiner, Anne Marie, ed. *Women and Catholic Priesthood: An Expanded Vision, Proceedings of the Detroit Ordination Conference.* New York: Paulist Press, 1976.

Hahn, Celia Allison. *Growing in Authority, Relinquishing Control: A New Approach to Faithful Leadership.* Bethesda, Md.: Alban Institute, 1994.

Hardesty, Nancy A. *Women Called to Witness.* 2nd ed. Knoxville, Tenn.: University of Tennessee Press, 1999.

Hassey, Janette. *No Time for Silence: Evangelical Women in Public Ministry Around the Turn of the Century.* Grand Rapids, Mich.: Academie Books, 1986.

Hearn, Virginia, ed. *Our Struggle to Serve: The Stories of 15 Evangelical Women.* Waco, Tex.: Word Books, 1979.

Henderson, Katherine Rhodes. *God's Troublemakers: How Women of Faith Are Changing the World.* New York: Continuum, 2006.

Hunt, Mary E. *Fierce Tenderness: Toward a Feminist Theology of Friendship.* New York: Crossroad, 1992.

Ingersoll, Julie. *Evangelical Christian Women: War Stories in the Gender Battles.* New York: New York University Press, 2003.

Isasi-Díaz, Ada María. En la Lucha *(In the Struggle)—Elaborating a* Mujerista *Theology: A Hispanic Women's Liberation Theology.* Minneapolis: Fortress Press, 1993.

———. La Lucha *Continues:* Mujerista *Theology.* Maryknoll, N.Y.: Orbis Books, 2004.

———. Mujerista *Theology.* Maryknoll, N.Y.: Orbis Books, 1996.

Jefferts Shori, Katharine. *Gospel in the Global Village: Seeking God's Dream of Shalom.* Harrisburg, Penn.: Morehouse, 2009.

Kassian, Mary. *The Feminist ~~Mystique~~ Mistake: The Radical Impact of Feminism on Church and Culture.* Rev. ed. Wheaton, Ill.: Crossway Books, 2005.

Kim, Eunjoo Mary. *Women Preaching: Theology and Practice through the Ages.* Cleveland: Pilgrim Press, 2004.

Maguire, Daniel C. *Sacred Energies: When the World's Religions Sit Down to Talk about the Future of Human Life and the Plight of This Planet.* Minneapolis: Fortress Press, 2000.

McEnroy, Carmel. *Guests in Their Own House: The Women of Vatican II*. New York: Crossroad, 1996.

Mercer, Joyce Ann. *Welcoming Children: A Practical Theology of Childhood*. Atlanta: Chalice Press, 2005.

Miller-McLemore, Bonnie. *Let the Children Come: Reimagining Childhood from a Christian Perspective*. San Francisco: Jossey-Bass, 2003.

Nesbitt, Paula D. *Feminization of the Clergy in America: Occupational and Organizational Perspectives*. New York: Oxford University Press, 1997.

Neuger, Christie Cozad, ed. *The Arts of Ministry: Feminist-Womanist Approaches*. Louisville: Westminster John Knox Press, 1996.

———. *Counseling Women: A Narrative, Pastoral Approach*. Minneapolis: Fortress Press, 2001.

Ruether, Rosemary Radford. *Catholic ≠ the Vatican: A Vision for Progressive Catholicism*. New York: New Press, 2008.

———. *Sexism and God-Talk: Toward a Feminist Theology*. Boston: Beacon Press, 1993.

———. *Women-Church: Theology and Practice of Feminist Liturgical Communities*. San Francisco: Harper & Row, 1985.

Russell, Letty M. *Church in the Round: Feminist Interpretation of the Church*. Louisville: Westminster John Knox Press, 1993.

———. *Just Hospitality: God's Welcome in a World of Difference*. Edited by J. Shannon Clarkson and Kate M. Ott. Louisville: Westminster John Knox Press, 2009.

Schneiders, Sandra M. *Beyond Patching: Faith and Feminism in the Catholic Church*. New York: Paulist Press, 1991.

———. *Finding the Treasure: Locating Catholic Religious Life in a New Ecclesial and Cultural Context*. New York: Paulist Press, 2000.

———. *New Wineskins: Re-Imagining Religious Life Today*. New York: Paulist Press, 1986.

———. *Selling All: Commitment, Consecrated Celibacy, and Community in Catholic Religious Life*. New York: Paulist Press, 2001.

Schüssler Fiorenza, Elisabeth. *But She Said: Feminist Practices of Biblical Interpretation*. Boston: Beacon Press, 1992.

———. *Discipleship of Equals: A Critical Feminist Ekklesia-logy of Liberation*. New York: Crossroad, 1993.

———. *In Memory of Her: A Feminist Theological Reconstruction of Christian Origins*. 10th anniv. ed. New York: Crossroad, 1994.

———. *Wisdom Ways: Introducing Feminist Biblical Interpretation*. Maryknoll, N.Y.: Orbis Books, 2001.

Sentilles, Sarah. *A Church of Her Own: What Happens When a Woman Takes the Pulpit*. New York: Harcourt, 2008.

Stevenson-Moessner, Jeanne, ed. *In Her Own Time: Women and Developmental Issues in Pastoral Care*. Minneapolis: Fortress Press, 2000.

———. *Through the Eyes of Women: The Handbook of Womencare*. Minneapolis: Fortress Press, 1996.

Stoltzfus, Louise. *Quiet Shouts: Stories of Lancaster Women Leaders*. Scottdale, Penn.: Herald Press, 1999.

Swartley, Mary, and Rhoda Keener, eds. *She Has Done a Good Thing: Mennonite Women Leaders Tell Their Stories*. Scottdale, Penn.: Herald Press, 1999.

Taylor, Sarah McFarland. *Green Sisters: A Spiritual Ecology*. Cambridge, Mass.: Harvard University Press, 2007.

Winter, Miriam Therese, Adair Lummis, and Allison Stokes. *Defecting in Place: Women Claiming Responsibility for Their Own Spiritual Lives*. New York: Crossroad, 1995.

Yust, Karen M. *Real Kids, Real Faith: Practices for Nurturing Children's Spiritual Lives*. San Francisco: Jossey-Bass, 2004.

Zikmund, Barbara Brown, Adair T. Lummis, and Patricia Mei Yin Chang. *Clergy Women: An Uphill Calling*. Louisville: Westminster John Knox Press, 1998.

Reference Works, Journals, and Newsletters

72-27. www.eewc.com/72-27.

Christian Feminism Today. www.eewc.com/CFT.htm.

In God's Image. www.awrc4ct.org/igi.php.

Journal of Feminist Studies in Religion. www.fsrinc.org/jfsr.

Keller, Rosemary Skinner, and Rosemary Radford Ruether, eds. *Encyclopedia of Women and Religion in North America*. 3 vols. Bloomington, Ind.: Indiana University Press, 2006.

WATERwheel, the newsletter of the Women's Alliance for Theology, Ethics and Ritual (WATER). Silver Spring, Md.: WATERworks Press, 1985–. www.hers.com/water.

Organizations

FaithTrust Institute. www.faithtrustinstitute.org.

Resource Center for Women and Ministry in the South. www.rcwms.org.

Women's Alliance for Theology, Ethics and Ritual (WATER). www.hers.com/water.

Index of Contributors

AVAILABLE FROM BETTER BOOKSTORES. TRY YOUR BOOKSTORE FIRST.

Spirituality of the Seasons

Autumn: A Spiritual Biography of the Season
Edited by Gary Schmidt and Susan M. Felch; Illus. by Mary Azarian
Rejoice in autumn as a time of preparation and reflection. Includes Wendell Berry, David James Duncan, Robert Frost, A. Bartlett Giamatti, E. B. White, P. D. James, Julian of Norwich, Garret Keizer, Tracy Kidder, Anne Lamott, May Sarton.
6 x 9, 320 pp, b/w illus., Quality PB, 978-1-59473-118-1 **$18.99**

Spring: A Spiritual Biography of the Season
Edited by Gary Schmidt and Susan M. Felch; Illus. by Mary Azarian
Explore the gentle unfurling of spring and reflect on how nature celebrates rebirth and renewal. Includes Jane Kenyon, Lucy Larcom, Harry Thurston, Nathaniel Hawthorne, Noel Perrin, Annie Dillard, Martha Ballard, Barbara Kingsolver, Dorothy Wordsworth, Donald Hall, David Brill, Lionel Basney, Isak Dinesen, Paul Laurence Dunbar.
6 x 9, 352 pp, b/w illus., Quality PB, 978-1-59473-246-1 **$18.99**

Summer: A Spiritual Biography of the Season
Edited by Gary Schmidt and Susan M. Felch; Illus. by Barry Moser
"A sumptuous banquet.... These selections lift up an exquisite wholeness found within an everyday sophistication." — ★ *Publishers Weekly* starred review
Includes Anne Lamott, Luci Shaw, Ray Bradbury, Richard Selzer, Thomas Lynch, Walt Whitman, Carl Sandburg, Sherman Alexie, Madeleine L'Engle, Jamaica Kincaid.
6 x 9, 304 pp, b/w illus., Quality PB, 978-1-59473-183-9 **$18.99**
HC, 978-1-59473-083-2 **$21.99**

Winter: A Spiritual Biography of the Season
Edited by Gary Schmidt and Susan M. Felch; Illus. by Barry Moser
"This outstanding anthology features top-flight nature and spirituality writers on the fierce, inexorable season of winter.... Remarkably lively and warm, despite the icy subject." — ★ *Publishers Weekly* starred review
Includes Will Campbell, Rachel Carson, Annie Dillard, Donald Hall, Ron Hansen, Jane Kenyon, Jamaica Kincaid, Barry Lopez, Kathleen Norris, John Updike, E. B. White.
6 x 9, 288 pp, b/w illus., Deluxe PB w/ flaps, 978-1-893361-92-8 **$18.95**;
HC, 978-1-893361-53-9 **$21.95**

Spirituality / Animal Companions

Blessing the Animals
Prayers and Ceremonies to Celebrate God's Creatures, Wild and Tame
Edited and with Introductions by Lynn L. Caruso
5¼ x 7¼, 256 pp, Quality PB, 978-1-59473-253-9 **$15.99**; HC, 978-1-59473-145-7 **$19.99**

Remembering My Pet
A Kid's Own Spiritual Workbook for When a Pet Dies
by Nechama Liss-Levinson, PhD, and Rev. Molly Phinney Baskette, MDiv; Foreword by Lynn L. Caruso
8 x 10, 48 pp, 2-color text, HC, 978-1-59473-221-8 **$16.99**

What Animals Can Teach Us about Spirituality
Inspiring Lessons from Wild and Tame Creatures
by Diana L. Guerrero
6 x 9, 176 pp, Quality PB, 978-1-893361-84-3 **$16.95**

Or phone, fax, mail or e-mail to: SKYLIGHT PATHS **Publishing**
Sunset Farm Offices, Route 4 • P.O. Box 237 • Woodstock, Vermont 05091
Tel: (802) 457-4000 • Fax: (802) 457-4004 • www.skylightpaths.com
Credit card orders: (800) 962-4544 (8:30AM–5:30PM ET Monday–Friday)
Generous discounts on quantity orders. SATISFACTION GUARANTEED. Prices subject to change.

Children's Spirituality

ENDORSED BY CATHOLIC, PROTESTANT, JEWISH, AND BUDDHIST RELIGIOUS LEADERS

Remembering My Grandparent: A Kid's Own Grief Workbook in the Christian Tradition *by Nechama Liss-Levinson, PhD, and Rev. Molly Phinney Baskette, MDiv* 8 x 10, 48 pp, 2-color text, HC, 978-1-59473-212-6 **$16.99** *For ages 7 & up*

Does God Ever Sleep? *by Joan Sauro, CSJ*
A charming nighttime reminder that God is always present in our lives.
10 x 8½, 32 pp, Full-color photos, Quality PB, 978-1-59473-110-5 **$8.99** *For ages 3–6*

Does God Forgive Me? *by August Gold; Full-color photos by Diane Hardy Waller*
Gently shows how God forgives all that we do if we are truly sorry.
10 x 8½, 32 pp, Full-color photos, Quality PB, 978-1-59473-142-6 **$8.99** *For ages 3–6*

God Said Amen *by Sandy Eisenberg Sasso; Full-color illus. by Avi Katz*
A warm and inspiring tale that shows us that we need only reach out to each other to find the answers to our prayers.
9 x 12, 32 pp, Full-color illus., HC, 978-1-58023-080-3 **$16.95*** *For ages 4 & up*

How Does God Listen? *by Kay Lindahl; Full-color photos by Cynthia Maloney*
How do we know when God is listening to us? Children will find the answers to these questions as they engage their senses while the story unfolds, learning how God listens in the wind, waves, clouds, hot chocolate, perfume, our tears and our laughter.
10 x 8½, 32 pp, Full-color photos, Quality PB, 978-1-59473-084-9 **$8.99** *For ages 3–6*

In God's Hands *by Lawrence Kushner and Gary Schmidt; Full-color illus. by Matthew J. Baek*
9 x 12, 32 pp, Full-color illus., HC, 978-1-58023-224-1 **$16.99*** *For ages 5 & up*

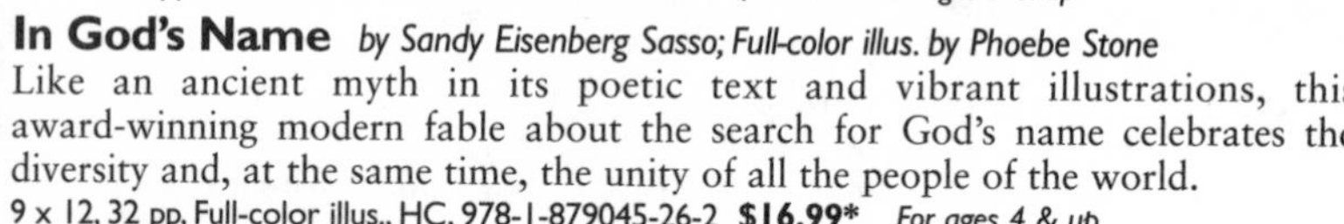

In God's Name *by Sandy Eisenberg Sasso; Full-color illus. by Phoebe Stone*
Like an ancient myth in its poetic text and vibrant illustrations, this award-winning modern fable about the search for God's name celebrates the diversity and, at the same time, the unity of all the people of the world.
9 x 12, 32 pp, Full-color illus., HC, 978-1-879045-26-2 **$16.99*** *For ages 4 & up*

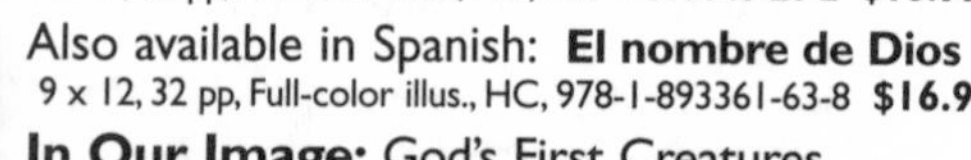

Also available in Spanish: **El nombre de Dios**
9 x 12, 32 pp, Full-color illus., HC, 978-1-893361-63-8 **$16.95**

In Our Image: God's First Creatures
by Nancy Sohn Swartz; Full-color illus. by Melanie Hall
A playful new twist on the Genesis story—from the perspective of the animals. Celebrates the interconnectedness of nature and the harmony of all living things.
9 x 12, 32 pp, Full-color illus., HC, 978-1-879045-99-6 **$16.95*** *For ages 4 & up*

Noah's Wife: The Story of Naamah
by Sandy Eisenberg Sasso; Full-color illus. by Bethanne Andersen
Opens young readers' religious imaginations to new ideas about the well-known story of the Flood. When God tells Noah to bring the animals of the world onto the ark, God also calls on Naamah, Noah's wife, to save each plant on Earth.
9 x 12, 32 pp, Full-color illus., HC, 978-1-58023-134-3 **$16.95*** *For ages 4 & up*

Also available: **Naamah:** Noah's Wife (A Board Book)
by Sandy Eisenberg Sasso; Full-color illus. by Bethanne Andersen
5 x 5, 24 pp, Full-color illus., Board Book, 978-1-893361-56-0 **$7.95** *For ages 0–4*

Where Does God Live? *by August Gold and Matthew J. Perlman*
Helps children and their parents find God in the world around us with simple, practical examples children can relate to.
10 x 8½, 32 pp, Full-color photos, Quality PB, 978-1-893361-39-3 **$8.99** *For ages 3–6*

* A book from Jewish Lights, SkyLight Paths' sister imprint

Bible Stories / Folktales

Abraham's Bind & Other Bible Tales of Trickery, Folly, Mercy and Love *by Michael J. Caduto*
New retellings of episodes in the lives of familiar biblical characters explore relevant life lessons. 6 x 9, 224 pp, HC, 978-1-59473-186-0 **$19.99**

Daughters of the Desert: Stories of Remarkable Women from Christian, Jewish and Muslim Traditions *by Claire Rudolf Murphy, Meghan Nuttall Sayres, Mary Cronk Farrell, Sarah Conover and Betsy Wharton*
Breathes new life into the old tales of our female ancestors in faith. Uses traditional scriptural passages as starting points, then with vivid detail fills in historical context and place. Chapters reveal the voices of Sarah, Hagar, Huldah, Esther, Salome, Mary Magdalene, Lydia, Khadija, Fatima and many more. Historical fiction ideal for readers of all ages.
5½ x 8½, 192 pp, Quality PB, 978-1-59473-106-8 **$14.99** Inc. reader's discussion guide
HC, 978-1-893361-72-0 **$19.95**

The Triumph of Eve & Other Subversive Bible Tales
by Matt Biers-Ariel
These engaging retellings of familiar Bible stories are witty, often hilarious and always profound. They invite you to grapple with questions and issues that are often hidden in the original texts.
5½ x 8½, 192 pp, Quality PB, 978-1-59473-176-1 **$14.99**

Also available: **The Triumph of Eve Teacher's Guide**
8½ x 11, 44 pp, PB, 978-1-59473-152-5 **$8.99**

Wisdom in the Telling
Finding Inspiration and Grace in Traditional Folktales and Myths Retold
by Lorraine Hartin-Gelardi
6 x 9, 192 pp, HC, 978-1-59473-185-3 **$19.99**

Religious Etiquette / Reference

How to Be a Perfect Stranger, 4th Edition: The Essential Religious Etiquette Handbook *Edited by Stuart M. Matlins and Arthur J. Magida*
The indispensable guidebook to help the well-meaning guest when visiting other people's religious ceremonies. A straightforward guide to the rituals and celebrations of the major religions and denominations in the United States and Canada from the perspective of an interested guest of any other faith, based on information obtained from authorities of each religion. Belongs in every living room, library and office. Covers:
African American Methodist Churches • Assemblies of God • Bahá'í • Baptist • Buddhist • Christian Church (Disciples of Christ) • Christian Science (Church of Christ, Scientist) • Churches of Christ • Episcopalian and Anglican • Hindu • Islam • Jehovah's Witnesses • Jewish • Lutheran • Mennonite/Amish • Methodist • Mormon (Church of Jesus Christ of Latter-day Saints) • Native American/First Nations • Orthodox Churches • Pentecostal Church of God • Presbyterian • Quaker (Religious Society of Friends) • Reformed Church in America/Canada • Roman Catholic • Seventh-day Adventist • Sikh • Unitarian Universalist • United Church of Canada • United Church of Christ

"The things Miss Manners forgot to tell us about religion."
—*Los Angeles Times*

"Finally, for those inclined to undertake their own spiritual journeys … tells visitors what to expect." —*New York Times*

6 x 9, 432 pp, Quality PB, 978-1-59473-140-2 **$19.99**

The Perfect Stranger's Guide to Funerals and Grieving Practices: A Guide to Etiquette in Other People's Religious Ceremonies *Edited by Stuart M. Matlins*
6 x 9, 240 pp, Quality PB, 978-1-893361-20-1 **$16.95**

The Perfect Stranger's Guide to Wedding Ceremonies: A Guide to Etiquette in Other People's Religious Ceremonies *Edited by Stuart M. Matlins*
6 x 9, 208 pp, Quality PB, 978-1-893361-19-5 **$16.95**

Prayer / Meditation

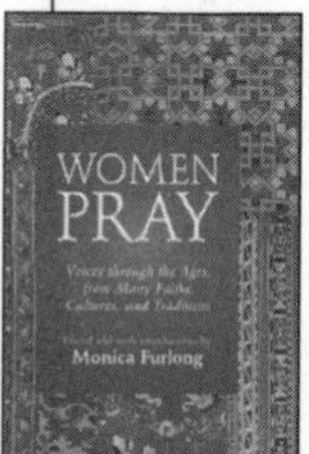

Sacred Attention: A Spiritual Practice for Finding God in the Moment
by Margaret D. McGee
Framed on the Christian liturgical year, this inspiring guide explores ways to develop a practice of attention as a means of talking—and listening—to God.
6 x 9, 144 pp, Quality PB, 978-1-59473-291-1 **$16.99**

Women Pray: Voices through the Ages, from Many Faiths, Cultures and Traditions
Edited and with Introductions by Monica Furlong
5 x 7¼, 256 pp, Quality PB, 978-1-59473-071-9 **$15.99**

Women of Color Pray: Voices of Strength, Faith, Healing, Hope and Courage
Edited and with Introductions by Christal M. Jackson
Through these prayers, poetry, lyrics, meditations and affirmations, you will share in the strong and undeniable connection women of color share with God.
5 x 7¼, 208 pp, Quality PB, 978-1-59473-077-1 **$15.99**

Secrets of Prayer: A Multifaith Guide to Creating Personal Prayer in Your Life *by Nancy Corcoran, CSJ*
This compelling, multifaith guidebook offers you companionship and encouragement on the journey to a healthy prayer life. 6 x 9, 160 pp, Quality PB, 978-1-59473-215-7 **$16.99**

Prayers to an Evolutionary God
by William Cleary; Afterword by Diarmuid O'Murchu
Inspired by the spiritual and scientific teachings of Diarmuid O'Murchu and Teilhard de Chardin, reveals that religion and science can be combined to create an expanding view of the universe—an evolutionary faith.
6 x 9, 208 pp, HC, 978-1-59473-006-1 **$21.99**

The Art of Public Prayer, 2nd Edition: Not for Clergy Only
by Lawrence A. Hoffman, PhD 6 x 9, 288 pp, Quality PB, 978-1-893361-06-5 **$19.99**

A Heart of Stillness: A Complete Guide to Learning the Art of Meditation
by David A. Cooper 5½ x 8½, 272 pp, Quality PB, 978-1-893361-03-4 **$18.99**

Meditation without Gurus: A Guide to the Heart of Practice
by Clark Strand 5½ x 8½, 192 pp, Quality PB, 978-1-893361-93-5 **$16.95**

Praying with Our Hands: 21 Practices of Embodied Prayer from the World's Spiritual Traditions *by Jon M. Sweeney; Photos by Jennifer J. Wilson; Foreword by Mother Tessa Bielecki; Afterword by Taitetsu Unno, PhD*
8 x 8, 96 pp, 22 duotone photos, Quality PB, 978-1-893361-16-4 **$16.95**

Three Gates to Meditation Practice: A Personal Journey into Sufism, Buddhism, and Judaism *by David A. Cooper* 5½ x 8½, 240 pp, Quality PB, 978-1-893361-22-5 **$16.95**

Prayer / M. Basil Pennington, OCSO

Finding Grace at the Center, 3rd Edition: The Beginning of Centering Prayer *with Thomas Keating, OCSO, and Thomas E. Clarke, SJ; Foreword by Rev. Cynthia Bourgeault, PhD* A practical guide to a simple and beautiful form of meditative prayer. 5 x 7¼, 128 pp, Quality PB, 978-1-59473-182-2 **$12.99**

The Monks of Mount Athos: A Western Monk's Extraordinary Spiritual Journey on Eastern Holy Ground *Foreword by Archimandrite Dionysios*
Explores the landscape, monastic communities and food of Athos.
6 x 9, 352 pp, Quality PB, 978-1-893361-78-2 **$18.95**

Psalms: A Spiritual Commentary *Illus. by Phillip Ratner*
Reflections on some of the most beloved passages from the Bible's most widely read book. 6 x 9, 176 pp, 24 full-page b/w illus., Quality PB, 978-1-59473-234-8 **$16.99**

The Song of Songs: A Spiritual Commentary *Illus. by Phillip Ratner*
Explore the Bible's most challenging mystical text.
6 x 9, 160 pp, 14 full-page b/w illus., Quality PB, 978-1-59473-235-5 **$16.99**
HC, 978-1-59473-004-7 **$19.99**

Sacred Texts—SkyLight Illuminations Series

Offers today's spiritual seeker an enjoyable entry into the great classic texts of the world's spiritual traditions. Each classic is presented in an accessible translation, with facing pages of guided commentary from experts, giving you the keys you need to understand the history, context and meaning of the text.

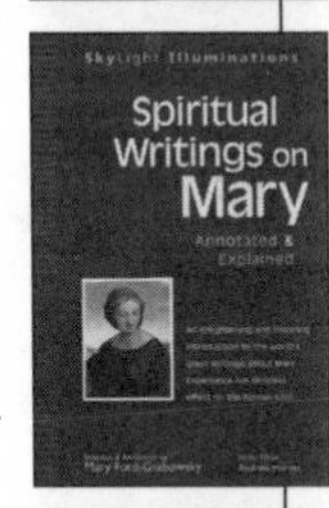

CHRISTIANITY

The End of Days: Essential Selections from Apocalyptic Texts—Annotated & Explained *Annotation by Robert G. Clouse, PhD*
Helps you understand the complex Christian visions of the end of the world.
5½ x 8½, 224 pp, Quality PB, 978-1-59473-170-9 **$16.99**

The Hidden Gospel of Matthew: Annotated & Explained
Translation & Annotation by Ron Miller Takes you deep into the text cherished around the world to discover the words and events that have the strongest connection to the historical Jesus. 5½ x 8½, 272 pp, Quality PB, 978-1-59473-038-2 **$16.99**

The Infancy Gospels of Jesus: Apocryphal Tales from the Childhoods of Mary and Jesus—Annotated & Explained
Translation & Annotation by Stevan Davies; Foreword by A. Edward Siecienski, PhD
A startling presentation of the early lives of Mary, Jesus and other biblical figures that will amuse and surprise you. 5½ x 8½, 176 pp, Quality PB, 978-1-59473-258-4 **$16.99**

The Lost Sayings of Jesus: Teachings from Ancient Christian, Jewish, Gnostic and Islamic Sources—Annotated & Explained
Translation & Annotation by Andrew Phillip Smith; Foreword by Stephan A. Hoeller
This collection of more than three hundred sayings depicts Jesus as a Wisdom teacher who speaks to people of all faiths as a mystic and spiritual master.
5½ x 8½, 240 pp, Quality PB, 978-1-59473-172-3 **$16.99**

Philokalia: The Eastern Christian Spiritual Texts—Selections Annotated & Explained *Annotation by Allyne Smith; Translation by G. E. H. Palmer, Phillip Sherrard and Bishop Kallistos Ware*
The first approachable introduction to the wisdom of the Philokalia, the classic text of Eastern Christian spirituality. 5½ x 8½, 240 pp, Quality PB, 978-1-59473-103-7 **$16.99**

The Sacred Writings of Paul: Selections Annotated & Explained
Translation & Annotation by Ron Miller Leads you into the exciting immediacy of Paul's teachings. 5½ x 8½, 224 pp, Quality PB, 978-1-59473-213-3 **$16.99**

Saint Augustine of Hippo: Selections from *Confessions* and Other Essential Writings—Annotated & Explained
Annotation by Joseph T. Kelley, PhD; Translation by the Augustinian Heritage Institute
Provides insight into the mind and heart of this foundational Christian figure.
5½ x 8½, 272 pp, Quality PB, 978-1-59473-282-9 **$16.99**

Sex Texts from the Bible: Selections Annotated & Explained
Translation & Annotation by Teresa J. Hornsby; Foreword by Amy-Jill Levine
Demystifies the Bible's ideas on gender roles, marriage, sexual orientation, virginity, lust and sexual pleasure. 5½ x 8½, 208 pp, Quality PB, 978-1-59473-217-1 **$16.99**

Spiritual Writings on Mary: Annotated & Explained
Annotation by Mary Ford-Grabowsky; Foreword by Andrew Harvey
Examines the role of Mary, the mother of Jesus, as a source of inspiration in history and in life today. 5½ x 8½, 288 pp, Quality PB, 978-1-59473-001-6 **$16.99**

The Way of a Pilgrim: The Jesus Prayer Journey—Annotated & Explained
Translation & Annotation by Gleb Pokrovsky; Foreword by Andrew Harvey
This classic of Russian Orthodox spirituality is the delightful account of one man who sets out to learn the prayer of the heart, also known as the "Jesus prayer."
5½ x 8½, 160 pp, Illus., Quality PB, 978-1-893361-31-7 **$14.95**

Sacred Texts—continued

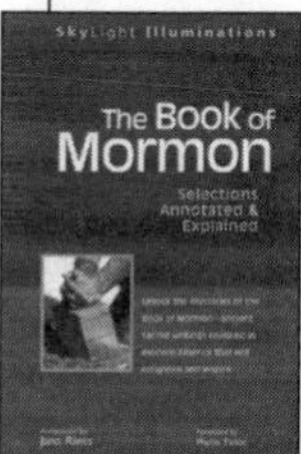

MORMONISM

The Book of Mormon: Selections Annotated & Explained
Annotation by Jana Riess; Foreword by Phyllis Tickle Explores the sacred epic that is cherished by more than twelve million members of the LDS church as the keystone of their faith. 5½ x 8½ , 272 pp, Quality PB, 978-1-59473-076-4 **$16.99**

NATIVE AMERICAN

Native American Stories of the Sacred: Annotated & Explained
Retold & Annotated by Evan T. Pritchard Intended for more than entertainment, these teaching tales contain elegantly simple illustrations of time-honored truths.
5½ x 8½, 272 pp, Quality PB, 978-1-59473-112-9 **$16.99**

GNOSTICISM

Gnostic Writings on the Soul: Annotated & Explained
Translation & Annotation by Andrew Phillip Smith; Foreword by Stephan A. Hoeller
Reveals the inspiring ways your soul can remember and return to its unique, divine purpose. 5½ x 8½, 144 pp, Quality PB, 978-1-59473-220-1 **$16.99**

The Gospel of Philip: Annotated & Explained

Translation & Annotation by Andrew Phillip Smith; Foreword by Stevan Davies
Reveals otherwise unrecorded sayings of Jesus and fragments of Gnostic mythology.
5½ x 8½, 160 pp, Quality PB, 978-1-59473-111-2 **$16.99**

The Gospel of Thomas: Annotated & Explained
Translation & Annotation by Stevan Davies; Foreword by Andrew Harvey
Sheds new light on the origins of Christianity and portrays Jesus as a wisdom-loving sage.
5½ x 8½, 192 pp, Quality PB, 978-1-893361-45-4 **$16.99**

The Secret Book of John: The Gnostic Gospel—Annotated & Explained
Translation & Annotation by Stevan Davies The most significant and influential text of the ancient Gnostic religion. 5½ x 8½, 208 pp, Quality PB, 978-1-59473-082-5 **$16.99**

JUDAISM

The Divine Feminine in Biblical Wisdom Literature
Selections Annotated & Explained
Translation & Annotation by Rabbi Rami Shapiro; Foreword by Rev. Cynthia Bourgeault, PhD
Uses the Hebrew Bible and Wisdom literature to explain Sophia's way of wisdom and illustrate Her creative energy.
5½ x 8½, 240 pp, Quality PB, 978-1-59473-109-9 **$16.99**

Ethics of the Sages: *Pirke Avot*—Annotated & Explained
Translation & Annotation by Rabbi Rami Shapiro Clarifies the ethical teachings of the early Rabbis. 5½ x 8½, 192 pp, Quality PB, 978-1-59473-207-2 **$16.99**

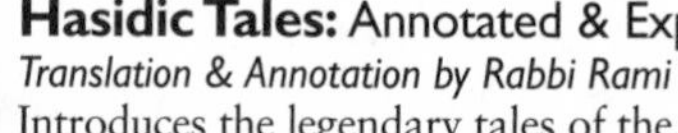
Hasidic Tales: Annotated & Explained
Translation & Annotation by Rabbi Rami Shapiro
Introduces the legendary tales of the impassioned Hasidic rabbis, presenting them as stories rather than as parables. 5½ x 8½, 240 pp, Quality PB, 978-1-893361-86-7 **$16.95**

The Hebrew Prophets: Selections Annotated & Explained
Translation & Annotation by Rabbi Rami Shapiro; Foreword by Rabbi Zalman M. Schachter-Shalomi
Makes the wisdom of these timeless teachers accessible.
5½ x 8½, 224 pp, Quality PB, 978-1-59473-037-5 **$16.99**

***Tanya,* the Masterpiece of Hasidic Wisdom:** Selections Annotated & Explained *Translation & Annotation by Rabbi Rami Shapiro; Foreword by Rabbi Zalman M. Schachter-Shalomi* Clarifies one of the most powerful and potentially transformative books of Jewish wisdom. 5½ x 8½, 240 pp, Quality PB, 978-1-59473-275-1 **$16.99**

Zohar: Annotated & Explained
Translation & Annotation by Daniel C. Matt; Foreword by Andrew Harvey
Brings together the most important teachings of the Zohar, the canonical text of Jewish mystical tradition. 5½ x 8½, 176 pp, Quality PB, 978-1-893361-51-5 **$15.99**

Spiritual Practice

Laugh Your Way to Grace: Reclaiming the Spiritual Power of Humor
by Rev. Susan Sparks A powerful, humorous case for laughter as a spiritual, healing path. 6 x 9, 176 pp, Quality PB, 978-1-59473-280-5 **$16.99**

Haiku—The Sacred Art: A Spiritual Practice in Three Lines
by Margaret D. McGee Introduces haiku as a simple and effective way of tapping into the sacred moments that permeate everyday living.
5½ x 8½, 192 pp, Quality PB, 978-1-59473-269-0 **$16.99**

Dance—The Sacred Art: The Joy of Movement as a Spiritual Practice
by Cynthia Winton-Henry Invites all of us, regardless of experience, into the possibility of dance/movement as a spiritual practice.
5½ x 8½, 224 pp, Quality PB, 978-1-59473-268-3 **$16.99**

Spiritual Adventures in the Snow: Skiing & Snowboarding as Renewal for Your Soul *by Dr. Marcia McFee and Rev. Karen Foster; Foreword by Paul Arthur*
Explores snow sports as tangible experiences of the spiritual essence of our bodies and the earth. 5½ x 8½, 208 pp, Quality PB, 978-1-59473-270-6 **$16.99**

Divining the Body: Reclaim the Holiness of Your Physical Self *by Jan Phillips*
8 x 8, 256 pp, Quality PB, 978-1-59473-080-1 **$16.99**

Everyday Herbs in Spiritual Life: A Guide to Many Practices
by Michael J. Caduto; Foreword by Rosemary Gladstar
7 x 9, 208 pp, 20+ b/w illus., Quality PB, 978-1-59473-174-7 **$16.99**

The Gospel of Thomas: A Guidebook for Spiritual Practice
by Ron Miller; Translations by Stevan Davies 6 x 9, 160 pp, Quality PB, 978-1-59473-047-4 **$14.99**

Hospitality—The Sacred Art: Discovering the Hidden Spiritual Power of Invitation and Welcome *by Rev. Nanette Sawyer; Foreword by Rev. Dirk Ficca*
5½ x 8½, 208 pp, Quality PB, 978-1-59473-228-7 **$16.99**

Labyrinths from the Outside In: Walking to Spiritual Insight—A Beginner's Guide *by Donna Schaper and Carole Ann Camp*
6 x 9, 208 pp, b/w illus. and photos, Quality PB, 978-1-893361-18-8 **$16.95**

Practicing the Sacred Art of Listening: A Guide to Enrich Your Relationships and Kindle Your Spiritual Life *by Kay Lindahl* 8 x 8, 176 pp, Quality PB, 978-1-893361-85-0 **$16.95**

Recovery—The Sacred Art: The Twelve Steps as Spiritual Practice *by Rami Shapiro; Foreword by Joan Borysenko, PhD* 5½ x 8½, 240 pp, Quality PB, 978-1-59473-259-1 **$16.99**

Running—The Sacred Art: Preparing to Practice *by Dr. Warren A. Kay; Foreword by Kristin Armstrong* 5½ x 8½, 160 pp, Quality PB, 978-1-59473-227-0 **$16.99**

The Sacred Art of Bowing: Preparing to Practice
by Andi Young 5½ x 8½, 128 pp, b/w illus., Quality PB, 978-1-893361-82-9 **$14.95**

The Sacred Art of Chant: Preparing to Practice
by Ana Hernández 5½ x 8½, 192 pp, Quality PB, 978-1-59473-036-8 **$15.99**

The Sacred Art of Fasting: Preparing to Practice
by Thomas Ryan, CSP 5½ x 8½, 192 pp, Quality PB, 978-1-59473-078-8 **$15.99**

The Sacred Art of Forgiveness: Forgiving Ourselves and Others through God's Grace
by Marcia Ford 8 x 8, 176 pp, Quality PB, 978-1-59473-175-4 **$16.99**

The Sacred Art of Listening: Forty Reflections for Cultivating a Spiritual Practice
by Kay Lindahl; Illus. by Amy Schnapper 8 x 8, 160 pp, b/w illus., Quality PB, 978-1-893361-44-7 **$16.99**

The Sacred Art of Lovingkindness: Preparing to Practice
by Rabbi Rami Shapiro; Foreword by Marcia Ford 5½ x 8½, 176 pp, Quality PB, 978-1-59473-151-8 **$16.99**

Sacred Attention: A Spiritual Practice for Finding God in the Moment
by Margaret D. McGee 6 x 9, 144 pp, Quality PB, 978-1-59473-291-1 **$16.99**

Sacred Speech: A Practical Guide for Keeping Spirit in Your Speech
by Rev. Donna Schaper 6 x 9, 176 pp, Quality PB, 978-1-59473-068-9 **$15.99**
HC, 978-1-893361-74-4 **$21.95**

Soul Fire: Accessing Your Creativity
by Thomas Ryan, CSP 6 x 9, 160 pp, Quality PB, 978-1-59473-243-0 **$16.99**

Thanking & Blessing—The Sacred Art: Spiritual Vitality through Gratefulness
by Jay Marshall, PhD; Foreword by Philip Gulley 5½ x 8½, 176 pp, Quality PB, 978-1-59473-231-7 **$16.99**

Spiritual Biography

Spiritual Leaders Who Changed the World

The Essential Handbook to the Past Century of Religion

Edited by Ira Rifkin and the Editors at SkyLight Paths; Foreword by Dr. Robert Coles

An invaluable reference to the most important spiritual leaders of the past 100 years.

6 x 9, 304 pp, b/w photos, Quality PB, 978-1-59473-241-6 **$18.99**

Bede Griffiths

An Introduction to His Interspiritual Thought

by Wayne Teasdale

The first study of his contemplative experience and thought, exploring the intersection of Hinduism and Christianity.

6 x 9, 288 pp, Quality PB, 978-1-893361-77-5 **$18.95**

The Soul of the Story

Meetings with Remarkable People

by Rabbi David Zeller

Inspiring and entertaining, this compelling collection of spiritual adventures assures us that no spiritual lesson truly learned is ever lost.

6 x 9, 288 pp, HC, 978-1-58023-272-2 **$21.99**

(A book from Jewish Lights, SkyLight Paths' sister imprint)

Spiritual Biography—SkyLight Lives

SkyLight Lives reintroduces the lives and works of key spiritual figures of our time—people who by their teaching or example have challenged our assumptions about spirituality and have caused us to look at it in new ways.

The Life of Evelyn Underhill

An Intimate Portrait of the Groundbreaking Author of *Mysticism*

by Margaret Cropper; Foreword by Dana Greene

Underhill was an early believer that contemplative prayer is not just for monks and nuns but for anyone willing to undertake it.

6 x 9, 288 pp, b/w photos, Quality PB, 978-1-893361-70-6 **$18.95**

Mahatma Gandhi

His Life and Ideas

by Charles F. Andrews; Foreword by Dr. Arun Gandhi

Examines the religious ideas and political dynamics that influenced the birth of the peaceful resistance movement.

6 x 9, 336 pp, b/w photos, Quality PB, 978-1-893361-89-8 **$18.95**

Simone Weil

A Modern Pilgrimage

by Robert Coles

A brilliant portrait of this strange and controversial figure and her mystical experiences.

6 x 9, 208 pp, Quality PB, 978-1-893361-34-8 **$16.95**

Zen Effects

The Life of Alan Watts

by Monica Furlong

Alan Watts did more to introduce Eastern philosophy and religion to Western minds than any figure before or since.

6 x 9, 264 pp, Quality PB, 978-1-893361-32-4 **$16.95**

Spirituality & Crafts

Beading—The Creative Spirit: Finding Your Sacred Center through the Art of Beadwork *by Rev. Wendy Ellsworth*
Invites you on a spiritual pilgrimage into the kaleidoscope world of glass and color. 7 x 9, 240 pp, 8-page color insert, 40+ b/w photos and 40 diagrams, Quality PB, 978-1-59473-267-6 **$18.99**

Contemplative Crochet: A Hands-On Guide for Interlocking Faith and Craft *by Cindy Crandall-Frazier; Foreword by Linda Skolnik*
Illuminates the spiritual lessons you can learn through crocheting.
7 x 9, 208 pp, b/w photos, Quality PB, 978-1-59473-238-6 **$16.99**

The Knitting Way: A Guide to Spiritual Self-Discovery
by Linda Skolnik and Janice MacDaniels Examines how you can explore and strengthen your spiritual life through knitting.
7 x 9, 240 pp, b/w photos, Quality PB, 978-1-59473-079-5 **$16.99**

The Painting Path: Embodying Spiritual Discovery through Yoga, Brush and Color *by Linda Novick; Foreword by Richard Segalman*
Explores the divine connection you can experience through art.
7 x 9, 208 pp, 8-page color insert, plus b/w photos, Quality PB, 978-1-59473-226-3 **$18.99**

The Quilting Path: A Guide to Spiritual Discovery through Fabric, Thread and Kabbalah *by Louise Silk*
Explores how to cultivate personal growth through quilt making.
7 x 9, 192 pp, b/w photos and illus., Quality PB, 978-1-59473-206-5 **$16.99**

The Scrapbooking Journey: A Hands-On Guide to Spiritual Discovery
by Cory Richardson-Lauve; Foreword by Stacy Julian Reveals how this craft can become a practice used to deepen and shape your life.
7 x 9, 176 pp, 8-page color insert, plus b/w photos, Quality PB, 978-1-59473-216-4 **$18.99**

The Soulwork of Clay: A Hands-On Approach to Spirituality
by Marjory Zoet Bankson; Photos by Peter Bankson
Takes you through the seven-step process of making clay into a pot, drawing parallels at each stage to the process of spiritual growth.
7 x 9, 192 pp, b/w photos, Quality PB, 978-1-59473-249-2 **$16.99**

Kabbalah / Enneagram

(Books from Jewish Lights Publishing, SkyLight Paths' sister imprint)

Cast in God's Image: Discover Your Personality Type Using the Enneagram and Kabbalah
by Rabbi Howard A. Addison 7 x 9, 176 pp, Quality PB, 978-1-58023-124-4 **$16.95**

Ehyeh: A Kabbalah for Tomorrow *by Dr. Arthur Green*
6 x 9, 224 pp, Quality PB, 978-1-58023-213-5 **$16.99**

The Enneagram and Kabbalah, 2nd Edition: Reading Your Soul
by Rabbi Howard A. Addison 6 x 9, 192 pp, Quality PB, 978-1-58023-229-6 **$16.99**

The Gift of Kabbalah: Discovering the Secrets of Heaven, Renewing Your Life on Earth
by Tamar Frankiel, PhD 6 x 9, 256 pp, Quality PB, 978-1-58023-141-1 **$16.95**

God in Your Body: Kabbalah, Mindfulness and Embodied Spiritual Practice
by Jay Michaelson 6 x 9, 272 pp, Quality PB, 978-1-58023-304-0 **$18.99**

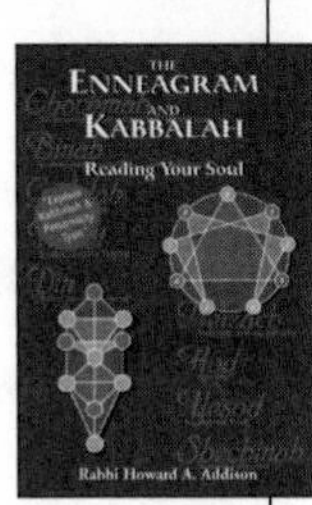

Kabbalah: A Brief Introduction for Christians
by Tamar Frankiel, PhD 5½ x 8½, 208 pp, Quality PB, 978-1-58023-303-3 **$16.99**

Zohar: Annotated & Explained *Translation & Annotation by Daniel C. Matt; Foreword by Andrew Harvey* 5½ x 8½, 176 pp, Quality PB, 978-1-893361-51-5 **$15.99**

Spirituality

Creative Aging: Rethinking Retirement and Non-Retirement in a Changing World *by Marjory Zoet Bankson*
Offers creative ways to nourish our calling and discover meaning and purpose in our older years. 6 x 9, 160 pp, Quality PB, 978-1-59473-281-2 **$16.99**

Laugh Your Way to Grace: Reclaiming the Spiritual Power of Humor *by Rev. Susan Sparks* A powerful, humorous case for laughter as a spiritual, healing path. 6 x 9, 176 pp, Quality PB, 978-1-59473-280-5 **$16.99**

Living into Hope: A Call to Spiritual Action for Such a Time as This *by Rev. Dr. Joan Brown Campbell; Foreword by Karen Armstrong*
A visionary minister speaks out on the pressing issues that face us today, offering inspiration and challenge. 6 x 9, 144 pp (est), HC, 978-1-59473-283-6 **$21.99**

Claiming Earth as Common Ground: The Ecological Crisis through the Lens of Faith *by Andrea Cohen-Kiener; Foreword by Rev. Sally Bingham*
Inspires us to work across denominational lines in order to fulfill our sacred imperative to care for God's creation. 6 x 9, 192 pp, Quality PB, 978-1-59473-261-4 **$16.99**

Bread, Body, Spirit: Finding the Sacred in Food
Edited and with Introductions by Alice Peck 6 x 9, 224 pp, Quality PB, 978-1-59473-242-3 **$19.99**

Creating a Spiritual Retirement: A Guide to the Unseen Possibilities in Our Lives
by Molly Srode 6 x 9, 208 pp, b/w photos, Quality PB, 978-1-59473-050-4 **$14.99**

Finding Hope: Cultivating God's Gift of a Hopeful Spirit
by Marcia Ford; Foreword by Andrea Jaeger 8 x 8, 176 pp, Quality PB, 978-1-59473-211-9 **$16.99**

Hearing the Call across Traditions: Readings on Faith and Service
Edited by Adam Davis; Foreword by Eboo Patel 6 x 9, 352 pp, HC, 978-1-59473-264-5 **$29.99**

Honoring Motherhood: Prayers, Ceremonies & Blessings
Edited and with Introductions by Lynn L. Caruso 5 x 7¼, 272 pp, HC, 978-1-59473-239-3 **$19.99**

Journeys of Simplicity: Traveling Light with Thomas Merton, Bashō, Edward Abbey, Annie Dillard & Others *by Philip Harnden*
5 x 7¼, 144 pp, Quality PB, 978-1-59473-181-5 **$12.99**; 128 pp, HC, 978-1-893361-76-8 **$16.95**

Keeping Spiritual Balance As We Grow Older: More than 65 Creative Ways to Use Purpose, Prayer, and the Power of Spirit to Build a Meaningful Retirement
by Molly and Bernie Srode 8 x 8, 224 pp, Quality PB, 978-1-59473-042-9 **$16.99**

The Losses of Our Lives: The Sacred Gifts of Renewal in Everyday Loss
by Dr. Nancy Copeland-Payton 6 x 9, 192 pp, HC, 978-1-59473-271-3 **$19.99**

Money and the Way of Wisdom: Insights from the Book of Proverbs
by Timothy J. Sandoval, PhD 6 x 9, 192 pp, Quality PB, 978-1-59473-245-4 **$16.99**

Next to Godliness: Finding the Sacred in Housekeeping
Edited by Alice Peck 6 x 9, 224 pp, Quality PB, 978-1-59473-214-0 **$19.99**

Renewal in the Wilderness: A Spiritual Guide to Connecting with God in the Natural World *by John Lionberger*
6 x 9, 176 pp, b/w photos, Quality PB, 978-1-59473-219-5 **$16.99**

Sacred Attention: A Spiritual Practice for Finding God in the Moment
by Margaret D. McGee 6 x 9, 144 pp, Quality PB, 978-1-59473-291-1 **$16.99**

Soul Fire: Accessing Your Creativity
by Thomas Ryan, CSP 6 x 9, 160 pp, Quality PB, 978-1-59473-243-0 **$16.99**

A Spirituality for Brokenness: Discovering Your Deepest Self in Difficult Times
by Terry Taylor 6 x 9, 176 pp, Quality PB, 978-1-59473-229-4 **$16.99**

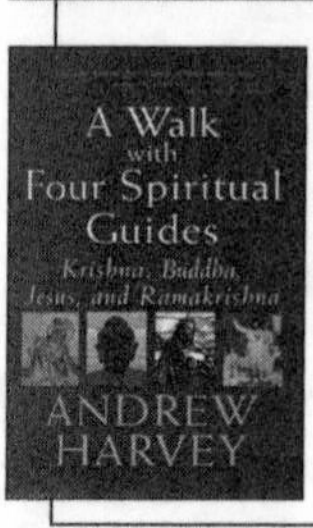

Spiritually Incorrect: Finding God in All the *Wrong* Places *by Dan Wakefield; Illus. by Marian DelVecchio* 5½ x 8½, 192 pp, b/w illus., Quality PB, 978-1-59473-137-2 **$15.99**

A Walk with Four Spiritual Guides: Krishna, Buddha, Jesus, and Ramakrishna
by Andrew Harvey 5½ x 8½, 192 pp, b/w photos & illus., Quality PB, 978-1-59473-138-9 **$15.99**

The Workplace and Spirituality: New Perspectives on Research and Practice
Edited by Dr. Joan Marques, Dr. Satinder Dhiman and Dr. Richard King
6 x 9, 256 pp, HC, 978-1-59473-260-7 **$29.99**

Women's Interest

New Feminist Christianity: Many Voices, Many Views
Edited by Mary E. Hunt and Diann L. Neu
Insights from ministers and theologians, activists and leaders, artists and liturgists who are shaping the future. Taken together, their voices offer a starting point for building new models of religious life and worship.
6 x 9, 384 pp, HC, 978-1-59473-285-0 **$24.99**

New Jewish Feminism: Probing the Past, Forging the Future
Edited by Rabbi Elyse Goldstein; Foreword by Anita Diamant
Looks at the growth and accomplishments of Jewish feminism and what they mean for Jewish women today and tomorrow. Features the voices of women from every area of Jewish life, addressing the important issues that concern Jewish women.
6 x 9, 480 pp, HC, 978-1-58023-359-0 **$24.99***

Dance—The Sacred Art: The Joy of Movement as a Spiritual Practice
by Cynthia Winton-Henry 5½ x 8½, 224 pp, Quality PB, 978-1-59473-268-3 **$16.99**

Daughters of the Desert: Stories of Remarkable Women from Christian, Jewish and Muslim Traditions
by Claire Rudolf Murphy, Meghan Nuttall Sayres, Mary Cronk Farrell, Sarah Conover and Betsy Wharton
5½ x 8½, 192 pp, Illus., Quality PB, 978-1-59473-106-8 **$14.99** Inc. reader's discussion guide
HC, 978-1-893361-72-0 **$19.95**

The Divine Feminine in Biblical Wisdom Literature
Selections Annotated & Explained
Translation & Annotation by Rabbi Rami Shapiro; Foreword by Rev. Cynthia Bourgeault, PhD
5½ x 8½, 240 pp, Quality PB, 978-1-59473-109-9 **$16.99**

Divining the Body: Reclaim the Holiness of Your Physical Self
by Jan Phillips 8 x 8, 256 pp, Quality PB, 978-1-59473-080-1 **$16.99**

Honoring Motherhood: Prayers, Ceremonies & Blessings
Edited and with Introductions by Lynn L. Caruso 5 x 7¼, 272 pp, HC, 978-1-59473-239-3 **$19.99**

ReVisions: Seeing Torah through a Feminist Lens
by Rabbi Elyse Goldstein 5½ x 8½, 224 pp, Quality PB, 978-1-58023-117-6 **$16.95***

The Triumph of Eve & Other Subversive Bible Tales
by Matt Biers-Ariel 5½ x 8½, 192 pp, Quality PB, 978-1-59473-176-1 **$14.99**

Also available: **The Triumph of Eve Teacher's Guide**
8½ x 11, 44 pp, PB, 978-1-59473-152-5 **$8.99**

White Fire: A Portrait of Women Spiritual Leaders in America
by Malka Drucker; Photos by Gay Block 7 x 10, 320 pp, b/w photos, HC, 978-1-893361-64-5 **$24.95**

Woman Spirit Awakening in Nature
Growing Into the Fullness of Who You Are
by Nancy Barrett Chickerneo, PhD; Foreword by Eileen Fisher
8 x 8, 224 pp, b/w illus., Quality PB, 978-1-59473-250-8 **$16.99**

Women of Color Pray: Voices of Strength, Faith, Healing, Hope and Courage
Edited and with Introductions by Christal M. Jackson
5 x 7¼, 208 pp, Quality PB, 978-1-59473-077-1 **$15.99**

Women Pray: Voices through the Ages, from Many Faiths, Cultures and Traditions
Edited and with Introductions by Monica Furlong
5 x 7¼, 256 pp, Quality PB, 978-1-59473-071-9 **$15.99**

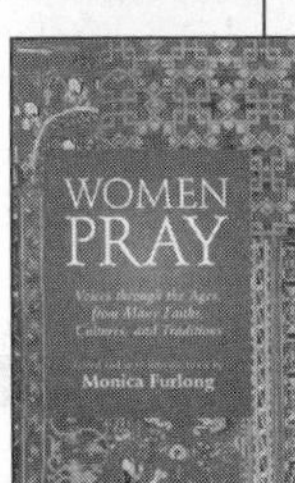

The Women's Haftarah Commentary: New Insights from Women Rabbis on the 54 Weekly Haftarah Portions, the 5 Megillot & Special Shabbatot *Edited by Rabbi Elyse Goldstein*
6 x 9, 560 pp, Quality PB, 978-1-58023-371-2 **$19.99***

The Women's Torah Commentary: New Insights from Women Rabbis on the 54 Weekly Torah Portions *Edited by Rabbi Elyse Goldstein*
6 x 9, 496 pp, Quality PB, 978-1-58023-370-5 **$19.99**; HC, 978-1-58023-076-6 **$34.95***

* A book from Jewish Lights, SkyLight Paths' sister imprint